Radical Spirits

Radical *Spirits*

Spiritualism and Women's Rights in Nineteenth-Century America

Second Edition

Ann Braude

INDIANA UNIVERSITY PRESS
Bloomington and Indianapolis

This book is a publication of

Indiana University Press
601 North Morton Street
Bloomington, IN 47404-3797 USA

http://iupress.indiana.edu

Telephone orders 800-842-6796

Fax orders 812-855-7931

Orders by e-mail iuporder@indiana.edu

Library of Congress Cataloging-in-Publication Data

Braude, Ann.
    Radical spirits : spiritualism and women's rights in nineteenth-century America /Ann Braude.— 2nd ed.
        p. cm.
    Includes bibliographical references and index.
    ISBN 0-253-34039-X (alk. paper) — ISBN 0-253-21502-1 (pbk. : alk. paper)
        1. Women's rights and spiritualism—United States—History—19th century. I. Title.

BF1275.W65 B73 2001
133.9'0973'09034—dc21

                                                                    2001039572

1 2 3 4 5 06 05 04 03 02 01

For

BEN BRAUDE

1898–1984

Contents

LIST OF ILLUSTRATIONS

Illustrations follow page 114

1. The Sisters Fox. *From* BALLOU'S PICTORIAL DRAWING ROOM COMPANION, *14 June 1856. Courtesy of the American Antiquarian Society, Worcester, Massachusetts.*

2. Amy Kirby Post and Isaac Post. *Courtesy of the University of Rochester Department of Rare Books and Special Collections.*

3. Margaret and Catherine Fox and Leah Fox Fish. *Lithograph by Currier and Ives, 1852. Courtesy of the University of Rochester Department of Rare Books and Special Collections.*

4. The séance table. *Courtesy of the Bettmann Archive, New York.*

5. The Boston Planchette. *Courtesy of the American Antiquarian Society, Worcester, Massachusetts.*

6. Fannie Davis. *From M. T. Shelhamer,* LIFE AND LABORS IN THE SPIRIT WORLD. *Courtesy of the Mary Evans Picture Library, London.*

7. Andrew Jackson Davis and Mary Fenn (Love) Davis. *From A. J. Davis,* THE MAGIC STAFF. *Courtesy of the American Antiquarian Society, Worcester, Massachusetts.*

8. Emma Hardinge. *From Emma Hardinge Britten,* NINETEENTH CENTURY MIRACLES. *Courtesy of the Watkinson Library, Trinity College, Hartford, Connecticut.*

ACKNOWLEDGMENTS

A historian is a bit like a spirit medium: one's goal is to allow the dead to speak as clearly as possible. Many people have assisted me in the attempt. This book began as a doctoral dissertation supervised by Sydney Ahlstrom and Nancy F. Cott. Although Sydney Ahlstrom's untimely death prevented his participation beyond the initial stages of this project, I hope that the final product reflects the model of humane scholarship he tried to impart to a sometimes unwilling student. In his absence, Nancy Cott served as an exemplary adviser. Always a thoughtful reader, she took my work seriously, but not too seriously, providing an ideal blend of criticism and encouragement. Her own work served as both a model and an inspiration throughout this project. My early teachers, Virgene Bollens, H. Patrick Sullivan, Martin Marty, and Rosemary Ruether set me on the path that led to this study.

The project received financial support from a faculty development grant from Carleton College. The American Antiquarian Society supported it with the Francis Hyatt Fellowship and provided an extraordinarily productive research home. During my stay there, I came to value many of the staff as both friends and colleagues. I would like to thank the entire staff of the society for its support and for its continuing interest in this book and its author. Thanks to Richard Fyffe for locating the stereograph reproduced on the cover. The project benefited greatly from the unusual personal interest shown by a few librarians and archivists, including Mary Huth and Karl Kabelac of the University of Rochester and the staff of the Vermont Historical Society. Christine and Dana Morgan, resident curators of Rokeby, home of the Rowland E. Robinson Memorial Association, kindly transformed their living room into a reading room for my research. Michael Kehoe and his family opened their homes to me during my Rochester research. Thanks also to the many other friends whose hospitality I enjoyed while traveling for research.

The following institutions graciously extended to me the use of their collections: The American Antiquarian Society, the Boston Athenaeum, the Boston Public Library, Carleton College, the Chicago Historical Society, Cornell University, the Free Library of Philadelphia, the Historical Society of Pennsylvania, the Newberry Library, the New York Public Library, the Rochester Public Library, the Rockford Museum Association in Rockford, Illinois, the Rowland E. Robinson Memorial Association in Ferrisburg, Vermont, the Arthur and Elizabeth Schlesinger Library, Smith College, the Stowe-Day Foundation, Syracuse University, the Townshend Public Library, the University of Illinois at Chicago, the University of Minnesota, the University of Rochester, the University of Wisconsin, the Vermont Historical Society, the Vermont State Library, the Watkinson Library at Trinity College, and Yale University. Permission to quote from manuscripts in their possession has been granted by courtesy of the University of Rochester, the Vermont Historical Society, and Richard and Helen Post.

Scholarship is a solitary endeavor. It might have been unbearably so if not for the many people who shared with me their enthusiasm for historical inquiry, whether in libraries, in conference sessions, or while following me through damp nineteenth-century graveyards. Two deserve special mention. Molly Ladd-Taylor has read virtually every word I have written from my early days in graduate school until the present day. Her generous partnership has added clarity and depth to my writing and has frequently saved me from embarrassment. Mark Greene, the Carleton College archivist, rendered tireless assistance at the final stages of writing. His keen editorial eye was invaluable in transforming the dissertation into a book. At that point, the manuscript also benefited from the comments of Liza Braude and R. Laurence Moore. In addition, I would like to thank Claire Rossini, Sally Stein, Bill Silva, Bruce Mullin, Richard Crouter, Ann Gordon, Marie Morgan, and Jonathan Butler as well as the host of friends and colleagues who read sections of the manuscript at various stages. I am grateful to Steve Seibert of Dragonfly Software, the designer of the computer program Nota Bene, on which this book was written, for his commitment to academic computing in the humanities. I would also like to thank my colleagues in Re-Evaluation Counseling for suggesting the possibility that writing a book might be a delightful activity and for helping to make it one.

I feel deeply indebted to the women and men who form the subject of this study. I am grateful to them for their commitment to their own convictions and for entering their lives, hopes, and dreams into the historical record. Finally, I thank my family, Liza, Marjorie, and Marvin Braude, and Vicci Sperry for their support and confidence in me over the years. This work is for my grandfather, Ben Braude, who wanted the best for me.

Introduction to the Second Edition

Women's rights and spiritualism. This book explores the intersection between two movements that may appear unlikely bedfellows. One of its goals is to suggest that they are not. I portray the compatibility of women's rights and Spiritualism as a manifestation of the intersection of religion and gender at the deepest levels of American culture. Every religious worldview must participate in the construction of gender if it is to provide a comprehensive vocabulary of meanings and actions for managing experience and interpreting reality. We should not be surprised, then, that a reform movement aimed at altering the roles and relations of men and women should find allies—sometimes unwelcome—within a religious movement committed to critiquing basic theological principles and religious structures.

While it should not be surprising to find a political movement and a religious movement sharing leaders, concepts, participants, and platforms, the coalescence of this particular political movement with this particular religion is in some ways surprising. The nineteenth-century women's movement eventually succeeded in some (though not all) of its central goals. Although often ridiculed in its own day, it is now regarded with respect for advancing universal suffrage and civil rights, key components of America's identity as a democratic nation. Spiritualism, in contrast, still attracts controversy and ill repute among critics who view it as a deception of the credulous. It is a testimony to the radicalism of the call for women's rights in the 1840s and 1850s that the religious movement with which it found most sympathy was one so much at odds with conventional beliefs. A second goal of the book, therefore, is to suggest that Spiritualism should be taken seriously as a religion making a legitimate response to nineteenth-century theological challenges.

The first and second goals merge in the focus on women's history.

Taking Spiritualism seriously as a religion means that the cadre of female mediums who spread the movement should be seen as religious figures, rather than as impressionable dupes. When I embarked on the research that eventually became *Radical Spirits*, more than one person asked whether I really wanted to tar women's rights with the taint of Spiritualism. Wouldn't that be bad for the movement? At the time I viewed these questions as curiously inconsistent with the goals of women's history and religious studies. All historians, I believed, were committed to the quest for truth, whether or not they liked where it led. Historians of women, in particular, needed to restore what had been excluded from the historical record, not to impose new sets of blinders. Students of religion aspired not to judge specific faiths but rather to understand and interpret them.

Ten years later, it is clear that just such contemporary issues shaped both the book and its reception. The choice of the subject was prompted by the desire to study a religious group in which women were visible as leaders. While casting a broad net for sources that would allow me to investigate these interests, I came upon the Achsa Sprague Papers at the Vermont Historical Society. Here was an unmarried woman from a small town who traveled the country as a public speaker in the 1850s—and she was a Spiritualist medium. Hundreds of letters from her admirers demonstrate that the trance lectures she delivered under spirit inspiration were experienced by many as a transformative source of religious teaching. Her personal papers revealed beyond the shadow of a doubt that she was absolutely sincere, that she resented and rejected any attempts to use her spiritual gifts for profit or deception, and that she viewed her religious teachings as part of advancing the reform agenda championed at the abolitionist and women's rights conventions she attended, as well as at Spiritualist conferences and meetings. Further investigation showed that Sprague was not an isolated figure, but was one of a substantial group of women who traveled as trance speakers during the 1850s. This group, it seemed to me, afforded an unusual opportunity to analyze an early example of women's religious leadership in America. Simultaneously, and unknown to me, a British historian concluded that the study of nineteenth-century spirit mediums afforded fruitful unexploited opportunities to explore the construction of gender in Victorian England.[1]

The publication of *Radical Spirits* in 1989 occurred in the midst of increased efforts in the humanities and social sciences to incorporate the experience of previously excluded groups. Women's studies, itself among the most massive efforts in this direction, embraced the principle of inclusion. African-American studies led the call for attention to racial and ethnic diversity. Something of a sea-change occurred in 1992, when the Columbus Quincentennial focused attention on issues of contact and colonialism, raising new questions about the most fundamental assumptions of both American and world history.

In the reorientation of the study of American culture along pluralistic lines, the place of religion remains ambiguous. Is religious affiliation akin to ethnicity in defining community identities and institutions? Or is it more like other voluntary associations, like belonging to a political party or a soccer league? Should religious diversity be included with race, class, and gender among the forms of difference that must be accounted for in analyses of American culture? While students of religion find that our subject partakes of elements of each model, we are consistently challenged to find ways to communicate this insight to those beyond the field of religious studies.

An important goal of *Radical Spirits* was to suggest the importance of religion as a factor in women's history, and, therefore, in the project of writing a more inclusive and accurate account of America's past. It seemed to me then, and does now, that a certain squeamishness about religious faith on the part of some scholars (many feminists among them) obscured important aspects of women's cultures. The rejection of religious belief and practice as analytic categories seemed, in some sense, to presuppose an opposition between faith and reason and to privilege the side of the binary historically associated with masculinity. By ignoring or downplaying the role of religious motivations, experiences, and meaning-systems, it seemed to me, historians downplayed arenas of American culture in which women might be more important than in—say—politics, business, or international affairs. I hoped that by demonstrating the religious motivations of historical actors who would appeal to contemporary readers, I might convince my colleagues to take religion more seriously. I hoped, for example, that by introducing the Rochester rappings from the point of view of dedicated Quaker abolitionists, I would encourage readers to question their own easy dismissal of Spiritualists. My goal was not that readers should take spirit communication more seriously, but rather that they should take those who spoke to spirits more seriously, and that they should accept the belief in spirit communication as an aspect of those people's worldview.

Whether as a result of *Radical Spirits* or not, Spiritualism has been taken more seriously as a theological, intellectual, and social movement in subsequent scholarly treatments. Bret Carroll locates Spiritualism among the primitivist and restorationist movements (Mormons, Shakers, Baptists, Disciples of Christ, and of course, Puritans) that sought to recapture Christianity's original order by eliminating later institutional and doctrinal developments. In his study of Henry Steel Olcott, Stephen Prothero depicts Spiritualism as a stage in Olcott's journey toward Buddhism. Notably, both of these works appear in the Indiana University Press Religion in North America series, co-edited by Catherine L. Albanese, who has herself become a serious student of the thought of Spiritualism's philosopher, Andrew Jackson Davis.[2]

Respectful treatments of Spiritualist history have informed new efforts to understand contemporary Spiritualist communities. The photographer Bill McDowell has documented the community of Lilydale, creating haunting images evoking universal longings for immortality and harmony. In *Cassadaga: The South's Oldest Spiritual Community*, a group of authors present a living Spiritualist community with roots reaching back into the nineteenth century. Combining architectural history, oral history, and photography with more conventional scholarly approaches, the book made an unusual departure by including an essay by a community resident about one of its prominent teachers—something that would have been difficult to imagine ten years ago. By studying a successful community dedicated to a controversial faith assumed by many to have been anathema in the evangelical South and to have died out long ago, they link contemporary movements to nineteenth-century Spiritualism. At Cassadaga the New Age does not appear as a foreign element on America's religious landscape, but rather as a domestic product that is as American as the Bible Belt and as deeply rooted in our national religious longings.[3]

This last publication builds on several trends in scholarship that point away from perspectives that would dismiss Spiritualism out of hand. Historians of American religion have begun to break down the barriers between margin and mainstream, between orthodox and heterodox, and especially between popular practice and official religious teachings. David Hall and Jon Butler pioneered this approach in seventeenth- and eighteenth-century studies. More recently, Ann Taves and Leigh Schmidt have extended it into the study of the nineteenth century, with important repercussions for the study of Spiritualism. Each continues the tradition of interpreting Spiritualism as an expression of both rationalism and romanticism, but departs from earlier accounts by considering other large religious departures under the same rubric. While I explored Spiritualism's interaction with Universalism, the Society of Friends, Transcendentalism, Christian Science, and Theosophy, they have brought in Methodism, a movement the membership of which outnumbered all of the others combined. Schmidt reminds us that angelic intimations of divine revelation continued to disrupt the world disciplined by enlightenment rationalism, for scientific elites as well as for revival converts. He also draws attention to the broad and multifaceted influence of the writings of Emmanuel Swedenborg, a key source of Spiritualist cosmology. Taves, meanwhile, finds evangelicals and Spiritualists sharing common cultural precedents and models in the mesmeric trance.[4]

In addition to addressing Spiritualist history, *Radical Spirits* was part of the expansion of the application of gender analysis to the study of religious history. As such, it found a warm reception among those interested in women's religious experience, expressions, and leadership. Contemporary readers found surprising resonance with the mediums' struggles to find a public voice, sometimes inserting the discussion of mediumship into the debates engendered by Carol Gilligan's assertion that women express values *in a different voice* (in her book of the same name—see n. 5). The question of women's religious leadership, its relation to theological innovation and to worship style has been deepened and strengthened by a number of subsequent studies. The connection between religion and reform has been explored in Nell Painter's biography of Sojourner Truth, as well as in Carolyn Gifford's careful selection from the diaries of Frances Willard.[5] Meanwhile, Judith Butler has pioneered a new approach to the discussion of gender, portraying it as a "performance" that constitutes an ongoing and contested process of cultural construction. The performances of mediums, both on the public platform and at private séances, highlighted a gendered division of labor in communication with the Divine. Such behavior suggests religion's substantial role in the construction, contestation, renegotiation, and performance of gender.[6]

Among the more audacious claims in *Radical Spirits* is the assertion that spirit mediums formed the first large group of American women to speak in public or to exercise religious leadership. The book documents the existence of 200 or so women whose careers as trance speakers during the 1850s and 1860s can be followed in the Spiritualist press. The happiest possible outcome of such an assertion, and, indeed, part of the motivation for making one, is the hope that further research will disprove it. The most probable exception to this claim, Quaker women preachers, has received substantial additional attention. Rebecca Larson's study of eighteenth-century Quaker women preachers asserts that "Never before had so many women spoken in public before audiences composed of both sexes."[7] Catherine Brekus also took up the challenge, and located 200 women preachers over the hundred years prior to the advent of Spiritualism, in a study that excluded Quakers. She found that this group, for the most part, were theologically conservative evangelicals whose defense of women's preaching was limited to their special call and did not extend to advocacy of women's rights. Likewise Susan Juster has examined Baptist women in eighteenth-century New England and argued for their loss of authority following the revolution.[8]

These studies, and those of the late nineteenth and early twentieth centuries begin to provide a framework for a periodization of women's leadership in American religion, and, indeed, for the symbolically important appearance of women as public speakers. While Quaker and evangelical women preachers preceded trance lecturers on the public platform, each, in turn, became mired in the fate of their own religious group, and ceased their effective public presence. The same would happen to spirit mediums in the 1870s and 1880s, as their faith became embroiled in scandals concerning materialization. Perhaps instead of looking for the first women religious leaders, historians need to analyze the cyclical rise and fall of women's leadership. Women play significant leadership roles in a variety of new or emerging movements, only to have their leadership repressed and forgotten as those movements become either institutionalized or marginalized. One of the most striking features of this cyclical pattern is the extent to which women's religious leadership is obliterated from historical memory, so that each subsequent emergence appears as something unprecedented, and indeed, ungodly. One possible outcome of a fuller portrait of the religious history of American women may be to normalize the notion of women's ministry, as well as exposing the repeated construction of bulwarks against it.

What distinguished spirit mediums from other religious women who rose to public roles at certain moments of enthusiasm within their religious communions was their commitment to women's rights. Perhaps *Radical Spirits*'s least explored contention is that Spiritualism formed a major—if not *the* major—vehicle for the spread of women's rights ideas in the mid-nineteenth century. Spiritualist mass meetings and lectures provided frequent, appreciative audiences for advocates of women's rights throughout the 1850s, while women's rights conventions were rare events, continuing into the 1860s, when the Civil War and the abolitionist cause placed those conventions in abeyance. Another argument about periodization suggests itself at this point—an argument concerning the history of feminism. Spiritualism's role in promoting women's rights was especially important during the movement's opening decades when its primary advocates were a vanguard far out of sync with national culture. Following reconstruction, the temperance and missionary movements became a focal point for religious women, and a means for many of them to become involved with women's rights. This broad acceptance of women's public moral role by Protestant church women laid the groundwork for the passage of woman suffrage in 1920. The work of Beryl Satter demonstrates that as the twentieth century dawned, radical religious views continued to inspire and support new forms of feminism. The desire of many women's rights leaders to perfect the self as a path to improving society drew them to the New Thought Movement. Once again religious radicals formed an important but controversial minority on women's issues, providing new intellectual frameworks that grew out of basic critiques of contemporary culture.[9]

While the discussion of an overlap between Spiritualism and the women's rights movement was greeted with interest by religious and cultural historians, it has been received more coolly by political historians and historians of the women's rights movement. When this overlap is mentioned, I am frequently asked for the names of women's rights activists who became adherents. Upon learning that the Spiritualists were not among the handful of well-known suffrage leaders, many dismiss the overlap as insignificant. They are disappointed to learn that among those in the vanguard of women's rights it was Lucy Stone's sister-in-law (Anna Blackwell), Susan B. Anthony's cousin (Sarah Anthony Burtis), Elizabeth Cady Stanton's neighbors (Mary Ann and Thomas McClintock), and Lucretia Mott's dinner guests (too numerous to name), not the famous leaders themselves, who espoused Spiritualism. Separated by one degree from the most important women's rights activists, these figures, in part because of their unconventional religious views, play only a small role in histories of the women's rights movement.

What distinguished those who adopted the new faith from those who did not? Often—not always—it was their radicalism. Sarah Grimké was probably the most important adherent among famous activists, along with regional leaders like Paulina Wright Davis and Laura de Force Gordon. Recent treatments of the nineteenth-century women's rights movement have tended to focus on the two giants: Stanton and Anthony, as well as on the notorious Victoria Woodhull. The tone-deafness to religion in this literature may be exemplified by the otherwise excellent Ken Burns documentary, *Not for Ourselves Alone* (1999). Here Frances Willard, who led the largest nineteenth-century organization to support woman suffrage, is described as an enemy of freedom who hoped to use the vote to enforce Christian morality. Barbara Goldsmith's book, *Other Powers,* worse than ignoring religion, holds up the involvement of suffragists with Spiritualism as a source of shock and sensationalism, exactly what *Radical Spirits* hoped to prevent.[10]

Why has the attempt to draw religious history and women's rights into a common narrative been the most difficult "sell" of the book's goals? The answer may lie in a similar pattern beginning to appear in accounts of modern feminism. In order to understand the continuing concerns effecting the reception of discussions of religion and the nineteenth-century women's movement, I would now like to explore the same issues in the emerging historiography of contemporary feminism.

After 30 years, the history of the "second wave" is being written. A new literature of memoirs, chronicles, and historical narratives looks back on the activism of the 1960s and 1970s in order to recapture its excitement and distill its lessons for the generation that has come of age in the world that feminism helped to shape. This literature suggests that the squeamishness about religious faith evident in the nineteenth-century historiography likewise pervades these accounts, and perhaps for the same reason. In accounts of the nineteenth-century women's movement, incorporating religion requires attention to popular activism in a variety of sectors of American culture, reaching far beyond the handful of famous leaders. In the new accounts of modern feminism, incorporating religion into the narrative would also require the depiction of a broad movement, manifesting itself in diverse forms in different cultural arenas.

The inclusion of religion within the historical assessment of feminism in both the nineteenth and twentieth centuries is important for several reasons. First, it can help dispel the idea that religion and feminism are opposing forces in American culture. This assumption undergirds many positions articulated both within conservative religious circles and within progressive feminism. Some contemporary feminists assume that religious women suffer from false consciousness and that their allegiance to patriarchal religious organizations makes them incapable of authentic work on behalf of women. However, religious hierarchies often discourage or prohibit women's public leadership and assume that those who work to improve women's status lack authentic faith. Both assumptions are based on misconceptions about the relationship between religion and feminism. Both make recurrent references to "secular feminism," most often exemplified by the National Organization of Women (NOW). Even the history of NOW itself suggests problems with the characterization of feminism as an exclusively secular movement.

An oft-reprinted photograph of the founders of NOW begins to tell the story. It shows a nun in full habit standing next to Pauli Murray, the first African-American woman ordained as an Episcopal priest, standing next to Betty Friedan. In addition to including religious women among its founders, NOW in its early years included religion as an arena of feminist activism, sponsoring an Ecumenical Task Force on Women and Religion among its early priorities. Similarly, *Ms.* magazine, from its inception, reported on feminist activity within religious groups. In 1974, for example, the December issue featured the first ordination of women in the Episcopal Church as well as an excerpt from Mary Daly's *Beyond God the Father,* while the July issue included the response of three religious Jews to the question, "Is It Kosher to Be a Feminist?"

Including religion in analyses of feminism's history is also necessary in order to provide an accurate assessment of the movement's impact. Just as the exclusion of Spiritualists leaves a small number of public leaders identified with the women's rights movement, the exclusion of religious women from the "second wave" makes it appear to effect a relatively narrow and homogeneous group. Attention to Catholic, Evangelical, Mormon, Jewish, and Muslim feminists, for example, suggests the movement's deep and broad reach into every region and sector of American life. Even attention to Protestants points away from stereotyped images, highlighting the participation of African-American women such as the Methodist leader Theressa Hoover or the Pentecostal minister Addie Wyatt. Most importantly, many religious feminists chose to maintain ties to their communities of faith while participating in the struggle for women's rights. Activists working for the equality of women within their denominations understood their work as part of the feminist movement. Movements for the ordination of women, for lay voting rights for women, and for inclusive language and liturgical reform reflected feminism's reach into a wide variety of religious groups. Explicitly feminist agendas animated the Women's Ordination Conference (Catholic), Woman Church Convergence, United Methodist Women and the Re-Imagining Conference, as well as Church Women United.

While many feminists chose their religious communities as their sphere of feminist activism, others became convinced that their faith traditions could not be cleansed of sexism, and left them behind. But even among this group, religion was often a focus of feminist activity. The feminist spirituality movement emerged as an alternative for those who hoped to abandon patriarchal traditions without abandoning religious experience. Feminist witchcraft, goddess worship, and a variety of

New Age spiritualities incorporated feminism and spread it into new arenas. As in Spiritualism, many of these groups eventually found kinship with male co-religionists in neopaganism.

While I hope that the reissuing of *Radical Spirits* will contribute to the continuing challenge of incorporating feminism into religious history and religion into the history of feminism, surely the most salient and unique feature of women's—and men's—involvement with nineteenth-century Spiritualism lay in its promise to bridge the final separation of death. Some readers found the author of *Radical Spirits* overly circumspect about whether Spiritualism could actually accomplish this, that is, about the authenticity of spirit communication, and about the continuation of individual identity after death. As much as I protested that it was the cultural meaning of spirit communication, not its authenticity, that was the subject of my research, questions persisted. While the promise of communication with those who have passed beyond death continues to attract Americans to Spiritualism, the continuing salience of this issue beyond Spiritualist circles was brought home to me by one of the most unexpected uses of *Radical Spirits* that has come to my attention. A Presbyterian who leads a monthly regional service commemorating the losses of pregnancy uses the book in her ministry to those who have experienced abortion, miscarriage, or stillbirth. The book's graphic portrayals of the reunion of mothers with lost infants, she told me, helped to heal the self-inflicted wounds of abortion. She said that she had named each of her own three aborted fetuses, and that she was glad that she had been able to be their mother even for the few months she carried them, although she was estranged from her three adult children. Moreover, the assertion that the potential children of terminated pregnancies are not lost but are in heaven with Jesus has become a staple of evangelical post-abortion counseling, as has the advice to name and mourn aborted fetuses.[11]

I did not know whether to be more shocked that a conservative Presbyterian would use a book filled with heterodoxy in her ministry, or that an anti-abortion activist would find kinship with the radical feminists who populate this book. The implications of joining aborted or miscarried fetuses with lost children were never contemplated by nineteenth-century Spiritualists, who, like their contemporaries, did not acknowledge fetal life before "quickening." Abortion was not uncommon during the rise of Spiritualism, and miscarriage is common in all times and places, yet I had never seen any indication that spirit communication included miscarriages or abortions.[12] Indeed, the expectation that spirit communication might be possible following pregnancies that only lasted a few weeks seems to reflect the heightened expectations of modern medicine that very premature infants might in fact grow to maturity, as well as new technologies permitting much more knowledge of early pregnancy. My own inclination was to agree with my nineteenth-century subjects, who mourned those who had joined them as living family members in a different way from abbreviated pregnancies. But the experience of separation and loss, apparently, reaches across religious and political divides, and across the centuries. Evangelical women who participate in ministries for those who have terminated pregnancies report a paralyzing sense of isolation. Exacerbated by the secrecy that perforce attends their choices, their isolation contributes to a sense of loss apparently as devastating as that suffered by nineteenth-century parents whose living infants died at a much higher rate than in our day. Finally, coping with grief is part of the human condition, linking those of every theological or political orientation.

One event in my own life has changed my personal perception of the issues leading to spirit communication. Since the birth of my daughter in 2000 I appreciate in a new way how connection to another human being could be so fundamental to one's existence that one would pursue any available avenue to continue it. The book's opening narrative, depicting a mother's loss of her infant, resonates for me in an entirely different way than when I initially selected it to open the book. While I had lost various elderly relatives and friends before writing *Radical Spirits,* I wrote about bereavement primarily as an observer, not as a participant. Ironically, it is not the loss of a loved one but rather the gift of a life entrusted to me to witness its miracle that has heightened my sensitivity to the difficulty of enduring a final separation. I do not know, now, if I could write about the loss of Annie Denton Cridge's baby in the unadorned fashion that I did ten years ago. I suspect that were I to broach this subject anew I would feel compelled to comment on the universality and tragedy of her grief, on the difference between losing an elder relative whose passing in some sense marks the progress of one's own maturation, and of losing a baby, "the fond great hope of my life," as Annie Denton Cridge called her son, the forward-looking promise of one's own legacy into the future. While I did comment on the refusal of Victorian women to accept that their innocent children could be damned to eternal suffering, I now see these issues in a more concrete way. I wonder daily how a parent could find the new life lying in their arms anything but good to the core, and what it meant for Calvinists to believe that infants were born with a Fallen nature, that a little baby who gladdens so many hearts could have a will inclined toward evil. I wonder how the incomparable serenity of my sleeping child could appear anything but innocent, and what effort it would take for a parent to convince herself otherwise.

While the book opens with a young mother's loss, it concludes with the aging reformers who worked for women's rights contemplating their own passage from the scene at the end of the nineteenth century. For some the principles that motivated reformers to work for a better world proved more enduring, and more consoling, than any human connections. But for others the desire to continue contact with loving companions who had given meaning to their lives by sharing their missions and their journeys superseded all. If this desire cancels out the words and deeds of those who experience it as significant, much will be erased from history.

NOTES

1. Alex Owen, *The Darkened Room: Women, Power, and Spiritualism in Late Nineteenth Century England* (London: Virago, 1989). Reprinted 1990 by University of Pennsylvania Press as *The Darkened Room: Women, Power and Spiritualism in Late Victorian England.*

2. Bret E. Carroll, *Spiritualism in Antebellum America* (Bloomington: Indiana University Press, 1997). Stephen R. Prothero, *The White Buddhist: The Asian Odyssey of Henry Steel Olcott* (Bloomington: Indiana University Press, 1996). Catherine L. Albanese, "On the Matter of Spirit: Andrew Jackson Davis and the Marriage of God and Nature," *Journal of the American Academy of Religion* 60 (Spring 1992): 1–17; "The Magical Staff: Quantum Healing in the New Age," *Perspectives on the New Age* (Albany, N.Y.: SUNY Press, 1992): 68–84, 307–310; "The Subtle Energies of Spirit: Explorations in Metaphysical and New Age Spiritualities," *Journal of the American Academy of Religion* 67 (June 1999): 305–325.

3. Michael Duncan, "Bill McDowell at Jan Kesner," *Art in America* (July 1999); John J. Guthrie, Jr., Phillip Charles Lucas, and Gary Monroe, *Cassadaga: The South's Oldest Spiritualist Community* (Gainesville, Fla.: University Press of Florida, 2000).

4. Ann Taves, *Fits, Trances, and Visions: Experiencing Religion and Explaining Experience from Wesley to James* (Princeton: Princeton University Press, 1999). Leigh Eric Schmidt, *Hearing Things: Religion, Illusion, and the American Enlightenment* (Cambridge: Harvard University Press, 2000).

5. Carol Gilligan, *In a Different Voice: Psychological Theory and Women's Development* (Cambridge: Harvard University Press, 1982); Nell Irvin Painter, *Sojourner Truth: A Life, a Symbol* (New York: W.W. Norton, 1996); Carolyn De Swarte Gifford, ed., *Writing Out My Heart: Selections from the Journal of Frances E. Willard, 1855–96* (Urbana: University of Illinois Press, 1995).

6. Judith P. Butler, *Gender Trouble: Feminism and the Subversion of Identity* (New York: Routledge, 1990).

7. Rebecca Larson, *Daughters of Light: Quaker Women Preaching and Prophesying in the Colonies and Abroad, 1700–1775* (New York: Knopf, 1999): 289.

8. Catherine A. Brekus, *Strangers and Pilgrims: Female Preaching in America, 1740–1845* (Chapel Hill, N.C.: University of North Carolina Press, 1998). Susan Juster, *Disorderly Women: Sexual Politics and Evangelicalism in Revolutionary New England* (Ithaca, N.Y.: Cornell University Press, 1994).

9. Beryl Satter, *Each Mind a Kingdom: American Women, Sexual Purity, and the New Thought Movement, 1875–1920* (Berkeley: University of California Press, 1999).

10. Barbara Goldsmith, *Other Powers: The Age of Suffrage, Spiritualism, and the Scandalous Victoria Woodhull* (New York: A.A. Knopf, 1998).

11. Linda Cochrane, *Forgiven and Set Free: A Post-Abortion Bible Study for Women* (Grand Rapids, Mich.: Baker Books, 1996); Sydna Massé and Joan Phillips, *Her Choice to Heal: Finding Spiritual and Emotional Peace after Abortion* (Colorado Springs, Colo.: Chariot Victor, 1998). Sydna Massé worked with James Dobson as Manager of Focus on the Family's Crisis Pregnancy Ministry before founding Ramah International Inc., a ministry aimed at helping individuals heal from the experience of abortion by reaching out to those considering abortion.

12. While a lively literature documents the similar religious treatment of aborted fetuses and infants who have died in Japan, this is highly unusual in the American context. Helen Hardacre, *Marketing the Menacing Fetus in Japan* (Berkeley: University of California Press, 1997).

Radical Spirits

"My Soul's Thraldom and Its Deliverance"

I n 1857, Annie Denton Cridge lost her first child within months of his birth. "My darling is gone! the fond great hope of my ___ life!. . . . How bitter the separation!" mourned the twenty-three-year-old socialist and woman's rights advocate.[1] She poured out her grief in the pages of the *Vanguard,* the newspaper she published with her husband in Dayton, Ohio. Three obituaries recounted the brief life and lamented death of little Denton Cridge. According to the longest tribute, authored by the grieving mother, the conditions that separated Cridge from her baby, however bitter, were short lived. During Denton's final moments, she saw the spirits of her own dead parents above his couch, "waiting to bear his sweet spirit away." She watched her baby's spirit withdraw from his body and assume a spiritual body, with the help of his grandparents. Since then, Cridge told her readers, she held her child in her arms every day. He weighed nothing and within a week had recovered from the illness that took his life. Her spirit mother held the baby while she dressed.[2]

For Anne Denton Cridge, her son's death marked the beginning of her ability to perceive the spirits of the dead and the beginning of a new religious faith. Her experiences as a medium dispelled the skepticism that resulted from her evangelical upbringing in England. "Though a member of an orthodox church for years, I never derived that satisfaction that must arise from positive knowledge," she told her readers. "What we believed was on the authority of someone else, and hence could not possibly effect us as a faith does based on what we know and have seen."[3] A year before the birth of her baby, at the

tender age of twenty-two, Cridge wrote a serial autobiography entitled "My Soul's Thraldom and Its Deliverance," which recounted her
rejection of evangelicalism.[4] Her parents' Methodist doctrines, she recalled, "made heaven into Hell." She described her search for truth
among the various progressive alternatives available in England: mesmerism, Owenism, and socialism. Although she had been exposed to
the Spiritualist doctrines that engrossed other American radicals, including her husband, before her son's death, it was not until Anne
Cridge saw spirits herself that communication with the dead changed
from a theory to a compelling faith. The firsthand knowledge she
now possessed of the fate of the soul after death countered the theological terror of her youth. Her baby's death and the advent of her
mediumship culminated her emancipation from the religious perspective that dominated her family and her era. When Anne Denton
Cridge became a Spiritualist, she joined a popular and controversial
movement that assumed a self-conscious identity in North America
in the mid-nineteenth century.[5] Spiritualism was a new religious
movement aimed at proving the immortality of the soul by establishing communication with the spirits of the dead. Whether reverenced
or ridiculed, Spiritualism was ubiquitous on the American scene at
mid-century. For some it provided solace in the face of bereavement,
for some entertainment, for some a livelihood earned from the credulous. For many it provided evidence of the immortality of the soul
that formed the basis of a sincere religious faith. For iconoclasts and
nonconformists it provided an alternative to the established religious
order. It held two attractions that proved irresistible to thousands of
Americans: rebellion against death and rebellion against authority.

Spiritualism held a special attraction for activists such as Anne Denton Cridge and her husband Alfred, who felt oppressed by the traditional roles assigned to men and women, found the entire social
order in need of revision, and condemned the churches as perpetua-
tors of repressive conventions. "The only religious sect in the world
. . . that has recognized the equality of woman is the Spiritualists,"
claimed the *History of Woman Suffrage*, edited by Elizabeth Cady Stanton and Susan B. Anthony. Written in the 1880s, the official history
of the nineteenth-century woman's rights movement recorded the
equality of women as speakers and leaders throughout Spiritualism's
thirty-seven-year history and the movement's vocal support for
woman suffrage. The *History of Woman Suffrage* described a religious
group whose beliefs and practices committed it to fostering female

leadership. "They have always assumed that woman may be a medium of communication from heaven to earth," the *History* observed, "that the spirits of the universe may breathe through her lips."[6]

Like the woman's rights movement, Spiritualism dated its inception to 1848 in upstate New York. The two movements intertwined continually as they spread throughout the country. Not all feminists were Spiritualists, but all Spiritualists advocated woman's rights, and women were in fact equal to men within Spiritualist practice, polity, and ideology. Certainly, as the *History of Woman Suffrage* stated, Spiritualists were the only religious group of which this could be said.* Detractors concurred in linking "Women's Rights and Spiritualism, [as] illustrating the follies and delusions of the nineteenth-century."[7] At a time when no churches ordained women and many forbade them to speak aloud in church, Spiritualist women had equal authority, equal opportunities, and equal numbers in religious leadership. While most religious groups viewed the existing order of gender, race, and class relations as ordained by God, ardent Spiritualists appeared not only in the woman's rights movement but throughout the most radical reform movements of the nineteenth century. They led so-called ultraist wings of the movements for the abolition of slavery, for the reform of marriage, for children's rights, and for religious freedom, and they actively supported socialism, labor reform, vegetarianism, dress reform, health reform, temperance, and antisabbatarianism, to name a few of their favorite causes.

The goal of this book is to examine the nature and extent of the overlap between the woman's rights movement and Spiritualism in nineteenth-century America. Why did Spiritualism's heterodoxy appeal to men and women anxious to depart from the traditional social order and especially from existing gender roles? What made the new religious movement as a whole sympathetic to woman's rights and to other reforms that horrified most pious Americans? This study analyzes the relation between the religious content of Spiritualism and the radical social views espoused by its adherents. It explores why and how Spiritualists made this unprecedented departure from accepted views about the proper roles and relations of men and women in religion and society. The outcome, I hope, illuminates the elusive con-

---

* Quakers, as the *History* noted, did have women ministers but did not appoint women to select meetings that had authority over both men's and women's meetings and censured members who spoke out on any political or reform subject.

nection between religious and political radicalism in American culture.

Spiritualism was a religious response to the crisis of faith experienced by many Americans at mid-century. Based on the view that contact with the spirits of the dead provided empirical proof of the immortality of the soul, Spiritualism appealed to people in search of new justification for a wavering faith. For those no longer convinced by the "evidences" of Christianity, Spiritualism provided "scientific" evidence of religious truth. Initially, it required people to believe nothing. Rather, it asked them to become "investigators," to observe "demonstrations" of the truth of Spiritualism produced under "test conditions" in the séance room. It provided a way to remain religious for those disaffected from Calvinism or evangelicalism in the antebellum years and for those disillusioned by Darwinism, biblical criticism, and the rise of science later in the century. Considering its own methods to be scientific, the movement participated in the optimistic equation of science and progress that bolstered the conviction of so many nineteenth-century reform groups.[8]

Spiritualism's claim to be scientific may draw smiles from twentieth-century readers, but the contention was not unreasonable within the context of popular scientific knowledge at mid-century. Few people viewed science and religion as enemies before the Civil War. Rather, investigators of each understood themselves as pursuing related inquiries into the nature of reality. Antebellum churchmen and scientists alike viewed the physical world as "one volume of God's Bible" in which God's will might be discovered in the laws he established to govern his creation.[9] All scientists saw God's hand in nature, although Spiritualists may have seen it more clearly than some. Furthermore, the major scientific discoveries of the nineteenth century initially appeared no more credible than the claims of Spiritualists. When Samuel F. B. Morse went to Congress to request $30,000 to construct an experimental telegraph line linking Washington and Baltimore in 1842, he found little understanding of the principles of electricity in the nation's governing body. Congressman Cave Johnson of Tennessee sarcastically suggested that, if the Congress wished to encourage science, half the appropriation should support experiments in mesmerism. His colleague from Alabama then moved that the Millerites—a sect predicting the second coming of Christ in 1844—should also share the appropriation. Although these proposals met with laughter, Chairman Winthrop of Massachusetts refused to rule that the amendment was not sufficiently analogous in character to the original bill and therefore was out of order. "It would," the chair opined, "require a scientific analysis to determine how far the magnetism of mesmerism was analogous to the magnetism to be employed in telegraphs." Two days later, when the bill finally came to a vote, seventy congressmen left their seats, many hoping "to avoid spending the public money for a machine they could not understand." Morse won his appropriation by a margin of three votes.[10]

If the U.S. Congress found the use of electricity in the telegraph incomprehensible in 1842, the general public can hardly have had a firm grasp of the principles of telegraphy six years later, when many of them found parallels between the instantaneous communication of messages over long distances by wires and what came to be known as "the spiritual telegraph," the communication of messages between this world and the next through human mediums. Indeed, both those who wished to prove such communication authentic and those who wished to expose it as fraud used inaccurate descriptions of electricity to explain its source.[11] Skeptics who wanted to discredit mediums required them to stand on materials presumed to be nonconductors of electricity, hoping to show that phenomena attributed to spirits was actually caused by electricity. One Spiritualist called electricity "the God principles at work," while another believed that "the delicate organization" of spirits enabled them to produce a "refined species of electricity" through which they communicated with living people. An early message attributed to Benjamin Franklin (a frequent communicator) gave credit for the success of the telegraph to "the intelligence of disembodied spirits." Franklin's spirit message asserted that scientific advancement on earth depended on the interest and cooperation of scientifically inclined spirits like himself.[12] Science, as Robert Darnton has observed about late eighteenth-century France, "captivated [the public] by revealing to them that they were surrounded by wonderful invisible forces." Gravity and electricity could be proved to exist but remained miraculous and inexplicable to most people. The strange forces that Congressman Johnson found equally absurd impressed many Americans as equally plausible.[13] The first chapter of this study will describe the manifestations that struck Spiritualists as convincing evidence of the possibility of communication with the dead.

Most people initially investigated Spiritualism in hope of communicating with a beloved friend or family member removed by death.

The new faith offered consolation and reassurance to bereaved Americans who, like Anne Denton Cridge, could no longer accept the harsh views of evangelicalism about the fate of their loved ones. Chapter 2 explores the immediate religious causes that led investigators to Spiritualism. It outlines Spiritualist theology and locates it within the spectrum of nineteenth-century attitudes toward death and the hereafter.

Because Spiritualism asserted that divine truth was directly accessible to individual human beings through spirit communication, the new faith provided a religious alternative that supported the individualist social and political views of antebellum radicals. Spiritualists in turn adopted a radical social program based on the same individualist principles that supported its unconventional religious practice. If untrammeled by repressive social or religious strictures, Spiritualists believed, individuals could serve as vehicles of truth because each embodied the laws of nature in his or her being. Such individualism laid the foundation for Spiritualism's rejection of male headship over women—or indeed of any individual over any other—whether in religion, politics, or society. Spiritualists believed that the advent of spirit communication heralded the arrival of a new era, one in which humanity, with spirit guidance, would achieve hitherto impossible levels of development. The new era would be characterized by the accomplishment of a broad program of progressive social reforms and a complete reformation of personal life. While other radicals struggled to reconcile their commitment to individualism with their belief in the sovereignty of God, Spiritualists found in their faith direct divine sanction for advancing social change. Chapter 3 discusses the common personnel and the ideological basis that Spiritualism shared with the early woman's rights movement and the ties that bound both to the radical wing of the movement for the abolition of slavery.

The prominence of women within Spiritualism resulted from a staunchly individualistic form of religious practice. Feminist scholars have found that women have been able to exercise leadership where religious authority derives from direct individual spiritual contact or experience rather than from office, position, or training.[14] Spiritualism produced an extreme case of these conditions, offering a unique opportunity for women to assume leadership. The movement viewed the individual as the ultimate vehicle of truth. Spirit communication could occur only through human mediumship. Individuals served as mediums for communication with spirits who revealed information about the divine order and the ultimate fate of the soul. Chapter 4 will analyze the role of spirit medium in order to explain Spiritualism's unprecedented success in accepting and promoting women's religious leadership.

Of all the changes in the social order advocated by Spiritualists in order to improve the status of women, two stand out. Chapter 5 explores the critique of marriage that made Spiritualism infamous for its association with free love. Chapter 6 discusses a second issue that Spiritualists viewed as crucial for women's emancipation: health. Mediums offered a variety of unorthodox diagnostic and therapeutic techniques. Both their gender and the benign nature of their treatments appealed to many who sought healing and brought mediums into direct conflict with the orthodox medical profession. Finally, Chapter 7 chronicles the decline of Spiritualism as a progressive social force in the 1870s and the competition it received from two new movements: Theosophy and Christian Science. In Spiritualism, the romanticism and perfectionism of antebellum reform outlived the Civil War. Even though its extreme individualism lost broad appeal after the war, it continued to motivate and support a small cadre of committed radical activists. Spiritualists never accepted the compromise with individualism that characterized the reform movements of the late nineteenth century. This may explain the movement's appeal to aging abolitionists as well as its dwindling influence among the reformers who superseded them as the century wore on.

Spiritualism never gave rise to permanent institutions of any consequence. Spiritualists held conventions like any other movement of the period, but these did not result in an organized church or even a national council.* Spiritualists resisted the sectarian impulse that so many denominations decried before splitting from their parent bodies. These conditions present certain problems for the researcher. It is not absolutely clear who or what to study under the title "Spiritualism." The movement had no orthodoxy because it had no governing body or power that could label a subgroup as heterodox. Spiritualism accommodated a fairly broad spectrum of views. In keeping with the

* The National Association of Spiritualists, the first of several organizations that still exist, was not founded until 1893.

extreme individualism of the movement, many lecturers presented descriptions of reality so unique that they had to invent their own terms to communicate their ideas.

Not only did the movement have no orthodox doctrine; it had no membership because it had nothing for adherents to belong to. It had no official leadership because it had no offices for leaders to hold. Mediums received no training and no ordination. Who, then, was a Spiritualist? Certainly, anybody who claimed to be may be regarded as a Spiritualist, but how shall we regard the many people who shunned public identification with the notorious movement but quietly attended séances, consulted the planchette (ouija board), or subscribed to Spiritualist periodicals? If it is difficult to determine who was a Spiritualist, it is also difficult to determine who was not. Many nineteenth-century figures who were not associated with the movement turned to Spiritualism in old age, frequently on the death of a beloved parent, child, or spouse. Spiritualism was in the air. It was available when it was needed, answering the religious needs of many who did not contribute to it as a movement. Because Spiritualists have no genetic identity, I will presume that a Spiritualist is anyone participating in a Spiritualist activity or idea.

Some may object that self-identification is insufficient evidence that a person is a Spiritualist, that frauds and charlatans must be distinguished from genuine inquirers. I see no reason to make retrospective judgments on this question. It concerns me only insofar as it concerned nineteenth-century Spiritualists. If someone was judged to be a fraud by contemporary coreligionists, I take that view into account. Any further judgments on my part would be comparable to judging the miraculous origins of any religion, a task that I do not understand to be within the competency of the historian.

Many people have asked my views about the authenticity of spirit communication. This question has increased interest because of the current popularity of "New Age" spiritual expressions that share many features with nineteenth-century Spiritualism. The practices of "channels" in the 1970s and 1980s who attribute the messages they voice to external intelligences closely parallel those of nineteenth-century mediums. Groups devoted to the recovery of "past life" experiences share much of the progressive outlook fueled by a sense of discovery that distinguished the Spiritualist movement of the last century. These phenomena have reached a broad audience through the autobiographical writings of the actress Shirley MacLaine, whose interest in investigating spirit communication was strengthened by learning of the existence of nineteenth-century mediums.[15] The acceptance by many Americans of channeled documents such as "A Course in Miracles" and "Seth Speaks" have rekindled nineteenth-century debates about what constitutes convincing evidence of spirit presence.[16]

As far as my own conclusions about the reality of spirit communication, I can say only that this is not the question that has motivated my inquiry and that this study does not address it. To me, nineteenth-century Spiritualism, like many of the spiritual explorations associated with the New Age, appears as an example of profound mystical experience and extraordinary self-deception tangled together in a hopeless mélange. If this study sheds any light on New Age phenomena, it will be by increasing our understanding of the relation of comparable religious expressions to their social and historical contexts, not by making judgments about their authenticity.

The mystery that has engaged my curiosity throughout this project is not the mystery of spirit communication but rather the mystery of faith. I want to know why and how people believe the things they believe and how social, political, and religious beliefs combine to form a comprehensive understanding of reality. In all times and places, some people talk to the spirits of the dead, and they persist in doing so whether it is regarded as revelation, heresy, or insanity. I am interested in exploring this phenomenon because I believe that faith is a crucial and little understood element of the social structure. It provides a window into the complex realm of human motivation. I hope that this study may contribute to our appreciation of the role of individual human intentionality and experience in shaping, as well as being shaped by, the world in which we live.

1

"Unbroken Communication between the Infinite and All Beings"

n 1848, the dedicated Quaker abolitionists Amy and Isaac Post, like the other residents of Rochester, New York, heard rumors of mysterious noises in the nearby village of Hydesville.[1] The rumors told of raps on the walls and furniture of an old farmhouse that occurred only in the presence of two young daughters of the family who inhabited it. The apparent intelligence of the mysterious sounds convinced the family and neighbors that the spirit of a murdered peddler buried in the basement made the raps. The residents of Hydesville crowded the house to hear the spirit demonstrate its superhuman knowledge by giving the correct number of raps when asked the age or number of their children. Initially, Amy and Isaac Post "paid no more heed" to the much touted raps than to "the Old Salem witch stories." Claims of unaccountable religious experiences were not unusual in western New York State, a section of the country "burned over" by repeated outpourings of the spirit and auspicious millennial tidings during the evangelical revivals of the Second Great Awakening.* But when the Posts learned that the family in which the mysterious sounds occurred was one with which they were "well acquainted," they took them more seriously. Isaac Post wrote to his brother and sister-in-law that Kate and Margaret Fox, in whose presence the raps occurred, were "Girls of 12 & 14 years who used to live in our house at Cornhill and with whom we always had good under-

* The same vicinity, the Finger Lakes region of New York State, gave birth to Mormonism in 1827 and to Millerism—which ultimately became Seventh-Day Adventism—in the 1840s.

standing." The Fox family deserted the apparently haunted house in hope of peace from the raps. Kate and Margaret were sent to Rochester to live with their older sister, Ann Leah Fish (See plates 1, 3).[2]

Here the story probably would have ended, but for the interest shown in the rappings by the Post family and the other indefatigable reformers who made up their circle of friends. The Posts' home at 36 Sophia Street served as Rochester's headquarters for reform lecturers and fugitive slaves, sometimes housing a dozen passengers on the Underground Railroad in a single night (See plate 2). Noted abolitionist speakers Abigail Kelly, William Lloyd Garrison, and Henry C. Wright relished Amy's hospitality and cherished her friendship. "I should love much to look into your home . . . about once in 24 hours," Rochester abolitionist Frederick Douglass wrote to Amy Post while absent on a speaking tour. Had Douglass looked in on an evening when the Posts had no guests, he would have found her sitting by the stove knitting stockings for the antislavery fair in Boston.[3]

Isaac Post reported that when Kate and Margaret Fox arrived from Hydesville "they felt very anxious that we should enjoy what they did there." Within a few days, one of the sisters visited the Posts, together with family friends Abigail and Henry Bush. The guests retreated into a bedroom with Amy, and the raps commenced. Isaac described what followed in a letter to his brother: "I suppose I went with as much unbelief as Thomas felt when he was introduced to Jesus after he had ascended. When I looked in the door with my countenance so doubting and saw Abigail & Henry looking as tho they stood before the judgment seat, I felt rebuked and much more so when Abbi in her most gentle manner asked some questions. I heard very distinct thumps under the floor apparently and several apparent answers." After this inexplicable experience, the Posts became the Fox sisters' mentors and confidants, gathering a small group to meet weekly in search of the truth that might be revealed by communicating with the dead through the girls' mediumship. Spiritualism joined the host of unpopular but heartfelt causes championed by the tireless reformers.[4]

Although later mediums would give verbatim messages from spirits, initially the raps were inarticulate, able to respond only "yes" or "no" to specific questions or to answer with a number, the number of raps made in succession. Isaac introduced the technique of reciting the alphabet so that the raps could spell words by sounding when the correct letter was reached. The process proved cumbersome and did not always improve the quality of the messages. On one occasion when the raps "demanded the alphabet" during dinner, Isaac found it difficult to divide the letters at which raps sounded into words. Finally, the raps revealed, "Put on as much molasses as he likes," hardly the profound revelation for which investigators hoped.[5] More satisfying communications resulted from direct questions such as those Isaac recorded during a session with Kate and Margaret in November 1848:

> Dr. Chase who had recently lost his mother, asked if his Mother's Spirit was present. The answer was, she was. Whether she was happy/ she was, whether her knowledge had increased since she passed away/ it had. Whether she continually watched over him/ she did. Then he asked about . . . a sister, whether his suspicions in regard to her death were correct. The answer, they were not. Would she have lived if other means had been used? The reply, she would not. Then he asked if [he] could be convinced that there could be spiritual manifestations, then he could get no more answers.[6]

Because the raps could communicate only in response to questions, the inquirers, rather than the mediums, set the agenda for the first spirit communications. True, even in Hydesville, a shower of affirmative raps greeted the question, "Are you a spirit?" But it was the direct inquiries of the Posts and their friends that revealed the presence of spirits other than that of the murdered peddler to whom the first raps were attributed. Persistent and repeated questions produced raps indicating the presence of other spirits, especially the spirits of dead relatives of those present. Investigators used sessions with the Fox sisters to pursue relief from the host of anxieties that accompanied separation at death, and many of them received it. The hunger for communion with the dead gave Spiritualism its content, transforming what may have been a teenage prank into a new religion. Americans wanted to talk to spirits, and they would have found a way to do it with or without Kate and Margaret Fox.

Most of the early investigators who set the course of the new movement were Quakers who, like the Posts, found themselves unable to participate in the Society of Friends because they believed it had strayed from its original principles. Quaker doctrine taught that the spirit of God lay within each individual and that this inner light was the primary vehicle for religious truth. The doctrine of the inner light produced an ongoing tension within Quakerism. Quaker tradition emphasized a simple life-style, and vested authority in meetings to ensure that members complied with rigorous standards of behavior and segregation from the non-Quaker "world." But, at the same time, Quaker doctrine undermined the authority of meetings and elders to enforce those standards by encouraging anyone who felt moved by the spirit to speak freely in meetings and by recognizing the authority of the inner light within each individual. During the antebellum period, Friends who felt moved to testify against the injustice of buying and selling human beings were silenced by an increasingly rigid disciplinary structure. Obedience to conscience clashed with obedience to Quaker elders and to the authority of meetings.

In 1827, the conflict between the authority of meetings and the freedom of the individual to act according to the promptings of the spirit caused a split within the Society of Friends. The followers of Elias Hicks, a cousin of Amy Post, withdrew to form separate meetings because they believed that orthodox Friends' meetings had become too formalized and no longer gave adequate freedom for individuals to act according to the dictates of the inner light. Hicks also believed that the Quaker establishment had become too enmeshed with the institutions and material comforts of "the world" and that tolerance of slavery confirmed this excessive worldliness. The Posts, like most antislavery Friends, withdrew from their meeting and joined the Hicksites. But even the Hicksite meeting imposed unacceptable restraints. When the Hicksites censured Amy and Isaac for participating in antislavery societies with non-Quakers, the Posts withdrew to help found yet another group, the Congregational Friends, in Waterloo, New York, composed predominantly of ex-Friends who wanted greater liberty to express their political views. The term *congregational* implied the adoption of a congregational form of polity, meaning that the Waterloo meeting did not recognize the authority of the Quaker hierarchy over the local congregation and would not answer to the Hicksite Genessee Yearly Meeting.[7]

The Waterloo Congregational Friends based their beliefs on the Quaker principle that the law of God is written in every human soul. Because human beings were created in the image of God, each one, "however less or more perfect be the manifestations of the principles of his nature," was in fact "a limited transcript of the perfect Architect." These views led the Waterloo friends to conclude that "an unbroken chain of communication" exists "between the Infinite and all beings." Of all known facts, they found "The existence of this communication between the finite and the Infinite" to be "first in magnitude and most absorbing in interest." Because God's image resided within each individual, they believed any limitation on absolute freedom of conscience impeded the divine will. In George Fox's exhortation to "Mind the light," they saw "the beginning and end of all religion." They left the Society of Friends because they viewed its increasing regulation of its members' freedom of expression as impeding communication with God.[8]

Within months of the formation of the Waterloo Congregational Friends, its members learned of the raps that occurred in the presence of the Fox sisters, and many accepted the spiritual origin of the mysterious noises. Communication with spirits appealed to devout Quaker reformers as an expression of the doctrine of the inner light. "It was some like friends preaching. They were relying on the spirit," observed Isaac Post. The "spiritual telegraph" reconnected the lines of communication with God that they feared had been severed by orthodox Quakerism's departure from its early practices. Congregational Friend Sarah Fish initially greeted the raps with skepticism. But, on reflection, she decided that they were within the bounds of Quaker teaching about communication between human and divine. "I became perfectly satisfied that I had resisted the Divine Spirit in my own heart by making light of what that child said," she wrote to Amy Post following an early séance. Sarah Fish laid down her pen after writing the above line, then heard raps on her own bedstand. She asked that the raps repeat if she was correct that they came at that moment to confirm the message of the light within. She heard more raps, which dispelled her last shreds of skepticism. "I am more than convinced of the truth that our departed friends are with us striving for our good," she concluded the next morning. Through networks of kin and friendship, news of the raps spread quickly to Quaker communities in Long Island, Nantucket, Philadelphia, and throughout New York State.[9]

The spiritual longings of the Waterloo Friends for intercourse with the infinite grew out of their Quaker heritage, but it overlapped with an urge shared by many Americans: the desire for communication with the dead. Investigators eager for news of departed loved ones, such as the Posts' friend Dr. Chase, asked for it directly. The Posts learned, in response to inquiries, that the mediums could see Isaac's three dead sisters as well as the Posts' recently deceased five-year-old daughter, Matilda. "They always speak of seeing Matilda [and] say she is happy around us," Isaac wrote to his brother and sister-in-law. A son, also lost at the age of five, but many years earlier, communicated as well. By addressing their own spiritual needs, and by asking the questions they did, the disaffected Quakers of upstate New York created a religious movement that would satisfy the yearnings of mid-century Americans across the country.[10]

More substantive communications began after Kate and Margaret's older sister, Leah Fox Fish, mother of three children, proved to be a medium. Leah was prone to headaches, from which she found relief when Isaac "put her asleep" by "magnetizing" her. In the resultant trance state, she communed freely with spirits, especially those of Hannah Kirby Post (Amy's sister and Isaac's first wife) and the Posts' departed children. "I should like she could remain so happy when awake and so judicious for she seems far in advance of her wakeful state," Isaac wrote to Amy. While in trance, Leah "reasoned very philosophical." She looked right at Isaac and said that "it was not true that first love was best for after the object was removed we are free to have the same feeling center on another." This remark held special significance for Amy and Isaac, both of whom lost a first love before marrying each other. The man whom Amy once regarded as her "only source of . . . earthly happiness" died shortly before they were to have been married. Amy then went to live in the household of her older sister, Hannah, and Hannah's husband, Isaac Post. When Hannah died, Amy stayed on to care for her sister's children and eventually married their father. Twenty years later, having produced four children and buried two of them, Amy and Isaac Post found affirmation from spirit communication for the shape their lives had taken as well as consolation for the many lost hopes they had once held dear.[11]

After a year of investigation, the spirits demanded a public demonstration of their intelligent communication. The spirits instructed Isaac Post and his cousin George Willets to rent the city's largest hall for three nights and charge the public seventy-five cents each to witness the Fox sisters' mediumship. Eliab Capron, a Congregational Friend from Auburn, New York, was assigned by the spirits to deliver an address explaining the nature of the manifestations. On November 14, 1849, four hundred people filled Corinthian Hall to hear the mysterious noises. The meeting appointed a committee of skeptics to investigate and report back to a similar assembly on a subsequent evening. When this committee announced itself unable to discover any fraud or trick by which the girls produced the raps, the second meeting turned rowdy. Throughout, Amy Post lent Catherine and Margaret "the aid of her gentle counsel and the strength of her irreproachable name." She accompanied them to the platform in Corinthian Hall and forced her way into a chamber where the girls were disrobed and subjected to minute examination.[12]

Eliab Capron subsequently tried to induce the Fox girls' mother to permit them to travel to New York City to demonstrate their mediumship. Mrs. Fox initially objected. But, in June 1850, she and her three daughters accompanied Capron to New York. They rented rooms at Barnum's Hotel, where Capron advertised public demonstrations, three times a day, admission one dollar. These demonstrations attracted enough attention to create a demand for private séances for select audiences. A notable array of literati gathered at the home of a New York clergyman to hear the raps. Guests included author James Fenimore Cooper, historian George Bancroft, poet William Cullen Bryant, poet and editor Nathaniel Parker Willis, reformer and publisher of the *New York Tribune* Horace Greeley, and George Ripley, Greeley's head editorial writer and founder of Brook Farm. According to Greeley, the séance puzzled most of those present but impressed Cooper, who received accurate answers to questions about a sister killed fifty years before. Willis described the "Post-Mortuum Soiree" less sympathetically to readers of the *Home Journal,* noting "the disinclination which these spirits seemed to have for any intercourse with editors."[13]

Greeley became a frequent investigator and invited the Fox family into his home. There they conducted a series of séances, at which Greeley's wife, Molly, received messages that she believed to be from her recently deceased five-year-old son. Greeley proclaimed himself "convinced beyond the shadow of a doubt of [the Fox sisters'] perfect integrity and good faith." He assured his readers in the *Tribune* that, "Whatever may be the origin or cause of the 'rappings,' the ladies in whose presence they occur do not make them."[14] Kate lived with the Greeleys the following fall, which brought much comfort to the bereaved family but little to the young medium. "How I hate her," Kate wrote of Mrs. Greeley to her brother. "Why did I leave my mother. . . . If you knew how sick at heart I am you would come after me. . . . My head aches so I can hardly write." The renown of the raps became a mixed blessing for the Fox sisters, who found themselves living among strangers, with little control over their lives. "I am very lonely: oh how I miss you," Kate wrote to Amy Post. But she also reported that "The dear spirits are doing wonderful things." The previous evening "the piano was sweetly played upon by spirit fingers, the guitar was played then taken up and carried above our heads each person in the circle was touched." She told Amy that the spirits "ring bells and move tables all when our feet are held. We have convinced many skeptical people." During the next few years, the Fox sisters demonstrated their mediumship in New York City, Buffalo, Pittsburgh, Philadelphia, Washington, D.C., and Ohio.[15]

Leah Fox Fish, the oldest sister, remained in New York, where she received calls from inquirers at her séance room. Several influential abolitionist leaders, having heard of the Fox sisters from their friends in Rochester, visited Leah and were converted by the experiences they had there. William Lloyd Garrison, who had been attending séances for several years, visited Leah in 1854. That evening in the séance room, six men and four women sat around a large table in what Garrison called "the usual manner," the hands of each resting on the table. The raps called for the alphabet and instructed the medium to "put her feet in the custody of one of the party . . . to convince everyone present that the medium had nothing to do with the phenomena by way of fraud or collusion." The first spirit to identify itself was Jesse Hutchinson, member of the famous family of reform singers. The spirit beat time in raps while the circle joined in singing a Hutchinson family favorite, "The Old Granite State." Another spirit, that of an antislavery pioneer whose daughter sat at the table, identified himself and rapped out by the alphabet that "Spiritualism will work miracles in the cause of reform." He then indicated that he wanted the circle to see the physical power of spirits. He directed the party to put a bell under the table, which, Garrison reported, was rung by "unseen power." He asked that paper be placed under the table, which when retrieved bore the first names of the two communicating spirits. Before leaving the séance, Garrison devised his own test to confirm the spirit presence. He asked that Jesse Hutchinson grasp his right hand. He then secured his hand between his knees to prevent access to it by other members of the circle. Garrison then felt the touch of a hand "with no warmth in it" while he saw the hands of all, including the medium, resting on the table.[16] Garrison's abolitionist coworker Henry C. Wright sat at Leah's séance table in 1851. He conversed with the spirit of Jesus, who rapped affirmatively to Wright's query whether he was "mortal like other men." Wright announced himself well satisfied with the communications.[17]

As the decade advanced, other mediums produced new types of manifestations. Instead of raps and reeling chairs, investigators found spirits moving their hands to produce automatic writing, controlling their voices to speak directly, and using a variety of devices designed to facilitate spirit communication. Isaac Post became a writing medium and published a volume of communications from deceased Quaker reformers in 1852.[18] Spirits began to control the voices of mediums, making communication much easier than the awkward alphabetic methods. Healing mediums appeared who could see inside the body and prescribe according to spirit instructions. "Test mediums" advertised their services to those who wished to question spirits regarding information that only a specific deceased friend or family member would know in order to confirm the spirit's identity. Speaking mediums might speak in the voice of a departed loved one or deliver a public lecture authored by their "control."

As more intelligent communications appeared from other sources, the public lost interest in the Foxes and their raps. The arctic explorer Elisha Kent Kane took an interest in Margaret and arranged for her support and education before departing for his second arctic expedition in 1853. After his premature death in 1857, Margaret claimed that they had been secretly married and that Kane had left her an annuity. Kane's respectable family, not surprisingly, denied his connection with the medium. Margaret responded by converting to Roman Catholicism. The oldest sister, Leah, married Daniel Underhill, a wealthy Spiritualist and insurance salesman, the same year. She continued to give private sittings but ceased to use her mediumship for profit. By the end of the decade, only Kate remained in public life. Engaged in a constant struggle with alcoholism, she eventually lost custody of her two sons when she was arrested for drunkenness in Rochester in 1888. Margaret, also addicted to alcohol, blamed Spiritualism for her own and her sister's woes.[19]

Although the Fox sisters converted many influential people and provided the model for other mediums, they never participated actively in the movement they began. Their own lives—riddled with alcoholism, poverty, instability, and loneliness—add little to an understanding of the role of Spiritualism in American history. They never appeared at conventions, contributed to publications, or cooperated with those interested in promoting the cause. They cooperated with, or perhaps more accurately were exploited by, only those interested in promoting the Fox sisters alone. By 1854, even the Foxes' early supporter George Willets lost interest in them, although he was still an ardent Spiritualist who frequently sought communications. "Few go to see her," he wrote of Leah Fox Underhill to his cousins Isaac and Amy Post. When the medium Emma Hardinge sought material for the first history of Spiritualism, she lamented Leah's unwillingness to contribute to the effort. However, she did not expect her proposed book to suffer because the Foxes' story had "been so much before the public that there can't be much to add." Clearly, she viewed their role in the movement as limited to the early events of their mediumship. "I only asked in compliment to them," she explained to Amy Post.[20]

The more recent historian of Spiritualism, Ernest Isaacs, concludes that "the Fox sisters did possess extra-normal powers of extra-sensory perception, telepathy, and telekinesis" but that there is no evidence that these derived from spirits. From a historical perspective, whether the Hydesville rappings were produced by the spirit of a traveling peddler buried in the basement or by a conscious or unconscious bid for attention by two imaginative young girls is of little consequence compared to the massive popular movement that resulted. Whether or not Kate and Margaret controlled the raps, they did not determine the meaning attributed to them by observers. The interpretations of investigators, rather than the manifestations themselves, provided the content of the new religion.[21]

Inside the Séance Room

Within months of the Rochester rappings, thousands of Americans across the northern states and eastern seaboard sat around their parlor tables to see whether they might not witness manifestations similar to those occurring in the presence of the Fox sisters. Fueled by rumor, curiosity, and persistent hunger for contact with the dead, Spiritualism spread "like a prairie fire," unhindered by the need for special facilities or trained emissaries. News of the raps aroused interest outside Rochester even before the first public demonstration. Eliab Capron claimed that Auburn, New York, where Margaret Fox lived briefly with her brother, housed one hundred mediums by the summer of 1850. Cincinnati heard its first raps in September in the presence of the clairvoyant Mrs. G. B. Bushnell, who had visited Rochester over the summer and witnessed manifestations at the Fox home.

By 1852, a Spiritualist in Woodstock, Vermont, reported the existence of "8 or 10 good mediums [and] 50 partially developed."[22]

Anyone might be a medium, and the only way to find out who could communicate with spirits was to try and see. "There is a very great excitement . . . in regard to the rappings. There is scarcely anything else to be thought of," wrote the sister of a Baptist elder when the raps arrived in Shaftsbury, Vermont. She sent her brother simple instructions for investigation that he or anyone could follow:

> Now if you would like to try to see if there is anything in it you and
> mother and Linus just sit around the stand or table and lay your
> hands down flat on it and let them remain a few minutes then say if
> there are any spirits in the room will they please raise the stand and if
> it does not move the first time wait a few minutes then ask again. You
> can try to satisfy yourself if you wish I don't know as it would be
> wrong.

She inquired of the raps for mediums and learned that her brother, his son, and mother as well as a female neighbor were all mediums, "so you can form a team among yourselves."[23]

Beyond such sisterly advice, detailed instructions for the formation of circles soon appeared in print. Most advised a maximum of twelve investigators, equally divided between men and women, seated close together around a table, hands either joined or laid on the table (See plate 4). They stressed the necessity of harmony among the circle's participants and encouraged the use of "means calculated to promote a harmonious calmness and concert of feeling." One set of instructions recommended opening with "serene silence, meditation, interior prayer, and the singing of appropriate hymns." "In order to obtain *good* and *lofty* communications," advised another, "it is positively essential that our thoughts and intentions be also *good* and *elevated*."[24] Many circles opened with singing to generate unity and equanimity of feeling among those present. In 1853, "in obedience to spirit authors," a Philadelphia circle published a volume of songs for use in spirit circles, received through a medium who had "never written poetry, and [had] been repeatedly surprised at the ease and rapidity with which she now receives it." To the tune of a familiar hymn, spirit circles sang, "Angel mother, thou art near me, Thou dost comfort, soothe and bless; Thou dost ever watch and cheer me, With a mother's tenderness," among other inspired lyrics.[25]

From November 1850 to March 1851, publisher and phrenologist Charlotte Fowler Wells kept a detailed transcript of séances at which her brother Edward Fowler served as medium. Josiah Warren visited the circle to inquire whether the communicating spirit approved the conduct of his communitarian settlement Utopia and whether the spirit would communicate with him at Utopia. Horace Greeley visited the circle and published the transcript of the 15 December séance in the *New York Tribune*, "to refute the common assumption that *nothing is ever communicated from the spirit world . . . that is of the slightest importance.*" Boston abolitionist editor LaRoy Sunderland remarked on the rapid spread of Spiritualism. He recalled that when he first proposed a Spiritualist periodical in 1850 "there was not one family known throughout the New England States, where responses from the spiritual world had been made to questions put by mortals." Manifestations had occurred, including musical manifestations produced through his daughter, Margaretta Sunderland Cooper, but no questions had been answered, except for those in the presence of the Foxes and a few other New York families. Sunderland reported that by mid-1851 the movement's opponents acknowledged the existence of a thousand mediums, witnessed in every state.[26]

Determined Americans sat in spirit circles even when manifestations were not easily forthcoming. The first circle formed in Philadelphia met twice a week for four months without response. Finally, in February 1851, sounds were heard that the circle attributed to spirits. A few days later, one of the circle's members, a physician, was attending a young woman whom he described as "a very sensitive clairvoyant and magnetic subject." Her family informed the doctor that they had heard mysterious noises around the patient's bed and that his brother's spirit had promised the medium he would rap that morning. The promised raps occurred, and the young patient produced manifestations that many Philadelphians found convincing. This news inspired the formation of other circles for weekly investigation, all of which enjoyed faster success than the first. Within a year, the city's six ongoing circles decided to organize a "Harmonial Benevolent Association," in accordance with instructions given by the spirits. The society met to hear lectures by its members and to read communications received in the circles. That summer, the Society rented a hall for Sunday lectures by Spiritualists and mediums. Weekly Sunday lectures continued in Philadelphia for decades.[27]

Most people initially investigated Spiritualism at home or in the homes of friends or neighbors, with untrained and unpaid girls or women acting as mediums. The experience of Ohio abolitionist Jo-

seph Barker was typical. On a winter evening in 1852, he visited the
home of his friends the Collinsons to meet a twelve-year-old girl who
played with their children and had a reputation for being a medium.
Barker described himself as "exceedingly wishful to witness some
proof of the spirit rapping theory" but as having "little or no hope"
that such proof would be forthcoming. According to Barker, "The
appearance of the girl was that of perfect simplicity, and ease border-
ing on carelessness, indifference or unconsciousness. It would be impossible to imagine anything more unlike fraud or deceit." After dinner, Barker, his friends, and another visiting reformer sat around a
table with the young medium. She placed her right hand on the table
and sat turned half away from the table, her left hand resting in her
lap. "Is there a spirit present that will communicate with me?" asked
Mr. Collinson. Three raps indicated an affirmative response. Collinson, who had the alphabet written out before him on a sheet of paper,
asked if the spirit would spell its name. Three more raps followed.
He moved his pencil slowly over the paper before him, pausing
briefly on each letter of the alphabet. When his pencil rested on *D,*
three raps sounded, followed by raps at *O, R,* and *A,* to spell *Dora,* the
name of the Collinsons' two-year-old daughter, who had died a few
months before. In response to her parents' questions, Dora reported
on her happy play life in heaven and her contact with other dead
relatives, including her twenty-year-old cousin, Mary Anne, who had
been her nurse. Dora announced the mediumship of two of her surviving sisters, implying that the family could hold further séances
without going beyond its own ranks for a medium. The Barker family, however, contained no mediums, so they would continue to rely
on the daughters of their friends for communications. Mary Anne
reported that Dora had teachers in heaven, although she had not yet
learned to read, and that she loved her parents and saw them often.

Joseph Barker was an English Methodist who had lost his faith and
now gave lectures against the divine origins of the Bible. He described the feelings with which he sat down at the séance table: "My
longing after immortality is intense. My longing for sensible, demon-
strative, irresistible evidence of a future life and of a spirit world is
intense." The Collinsons were English Mormons who had left England in order to join the Mormon settlement at Salt Lake. Mary
Anne died in Kansas, just as the family was about to start across the
plains to Utah. Her spirit expressed approval of the family's decision
to change its course and settle in Ohio instead of pressing on to Salt

Lake. The Collinsons took the opportunity of the séance to inquire whether Joseph Smith (the founder of Mormonism) was a true prophet, whether the Book of Mormon was a divine revelation, and whether polygamy was a correct principle. To all these questions, the spirit of Cousin Mary Anne rapped in the negative. Barker, however, received support for the religious path on which he had embarked. His brother's spirit rapped affirmatively when asked if he approved Barker's course in leaving Methodism and lecturing against the divine origins of the Bible. All this wisdom came through the mediumship of a twelve-year-old girl.[28]

As in Rochester, Americans throughout the country found messages from spirits most plausible when delivered through the agency of adolescent girls. Mediums appeared most frequently among the younger female members of families. A student at a girls' school in Ohio reported that there were sixteen mediums among her classmates in 1852, including herself. LaRoy Sunderland, the first to call public attention to Spiritualism in New England, held frequent circles in his home after learning about the Rochester rappings in 1848. He met with no success until he called for raps in the presence of his daughter Margaretta, who was rocking her baby in a cradle. She soon developed into a musical medium, inspired to play and sing by the spirits.[29]

Mediumship was closely identified with femininity. The popular Spiritualist writer Cora Wilburn heralded the advent of spirit communication "in the persuasive accents of inspired woman's tongue."[30] Not all mediums were women, but the association of mediumship with femininity was so strong that it was not dispelled by the contravening evidence of the existence of male mediums. "The medium may be man or woman—woman or man—but in either case, the characteristics will be *feminine*—negative and passive," said a longtime Spiritualist leader. Spiritualists used the language of electricity, also current in mesmerism and phrenology, to describe the relative positions of men and women in spirit communication. Women were "negative," and men were "positive." Circles should be composed of equal numbers of men and women "or of persons in whom respectively the positive and negative elements predominate." Experts agreed that "some males are comparatively feminine, or negative, as indicated by a lack of muscularity of organism, and of force of character; while some females are comparatively masculine or positive, as evinced by the possession of these characteristics." In order to facilitate the trans-

mission of electrical currents that spirits used to manifest their presence, circles should seat men and women, "or positives and nega-
tives," alternately in a circle, "the most positive and most negative
persons occupying opposite positions in the circle. By most negative
is here meant the one who is most susceptible to spiritual influences,
or the most of a medium."[31] Such advice closely equated femininity
and mediumship but also allowed for exceptions based on the characteristics of the individual. By identifying mediumship with characteristics believed to be inherent in women, Spiritualists echoed the
language of the larger culture, which identified the qualities of piety
with the qualities of femininity.

Spiritualism also reflected the Victorian view that the home was the
true locus of religiosity. Referring to the Fox sisters, one Spiritualist
wrote that, "Not in the church, not in the capitol, but in the family,
came the first demonstrable recognition of immortal life and immortal love—the holiest truth to the holiest place." Spiritualists secured
the place of religion well within women's sphere by relocating religious practice from the church to the home. Spirit circles gathered
around parlor tables, a most appropriate place for women to preside.
Charles Beecher claimed, "It is not in its published literature, its periodicals, its lectures and its public mediums that the strength of the
movement lies. It is in its family or home circles." The *Plain Guide to
Spiritualism* advised that, "During the long evenings, as friends and
families gather around the social board, no enjoyment can become
more genial and benign than that of seeking communion with those
who have passed on to the land of eternal spring and perennial summer."[32] The ritual of the séance perfectly suited the domestic environment. It required no participants beyond the family, no facilities beyond the home.

The introduction of the planchette facilitated the mediumship of
untrained family members within the home. A heart-shaped piece of
wood mounted on three casters, the planchette was believed to respond to magnetic forces passing through the bodies of those who
placed their fingers on it, thus communicating messages from spirits
(See plate 5). It could be used either with a copy of the alphabet, on
which it would point to letters to spell out communications, or with a
pencil inserted into a hole in its back, so that a spirit could use the
planchette to write. It was easy to use, required no experience or ex-
pertise, and could lead to the discovery or encouragement of mediumship in unsuspecting investigators. Although not commercially

mass-produced in the United States until the 1860s, planchettes imported from France were available in Spiritualist bookstores by the late 1850s.[33] The line between parlor game and religious inquiry blurred when families who tried the spirits in fun discovered mediums in their midst whose messages prompted serious investigation.[34]

For those unable to investigate Spiritualism within their own families, professional mediums offered a variety of services, ranging from public séances to clairvoyant medical examinations. A wealthy manufacturer engaged Kate Fox to give free sittings for the public in 1855. The Boston Spiritualist newspaper the *Banner of Light* sponsored a public free circle at its offices and published the communications received there in its pages each week. Mrs. J. H. Conant exercised her mediumship at the Banner Free Circle from its inception in 1857 until her death in 1875. Subscribers contributed to the support of free circles. Mediums advertised in the *Banner* and in other Spiritualist newspapers. Investigators determined to witness convincing manifestations might go from medium to medium until they found satisfaction.[35]

The Scope of the Movement

Unfortunately, any attempt to estimate the numerical scope of the movement is rendered questionable at best by Spiritualists' aversion to organization. The faith required no affiliation of any kind of its adherents or even of its leaders and mediums. While Spiritualists often organized at the local level, they staunchly opposed national organization or anything that would make a census of the group possible. Spiritualists formed a denomination whose affiliates could be counted only after the movement was on the decline in the 1890s. The 1890 census reported forty-five thousand Spiritualists in thirty-nine states and territories, but this included only those formally affiliated with an organized society.[36] Estimates of the number of Spiritualists by contemporary observers ranged from a few hundred thousand to eleven million (out of a total population of twenty-five million). Enthusiastic supporters and alarmed detractors proposed inflated figures, all equally without basis.[37]

Unlike most religious groups, Spiritualists avoided institutional form and frequently influenced people of other denominational affiliations. An estimate of the number of Spiritualists would vary

greatly depending on whether one included only regular practitioners of spirit communication or persons who expressed interest in investigation. Many believers based their faith on a single séance at
which convincing communication occurred, while other individuals
investigated for decades without success. In any case, Spiritualism's
influence was hardly limited to adherents. It received serious investigation from church-goers and scientists as well as from infidels and
mystics and provoked ire and ridicule from committed skeptics and
unsympathetic newspapermen as well as from orthodox clergy. One
observer counted Spiritualism high among "Certain Dangerous Tendencies in American Life" and estimated that "Perhaps a majority of
the members of evangelical Protestant churches in this country have
at sometime consulted the spirits of dead people, by the help of some
professional ghost-seer or medium." Medium historian Emma Hardinge wondered whether the movement benefited more from "the
zealous enthusiasm of its admirers or the bitter persecution of its an-
tagonists," as the latter sometimes generated more publicity.[38]

Spiritualists did not join organizations, but they did read and write.
Because the movement shunned the kind of structures that in other
American denominations served to foster cohesion and spread information, it relied heavily on the public press. Books and periodicals
helped fill the gap left by the lack of organization. Spiritualist publications linked isolated believers across America, providing a vehicle
for communication and solidarity for those who shared a belief that,
although widespread, could be extremely unpopular in a locality with
only a few adherents. Because the leading mediums and advocates of
the movement were itinerant and their movements were unpredict-
able, they could be followed only through the centralized information
provided by newspapers. By the end of the century, over a hundred
periodicals had reported news of spiritual manifestations and the
movement they began. Though many had small circulations and
short lives, between twenty and thirty were in print during most years
between the movement's beginning at the end of the 1840s and its
decline in the 1890s.[39]

The *American Booksellers Guide* of 1871 advised its readers that "The
sale of [Spiritualist] books is as steady as of books in any other department of the trade, and they should not be overlooked by the
bookseller," reporting that Spiritualist publications accounted for the
sale of fifty thousand books and fifty thousand pamphlets every
year.[40] Hardly a major novelist of the period could resist Spiritualism's

dramatic possibilities, and many a minor writer exploited its popularity. While Henry James, Nathaniel Hawthorne, and William Dean Howells expressed varying degrees of distaste for the new movement, they gave graphic portrayals of its practitioners in *The Bostonians, The Blithedale Romance,* and *The Undiscovered Country,* respectively. Jo March, scribbling heroine of Louisa May Alcott's *Little Women,* lamented that her first novel was accused of "spiritualistic ideas" even though she had none. Harriet Beecher Stowe, one of the best-selling authors of the nineteenth century, urged her publisher to send a review copy of her book *Old Town Folks* to the *Banner of Light.* "That paper commands an immense circulation and influence," she wrote, "and a notice of the 'spiritualistic features' of the book in it would ensure a sale of many copies." The publisher took her advice.[41]

Early converts included individuals whose prominence made the manifestations difficult to dismiss as frauds perpetrated on the credulous. Every notable progressive family of the nineteenth century had its advocate of Spiritualism, some of them more than one. Anna Blackwell, eldest and most radical sibling of pioneer doctors Elizabeth and Emily and abolitionists Henry and Sam, adopted Spiritualism by 1850 and became a vociferous lifelong advocate. The ubiquitous Beecher family contributed Charles Beecher and Isabella Beecher Hooker to the ranks, while Harriet Beecher Stowe became a serious investigator. The Baptist missionary dynasty fathered by Adoniram Judson gave its youngest member, Abby Ann Judson.[42] As already noted, abolitionist William Lloyd Garrison was an early convert and remained loyal to the movement until his death. The famous Grimké sisters, Sarah and Angelina, talked to spirits. The conversion of New York State Supreme Court judge John Edmonds in 1851 increased the movement's credibility. Edmonds resigned his position on the bench to become a full-time advocate and medium. The *New York Tribune* printed the pro-Spiritualist correspondence of U.S. senator N. P. Talmadge with the poet Sarah Helen Whitman, former fiancée of Edgar Allan Poe. These officials were joined by Ohio congressman Joshua Giddings. In 1854, thirteen thousand people signed a petition asking the U.S. Senate to appoint a scientific committee to investigate spirit communication. The petition received enough support to reach the floor of the Senate, but not enough to prevent it from being ridiculed once it arrived there. Mary Todd Lincoln spoke with her dead son, Willie, and brought mediums into the White House, where they conducted séances for senators and cabinet members.[43]

Although the new faith had some prestigious adherents, spirits were no respecters of class. The movement enjoyed support among both rural poor and urban laborers. Lydia Maria Child wrote in 1862 that "Spiritualism is undermining the authority of the Bible in the minds of what are called the common people faster than all other causes put together." Another observer thought it drew converts from the "larger class" of low "intellectual character" who "still believe in savage thoughts, omens, dreams, and signs." The recent work of Jon Butler suggests that there may indeed have been a substratum of non-Christian folk practice among Americans of both European and African descent that connected Spiritualism with earlier occult beliefs. Intellectuals like Child and fellow abolitionist Thomas Wentworth Higginson constantly tried to distinguish their own beliefs from those of the mass of Spiritualists who flocked to witness sensational demonstrations. This larger, less literate group left fewer accounts of their experiences than elite investigators did. The printed sources on Spiritualism, like most printed sources, derived mainly from educated middle- and upper-class adherents, but the halted prose of the letters preserved in the personal and professional correspondence of medium Achsa Sprague shows that setting pen to paper was an unusual event for many adherents, even among local leaders. Some writers even associated the abrogation of literary and religious conventions. "I hope you will excuse my writing and my spelling for this is the first letter I ever wrote to a woman in my life and I never went to school but a few days in my life and I think but little of forms and serrumonies [ceremonies]," wrote one correspondent.[44]

Americans of English Protestant descent dominated Spiritualism in the North, but others also participated. Two Jews became well-known advocates, Cora Wilburn and Louis Schlesinger. A sizable community of French-speaking Spiritualists, probably immigrants from Canada, founded a church in Wisconsin and published their own hymnal. German-speaking Spiritualists held circles in Waukesha County, Wisconsin, and in Wheeling, West Virginia, during the 1850s and were served by the biweekly *Tafelrunde: Spiritualische Blätter für Fortschritt und Reform,* published in Washington, D.C., from 1870 to 1872.[45]

Spiritualism found a natural resonance with African religious beliefs introduced by the slave population in the South. Mediumship and spirit possession existed in many of the cultures from which slaves came. The West African view that ancestors have a role in the social structure and continue to merit the obligations of kinship after death predated similar beliefs among American Spiritualists. The belief that "the dead can return to their living in visitations that are not necessarily ill-intended or dangerous" persisted among African-Americans both in the rural South and in the large cities to which they migrated following Reconstruction. Blacks did not identify themselves as Spiritualists in large numbers until the twentieth century, but they did contribute individual mediums to nineteenth-century Spiritualism and probably introduced ideas sympathetic to Spiritualism into the white population in the South.[46]

Unlike their coreligionists of European descent, African-American Protestants did not base their faith on regularized doctrines produced by a trained clergy and dependent on written texts. As a result, and because of their loyalty to their ancestors, they may have drawn the line of orthodoxy so as to include Spiritualism more frequently than did white Protestants, who generally placed it outside the limits of acceptable Christian belief. Black churches in Washington, D.C., welcomed the white medium Cora Hatch in their pulpits, something no white evangelical church ever did.[47] Some white Spiritualists recognized doctrines similar to their own in African-American religion. A Spiritualist lieutenant in the Union army reported on mediumship among contraband slaves, including a Methodist exhorter from Mississippi. He concluded that the "negro character" was "intuitive, inspirational, religious, and altogether mediumistic," implying that blacks shared with women the characteristics that made them susceptible to spirits. In the North, African-American Shaker leaders Rebecca Jackson and Rebecca Perot trained themselves as mediums and attended séances regularly in Philadelphia. Mr. Anderson, "a colored gentleman of Battle Creek," participated in a Michigan Spiritualist convention in 1866. Black historian and abolitionist William Cooper Nell met the Fox sisters at the Posts' home in Rochester and became an avid convert. The movement claimed Sojourner Truth as a convert in her old age.[48]

Spiritualism's association with abolition generated substantial antagonism to the movement among southerners of European descent. Nevertheless, believers willing to brave the rancor of their neighbors appeared in small numbers throughout the region. The *Banner of Light* claimed subscribers in every state and territory and received correspondence from throughout the country. Spiritualism flourished in New Orleans, which contributed two national leaders to the movement. One New Orleans observer commented that "Spiritualism has made much more rapid progress among the Creole and Catholic portions of our population than the Protestant; first, because most of them have more time for investigation than the rushing hurrying, money-making American, and secondly, the creed of the Catholic Church does not deny the possibility of spirit communion." Ex-Catholic French-speaking Spiritualists in New Orleans produced two periodicals: *Spiritualiste de la Nouvelle-Orleans; Echo-Mensuel* and *Le Salut* (Salvation).[49] Memphis had a number of circles by the mid-1850s, and a series of Spiritualist periodicals appeared in Tennessee during the 1870s. Circles abounded in Macon, Georgia, where a Universalist newspaperman published the *Christian Spiritualist* circa 1860. A second Spiritualist newspaper appeared in Georgia in the 1880s.[50]

In general, southern Spiritualists identified themselves as Christians more consistently than did northern Spiritualists. They tended to focus on communication with the dead while ignoring both the reform agenda and the heterodox theology that many believed such communication implied. A Methodist minister organized the leading séance circle in Memphis, which used a "pious young lady" from the Baptist church as its medium. Some white evangelicals in the South, who had more contact with African-Americans than did their northern counterparts, shared the view of their black coreligionists that spirit communication was compatible with Christian belief. Gertrude Thomas, a well-educated Georgia Methodist who became a suffragist, found attending séances compatible with a vibrant Methodism. The Southern Baptist Publication Society published Mary Dana Schindler's sympathetic account of investigation in *A Southerner Among the Spirits*.[51] As in the North, Southern Spiritualism attracted a few intellectuals who felt dissatisfied by the sectarianism of the churches, including the writer William Gilmore Simms. Spiritualism's association with abolition may have limited its appeal among slaveholders to urban professionals whose livelihood did not depend on slavery. Civil War diarist Mary Chestnut reported that her doctor in Columbia, South Carolina, adopted the new faith. Thomas Moore Fort, a lawyer and educator in Minden, Louisiana, during the 1850s, cherished a Spiritualist volume entitled *Epic of the Starry Heaven* and passed it down to his descendants.[52]

In all regions, mediums themselves hailed from varied class backgrounds, and mediumship sometimes served as a vehicle of upward mobility. Once mediumship showed a potential for profit, fraudulent mediums imposed themselves on the public, and some indeed profited from deception. But, for every charlatan, thousands of earnest investigators sought communication with spirits, many through unpaid mediums in their own homes. Profit, or the desire for profit, did not in itself prove deception. One early believer privately opined that the spirits would not have selected his wife as a medium unless "some *good* should come out of it," by which he meant pecuniary good. The historical significance of Spiritualism lies less in the few outstanding sensationalists than in the masses of faithful followers who made it a popular movement. Interpretations of Spiritualism that dismiss hordes of truth seekers as benighted kooks ignore the sincere longings that attracted people to the movement and fail to locate Spiritualism within the context of the cosmological alternatives available in the mid-nineteenth century.[53]

2

"The Blessedness of Sinless Childhood in the World Beyond"

M ary Robbins Post scoffed at the news of the spirit rappings.[1] She greeted the reports from her Rochester relatives with polite disbelief. "We should dearly love to visit you . . . and see whether it would be possible for us to be convinced in relation to spiritual manifestations," she wrote to her in-laws, Amy and Isaac Post. "But probably they would not converse freely with skeptics such as we and if they should deign to do so I cannot see that we should receive much aid and comfort thereby." In February 1850, Mary Post identified herself as having "combated strongly against the mysterious noises" but hoped that the bonds that united her and her husband with his brother's family would "not be severed by a difference of opinion on a subject of which we have never seen or known anything personally and which conflicts with our reason and preconceived notions." Within a few months, she had become more receptive to the idea of communication with the dead. By September, she wrote to the son of Amy Post's sister, also an investigator, that "your father and mother have told us so many wonderful things that if not fully convinced we have certainly become much more ready to hear." A month later, she was still skeptical but wrote to Isaac, "I would be so glad to be convinced relative to this matter whether it really be what it purports to be I can not help doubting."[2]

Mary Post's hope of being convinced of the reality of spirit communication may have been quickened by her attendance at the funeral of a friend's son. She wondered whether her bereaved fellow Quaker held "the same dark and sad view [of death] which the mass of mankind hold or those of a bright and progressive life which takes from death its sting and from the grave its victory." She had just obtained the first volume of Andrew Jackson Davis's *Great Harmonia,* a new work that would play a noteworthy role in the progress of Spiritualism. "His ideas are I think destined to change long established beliefs in regard to death, progression, and happiness of all," she wrote to Isaac. Shortly after writing this letter, she experienced a death in her own family and immediately accepted the spiritual origins of the manifestations.[3]

"Our dear our loved and precious Mary has entered on her higher life," the bereaved Mary Robbins Post wrote to Amy and Isaac. Her loss was an especially difficult one—the unexpected death of the daughter who bore her name, a healthy young woman who had served as nurse during an outbreak of measles and pox. She refrained from visiting her daughter during the fatal illness because she presumed the young woman would recover and wanted to avoid spreading the contagion. Following her daughter's internment, Mary Post turned again to the new book by Davis and felt "greatly comforted" by the section explaining his "Philosophy of Death," which she quoted in her letter announcing her daughter's death to Amy and Isaac. She found bereavement "far less afflictive and overwhelming" after she accepted Davis's view that nothing is lost by leaving this world "to pursue life's journey amid immortal beauties in the Spirit Land." "I sometimes ask myself," she wrote, "whether the time will ever come when we will cease to mourn for our friends." Apparently, Davis's philosophy comforted Post sufficiently to allow her to shift her attention from her grief to the progress of Spiritualism. She closed by expressing her satisfaction that "believers are multiplying" and her hope that the Fox sisters would visit her soon.[4]

Three events intervened between Mary Robbins Post's initial skepticism and her new faith. First, she visited the Fox sisters in New York City and witnessed manifestations through them. Second, she read the work of Andrew Jackson Davis, visionary prophet of the "Harmonial Philosophy," who offered a philosophic explanation of the significance of spirit manifestations. Finally, she experienced a death in her own circle and found comfort in the doctrines of Spiritualism. These three events parallel the three immediate factors that provoked popular interest in Spiritualism: the desire for empirical evidence of the immortality of the soul; the rejection of Calvinism or evangelicalism in favor of a more liberal theology; and the desire to overcome bereavement through communication with departed loved ones. No one of these alone accounts for the rise of Spiritualism, but together they explain much of its appeal. "Spirit manifestations," the observable evidence of spirit presence during a séance, addressed the first desire. Spiritualism's elaboration, through the writings of Andrew Jackson Davis and a host of self-proclaimed philosophers, of a cosmology that contradicted the tenets of orthodox Protestantism satisfied the second desire. The third desire was satisfied when the bereaved received messages from the deceased by either automatic writing or verbal communication through a human medium. Having witnessed the phenomena of the séance room in chapter 1, we turn now to the theological underpinnings of the rejection of death.

Andrew Jackson Davis and the Rejection of Calvinism

Investigators sought a new basis for faith in spirit communication because they found the teachings of existing churches either inadequate or incorrect. But the manifestations themselves were not sufficient to constitute a new religion. Spiritualism developed a fully articulated cosmology that offered an alternative to Protestantism, including a philosophic explanation of the place of spirit manifestations in the structure of the universe. The new movement found its metaphysics in the Harmonial Philosophy of Andrew Jackson Davis (see plate 7). A few years before the first raps, Davis proclaimed a vision of the unity of natural and supernatural truths revealed to him during mesmeric trances by the spirit of the eighteenth-century Swedish mystic Emanuel Swedenborg. Davis recorded the content of his messages from Swedenborg in a voluminous tome entitled *The Principles of Nature, Her Divine Revelations, and a Voice to Mankind.* Beginning in 1847, Davis and a small group of Universalist ministers labored to spread his message through the publication of his revelations and through their journal, the *Univercœlum and Spiritual Philosopher.* The "Divine Revelations" included the prediction that other spirits would communicate with other human beings, just as the spirit of Swedenborg spoke to Davis, and just as Swedenborg had conversed with a host of enlightening spirits during his own lifetime.[5]

The Harmonial Philosophy made slow progress. Its organ, the *Univercœlum,* lasted just long enough to welcome the mysterious noises produced in the presence of the Fox sisters as evidence of the truth of Davis's prediction of spirit communication. On hearing of the Rochester rappings, Davis invited the Fox sisters to his home in New York City. Davis investigated the Fox sisters' mediumship himself and explained it to the public in terms of his own philosophy in *Philosophy of Spiritual Intercourse*. In this work, he provided instructions for the formation of the circles that became the basis of much Spiritualist practice.[6]

Once Davis and his followers joined their cause to that of the manifestations, the Harmonial Philosophy began to enjoy greater success. Americans found the opportunity to observe communication with spirits far more compelling than the opportunity to read about Davis's communications with the spirit of Swedenborg. However, after becoming investigators of Spiritualism, they anxiously imbibed writing that provided a philosophic explanation of what they had seen or hoped to see. Davis would likely have remained an obscure prophet had he not tied his cause to the new manifestations. But, once linked to the "mysterious noises" and their echoes, Davis became the philosopher of a mass movement. Hundreds of sometime metaphysicians added their visions to Spiritualist literature, but Davis's writings retained a special role. Spiritualists recoiled from giving anything authority over individual conscience or inspiration and therefore refrained from according the status of scripture to Davis's writing or to anyone else's, including the Bible. However, if Davis's work was not viewed as authoritative, it commanded sufficient respect and popularity to earn its author a central leadership role in the movement. Davis's most significant contribution to Spiritualism was the articulation of a comprehensive worldview incorporating spirit manifestations, reform principles, and an anti-Calvinist theology into a single system.

At the beginning of the nineteenth century, Calvin's influence was still strong in American theology. The "New Divinity Men" who spoke for Protestant orthodoxy were devoted students of Jonathan Edwards, whose graphic portrayal of "Sinners in the Hands of an Angry God" moved many of his eighteenth-century parishioners to conversion. The popular understanding of Calvinism depicted a world created and governed by a God who predestined the majority of people to eternal suffering in Hell. Human beings deserved damnation in retribution for their inherent sinfulness passed down through the generations since Adam's original disobedience to God in the garden of Eden. Created free from sin and suffering, human beings, through Adam's Fall, caused pain and death to enter the world. God showed his mercy and graciousness by offering eternal life to his saints, those few human beings he elected to enjoy salvation and spend eternity at his right hand. He made it possible for these few to overcome death by sacrificing his only son, Jesus. Puritan divines, and their cohorts and descendants in the Congregational, Presbyterian, Baptist, and Reformed churches, encouraged human beings to strive for piety and righteousness in the hope of discovering themselves to be among God's elect. The Methodists, the new denomination that came to dominate American Protestantism during the nineteenth century, rejected election and predestination in favor of the belief that all people had the potential to experience Christian conversion and achieve salvation. But even the Methodists, like all revivalists, retained the view that those who failed to experience conversion were condemned to endless suffering in hell.[7]

Unlike their Christian contemporaries, Americans who adopted Spiritualism no longer had to rely on speculation or even revelation for information about the ultimate fate of the human soul. The details of life after death could now be described in concrete terms by those who had experienced them at firsthand. Information about the order of creation that was not described by spirits could be observed in the laws of nature. Spiritualist cosmology viewed nature as a benign reality that revealed the divine order. Andrew Jackson Davis described nature as "the only true and unchangeable revelation of the Divine Mind." In sharp contrast to the tenets of orthodoxy, an early spirit message claimed that Protestant churches "only look for the destruction of the earth's *wicked inhabitants,* whereas the true version is not the destruction of the Universe . . . but the development of true fraternal harmony." Spiritualism offered a rosy picture of reality that many Americans found more consistent with nineteenth-century optimism than the religious traditions from which they came.[8]

Spiritualism represented an extreme position in the liberal trend of theology that swept the mainstream Protestant denominations in the United States far from their Calvinist or Reformed origins. Spiritualists shocked their contemporaries by following the national liberal trend in theology so far that it led them to question the most fundamental Protestant doctrines: the divinity of Jesus and the divine origins of the Bible. Because Spiritualists believed that they had penetrated the veil of death, they could discard distasteful doctrines required by the Christian attempt to reach an explanation of death consistent with the benevolence of the deity and with a human moral order. Without a "final change" at death, the underpinnings of Christian theology lost their explanatory function. The system no longer needed original sin, which brought death into the world, or predestination, future punishment, final judgment, or infant damnation, which explained the fate of the soul after death. With no threat of judgment or punishment, humanity needed no redemption and therefore no atonement. Christ himself became logically unnecessary, as did the Gospels that announced his resurrection.

Although gentler doctrines were preached from a number of pulpits by mid-century, Spiritualists continued to identify themselves as foes of Calvinism. As late as 1890, Abby Ann Judson, member of the famous family of Baptist missionaries, attributed her conversion to Spiritualism to her conscientious objection to Calvinist doctrines.[9] Ignoring the watered-down forms of Calvinism that came to characterize many popular denominations, Spiritualists recalled with horror the religious education of their youth. The clairvoyant Semantha Mettler described her feelings after being "cut off without hope" as an unregenerate eleven-year-old by a debate with her Congregationalist Sunday school teacher. "Why has God made the birds so happy," she wondered, "and me, a little child that has a living soul, with this terrible fear, like a phantom coming between me and the beautiful earth, stealing into my dreams with its terrible grimaces and casting its black shadows athwart the cheering sunlight?" The following year, in 1830, she was converted at a protracted meeting during the height of the Second Great Awakening. She converted to Universalism in 1842, met Andrew Jackson Davis in 1845, and became one of the first public healing mediums when the Spiritualist movement began in 1848. Mettler, like many nineteenth-century Americans, found the orthodox teachings to which she had been subjected inconsistent with her own experience of nature as beautiful and benign.[10]

Spiritualists attributed dire tragedies to Calvinist beliefs and to the Catholic view that those who died unbaptized would spend eternity in limbo. Andrew Jackson Davis's newspaper, the *Herald of Progress*, described the fatal outcome of an Irish woman's Catholic beliefs about the fate of unbaptized infants. The paper reported that the "poor victim of superstition" committed suicide after giving birth to a still-born child because she was "so afflicted by her conception of its probable destiny because unbaptized." "We have looked in Protestant journals in vain to discover a recommendation for penal enactments, to restrain teachings so obviously tending to insanity," Davis editorialized. He condemned the Protestant failure to actively refute this Catholic doctrine.[11]

With the rise of revivalism and especially with the spread of Methodism in the nineteenth century, many Americans adopted the doctrine of "Arminianism." Condemned by Calvinists at the Synod of Dort (1618–19), Arminianism rejected the doctrine of predestination in favor of the belief that all human beings potentially had the ability to reach salvation.[12] Spiritualism concurred with the Arminian view that heaven was not reserved for an elect few, but it parted with all evangelicals by rejecting the existence of hell altogether. "[Spiritualism] is so much more comforting than the old theology," wrote a Kentucky advocate, explaining the movement's success to a friend in Wisconsin. "We get some heavy raps from the pulpit nearly every Sunday for taking away the scare crow *Hell* eternal torment etc by which they frighten sinners to repentance."[13] Revival preachers, however, intended not to comfort but to encourage conversions, so they emphasized the horrific fate of the unconverted. A medium raised as a Methodist in western New York State described her anxiety about "the doctrine of the final loss of unconverted souls" even after she experienced conversion herself at age fifteen. "Those who were out of the church, and whom I held especially dear, I carried as a burden on my soul, often feeling how miserable even heaven would be without the companionship of those I dearly loved." She prayed in vain for the conversion of loved ones. Finally, during a revival, an evangelist told church members that, if each selected one person to pray and labor for, that person would be converted. The revival lasted six weeks, and the faithful young woman prayed every day for her unconverted friends. She remembered the last night of the revival as the "deathnell to my faith . . . in such means of revival and the beginning of my awakening." She stopped attending Methodist meetings, sought the company of the one Spiritualist family in town, and became a medium at the third séance she attended. Spiritualists viewed the existence of hell as inconsistent with the benevolence of God and the essential goodness of human beings, each of whom, as part of the order of creation, reflected the divine mind in his or her own being.[14]

Spiritualism objected to Christian doctrine at precisely those points at which a "true woman" of the Victorian era would be appalled by Calvinism. As the nineteenth century wore on, American culture increasingly viewed women as the moral guardians of their families, in contrast to earlier Protestant views that placed the father firmly at the head of family religious life. This shift paralleled a trend away from the identification of women with the fallen Eve, the temptress who would lead man into sin and carnality, and toward a "secular Mariology," which viewed women as naturally pure and religious and emphasized their nurturing role as mothers who inculcated piety in their children. As the new industrial economy separated men's workplaces from the home, women, according to the popular religious thought of the day, were left behind to oversee a domestic sphere untainted by the amoral tendencies of the marketplace. Here they were expected to use their recently discovered inherent purity and piety to influence men who spent all day in the corrupting sphere outside the home.[15] The emergence of this Christian domestic ideal encouraged women to see the fulfillment of their spiritual obligations in the exercise of religious influence within the family circle rather than in the pursuit of their own salvation. As their roles as mothers increasingly determined their primary social and religious identities, women were less and less willing to accept that those who died without a Christian conversion experience were damned in spite of God's love and their mother's. Nineteenth-century women refused to believe that a benevolent deity would cause precious sons and daughters to be born knowing all along that he would condemn some, if not most, of them to eternal punishment in hell.

The new concept of "true womanhood" conflicted at several points with orthodox theology. It contributed to the appearance of an image of God as a loving parent, solicitous for the welfare of his children, which joined the old Puritan image of a God of wrath. Women who identified with the new ideology (and this included most American women outside slavery to some extent) began to dissent from orthodox doctrine. Antoinette Brown Blackwell, America's first woman minister, resigned her pulpit in 1854 when she recoiled from her congregation's expectation that she would hold up frightening images of punishment at the deathbed of an unconverted youth and at the burial of an illegitimate baby. She later left her orthodox tradition for Unitarianism.* The daughters of New England divines expressed

---

* Antoinette Brown (later Blackwell) was ordained in 1853 by the First Congregational church in Butler, Wayne County, New York. Because of its congregational polity, the Butler church could call whomever it chose to be its minister, without the advice or consent of its denomination. Thus, Brown's ordination did not imply the willingness of

their rejection of their fathers' harsh theology in sentimental novels
that became the best-selling books of the nineteenth century. These
authors explicitly connected their rejection of Calvinism with their
gender. Where "hard old New England divines . . . tread with sublime
assurance," wrote Harriet Beecher Stowe, "woman often follows with
bleeding footsteps." Spiritualism presented an extreme case of the
rejection of Calvinism that pervaded women's culture.[16]

In place of the vague assurances of sentimental literature and
mainstream Protestantism, Spiritualists offered concrete descriptions
of the fate of lost loved ones after death. They propounded the doctrine of progression, asserting that individual souls continued to grow
in grace after death, advancing through a series of successively more
perfect spheres, each one suited to promote spiritual development
for the attainment of the next sphere of heaven. Andrew Jackson
Davis's revelations described a series of six celestial spheres of increasing harmony, beauty, and wisdom through which the soul advances
after death. Davis's vision was based on the cosmology of Emanuel
Swedenborg, which described six progressive spheres following
death, three hells and three heavens. Davis explained that these were
actually six heavens but that the first sphere after earth (the second
sphere) was relatively chaotic and so had been misperceived as a hell
by Swedenborg. Spirit messages confirmed Davis's cosmology by spec-
ifying their sphere of origin. Davis believed the notion of spheres
provided a better incentive to lead a moral life on earth than the
concept of heaven and hell because the more spiritually advanced one
became during life on earth the more advanced would be the sphere
one entered at death. Spiritualists contrasted their own views with the
harsh doctrines of orthodoxy, which they considered to be destructive
of human hope and accountability.[17]

Because spirits continued to develop after death, those who died
young would mature in heaven. Both bodies and personalities would
continue to develop. Spirits assured bereaved parents that heaven
provided "suitable arrangements" for the care of infants. One spirit
message described the care of babies in heaven, declaring "If you
could but see them as we see them; could you but know the joy that
we find in pressing them to us, in watching over them, how soon
would the tear of sorrow be wiped from the parent's eye."[18] Departed

---

any beyond her immediate congregation to accept a woman minister. The first woman
to be ordained by full denominational authority was Olympia Brown, ordained by the
Universalists in 1863.

children would learn to talk and even to write from other spirits, thus enabling them to communicate with living parents. Through their ability to visit the land of the living at will, they would become acquainted with the families they had not lived to know and would follow events in the lives of their terrestrial relatives. Thus, a bereft parent could look forward not only to a heavenly reunion with a cherished child but also to constant and increasing intimacy, just as though the child still lived. "Gentle mother," read a typical message, "your little seraph boy is not *dead*, but *liveth*. In his uncontaminated love, find comfort for the ills of life." Spiritualism presented the most extreme version of the rejection of the Puritan view of the child as a vessel of imputed sin unredeemed by conversion. Like Romantics and sentimentalists, Spiritualists viewed the innocence of childhood as closer to God than the world-sullied character of adults. The idealized child, the mature version of a child who died before speech allowed the expression of human failings, could express superhuman love and provide superhuman comfort. In the message to "Gentle mother," the abiding love of a dead child replaces the love of Jesus as the source of comfort to the faithful during life on earth. Having eliminated sin, hell, and judgment, Spiritualism eliminated the need for a savior.[19]

In place of faith in a savior, Spiritualists saw God in the harmony and beauty of the natural world and in the inherent goodness of human beings. Unlike their evangelical contemporaries, who believed that the natural person was separated from God by sin and needed to receive a new nature through conversion to be transformed into a Christian, Spiritualists believed that human nature did not need to be transformed, that human beings were born good, each reflecting the image of God, and therefore did not need to be saved. This view came as a welcome relief to Spiritualists raised in the evangelical milieu of early nineteenth-century America. Mary Fenn Love, who would later marry Andrew Jackson Davis and join him as a leader of the movement, described her Baptist past in the revival-ridden "burned over district" of western New York. "Day by day and night by night did I narrowly scrutinize my conduct lest I grieve away the holy spirit," she recalled. "I faithfully studied the theological doctrines I professed to believe until the Atonement, Regeneration, Foreordination and the bodily resurrection grew into solemn mysteries which my reason vainly sought to penetrate, and from which I withdrew my sacrilegious fingers." Her own sins and the sins of others became constant sources of torture. "Heaven only knows," she wrote, "the agony I suffered lest those I loved on earth should be lost to me hereafter. A heavy gloom settled upon my spirit, and this beautiful earth, now so radiant with joy and promise, seemed little better than one great charnel house."[20]

Mary Fenn Love's escape from the agony of her orthodox belief and her conversion to Spiritualism occurred through the contemplation of nature. "When at last I dared to gaze into the opening Heavens, the tempest and darkness, the shroud and pall all vanished, and I saw only angels, with their deep calm eyes, so full of beauty and tenderness. Then like the rushing of mighty waters, came over my soul, a sense of harmony and glory and of the all pervading love of the Infinite Father. . . . None, *none* in the vast Universe of God were lost to Him."[21] Cora Wilburn described a similar scenario in recounting her conversion from Judaism first to Christianity and then to Spiritualism. "My child mind," Wilburn wrote of her Jewish upbringing, "was imbued with unwholesome fears; with pictures of a revengeful, changeful God. *I feared Him.* Consequently I could not love God or Humanity with a *perfect love.*" Later, when she turned to Christianity, she found that "the New Testament failed to inspire me with those glowing aspirations . . . that Nature, God's holy exponent of Principles, had never failed to present to heart and intellect."[22] Nature, in the Spiritualist view, not only became the source of truth but also served as an antidote to the repression of established religions.

In spite of the apparent logical conflict between the evidences of Spiritualism and the doctrines of Christianity, many investigators found support for their Christian faith at the séance table. Investigators loyal to the doctrine of the incarnation, as were those in the Beecher family, viewed the manifestations as support for the plausibility of biblical miracles. For them, Spiritualism's proof of God's unwillingness to sever families at death supported the new theology emerging at mid-century based on the love of Christ rather than the wrath of God. Some argued that Spiritualists should remain within their churches "and work for truth there" rather than withdrawing to form their own societies. One newspaper account of a trance speaker described her as "a young lady of intelligence and attested purity of life (being still a member in good standing of an Evangelical Christian Church, for the reason that after an investigation by the authorities of the church 'no fault was found in her')." Many believers in manifestations did remain within their churches, although a few were expelled for their beliefs.[23]

Excommunications were relatively rare. After all, people spoke to angels in the Bible, and talking to the dead apparently contradicted no basic tenet of Christian faith.* It was rather the conclusions that Spiritualists drew from spirit manifestations that brought their orthodoxy into question. The First Congregational Church of Oshkosh, Wisconsin, excommunicated a mother and her adult daughter for denying the plenary inspiration of the Bible, denying the divinity of Christ, and denying the equality of the Father and the Son as persons of the Trinity. The complaint charged the woman with saying, with reference to the Trinity, that she "believed there were more persons than three in God, that all who had the love of God in their hearts were to that degree a part of God." In her defense, she did not deny the charges but argued that "The real [charge] that has so agitated the mind of our pastor, and caused him to be the instigator of all the rest, is not named. . . . It is, that I am a Spiritualist." Her husband sympathized with her but was not charged in the complaint, either because he was not a Spiritualist or because he was not a church member. Orthodox clergy understandably condemned Spiritualism as fundamentally opposed to a Christian worldview. Oliver Wendell Holmes quipped that "with the crack of a toe joint" Kate and Margaret Fox had caused "such a crack of old beliefs that the roar of it is heard in all the ministers' studies in Christendom."[24]

Spiritualism and the Liberal Denominations

The Spiritualist critique of Calvinism offered little that was original or even of recent vintage. As has been noted, the trend of nineteenth-century culture mandated a liberalizing of theology. Even the Pres-

---

* The angels in the Bible cited by Spiritualists as evidence for their faith were not actually spirits of the dead but rather a distinct order of beings created by God. However, by the mid-nineteenth century, the biblical understanding of angels coexisted with a popular notion that virtuous people became angels after death. The only actual instance of spirit communication described in the Bible, the conversation between King Saul and the prophet Samuel through a ghost-seer (1 Sam. 28:3–25), is not portrayed as meriting divine approval. In fact, it was used to criticize Spiritualism as demonic because of the popular identification of the woman who contacted the spirit of Samuel as the "Witch of Endor."

byterians recoiled from infant damnation by mid-century. When
Spiritualism was born in 1848, liberal theologians had been using infant damnation to condemn Calvinism for a hundred years. Yet the
apparently appealing view that infants could not be damned only
slowly penetrated popular Protestantism. Early in the nineteenth century, Unitarians argued a position similar to the doctrine of progression. "Unitarians believe in many hells and many heavens, according
to the character and condition of each person," wrote James Freeman
Clarke. "They believe that the purpose of future suffering will be
reformatory and not vindictive." While Unitarianism offered a religious alternative to the harsh doctrines of orthodox theology, its emphasis on rationality limited its appeal to a small educated elite. The
"corpse-cold Unitarianism" of Brattle Street had little influence beyond the commercial and professional classes of Boston. Historian
Lewis Saum's reading of antebellum diaries and correspondence revealed that Unitarianism "came almost not at all to the attention of
the common people," while Spiritualism received broad exposure. In
Spiritualism, doctrines that Unitarianism offered to the few became
available to the many.[25]

Spiritualism's conception of nature as permeated with divinity received earlier and more elegant expression within Unitarianism's
more heterodox offshoot, Transcendentalism. Ralph Waldo Emerson's discovery in the 1830s that the divinity revealed in nature had
no need of the dogmas or rituals of an established church preceded
the same discoveries by Spiritualists, and the hostility he encountered
from his fellow Unitarian ministers when he questioned the divinity
of Christ foretold the acrimony with which Spiritualism would be met
even within the liberal denominations. Spiritualists acknowledged
their debt to Emerson. They enthusiastically attended his lectures
and quoted him in their publications and on their platform.[26] But
Emerson eschewed their praise and failed to return the compliment.
Spiritualism drew harsh invective from both Emerson and Henry David Thoreau. The giants of Transcendentalism found their neighbors
in Concord thoroughly infected with the new religion by 1852. Thoreau reserved some of his ugliest language for the manifestations.
Emerson condemned the rappings both in his private journal and on
the lyceum platform. In his famous lecture "Success," first delivered
in 1859, Emerson used Spiritualism to exemplify the immoral trend
of American society. "I hate this shallow Americanism which hopes to
get rich by credit, to get knowledge by raps on midnight tables, to

learn the economy of the mind by phrenology, or skill without study," he told the American public.[27]

Yet, whatever disdain Emerson and Thoreau felt for Spiritualism, it spread some of their most cherished ideas far beyond the ranks of those who identified with Transcendentalism. The birth of Spiritualism coincided almost exactly with the death of Transcendentalism as a social movement. Brook Farm closed its doors in 1847, and by 1850 the Transcendentalists had lost faith in the alternative social visions that they had hoped would reform the nation.[28] Transcendentalism's Unitarian origins and intellectual elitism limited the scope of its appeal. While the American public flocked to Emerson's lectures and were inspired by what he said, few of them responded by joining communes or becoming Transcendentalists. Instead, they followed his lectures with visits to séances, where the power of Emerson's ideas helped fuel the movement he despised. Those same ideas found a broad and dedicated audience among Spiritualists. The immanence of God, the destructive limitations of the Christian tradition as a path to truth, and the necessity of seeking truth instead in the natural world and within the self all found popular acceptance among the mass of Spiritualists. Spiritualist Cora Wilburn echoed the claims of her more sophisticated Transcendentalist predecessors. "Still monstrous evils afflict the dwellers of the earth, and as the Bible fails to apply the remedy, must there not be a higher and a safer guide?" she asked rhetorically in 1860. "There is," she answered, "*in the human soul.*" Like the Transcendentalists, she found "great and noble truths . . . in the Scriptures of all nations" but rejected the possibility of an "infallible and closed revelation" because she found it incompatible with "human progression."[29]

From a philosophical perspective, the basic similarities between the Transcendentalist and the Spiritualist outlook appear to outweigh the differences. Both movements based their metaphysics on the immanence of God in nature and in the human soul. Emerson's *Nature*, like Andrew Jackson Davis's *Principles of Nature*, was originally assumed to be the work of a Swedenborgian.[30] Transcendentalist editor William Henry Channing thought the appeal of the two movements similar enough to purchase the subscription list of Andrew Jackson Davis's *Univercœlum* when he embarked on the publication of *The Spirit of the Age*, which superseded both the first Spiritualist periodical and *The Harbinger*, the organ of the Transcendentalist Brook Farm community.[31] While investigation preoccupied many Concord residents, only a few Transcendentalists identified themselves as Spiritualists, notably Elizabeth Peabody and Georgianna Bruce Kirby.[32] What finally separated the apparently sympathetic movements was, of course, spirit communication. While direct communication with individual spirits struck Emerson as a vulgar distortion of the message of Transcendentalism, it struck many Americans as concrete proof of the immanence of God and as a literal interpretation of Emerson's advice to seek truth within their own souls. Spiritualism's concreteness liberated many of Emerson's ideas from their class-bound character by making them accessible to those without the intellectual bent to grasp their subtler implications. But, in the process, the new movement made itself reprehensible to some of its most important philosophical forebears.

While Spiritualism made liberal theology and transcendental visions widely available, it also confirmed liberal beliefs already held by other groups. The early twentieth-century historian of Spiritualism, Frank Podmore, observed that Spiritualism drew many followers from religious groups that "held some liberal or attenuated Christian doctrine," such as Unitarians, Universalists, and Quakers. In contrast to evangelical denominations whose theology Spiritualists attacked head-on, investigators from liberal groups found in the manifestations evidence for what they already believed. Spirit communications provided Unitarians with confirmation for their rejection of eternal damnation, Universalists found in them confirmation of the doctrine of universal salvation, and Quakers saw them as a concrete illustration of the doctrine of the inner light. Like the Spiritualists, all these groups at various times drew the ire of the orthodox clergy.

Podmore went on to claim that "no religious body gave a larger contingent to the new faith than the Universalists." Winthrop Hudson, writing in the 1960s, concurred with Podmore, concluding that Universalism never completely recovered from the enthusiasm shown for Spiritualism among both its clergy and its laity. Universalism added to the Arminian view that all people *can* be saved the claim that all *will* be saved. Universalism shared much of Unitarianism's liberal theology, but it drew its adherents from a less urban and less educated population. Although never a large denomination, by 1850 Universalism had twice as many churches as Unitarianism and a wider geographic distribution. In the western states of Ohio, Indiana, and Illinois, Universalism established a presence in agricultural regions untouched by Unitarianism.[33]

Universalist ministers made up Andrew Jackson Davis's first follow-ers. In 1852, the Universalist minister and reformer John Murray Spear recorded a series of messages delivered through him from his namesake, the founder of Universalism, John Murray. Universalist minister Olympia Brown reported in the 1870s that "half of Univer-salist ministers are Spiritualists and make no secret of it." One of her colleagues disagreed. Rev. N. Gunnison opined that Spiritualism was "dying out" in 1869. "Few of my acquaintances who were firm believ-ers fifteen years ago have any faith in it now." Yet even Gunnison's claim that the heterodox faith was on the decline confirms that Spir-itualism had indeed flourished among Universalist clergy and that it continued to be a point of controversy.[34]

Universalist leader Rev. T. Starr King thought Spiritualism impor-tant enough within Universalism to address it in an 1858 sermon en-titled "The meaning and methods of communication with the Spiri-tual World." The Spiritualist *Banner of Light* applauded the sermon but criticized its failure to openly condone Spiritualism. According to the editor, "Every *Spiritualist* would accept with heart and soul" King's insistence that "spiritualism . . . centers in God," but "the keen sar-casm with which he assailed some parts of the faith, that is so pre-cious, not only to many of his own congregation, but to a very large proportion of the Christian community, bears with it, its own con-demnation." The Spiritualist press reported conversions of Univer-salist ministers, such as J. Merrifield of Mishawka, Indiana.[35]

While most denominations shuddered at the thought of Spiritualist heterodoxy within their ranks, Universalist ministers sometimes iden-tified themselves as Spiritualists without suffering the excommunica-tion that attended such actions in other churches. The Universalist minister J. M. Peebles separated from his denomination to become a Spiritualist but was installed as pastor of a Universalist church in Bal-timore in 1856 and preached Universalism in San Francisco in 1862 while holding office in several Spiritualist organizations. Even as an ex-minister, Peebles enjoyed a respectability through association with the ministry that aided Spiritualist efforts. Spiritualists in White Pi-geon, Michigan, felt that clerical opposition diminished once Peebles endorsed their cause. L. F. W. Andrews briefly interrupted his forty-year Universalist ministry to publish a Spiritualist periodical in the 1860s. Spiritualists often used Universalist facilities for funerals or conventions, possibly because all other denominations refused. In a few towns, Spiritualists attempted to unite with Universalists to construct meeting houses, but these experiments rarely succeeded. Spiritualists who participated in such an effort in Manchester, Iowa, complained that they were rarely allowed to use the building.[36]

In a few cases, Universalist congregations abandoned their denomination to embrace Spiritualism. An early Philadelphia-area Spiritualist circle formed from the remnant of a Universalist church closed in 1850. In 1863, a Universalist congregation in the same city accepted Spiritualism and rededicated their meeting house as "the First Spiritualist Church of Philadelphia." More frequently, Spiritualism flourished within Universalist congregations without upsetting their denominational loyalty. After attending a Universalist funeral at which the minister "was in a state of extatic [*sic*] faith concerning immortality, which he plainly said had been very much strengthened by the phenomena of modern Spiritualism," Lydia Maria Child concluded that "in all the sects more or less of the preachers are inoculated with Spiritualism." She noted that the Universalist minister in the next town had also been influenced by Spiritualism. He "quotes phenomena in his sermons as heralds of new dispensations."[37]

"Most of the Universalists" in Vermont had become Spiritualists, trance speaker Warren Chase reported during an 1859 visit to the state. Spiritualism won enough Universalist support in Vermont to spark controversy within the denomination. In 1856, the medium Achsa Sprague debated Spiritualism against a Universalist clergyman before a crowd of one hundred people. In 1871, the Universalist Vermont State Convention considered a resolution prohibiting the use of Universalist churches "for the dissemination of spiritualist teachings which failed to acknowledge the unique primacy of the Scriptures as an indispensable element in historic Universalism." No other denomination would have felt compelled to specify the particular type of Spiritualist teaching that it prohibited, as most churches would brook no Spiritualism of any kind within their walls. Even this mild prohibition, however, failed, and the convention ultimately left it to each church to decide about Spiritualist teachings independently. Only a strong Spiritualist presence within the denomination could have resulted in such an action.[38]

Spiritualism also appeared within Unitarianism, although less frequently. The Harvard-trained Unitarian minister Herman Snow transferred his allegiance from William Ellery Channing to the spirits during a winter spent at the Spiritualist-leaning Hopedale community and published a volume on "spirit-intercourse." He subsequently resumed his ministry, called by a Unitarian congregation fully aware of his unorthodox views. Theodore Parker's Unitarian congregation in Boston included a practicing medium among its choristers.[39]

Although Spiritualism shared important doctrines with liberal Christian denominations, to hold these views in conjunction with belief in spirit communication was very different from holding them without it. Spiritualists viewed liberal theology as a necessary but insufficient basis for religious faith. Even those introduced to Spiritualism by the philosophical writing of Andrew Jackson Davis looked for manifestations to confirm what they read.[40] Séances provided two features that no amount of philosophy could offer: an opportunity to seek communication with spirits of those one had known while alive and an empirical demonstration of the doctrines Davis taught. "If you have communication with those who have cast off the natural body will you not enquire if the same be not possible to us at Santa Cruz[?]" Transcendentalist Georgiana Bruce (Kirby) wrote from California to Charlotte Fowler Wells in New York. Bruce hastened to add, "Our Interest . . . grows out of no idle curiosity—for both Mrs. [Eliza] F[arnham] and myself are firm believers and do not stand in need of evidence but we want religious teaching and advice."[41] However philosophical some Spiritualists might wax, manifestations formed the foundation of the new faith. Andrew Jackson Davis himself dated the "external" beginning of Spiritualism to the Hydesville rappings.[42]

The Fate of Sinless Infants

Many investigators first approached the séance table in hope of continuing communication with a beloved friend or family member whose voice had only just been silenced. In the nineteenth century, more frequently than today, death entered every life, and each individual had to find a way to continue in its face. For many Americans, Spiritualism offered a real and effective source of consolation. This attraction reinforced the primacy of manifestations because only manifestations could reestablish bonds severed by death. "The world grows dark with us," Horace Greeley confided to Margaret Fuller following the death of his five-year-old son in 1849. "The one sunburst of joy that has gladdened my rugged pathway has departed." Having buried three infant girls, Greeley and his wife idolized "Pickie" (Arthur Young Greeley) and were disconsolate when he died suddenly of cholera. Greeley feared for his wife's sanity and spent evenings with her talking about Pickie's brief life. The Greeleys invited the Fox sisters into their home in the hope that Pickie's presence would brighten the dark world they now inhabited. Greeley later attributed the attempt to reach Pickie through Spiritualism to his wife, who "talked to dear Pickie daily for weeks when Catherine Fox was with her." But he also longed to hear his son's voice and recounted séances at which he conversed with Pickie. The Greeleys' experience typified that which drew many investigators to Spiritualism.[43]

In her study of the Beecher family, Marie Caskey has shown that orthodox Christians of the early nineteenth century reconciled themselves to death by developing concepts of the hereafter that pointed in the direction of Spiritualism. Patriarch Lyman Beecher, one of the best-known evangelists of the early nineteenth century and father of Harriet Beecher Stowe and Henry Ward Beecher, described heaven as a place of great beauty, where individuals would retain characteristics and proclivities of their earthly personalities. He taught his children that their dead mother, Roxanna, watched over them from heaven and continued to play an active role in their spiritual development. The personal presence of the sainted Roxanna Beecher was strong enough to prompt some of the Beecher children to investigate Spiritualism, while it moved all of them toward a more liberal theology. Caskey argues that the Beechers' Spiritualism resulted from the persistence into the nineteenth century of their Calvinist anxiety about the fate of the soul after death.[44]

In keeping with the nineteenth century's elevated estimation of the power of human beings, the developing evangelical consensus gave new weight to the role of human agency in the drama of salvation. Ministers no longer relied on God alone to kindle revivals of religion. They developed the protracted meeting, the "anxious bench," and other techniques through which human beings created conditions conducive to conversion. Because evangelicals believed that individuals could influence their own salvation, they emphasized preparation for death, as the possibility of conversion existed up until the moment of death, but not thereafter. While earlier Protestants placed their fate in the hands of God, nineteenth-century evangelicals anxiously labored with the dying. The focus on human agency and moral accountability suggested that individuals were responsible for their failure to receive the spirit. Because of the new possibility that human beings might cause a conversion, "the death of an unregenerate individual engendered more anxiety than in the Puritan era when people left election in God's hands alone." This was especially true in the case of infants and children, who died before they had an opportunity to exercise their own agency toward conversions.[45]

Death presented a greater cosmological problem for emerging worldviews that emphasized human agency than for earlier visions based solidly on the sovereignty of God. Death's uncontrollability and finality belied the claims of nineteenth-century optimists who hoped to control the universe through feats of human technology. Death also challenged romantic outlooks that viewed nature as benign and harmonious. Although death rates fell throughout the nineteenth century, or perhaps because of it, a cultural preoccupation with death and mourning flourished.* A vast body of consolation literature addressed the relocation of death in American culture. Urbanization and industrialization transformed death from an event that deprived the community of a unique social actor into a personal loss felt only by family and friends. Individuals compensated for the "callous indifference of the 'tearless throng'" by intensifying private bereavement. Mourning rituals expanded, and the rural cemetery movement and the new profession of undertaking launched commercial and material changes that paralleled new religious interpretations of death.[46]

By seeking, and sometimes finding, intimate contact with the dead, Spiritualists found evidence for the rejection of death as a final separation. "Believe not that what is called death is a final termination to human existence, nor that the *change* is so entire as to alter or destroy the constitutional peculiarities of the individual," wrote Andrew Jackson Davis, "but believe righteously, that death causes as much *alteration* in the condition of the individual as the *bursting* of a rose-bud causes in the condition and situation of the flower." If death did not change beloved friends, then it need not silence their voices. Spiritualists not only asserted the possibility of hearing the dead speak but proposed this as *the* normative religious experience.[47]

For the bereft, death, especially premature death, challenged the meaning of life. In "To My Spirit-Brother," Spiritualist poet Fanny Green asked the questions that bothered many Americans. "But why did cruel nature e'er entwine / Each heart so closely, dearly with the

* Although overall death rates declined, epidemics of cholera and diphtheria occurred every ten years or so, reminding Americans that death could suddenly appear in the midst of any family.

other / If we must never hope that mine and thine / Should bind us, O, my dear, my more than brother!"[48] Sentimental values and an increasing emphasis on the nuclear family as the focus of emotional life encouraged a rebellion against death. "Why were we made to love so ardently, with sympathies so warm—with hearts so dependent on others for enjoyment—if death must come to sunder such ties?" asked a character in a typical work of Spiritualist fiction. She then describes the "intense desire [that] took possession" of her to follow her beloved brother into death, "to feel the chill of the dark valley." According to the story, she overcame the despair of bereavement when her brother appeared to her in a dream and described the idyllic setting in which he found himself after death. "Tell my father and mother of my home and they will cease to mourn for me," the spirit told his sister.[49]

Spiritualism's denial of death offered a unique kind of consolation to the bereaved. Messages frequently focused on the spirit's happiness after death and continued concern for surviving family members. "Dear Mother, all is well," a daughter's spirit assured her parent in a typical message. Spirits claimed that their estate after death was a pleasant one and did not merit mourning. "Do not weep, it grieves me to hear you weep," the spirit told her mother.[50] While others hoped and prayed over the fate of their loved ones after death, Spiritualists could rest assured by concrete statements from beyond the grave. With the separation of a public man's sphere of the world and the market from a private woman's sphere of home and family, Americans imagined heaven as an extension of woman's sphere. No commercial or industrial establishments lined the streets of heaven. In fact, American visions of heaven often omitted the street altogether as an urban intrusion unnecessary to the pastoral images generated by nostalgia for an agrarian world. As the home became a haven from the heartless world, heaven began to share many of its attributes. God called people not to the marketplace or the shop but to the home. "Death," said Henry Ward Beecher, "is only God's call, 'Come home.'"[51] The rural cemetery provided a permanent resting place that ignored the existence of the marketplace. Instead, its tree-lined lanes and neatly fenced family plots replicated the suburbs that increasingly insulated the middle-class Christian home against the moral dangers of the world.

As liberal Protestantism and sentimental fiction brought heaven closer and closer to earth, it is not surprising that some people found the distance short enough to bridge. While Spiritualists were criticized for their materialistic portrayal of life after death, churchgoers across the country enthusiastically peered through *The Gates Ajar* to see the apple trees and meadows of a heaven that looked very much like the New England village of novelist Elizabeth Stuart Phelps's girl-hood.[52] Spiritualists embraced the rural cemetery movement, in which the rejection of death was expressed in the transformation of the burial ground from a reminder of the inevitability of death and decay into a site designed for the contemplation of happy memories and heavenly reunions.[53] Spiritualist surveyor John Shoebridge Williams provided the plan for the new Oak Dale Cemetery in Urbana, Ohio, in 1856, clearly indicating the innovations that made a rural cemetery a place of spiritual uplift. In addition to mapping plots and lanes with pastoral names, his plan included "contemplation seats," a "poets' bower," and "vistas" indicated by broken lines. The cemetery emanates from a central rostrum, surrounded by "seats for instruction." Shoebridge's plan provided the mourner with comfortable accommodations for the contemplation of heaven. Spiritualists articulated and acted on unorthodox thoughts that they shared with many other Americans.[54]

Death literally occurred in woman's sphere. Most people died at home in bed, attended by female relatives. In New York City in 1853, 49 percent of those who died were children under five, who presumably had been under primarily female care. Women, who were expected to focus their lives on the nurture of family members during life, were also expected to feel losses through death more deeply than men, who might turn their attention to other duties. Middle-class women remained at home by empty cribs and unoccupied seats at the dining room table and produced and purchased a variety of memorial artifacts, from postmortem photographs to jewelry woven from the hair of the deceased. Etiquette prescribed longer periods of mourning for women than for men. Probably a husband's death did have a greater impact on the survivor than a wife's, and the widow's longer mourning reflected this.[55]

Like Queen Victoria, the moral emblem of the era, who assumed mourning permanently following the death of her husband, nineteenth-century women could adopt mourning as a full-time occupation. Spiritualism provided a way to show love and interest in the dead without submitting to the restrictions on one's activities that accompanied mourning. Spirit messages frequently assured the survivor that mourning was unnecessary. Andrew Jackson Davis argued that "the excessive weeping and lamentation of friends and relatives, over the external form of one departed, are mainly caused by the sensuous and superficial mode by which the majority of mankind view the phenomena of death." If, as Davis claimed, "*Death* is but a *Birth* of the Spirit from a lower into a higher state," then it did not justify mourning. If death did not cause separation and there were no reason to fear for the fate of the individual after death, then the bereaved might dispense with dwelling on death and commence efforts toward uplifting the world of the living. In his final condemnation of American attitudes toward death, Davis described it as infinitely preferable to a loveless marriage: "You may clothe yourselves with the dark habilments of wo, when you consign at the altar, a heart to a living grave . . . but robe yourselves with garments of light to honor the spirit's birth into a higher life!"[56]

Spiritualists responded to Davis's advice by wearing white at funerals and by transforming internments into events that emphasized continuity rather than the finality of death. Instead of delivering eulogies, mediums who presided at funerals delivered messages from the deceased, often describing the journey away from earth, the beautiful destination at which the spirit arrived, and its continued love and concern for survivors.[57] While other tombstones recorded the date on which the deceased "died," Spiritualist gravestone inscriptions report the date on which the ones there interred "entered the Summerland" (the Spiritualist term for heaven), or "awakened to the newness of life in the Spirit World," or "passed to the Spirit Land," or, simply, "Translated."[58]

As such grave inscriptions indicate, Spiritualism echoed the themes popular in mid-century consolation literature, but as always insisted that they be extended to their logical conclusion. Few Americans would have objected to the response non-Spiritualist author Sarah Payson Willis (Fanny Fern) gave to a "broken Hearted mother" who asked for "a word to comfort me for the death of my baby." Willis replied in words that any Spiritualist might utter. "But one thing I know," she wrote, "that in the other world your baby and mine will know us—their mothers, else God were not God."[59] Spiritualists viewed as hypocritical conventions that justified such statements as Willis's, encouraging the gentle language of consolation but refusing to accept its implied message of continuing contact with the dead. They complained that orthodox ministers did not really believe the words of comfort they spoke at funerals. Leader William Hayden noted that orthodox clergy often sounded like Spiritualists when consoling the bereaved, assuring them that the deceased "are not gone, but often with you, watching over you and loving you, far more than ever before, coming to you in the still hours of the night, with sweet words of comfort and hope." But, Hayden complained, "the very moment you say to them that you have realized the sublime truth of their teachings, that you have communicated with the dear ones, whose bright dwellings are on the glorious hills of heaven . . . they look at you to see if you are not mad, and assure you that it is all wicked delusion . . . the work of the devil." When his own child died, Hayden called on Louisa Bridge to act as "medium for the funeral sermon." [60]

Spiritualists found a pragmatic demonstration of the superiority of their philosophy in the effectiveness of the coping strategies it provided for the bereaved. Andrew Jackson Davis attributed conventional mourning practices to the false teaching that death caused the annihilation of the individual personality. "Could you but turn your gaze from the lifeless body, which no longer answers to your look of love; and could your spiritual eyes be opened; you would behold— standing in your midst—a form, the same, but more beautiful, and living!" he told his readers. "There is great cause," Davis concluded, "to rejoice at the *birth* of the spirit from this world into the inner sphere of life." [61] These were the words Mary Robbins Post found so comforting when she buried her beloved daughter.

3

"Thine for Agitation"

The emphatic individualism that placed Spiritualists in opposition to established religion had social and political implications as well.[1] Dependent for spiritual knowledge on the unhindered autonomy of female mediums, believers vigorously applied the principle of individualism to the role of women. As a result, they became ardent advocates of woman's rights. " 'Equals Rights' is my motto," declared the medium Elizabeth Kingsbury in 1857. But she found that "Woman has been so long subject to customs degrading to herself, that neither she nor the men are sensible where, and to what extent, they [equal rights] exist!"[2] When Spiritualists applied their individualist convictions to women's situation, they found a need for drastic changes to allow women to express their true natures as human beings. They found that the norms imposed by society dictated both an immoral theology and an immoral structure of relations between human beings. In response, they argued that women needed to be freed from limited education that restricted the development of their intellects, from unjust laws that denied them access to their property and custody of their children, from unequal marriages that subjugated them to men, and from economic restrictions that forced them into dependence. Spiritualists' commitment to the emancipation of women formed one plank of a broad reform platform designed to overthrow conventions imposed by church or state between the individual and his or her God-given nature. They denounced the authority of churches over believers, of governments over citizens, of doctors over patients, of masters over slaves, and, most of all, of men over women.

Spiritualists' radical vision for the reformation of society paralleled the extreme individualism of their religious practice. Their faith was antithetical to institutional religion because it asserted that truth came directly to the individual without mediation by minister, Bible, or church. The ability of spirits to reveal the fate of the human soul directly to human beings at the time and place of the spirit's choosing obviated the need for scripture, sacrament, or sanctuary—even for worship. Unlike church attendance, which reinforced the worshiper's identity as a member of a congregation, attending a séance was an intensely individual action. Investigators consulted mediums in hope of personal communications from intimate family members, "mother to child, brother to sister, teacher to pupil."[3] By providing a form of religious practice in which truth revealed itself to individuals without recourse to external authority, Spiritualism became a magnet for social and political radicals throughout the nineteenth century.

Spiritualists adopted much of their social program from individualist rhetoric already articulated within the left wing of the movement for the abolition of slavery. However, as a group, they differed from other abolitionists by lifting woman's rights out of the reform platform as preeminent. The new religion injected its followers' priorities into the radical agenda as it came to permeate several groups central to the progressive audience of the period. Members of the New England Non-Resistance Society, the Christian socialist Hopedale Community, and the schismatic Quaker "Friends of Human Progress" adopted the new faith because it offered a religious outlook that incorporated their individualist principles. Many radical abolitionist leaders also became adherents. In addition, the large audiences assembled by Spiritualists at their own conventions became crucial to the dissemination of radical ideas. At these events, woman's rights was not presented as just another reform. Rather, Spiritualists believed, as one advocate put it, that "woman's freedom is the world's redemption."[4] As investigation of the manifestations swept the nation, Spiritualism became a major—if not *the* major—vehicle for the spread of woman's rights ideas in mid-century America.

Spiritualists at Seneca Falls

The same summer that the Fox sisters arrived in Rochester, the historic Seneca Falls Convention met to consider the "social, civil, and religious" rights of women.[5] Dissident Quakers in upstate New York provided the nucleus for investigation of the two equally controversial innovations: Spiritualism and woman's rights. In June 1848, Lucretia Mott, a Quaker preacher from Philadelphia, participated in the organization of the Congregational Friends in Waterloo, New York, and then remained in the region to visit her sister, Martha Coffin Wright. It was then that Mott was reunited with Elizabeth Cady Stanton, whom she had met at the World Anti-Slavery Convention in London in 1840, and the two sent out the call for the first woman's rights convention. The American woman's rights movement drew its first breaths in an atmosphere alive with rumors of angels. Members of the Waterloo Friends flocked to nearby Seneca Falls and figured prominently in the convention's proceedings.[6] Raps reportedly rocked the same table where Lucretia Mott and Elizabeth Cady Stanton penned the "Declaration of Sentiments," which formed the convention's agenda. The table stood in the parlor of progressive Quakers (and future Spiritualists) Thomas and Mary Ann McClintock. Raps were reported at Stanton's home as well.[7]

From this time on, Spiritualism and woman's rights intertwined repeatedly as both became mass movements that challenged the existing norms of American life. The two movements shared many leaders and activists. While not all feminists were Spiritualists, all Spiritualists advocated woman's rights. Andrew Jackson Davis allied himself in marriage with an adamant woman's rights activist from Western New York, Mary Fenn Love, who joined Stanton and Anthony, as well as a half dozen Rochester Spiritualists, in calling the first New York State Woman's Rights Convention in 1853 (see plate 7). According to the Spiritualist press, Mary Love had "consecrated her life—her all for the redemption of her sex." After her marriage in 1855, Mary Fenn Davis quickly outstripped her husband as a public spokesperson in both movements. "In point of pleasing oratory," observers found her "even more acceptable" than her husband. "Spiritualism has inaugurated the era of woman," Mary Davis proclaimed. She recalled the common birthdate of the new religion and woman's rights in 1848. "Since that time Spiritualism has promoted the cause of woman more than any other movement," Davis explained.[8] Speakers and mediums participated in the general woman's rights agitation and promoted woman's rights from their own platforms. Announcing the 1851 Woman's Rights Convention, the *Spirit Messenger and Harmonial Guide* called its topic "the most important reform issue of the day." Spiritualist conventions called for the "Emancipation of women from all legal and social disabilities."[9]

Incipient Spiritualists among the Progressive Friends asserted the rights of women with a boldness that shocked even Elizabeth Stanton and Lucretia Mott. When the Seneca Falls Convention adjourned, its participants agreed to reconvene in Rochester two weeks later, appointing ex-Hicksites Amy Post, Sarah Hallowell, and Sarah Fish and ex-Presbyterian Sarah Owen a committee on arrangements. When this group made the unprecedented proposal that a woman preside over the convention, Mott and Stanton "stoutly opposed it" as "a most hazardous experiment" and urged the election of Lucretia's husband, James. The convention threatened to break up, but, after convincing reassurances from Amy Post and Rhoda De Garmo about the ability of women to preside at conventions, Abigail Bush was elected and took the chair.[10]

Consistently, those who assumed the most radical positions on woman's rights became Spiritualists. Nancy Hewitt has analyzed the group of Rochester "ultraist" women who led local campaigns for woman's rights, abolition, and Spiritualism. She found that they came from Hicksite farming villages in western New York, where they had imbibed a tradition of isolation from the world but activism within their own communities. In Rochester, Hewitt located the ultraist reformers on the "lower rungs of the new urban bourgeoisie."[11] Amy Post, Rhoda De Garmo, Mary Ann and Thomas McClintock, Sarah D. Fish, Catherine Ann Fish Stebbins, Sarah Hallowell, Sarah Anthony Burtis (cousin of Susan B. Anthony), Lucy Coleman, and Eliab Capron were among Progressive Friends who participated in the Seneca Falls convention and the follow-up convention at Rochester. All became Spiritualists. Three of this group, Amy Post, her sister Sarah Hallowell, and Sarah Fish, made the historic recommendation that the Rochester Woman's Rights Convention elect a female president.[12] Abigail Bush, who filled the office, described herself as "born and baptized in the old Scotch Presbyterian church . . . [whose] sacred teachings were 'if a woman would know anything let her ask her husband at home.' " The only non-Quaker among the original group that witnessed the Fox sisters' manifestations at the Posts' home, Bush became a lifelong Spiritualist.[13]

Spiritualism and woman's rights spread simultaneously through the network of Quaker abolitionists that produced the first supporters for both movements. Susan B. Anthony, daughter of a Rochester Quaker family and member of the Waterloo Friends, missed the Seneca Falls Convention but had become Elizabeth Cady Stanton's partner in leading the agitation for woman's rights by the early 1850s. She recorded in her diary that "Spiritualism as usual [was] the principle topic" when she dined with a group of Quaker abolitionists and woman's rights pioneers at the Philadelphia home of Lucretia Mott in 1854. She noted each reformer's opinion of the topic in her diary. Pioneer abolitionist and feminist Sarah Grimké, an ardent believer, "was all enthusiasm in the faith." The Jew-turned-atheist Ernestine Rose and a Mrs. Curtis, "believing the spirit inseparable from the body," expressed their disbelief. Anthony reported that Eliab Capron, the early promoter of the Fox sisters, "doesn't believe, he *knows* there is a reality in spirit disembodied, communicating with the living." But Anthony herself did not take sides in the debate. "The rest of the company," she wrote, "with myself, seemed not to know whether or not there is any truth in these modern manifestations." The uncommitted group included her hosts, James and Lucretia Mott, whose extensive investigations never convinced them of the reality of spirit communications.[14] Similar scenes occurred among black reformers in Boston, where Charlotte Forten struggled with the avid faith of William Cooper Nell.[15]

The early woman's rights movement, like Spiritualism, drew both inspiration and leadership from the left wing of the movement for the abolition of slavery. Radical abolitionists, in turn, found in Spiritualism a religion in harmony with their individualist principles. Abolitionists' interest in both woman's rights and Spiritualism derived from their fierce loyalty to the principle of individualism. They opposed slavery because it depended on the unjust usurpation of the individual autonomy of one person by another, and they found the same injustice in the relations between men and women and in the dogmatic teachings of the churches. Although slavery was the issue whose urgency awakened abolitionists to the need for action, the individualist basis of their agitation sensitized them to an array of injustices, which at times included the appropriation of Indian lands, capital punishment, the abuse of alcohol, and legal enforcement of the Christian sabbath, to name a few examples. A "sisterhood of reforms," composed of peace, temperance, and health reform as well as antislavery, came to occupy many who entered public life through abolition. The issue of women's public participation split the abolition movement. The evangelically inclined conservative group argued that assigning public roles to women was so controversial that it would detract from the achievement of freedom for the slave. The more radical followers of William Lloyd Garrison believed that they were fighting for freedom as an ideal and that denying it to women would not hasten its approach for slaves. Once the two groups split in 1840,

Garrisonians were free to mix both woman's rights and religious radicalism with antislavery agitation. The Garrisonian American Anti-Slavery Society put the leading woman's rights speakers on its payroll during the 1850s, although it required them to allot a portion of their lectures to abolition. For most Garrisonians woman's rights became a part of the "sisterhood of reforms," and for many Spiritualism did also.[16]

Spiritualist reformers found adherence to prescribed gender roles inconsistent with the principle of individual sovereignty. "Let every *woman*, who feels the chains imposed on her by tyrant custom, resolve to break them, cost her what it may," declared Miss S. Hill, writing on "Individualism" in the *Agitator*, a Spiritualist periodical. She enjoined women to disregard customs that limited their freedom to follow their own consciences. "How can we be our own sovereigns as long as we allow others to think, feel, and act for us, and are content to be ourselves, the mere appendages of those who presume to prescribe for us our appropriate spheres?" Hill asserted, and many Spiritualists concurred, that men also compromised their individuality by conforming to accepted gender roles. "Let man too, the slave of passion, of prejudice, and of ignorance, become his own sovereign," she proposed.[17] Society's notions of appropriate behavior for men and women should not be allowed to preempt the divine order expressed in human nature. Spiritualist rhetoric gave the reform of gender roles the same urgency that others saw in winning freedom for the slave.

Spiritualism and Radical Individualism

The individualist ferment within abolition produced a moral critique of the churches that underscored the theological dissent discussed in the last chapter. Radical abolitionists agreed with Romantics and Transcendentalists that the church, the clergy, and the Bible were so many enslavers of the human spirit. They also believed that individualist principles required constant agitation in order to effect a transformation of society. While the more moderate majority of reformers based their programs on Christian teachings, radicals urged men and women of conscience to "come out" from the churches. They viewed the churches as corrupt because their failure to take a stand against the ungodly institution of slavery proved them untrue to Christian principles. The Garrisonian critique of the churches stemmed from Christian perfectionism, the doctrine that it is possible to attain complete freedom from sin in this life. Perfectionism contrasted with the orthodox view that we are bound to sin as long as we are bound to our bodies. Abolitionist "come-outers" discovered their churches to be tainted by the sin of slaveholding and fled in search of more pristine alternatives.[18]

Most radical reformers were intensely religious. Their rejection of the churches was a rejection not of religion but rather of the corruption of religion. The abolitionist and woman's rights advocate Lucy Coleman recalled that, when she became a Spiritualist, she gave up the church "more because of its complicity with slavery than from a full understanding of the foolishness of its creed."[19] Like other reformers, her antislavery led her out of the church, but the Garrisonian program provided no alternative spiritual outlet. It asked abolitionists to take a religious stand against the churches, the clergy, and the Bible, but it offered nothing in place of these cherished institutions. The religious anarchism of Spiritualism provided a positive religious expression that harmonized with the extreme individualism of radical reform.

While the Garrisonian critique began with the churches' acceptance of slavery, it did not end there. The fullest elaboration of the radical critique of established religion found expression in the New England Non-Resistance Society, founded by abolitionists whose moral encounter with slavery led them to condemn any institution based on the use of force. They took their name from their extreme pacifist position, which condemned the use of force even in self-defense. Nonresistants followed the logic of these ideas to condemn the authority of any human being over any other human being because it usurped the authority of God by interfering with the autonomy of a moral agent. They believed that individuals should look within themselves and act according to the convictions placed there by the creator. Nonresistants found immoral attempts at coercion in virtually everything associated with Protestant religious practice: in the hierarchies of denominations, in the exercise of discipline over church members, in the power of the clergy, and in the use of the Bible as the test of truth. They coined the term *self-sovereignty* to describe the state of absolute individual autonomy they believed to be God's intention for every person. Consistent application of the principle of self-sovereignty that emerged from the struggle against slavery required a complete transformation of the existing power relations between men and women.[20]

Nonresistance and self-sovereignty, especially when their feminist implications were spelled out, proved to be controversial and divisive ideas even within the ranks of abolition. When the short-lived New England Non-Resistance Society declined in the late 1840s, the antiauthoritarianism of Spiritualism attracted the movement's leaders.[21] Henry C. Wright, the "voluntary, unhired agent" of the New England Non-Resistance Society who helped plan the Grimké sisters' famous speaking tour in 1838, became one of Spiritualism's earliest and most energetic converts. When Wright adopted views on individual moral autonomy extreme even among radical abolitionists, his political position found full support in Spiritualist religious practice. Assuming the role of self-appointed, unpaid agent for Spiritualism as well as nonresistance, he supported Spiritualism publicly as early as 1850 and received convincing communications at Leah Fox Fish's séance table the following year. He was ubiquitous on the Spiritualist platform, frequently using it to criticize gender roles, until his death twenty years later. According to the *American Booksellers Guide,* Wright was second in popularity only to Andrew Jackson Davis among Spiritualist readers.[22]

Spiritualism reached deep into the ranks of radical reform when it penetrated the Christian socialist community of Hopedale, near Milford, Massachusetts. The most long lived of the antebellum socialist communes, Hopedale was known as a stronghold of nonresistance. Henry C. Wright made his headquarters there, where reformers attempted to emulate the communal life of the first Christians. Spiritualists remembered Hopedale as "a sound theoretical and practical Woman's Rights Association." Resident Abby Price, an early woman's rights activist, was ever present to provide eloquent rebuffs if the community failed its principles.[23] Spirit manifestations appeared at Hopedale early in 1851, following reports of the rappings from Henry Wright and in Hopedale's newspaper, the *Practical Christian.* Hopedale's founder and leader, Adin Ballou, longtime president of the Non-Resistance Society and former Universalist minister, found the manifestations convincing and adopted the new faith. A few months later, Ballou's promising nineteen-year-old son, Adin Augustus, died suddenly of typhus. The community sank into grief, consoled only by the hope of spirit communication. Their hopes were realized when the spirit of Adin Augustus Ballou moved the hands of two young residents known as writing mediums. Séance circles multiplied at Hopedale.²⁴

The prominence of Spiritualism at Hopedale tied the new religion more closely to the network of radical reform. Ballou served as president at two of the earliest Spiritualist conventions, at which other Hopedale residents also served as officers.²⁵ Two Hopedale residents, Bryan J. Butts and Harriet N. Greene, produced a newspaper entitled the *Radical Spiritualist,* which advocated "Spiritualism, Socialism, Anti-Slavery, Non-Resistance, Woman's Rights, Anti-Oath-taking and Office-holding, Temperance, Vegetarianism, Anti-Tobacco (Tea, Coffee) and every other Reform which requires the practice of a higher life." The coeditors were married, but Harriet Greene retained her own name because she "had no intention of delivering up soul and body to the keeping of any man, however worthy that man might be." Hopedale's favorite medium, Fanny Davis,* advocated both woman's rights and nonresistance even while speaking in trance.²⁶ Other socialist communities, some exceeding Hopedale in their assault on gender roles, also showed a propensity for Spiritualism. Manifestations appeared in 1853 at the radical North American Phalanx in New Jersey, from which Abner French went on to become a leading Spiritualist. They also appeared at Josiah Warren's "Modern Times" community and at the Wisconsin Phalanx, where leader Warren Chase, a forceful midwestern advocate of Spiritualism, adhered to both nonresistance and woman's rights.²⁷

In addition to members of the New England Non-Resistance Society and residents of socialist colonies, disaffected members of the Society of Friends constituted an important element of those who adopted Spiritualism as a faith in harmony with radical politics, both feminist and abolitionist. "Quakerism furnishes a good substratum for steady and permanent progress in reform," observed Alfred and Anne Denton Cridge, who found that Spiritualist and reform lectures attracted four or five times as many people in the Quaker city of Richmond, Indiana, as in their larger hometown of Dayton, Ohio.²⁸ Quakers adopted Spiritualism with relative ease because of its similarities with their own practices and ideas. Many of the Quakers who adopted Spiritualism, like Amy and Isaac Post, had already withdrawn from the Society of Friends in search of greater freedom of conscience on political issues. Although the Hicksite Separation attempted to re-

---

* For a depiction of Fanny Davis's mediumship many years later, see plate 6.

solve the relative positions of Quaker discipline and spiritual freedom, the debate continued to divide local meetings throughout the antebellum period. Small groups withdrew in search of greater freedom of expression. Like the Waterloo Congregational Friends in upstate New York, they were often spurred by antislavery sentiment. By 1850, about sixteen groups had formed in New York, Ohio, Indiana, Iowa, and Michigan, variously called Congregational Friends, Progressive Friends, or Friends of Human Progress. The Pennsylvania Progressive Friends withdrew to form a separate meeting in 1852, which met annually until 1905. According to Albert J. Wahl, historian of the movement, "they all claimed to be throwing off the authority and formalism of superior church bodies to return to the liberty and simplicity of primitive Quakerism."[29]

The Friends of Human Progress filled a gap created when comeouters left the meetings that had previously nurtured their faith. Progressive Friends came together to replace the sense of community formerly provided by Quaker fellowship. But their phobia of infringements on individual religious freedom meant that their reason for association lacked religious content. Like other come-outers, disaffected Quakers found in Spiritualism a positive religious expression of their commitment to freedom of conscience.

Across the Midwest and New York State, Quaker splinter groups investigated Spiritualism and discussed it at yearly meetings and quarterly conventions. Quakers sought in Spiritualism an intensity of religious experience that their own tradition had trained them to expect but no longer satisfied. Sarah Thayer, a former Hicksite, "never enjoyed a Quaker meeting with such pure zest" as she did an 1857 Spiritualist convention in Rochester. She rejoiced that "there was much good speaking" and considered it a "blessing" that she was able to hear the Spiritualist lecturer Charlotte Beebe (also an ex-Quaker). The leader of the Spiritualist community in Troy, New York, wrote that his own and another ex-Quaker family preferred Spiritualism to Quakerism because the Quakers "feed their followers on husks and they are indeed very dry." These friends drew their expectations for religious experience from Quakerism but satisifed them with Spiritualism.[30]

The cultivated antiauthoritarianism of the Friends of Human Progress provided fertile soil for Spiritualist belief as well as an open platform for its promulgation. Spiritualism was the "ruling element" at the 1856 Michigan Yearly Meeting, where Henry C. Wright played a prominent role.[31] The following year the same group resolved that "modern Spiritualism had promoted human progress, physically and spiritually." Susan B. Anthony, clerk of the Waterloo Friends of Human Progress (they changed their name from Congregational Friends in 1854), reported, "The more advanced and rational class of teachings of the harmonial or Spiritual views and ideas were commended as worthy of acceptance." In Richmond, Indiana, a circle of mediums formed on the platform at the 1857 meeting of the Friends of Progress, and a clairvoyant answered questions and described diseases. Spiritualism occupied a day and a half of the four-day meeting of the Progressive Friends of Pennsylvania in 1859. Thomas Wentworth Higginson spoke in support, "presenting an outline of the argument which satisfied his own mind that the so-called spirit manifestations are genuine." Finally, the meeting adopted a testimony that condemned opposition to investigation and expressed gratitude for "the power [Spiritualism] is exerting to break up sectarianism, enlighten individual minds, and elevate the lives of many." Andrew Jackson Davis presented the Harmonial Philosophy to Progressive Friends in Pennsylvania, Michigan, and New York. By the late 1850s, most Quaker splinter groups accepted Spiritualism.[32]

Mediums emerged from the leading women in the Progressive Friends. Charlotte Beebe worked as a medium in Massachusetts in 1855 and soon became a popular Spiritualist lecturer. She wrote her lectures in trance and delivered them in a conscious state. In 1857, she served as secretary of the Michigan Yearly Meeting of the Friends of Human Progress and addressed the meeting on the "Unity and Diversity of all things in the Universe,—especially of religions, and of all movements for the amelioration of the condition of the Race."[33] Mary Thomas Clark, a minister of the Congregational Friends of Indiana, spoke at Spiritualist conventions throughout the 1860s. Mediums also participated in the Indiana yearly meeting and the Friends of Human Progress meeting in Cattaraugus County, New York.[34]

As with both woman's rights and abolition, the attraction between the Friends of Human Progress and the Spiritualists was mutual. Meetings were advertised in the *Banner of Light* and other Spiritualist papers as well as in abolition newspapers. Spiritualists and Progressive Quakers endorsed an identical reform platform. By the 1860s, the intermingling of the two movements was so extensive that it was difficult to tell them apart. A Spiritualist convention held at Rockford, Illinois, in 1857 proposed "sharing the name, as we do the goals, of the Progressive Friends of Pennsylvania." After this, Spiritualist groups calling themselves "Friends of Progress" dotted the Midwest, but it is difficult to determine how many originated with dissident Friends. In Decatur, Wisconsin, the 1862 meeting of the Friends of Progress featured the trance speakers Miss M. J. Woodbury. The medium Mrs. Kutz was the main speaker when the Friends of Progress met in Leighton, Michigan, in the same year.[35]

The Quaker historian Allen C. Thomas found no record of meetings of Progressive Friends after 1865 and attributed their demise to the abolition of slavery, which he believed put an end to their reason for being.[36] However, several groups did not disband, evolving instead into Spiritualist meetings. The most explicitly Spiritualist of all the Quaker groups, the North Collins (New York) Friends of Human Progress, continued meeting throughout the 1860s and 1870s. They arranged their fourteenth annual meeting so that "those wishing to attend both this and the annual spiritualist meeting in Buffalo can do so in one trip." In 1869, when mediums were under attack, they passed a resolution in their support. In 1883, they incorporated in order to rebuild their meeting place, Hemlock Hall, which was ultimately replaced by Lily Dale, a Spiritualist summer meeting ground that still flourishes today.[37]

In Indiana, the same radical Quakers who led the Friends of Human Progress during the late 1850s and early 1860s subsequently participated in a series of meetings whose names slowly transmuted from denoting Quaker roots to asserting Spiritualist identity. Progressive Friends Agnes Cook, Valentine Nicholson, Mary Thomas (Clark), and James Cooper attended the "Yearly Meeting of Progressive Friends and Spiritualists" in 1862, the "Quarterly Meeting of the Progressive Spiritualists" in 1863, and the "quarterly meeting of the Friends of Spiritual Progress" in 1864. By 1865, the words *Friends* and *Progress* were gone, but Cook and Cooper served as officers at the "Three Days Meeting of Spiritualists" at Greensboro, which apparently replaced the other groups. In 1866, Michigan hosted the "First State Convention of Spiritualists and Friends of Progress."[38]

In New England, disaffected Quakers of radical political views never formed separate meetings, but some became Spiritualists without group support. The Buffum family in Rhode Island and the Robinson family in Vermont, for example, each welcomed Spiritualism. Both families were active in the woman's rights movement and used their homes to house fugitive slaves traveling on the underground railroad to freedom in Canada. Rowland and Rachael Robinson had withdrawn from the Society of Friends because of its indifference to abolition several years before the Rochester rappings.[39] Ann King of the Robinson household described her alienation from her Quaker meeting. "I always stood in everything with the liberal part of society, until in search of still greater freedom I found myself outside of the pale of sectarianism altogether; and could not bind myself again, yet should like to attend meetings with the progressives were I near enough," she wrote to Amy Post. Ann King's commitment to individual spiritual autonomy took her "outside the pale" of all organizations, yet she still longed for the fellowship of association.[40]

Quaker splinter groups used their new freedom to explore both radical religion and radical politics. While emanating from the Society of Friends, they were motivated by the same anarchist leanings that prompted other reformers to blend religious and political concerns. Feminist editor Mrs. H. F. M. Brown found the 1857 meeting of the Geneva, Ohio, Friends of Progress to be the "most progressive, most radical meeting we have every attended."[41] Splinter groups discussed the host of issues on the reform agenda. In addition to the equality of the sexes, Spiritualism, and abolition, the 1855 Ohio Yearly Meeting of Progressive Friends, for example, considered "the abolition of capital punishment, the overthrow of intemperance, . . . writing and spelling reform, the use of tobacco, [and] the land monopoly."[42] They found their three-day conference inadequate for the full examination of their many concerns.

Other meetings addressed health reform, marriage reform, and the exploitation of labor by capital as well as condemning sectarianism, the authority of the Bible, and the setting aside of the Sabbath. The 1857 Michigan Yearly Meeting of Progressive Friends claimed that its resolutions embodied "the highest ideals of the friends on nearly all the subdivisions of Progress" during their four-day meeting. Speakers included Sojourner Truth, Martin, a fugitive slave, Charles Burleigh, and Parker Pillsbury on "freedom without distinction of color"; Friend Pease of Cincinnati on "Freedom of the Public Lands"; and Charles K. Whipple on "the principle of Freedom of Religious Opinions." On Sunday, Mary Fenn Davis spoke on "Freedom, without distinction of sex" to an audience so large that it "could be accommodated under no roof in the place."[43]

The Friends of Human Progress joined in the condemnation of the churches as agents of oppression in general and as oppressors of women and slaves in particular. The proceedings of the 1857 meeting of the Geneva, Ohio, Friends of Progress resolved "That making merchandise of men is a legitimate outgrowth of Bible Religion; therefore all attempts to eradicate slavery from our land, while we continue to nurture and nurse the parent stem, must of necessity prove a failure." A speaker then made "a very *strong* speech," in which she argued that "women were in an enslaved and crushed condition, and that the 'Old Theology' was responsible for it" because the Bible and the church "taught that man was far superior to woman." According to the Waterloo Friends, any attempt to base reform on the established churches was "in the first place . . . a piece of arrogance intensely narrow and Romish; and in the next . . . a wild hallucination, and an utter futility." These conventions made explicit the bonds between religious and political reform.[44]

The Spiritualist network, including Progressive Friends, assembled large audiences for promoters of radical causes. These meetings allowed for the dissemination of woman's rights ideas beyond the occasional convention devoted to them exclusively. Speakers more skilled in agitation than organization welcomed the opportunity to address receptive groups. A large convention in Providence, Rhode Island, found that "all departments of human improvement and practical reform come legitimately within the scope of a broad Spiritualism" because "the present selfish and antagonistic relations of society are unsuited to a higher spiritual condition." This justification was frequently offered for the introduction of social and political reforms at Spiritualist conventions. The Providence meeting then adopted resolutions addressing a variety of specific reforms because "spiritual growth and welfare depends on [one's] physical health and surroundings." Most Spiritualist meetings during this period adopted similar platforms. The Providence convention combined virtually every radical plank into a single resolution endorsing the "Equal enlightenment, enlargement, and consequent ultimate liberty of all human beings, and the abrogation of all oppression, civil inequality, domestic tyranny or mental or spiritual despotism, because freedom is the birthright of all, and the instinctive demand of every growing spirit." Abby Kelly Foster, the abolitionist and feminist agitator, "rejoiced to see that the tendency of Spiritualism was to elevate woman."[45]

The Rutland Free Convention of 1858, remembered by reformers as one of the great radical events of the period, illustrated both the central position of Spiritualists within the radical audience and their role in keeping woman's rights central to the radical agenda. "I am just returned from attending one of the largest and most important Reformatory Conventions ever held in this or any other country," wrote the non-Spiritualist woman's rights advocate and antislavery militant Parker Pillsbury on his return from Rutland. "The most numerous class in the audience," he reported, "was the Spiritualists." The Vermonters who called the Rutland Convention did not mention Spiritualism. Yet the 160 signatures to the call included the state's leading Spiritualists and its favorite trance speakers, Achsa Sprague, Sarah Horton, Newman Weeks, and Melvina Townsend. The call was published in the *Liberator* as well as in the Spiritualist press. The meeting was called to order by a prominent Spiritualist, John Landon, and presided over by another, Jason F. Walker, also known for his abolitionist activities. Radical religion and radical politics attracted the same people.[46]

The convention's first resolution expressed the common base of antiauthoritarianism and extreme individualism shared by Spiritualism and radicalism. It resolved that "the authority of each individual soul is absolute and final" and condemned "the individual, the Church or the State, that attempts to control the opinions or practices of any man or woman by an authority or power outside of his or her own soul." The convention affirmed the truth of Spiritualism in its third resolution, nestled between the second, which proclaimed the immorality of slavery, and the fourth, which opposed capital punishment. A strong woman's rights resolution asserted that because of her individual autonomy woman should be placed "politically, educationally, industrially and socially on perfect equality with man." In other resolutions, the convention opposed economic tyranny imposed by tariffs and by the private ownership of land and the tyranny of the churches expressed in the Sunday Sabbath and in the use of the Bible as a test of truth.[47] The resolution endorsing Spiritualism emphasized its social and political implications. The convention found that belief in "spirit-intercourse *is opposed to all despotism, impurity and sensualism,* and conduces to the only authority consistent with the human soul, or favorable to sound morality." Spiritualism was presented as an integral part of the program of radical reform. Like every other plank, its goal was emancipation.[48]

The strongest statements on woman's rights came from Spiritualist speakers. Henry Wright won passage of the resolution he proposed supporting woman's right to decide when and under what circumstances she will bear children. Mary Davis spoke in support of Wright's resolution and about other disabilities women suffered in marriage. The medium Mrs. Julia Branch gave one of the century's most fiery defenses of free love and then offered the following resolution:

> Resolved, That the slavery and degradation of woman proceed from the institution of marriage; that by the marriage contract, she looses control of her name, her person, her property, her labor, her affections, her children, and her freedom.

Branch's resolution preoccupied the rest of the convention and was responsible for its reputation as a meeting of "free lovers." Although it received more debate than any other resolution, Branch's proposal was voted down.

While a few reformers objected that the convention wasted its time on Spiritualism, and a few Spiritualists thought their cause should take precedence, most of the two or three thousand in attendance found Spiritualism and radical reform a harmonious combination and felt well satisfied with a program that interspersed trance mediums with speakers on woman's rights, abolition, and free trade. The assembly vetoed Parker Pillsbury's motion to subject Andrew Jackson Davis's lecture on Spiritualism to the same ten-minute limit applied to other speakers. Davis used his time to argue that "belief in Spiritualism is simply the door to . . . acceptance of the various reforms for which this Convention has assembled." Two mediums, fourteen-year-old Flora Temple and the popular Achsa Sprague, addressed similar themes in trance. Only the indomitable atheist, Ernestine Rose, argued that Spiritualism was incompatible with the convention's reform objectives. "Why employ our precious moments in discussing a subject which, at best, it is a matter of indifference whether we know it or not," asked Rose, following a speech on "The Natural Evidences of Immortality." "Suppose your child falls into a well, and while it is struggling in the water, a man comes to help you take him out," she pleaded with the audience; "will you stop to convince him of the immortality of the soul before you pull the child out?"[49]

Although Rose's appeal to pragmatism drew applause, it did not express the consensus of the meeting. The majority concurred with the convention's resolution that Spiritualism and radical reform expressed complementary aspects of the single goal of human progress.

Some of the most prominent Spiritualists present did not mention religion during the ten minutes allowed to each speaker, choosing rather to address some other reform issue. Mary Fenn Davis confined her remarks to woman's rights, while a Boston Spiritualist focused on free trade. At the opposite extreme from Rose and Pillsbury, two speakers advocated the priority of Spiritualism over other reforms. These Spiritualist extremists proved to be more in harmony with the spirit of the Free Convention than Rose and Pillsbury, who sought to abridge Spiritualists' free speech. When Pillsbury tried to interrupt a lengthy debate over Spiritualism's compatibility with the Bible, the audience shouted him down. A speaker from New Hampshire asserted the greater liberty of the Spiritualist position. He expressed his willingness to listen to other reforms, although he viewed Spiritualism as "the foundation on which all reforms must rest" because "no man or woman can be a true Spiritualist who does not believe in the abolition of all slavery, whether of the mind or the body." He was himself an active abolitionist and an admirer of Parker Pillsbury, but he was shocked to hear Pillsbury challenge the right of Spiritualists to address the convention. "While I honor the man, and honor the work in which he is engaged, I cannot honor that feeling," the protester continued, "which would make this any other than a perfectly free convention."[50]

Some dissatisfied Spiritualists, who felt that other matters received too much attention, proposed to divide the convention on Sunday and hold a meeting of Spiritualists in the town hall. Andrew Jackson Davis emerged as the hero of the event. He satisfied the reformers by declaring that he disapproved of conventions narrowly limited to Spiritualism and that he came to this one only "because it was announced as one where all the interests of benighted and oppressed humanity should find voice." But he also pleased the dissatisfied Spiritualists by consenting to address the entire assembly on Spiritualism when the crowd demanded it.[51]

Parker Pillsbury's unsuccessful attempt to divorce radical reform from Spiritualism at the Rutland Convention illustrates a basic tension between the two causes. Although ideologically compatible, they could conflict in practice. One might believe in both, but partisans urged that, as a matter of expediency, one or the other must be put first. Abolitionists both inside and outside Spiritualism objected to assertions that the promulgation of the new faith must take precedence over reform efforts. On the other hand, consistent advocates of individual sovereignty balked at the ideological impurity of reformers who participated in the political process or in organizations that compromised their autonomy.

The pervasive overlap of Spiritualism with radical reform exacerbated the tension between the new religion and the political concerns of its adherents. Spiritualism preoccupied Garrisonians during the early 1850s but elicited a wide range of responses. Many reformers believed in Spiritualism but rarely identified themselves with the movement, focusing their public activities first on abolition and second on woman's rights. This group included Garrison, Lucy Coleman, Elizabeth Buffum Chace, Betsey Mix Cowles, Thomas Wentworth Higginson, Francis Jackson, Ellis Gray Loring, William Cooper Neil, Oliver Johnson, and the Grimké sisters, for example.[52] Probably many of this group shared Thomas Wentworth Higginson's reservations about the Spiritualist platform. Although he claimed that "nothing but want of time" prevented him from accepting the many invitations he received to speak on Spiritualism, he took exception to the content of Spiritualist lectures. "Undoubtedly the *facts* of Spiritualism are the most important yet launched upon the history of humanity," Higginson concluded after eight years of investigation. "But the *philosophy* of Spiritualism is not yet born, and the more boldly one talks about it, the less attention he usually deserves." Yet, during the next two years. Higginson found time to deliver and publish two addresses endorsing Spiritualism. Radicals may not have cared for the metaphysical excesses of some Spiritualists, but their distaste was insufficient to dispel their faith in a religion that harmonized so well with their social and political ideas.[53]

Non-Spiritualist Parker Pillsbury criticized believers' lack of militancy on abolition, but he nevertheless remained alert to their significance as an audience for radical reform. In spite of reservations, Pillsbury and Ernestine Rose shared the platform with Spiritualists repeatedly during the 1850s and 1860s. They both participated in the sequel to the Rutland Convention called by Mary and Andrew Jackson Davis at Utica, New York. While Pillsbury thought the attendance of two or three thousand at the Rutland Convention placed it among the largest reform conventions ever held, Henry Wright was able to give a report of the Utica Convention to a crowd of five thousand at a Spiritualist picnic the next month. Spiritualist meetings were large and frequent and provided an important platform for radicals, who were invited to speak freely whether they were Spiritualists or not. In the 1870s, Pillsbury still frequented Spiritualist conventions and claimed that he had always been a friend of the movement. Spiritualists made up such an important audience for radical views that they could not be dismissed.[54]

Abolitionists complained that a few of their number had given up the cause of the slave in favor of the spirits. John Murray Spear and Stephen Pearl Andrews did become preoccupied with Spiritualism to the exclusion of antislavery. LaRoy Sunderland was accused by a *Liberator* correspondent of having "apostacized from anti-slavery" and "selling ghosts by the dollar." Garrison defended Sunderland's character, finding that his "course [regarding Spiritualism] has been disinterested, upright and honorable," but confirmed that Sunderland "has not been visible, as a public labourer, in the anti-slavery cause, for several years (having devoted himself with enthusiastic zeal to scientific investigations and experiments)."[55] The Salem, Massachusetts, abolitionist Eliza Kenney drew criticism from the local antislavery society when she gave up organizing antislavery fairs on becoming a medium. She explained to the black abolitionist Spiritualist William Cooper Nell that "she considered antislavery *included* in her spiritualism." Kenney, who signed the call to the second national Woman's Rights Convention, in 1850, was lost to the cause of both woman and the slave after she became a follower of the idiosyncratic medium John Murray Spear.[56]

Lucy Coleman, also a participant in the 1850 Woman's Rights Convention and a woman's rights canvasser, encountered similar defections among abolitionists in Michigan, where "Spiritualism was rioting like some outbreak of disease." Throughout the state, "circles were the order of the day, and of the night." When Coleman traveled with Amy Post from western New York to Michigan for the annual meeting of the Western Anti-Slavery Society, the meeting's attention focused on Spiritualism. "My friend Mrs. Post, as well as myself, was a Spiritualist, but we could see no propriety in turning an Abolition meeting into an 'experience meeting' for Spirits," Coleman complained. "Even the veteran Henry C. Wright seemed to have lost all zeal for the slave, saying that now the *spirits* would, without doubt, bring the emancipation of the race; just as the Christian would have said, 'God will in his own good time, take care of the slave.'" Coleman's partner on her speaking tour for the American Anti-Slavery Society, Andrew Foss, accepted Spiritualism the following year when he received a message from his deceased daughter. He continued his abolitionist labors but also spoke at Spiritualist conventions.[57]

The tensions created by Spiritualist sympathy for reform generated hostile editorial debates within the Spiritualist press. "With one or two exceptions, the Spiritual papers of the North are more or less tinctured with the peculiar fanaticism of that section," complained L. F. W. Andrews, editor of the single proslavery Spiritualist newspaper, about the antislavery bias of the Spiritualist press. Most Spiritualist newspapers were proud of their antislavery reputations, but the largest and most moderate, the *Banner of Light*, tried to remain neutral.[58] In 1858, the two-year-old *Banner*, anxious to appeal to a broad national readership, tried to separate its unorthodox religious views from the unpopular political positions that usually accompanied them. It published a series of sermons by Theodore Parker but omitted the sermon on slavery because it was too controversial.* "Our object in publishing the Banner is to aid in the dissemination of Spiritualism, and much as we admire Mr. Parker, and we do certainly love him and his theology, we cannot take grounds which will contract the sphere of our usefulness," explained the editors. "We have no desire to single out one evil more than another, particularly when the combat shall affect the legal rights of our brethren." [59]

The *Banner*'s defense of the legal rights of slaveholders may have sustained subscriptions in the South, but it drew criticism from the abolitionists who were a vocal part of the Spiritualist public. "I solemnly protest, as a *Spiritualist*," wrote antislavery activist E. R. Place, "against the Spiritualism that could utter, or that can endorse the sentiments quoted above." A second correspondent decried the inconsistency of the *Banner*'s position with the resolutions of Spiritualist conventions opposing despotic authority, whether spiritual or temporal.[60] Editor Luther Colby responded with a plea that politics be kept out of religion, a cry heard often from other churches but only rarely from Spiritualists. In 1860, Andrew Jackson Davis, frustrated by the *Banner*'s apolitical stance, started his own newspaper, the *Herald of Progress*. The opening editorial condemned "any serial or journal . . . which, because lacking something, either in purse or principle, attempts to maintain positions of amiable *neutrality* on questions

---

* Theodore Parker was not a Spiritualist, but he espoused a critique of established religion that made him very popular among Spiritualists.

of great moment to mankind." This thinly veiled attack on the *Banner of Light* inaugurated a policy of forthright support for abolition, which indeed drew criticism from Southern readers who received the *Herald* to fill out their subscriptions to the defunct *Spiritual Telegraph.* Two correspondents canceled their subscriptions because "even if it was acceptable to us on the subject of slavery, *which it is not . . .* it is against both the law and public sentiment here to distribute or circulate incendiary and Abolitionist publications." They warned Davis that he had ended his usefulness to Spiritualism in the South. Davis replied that this warning proved "that free speech and slavery cannot go hand in hand, and that the facts of Spiritualism alone do not convey its true message of freedom without Spiritualist philosophy and principles."[61]

While the *Banner of Light* drew fire for being weak on antislavery, Garrison's *Liberator* attracted equal criticism on the rare occasions when it appeared critical of Spiritualism. The *Liberator* received a flurry of angry correspondence when it printed a letter that objected to medium Cora Hatch's attribution of a trance lecture to the spirit of Theodore Parker and criticized her mediumship and Spiritualism in general. Indignant Spiritualist readers rushed to the defense of their faith. Progressive Friend Giles Stebbins dissented from both the *Liberator*'s criticism of Spiritualism and the *Banner*'s attempt at neutrality.[62] Although neutrality on abolition was good business, judging from the *Banner of Light*'s stability and wide circulation, activists supported a host of smaller, more daring papers. The *Agitator,* the *Social-Revolutionist,* the *Vanguard,* and the *Radical Spiritualist* announced their sympathy with Garrisonian tactics in their titles. "What has [Spiritualism] to do with anything if it ignores the discussion of the three great questions of the day?" asked *Agitator* editor Mrs. H. M. F. Brown in response to a coreligionist who claimed that Spiritualism had nothing to do with abolition, woman's rights, or free love.[63]

Woman's Right to Self-Ownership

Ironically, Spiritualism's conflicts with abolition increased its efficacy in nurturing woman's rights agitation. During the 1850s, feminists whose first loyalty was to antislavery shared a common agenda with those whose first loyalty was to Spiritualism. Both groups based their program on the condemnation of men's power over women implicit in the doctrine of individual sovereignty. As they labored to make that critique explicit during the 1850s, all advocated far-reaching changes in women's status, focusing on a woman's right to self-ownership in all legal and social relations, including her right to control her property, to control sexual access to her body, to have custody of the children she bore, and to wear healthful and unrestrictive clothing. But, during the 1860s, the course of woman's rights within Spiritualism and within abolition began to diverge. While Spiritualists continued to fight for the radical reform agenda of the 1850s throughout the nineteenth century, a narrower program concentrating on the right to vote arose among activists who identified themselves with abolition but not with Spiritualism.

Although woman's rights agitators held their own conventions during this period, the women who led these meetings remained a subgroup within the abolition movement. Although many of them had faith in spirit communication, with the exception of those who organized the very first conventions in New York State, most of these women did not publicly identify themselves with Spiritualism and did not contribute to its progress as a movement.[64] They perceived themselves as working for equal rights for all people, black and white, male and female, but their concerns remained secondary in the larger movement, which was aimed primarily at the abolition of slavery. The full implications of this subordinate status within the abolition movement did not become clear until after the Civil War, when women were asked to set aside their claims until full rights were secured by black men.

Because the woman's rights movement was essentially ancillary to the abolition movement, internal and external developments affecting antislavery determined its course. Abolitionists set the agenda, and woman's rights activists either followed their lead or reacted against it. During the Civil War period, non-Spiritualist woman's rights advocates abandoned agitation for women. When Abraham Lincoln signed the Emancipation Proclamation, Elizabeth Cady Stanton and Susan B. Anthony immediately formed the Women's Loyal League to lobby for a constitutional amendment outlawing slavery. Following the war, the struggle over the Fifteenth Amendment to the Constitution, granting voting rights to freed slaves, convinced the abolitionist woman's movement that voting was the most important right for women to obtain and transformed the woman's rights movement into the woman suffrage movement.[65]

Spiritualist agitators did not depend on the antislavery movement for resources or networks and did not determine their reform program in response to abolition. In contrast to their non-Spiritualist sisters, they did not abandon woman's rights agitation during the Civil War, nor did they assume a narrow focus on suffrage after the war. They continued to pursue the broad woman's rights agenda of the 1850s, pressing for dress reform, marriage reform, and economic rights, all of which disappeared from the postwar suffrage movement.

Although Spiritualists universally condemned slavery, their organizational independence from abolition allowed them to assert that woman's rights should be the preeminent reform. Like other abolitionists, Spiritualists believed that the oppression of African Americans and of women stemmed from the same cause. A typical speaker "protested against the ownership of souls" and called for "freedom for the black man and the white woman." While most abolitionists felt that the dire conditions of freed slaves required that their cause take priority even after the Civil War, some Spiritualists asserted that white women suffered the worst slavery. Both groups ignored the double disabilities of black women. As one male Spiritualist put it, he wanted "equality for all before the law, regardless of sex or color (and I place woman before the Negro)." Even a speech by "a colored gentleman," an unusual event at a Spiritualist convention, endorsed universal suffrage, enfranchising African Americans and women simultaneously.[66]

Spiritualists' assertion of woman's rights could have racist overtones. "The woman of refined sensibilities, more than the stolid slave of the south, needs emancipation," wrote the editor of the *Social Revolutionist*. Trance speaker Warren Chase, member of the Wisconsin legislature in the early 1850s, concluded from his efforts to extend suffrage to blacks and women that "the slavery of women was deeper and mose lasting that that of Negroes in the hearts and prejudices of the people." Mrs. H. M. F. Brown told a convention that white women endured the worst slavery, but the resolution she put before the assembly protested the slavery of both blacks and women.[67] While Frederick Douglass implored equal rights advocates to make the years after the war "the Negro's hour," a reporter at a Spiritualist convention observed that "the interest and appreciation" shown Juliet Stillman's woman's rights speech "told plainer than words that now is woman's hour, and she has but to work and wait for the harvest that is ripening, when she can gather for herself and her daughters the rich fruits of freedom, equality, and justice." Even the *Banner of Light*, which defended ideological neutrality regarding abolition, felt free to voice fighting words for woman's rights. "The Banner shall continue to wave until all humanity are completely disenthralled, and WOMAN, the brightest gem in the human galaxy, placed on an equality in every respect with her . . . companion MAN!" the paper editorialized in 1866.[68]

At Spiritualist conventions, abolitionists were joined in their advocacy of woman's rights by Spiritualist reformers who shared their ideological individualism but not their commitment to antislavery as preeminent among all reforms. Mediums often lectured on woman's rights while in trance, and Spiritualism's national speakers helped spread the new movement more widely than could the few abolitionist agitators unaided. In Illinois, for example, the suffrage movement's official history reported "but little agitation" for woman's rights before the Civil War. But an 1860 Spiritualist conference resolved that any abridgment of woman's rights constituted "an unwarrantable assumption of power unbecoming of an enlightened people," and Illinois Spiritualist conventions were a hotbed of woman's rights agitation throughout the early 1860s.[69]

The minutes of a large Spiritualist convention held in Chicago in 1865 reflect the prominence that Spiritualists gave to woman's rights while much of the women's movement was in abeyance during the Civil War years. The first speaker from the floor "spoke in favor of the elective franchise for woman, as the foundation of all future guarantees of rights." Next, Juliet Stillman of Whitewater, Wisconsin, rose to speak. According to the minutes, she "ridiculed the idea of women going to the polls in a fashionable dress; while she was in favor of women's voting, she claimed that the reform dress must be adopted as a precedent movement; that the great demand of the day was health." The minutes then quote Mrs. Dr. Stillman as saying, "If women compress the chest so as to press out the very life, would they not vote, if fashion said so, for a very bad measure?" At the conclusion of Dr. Stillman's lengthy indictment of tightlacing, petticoats, and insufficient exercise, the assistant secretary of the Society, Lois Waisbrooker, presented an opposing view. "I believe every individual should wear that dress they feel most at home in. I have all the opposition which my spirit feels strong enough to bear."[70] Waisbrooker, a free love advocate, had been subject to much derision for her Spiritualism and for her radical social views. She felt unable to withstand the additional ridicule heaped on those who wore the "American Dress," composed, like the bloomer costume, of a shortened skirt over loose trousers.[71] Spiritualists not only kept woman's rights before the public during the Civil War years but also provided for the expression of a diversity of opinions among agitators of the cause.

Spiritualism provided a platform and a network of support for a relentless group of woman's rights advocates who operated outside the mainstream of the women's movement. Inspired by the principle of individualism, nonmedium leaders Dr. Juliet Stillman Severance, Hannah (Mrs. H. F. M.) Brown, Annie Denton Cridge, Lois Waisbrooker, Louise T. Whittier, Mary Fenn Davis, and Dr. Alcinda Wilhelm focused almost exclusively on woman's rights during their frequent appearances before Spiritualist audiences. In pursuit of woman's emancipation, they edited newspapers, wrote books, led organizations, chaired conventions, and addressed large audiences regularly for several decades. In addition, a host of lecturers, trance and normal, male and female, included woman's rights prominently among the subjects they addressed.

In spite of their ardent dedication to the cause, Spiritualist woman's rights agitators are strangely absent from the chronicles of the nineteenth-century women's movement.[72] Mrs. H. F. M. Brown published the *Agitator,* a newspaper devoted to Spiritualism and woman's rights, in Cleveland in the late 1850s. One of the earliest and most radical of American women's newspapers, neither the *Agitator* nor its editor found their way into accounts of the nineteenth-century woman's movement.* Hannah Brown became an agent for Stanton and Anthony's new paper, the *Revolution,* probably selling it in her bookstore, and Alcinda Wilhelm wrote exuberant praise for the new publication, but its editors left the activities of their Spiritualist coworkers unnoticed. Lois Waisbrooker published more than a dozen novels and tracts advocating woman's rights and published and edited a series of feminist newspapers, but she drew no attention from non-Spiritualist reformers. Spiritualists distinguished themselves among woman's rights activists by their radicalism, their association with anarchism and socialism, and their critiques of marriage, which earned them all the label "free lover." Their pursuit of absolute self-determination for women prohibited them from focusing on a single issue such as tem-

---

* Hannah F. M. Brown's paper should not be confused with the *Agitator,* published by Mary Livermore in Chicago ten years later.

perance or suffrage, the movements that provided most of the strong female leaders of the nineteenth century.[73]

The absence of Spiritualist agitators from standard chronicles may result from the canonization of the history of the woman's rights movement in the three-volume *History of Woman Suffrage,* edited by Elizabeth Cady Stanton, Susan B. Anthony, and Matilda Joslyn Gage.[74] It is unclear whether the editors intentionally excluded Spiritualists from their account or whether they were simply unfamiliar with them. The editors depended for much of their text on local leaders, who, with the exception of Catherine Stebbins of Michigan, may have preferred to exclude Spiritualist coworkers because of their heterodoxy. It is also possible that Spiritualist agitators and other reformers worked on parallel tracks, that they were each unaware of the other's activities yet nonetheless in pursuit of similar goals.

In either case, Spiritualists' exclusion from the historical record did not reflect their impact at the time. Spiritualism provided an important audience for radical reform and a source of affirmation for embattled radical leaders. In their zeal for "self-ownership," Spiritualists advocated a broad woman's rights program, combating every disability imposed by church, state, or social convention. They spread the message of woman's emancipation to large audiences, lecturing tirelessly across the country. The annals of Spiritualism contain the history of another women's rights movement in addition to the one that became the woman suffrage movement.

4

The Meaning of Mediumship

Spiritualism's greatest contribution to the crusade for woman's rights probably lay in the new role of spirit medium. While reformers talked about women's autonomy, mediumship cast women in a central public role in the new religion. Far from requiring guidance from men, mediums led both men and women on the path to truth. The example of mediums, whose religious role encouraged them to take charge of their own lives, reinforced the application of the principle of individual sovereignty to women. In mediumship, women's religious leadership became normative for the first time in American history. Yet mediums did not model a simple abrogation of accepted feminine norms. Instead, mediumship gave women a public leadership role that allowed them to remain compliant with the complex of values of the period that have come to be known as the cult of true womanhood.

The cult of true womanhood asserted that woman's nature was characterized by purity, piety, passivity, and domesticity.[1] While this ideology held that women were especially suited to religion and that religion was especially important to women, it nevertheless required them to defer to men in all religious matters. Every Sunday women saw more of their sisters than their brothers in the churches they attended, yet they, the majority of members, were excluded from all decisions regarding church operations. The religious instruction of the young was entrusted to them in Sunday schools, but they were forbidden to speak out loud during regular services. Told to serve God through their influence in the home, they saw men rule an ungodly and immoral society outside the home. The increased leadership of women during the Second Great Awakening in the early decades of the nineteenth century deepened the existing contradictions. Women's spiritual prowess was affirmed, but they were still denied ordination or positions of authority in church organizations.

Spiritualism embraced the notion that women were pious by nature. But, instead of concluding that the qualities that suited women to religion unsuited them to public roles, Spiritualism made the delicate constitution and nervous excitability commonly attributed to femininity a virtue and lauded it as a qualification for religious leadership. If women had special spiritual sensitivities, then it followed that they could sense spirits, which is precisely what mediums did. Nineteenth-century stereotypes of femininity were used to bolster the case for female mediumship. "Women in the nineteenth century are physically sick, weak and declining," wrote one Spiritualist leader. But if "the functions depending on force and muscle are weak . . . the *nerves* are intensely sensitive. . . . Hence sickness, rest, passivity, susceptibility, impressionability, mediumship, communication, revelation!"[2] The very qualities that rendered women incompetent when judged against norms for masculine behavior rendered them capable of mediumship. Mediumship allowed women to discard limitations on women's role without questioning accepted ideas about woman's nature.[3]

Women did not consciously choose to be mediums. Rather, they and their coreligionists believed that the spirits chose them and that they passively allowed spirits to communicate through them. Even the process of becoming a medium was referred to in the passive form: one was said to be "being developed as a medium," the active role being attributed to spirits. Thus, the advent of mediumship did not require a decision to rebel against a domestic role. With the encouragement of spirits, women did things that they themselves believed women could not do. A medium in Philadelphia greeted her new calling with proper feminine hesitation. "If it will make me better, purer, or more useful, I will welcome it. . . . [But] I fear I am an unworthy servant, and unfitted for so high a calling," she wrote to a more experienced medium.[4] Spirit presence helped women overcome internal doubts as well as external sanctions. The medium Amanda Britt Spence, addressing a Spiritualist convention, "rejoiced that Spiritualism had called out woman" from the "duties and trials in which none but angels could sympathize." She reported that women shrank from the new burdens occasioned by mediumship. Spence summed up the typical response to mediumship in the words,

"If it be possible, let this cup pass from me, nevertheless, not my will, but thine Oh God, be done!" But, with whatever hesitation women might greet their new role, she concluded, "There is no power to resist the overwhelming influences of the spirit world."[5]

Once spirits were in evidence, they could provide women with encouragement and motivation to assume leadership against public criticism. Emma Hardinge, a leading trance lecturer (see plate 8), described how spirits overcame her own ideas about activities proper for women when she embarked on the lecture circuit:

> that I, a woman, and moreover, "*a lady by birth*," and *English*, above all,
> that I would go out, like "strong minded women," and hector the
> world, on public platforms! oh, shocking! I vowed rebellion—to give
> up Spirits, Spiritualism, and America; to return to England and live "a
> feminine existence" once again. With these magnanimous resolves
> upon me *one week, the next* saw me on a public platform, fairly before
> the world as a trance speaker.[6]

With spirit guidance, women spoke in public, wrote books, and went on lecture tours. Mary Dana Shindler, for example, visited a test medium in New York and asked the spirits, "Do you wish me to write the work I am thinking of?" "Yes—go on; it will sell well," was the encouraging reply. She took the spirit's advice and wrote *A Southerner Among the Spirits*. As mediums, women became sources of religious truth and, as such, assumed the authority of religious leaders. Spirits, it seemed, encouraged women to do things that other forces militated against.[7]

Mediumship circumvented the structural barriers that excluded women from religious leadership. By communicating directly with spirits, mediums bypassed the need for education, ordination, or organizational recognition, which secured the monopoly of male religious leaders. While men might bar women from church councils or from theological education, human authority could not supersede that given to mediums by the spirits who spoke through them. Spirit communcation carried its own authority. If one accepted the message, one had little choice but to accept the medium.

Trance Speakers

Spiritualism departed from accepted social norms by encouraging women to speak in public, but the manner in which they spoke had a cultural significance of its own. Equal numbers of men and women spoke from the Spiritualist platform, both on the lecture circuit and at conventions, picnics, and grove meetings. But speakers observed a rigorous sexual division of labor. Men called meetings to order, forcefully presiding over gatherings that could number in the thousands. They addressed audiences in a "normal" state, expressing their own views on Spiritualist subjects. In contrast, the women at the podium were unconscious. Trance mediums were understood to be passive vehicles, whose physical faculties were used by spirits to express the sentiments of these unseen intelligences. Mediums presented not their own views but those of the spirits who spoke through them. The juxtaposition of men officiating at large assemblies with unconscious women voicing extemporaneous visions of heaven in verse both satisfied existing sexual stereotypes and pushed them a step further. The essential passivity of women was asserted in a public arena, displayed before thousands of witnesses.[8]

Sparse qualifications in a trance speaker reinforced the claim that the lecture originated not with the speaker but with spirits. While men qualified for the public platform by wisdom, education, and experience, trance speakers qualified by innocence, ignorance, and youth.[9] The fact that a woman stood up in public and gave a lecture in itself evidenced spirit agency since few believed a woman could do such a thing unaided. A correspondent to the *Banner of Light* argued that the doctrines of Spiritualism must be true because the great "lady trance speakers," Rosa Amedy, Cora Hatch, Emma Hardinge, Emily Beebe, Emma Jay Bullene, and Anna Henderson, "have never been able, nor even attempted, as far as we know, to give such lectures in the normal state." A New York City lecture by Emma Jay (later Bullene) given "in the abnormal state" offered one clear example. "That a young lady not over 18 years of age should speak for an hour and a quarter, in such an eloquent manner, with such logical and philosophical clearness," proved to one observer the presence of "a power *not* natural to the education or mentality of the speaker."[10]

Women, in contrast to men, could be public teachers of religion without education because they were pious by nature. According to the well-respected trance speaker Lizzie Doten, "Woman does not need to cultivate her intellect in order to perceive spiritual truths. Let her live, only, true to her Divine nature and her spiritual perceptions." "Make a home in your heart for God," Doten told the women in her audience, "and His angels shall come, and all that is needed for spiritual perception and development comes in with that inspiration." She conceded that women received inadequate education, but she did not view lack of training as a block to religious leadership. "Woman . . . has been forced into a narrow circle of life, a dull routine of duties; and that is declared to be woman's sphere," Doten complained. "But God does not wait for this [education]. He has made woman a religious teacher." Doten predicted correctly that, "as the generations pass, there shall be women, as well as men, with these exceptional educations." But the training that prepared men to become religious leaders could never replace "the unconscious inspiration" that gave women direct access to religious knowledge. Ultimately, Doten believed, all people would recognize the superiority of women's natural piety in trance to male theological education. "She is the divine Shekinah, the Holy of Holies, in her man shall recognize the image of his God, and kneel and adore." Although the views expressed here are consistent with those Doten expressed while conscious, they were delivered in trance.[11]

Youth also proved that the trance medium did not compose her own speech. Cora Hatch, who, under a variety of married names became one of the most celebrated trance speakers of the nineteenth century, made her first appearance at the age of eleven, in 1851, in Lake Mills, Wisconsin, and spoke throughout the state the following year.* At fourteen, she was employed as a regular speaker by a Spiritualist society in Buffalo, New York, a position she held for two years. She then moved to New York City, which became her base for tours to the major cities of the East and Midwest by the age of seventeen.[12] Fourteen-year-old Flora Temple, of Bennington, Vermont, traveled to the Rutland Free Convention to speak in trance, "though apparently in a normal state," before several hundred people in 1858. Susie Cluer, aged thirteen, was popular for her poetic presentations. For audiences that had never witnessed a woman speaking in public, the spectacle of a teenage girl at the podium must have appeared impressive, if not miraculous. Martha Hulett, a farmer's daughter from Illinois, began her career at sixteen and was lecturing as far away as Tennessee by eighteen. A biographical account in 1860 observed that

---

* Born Cora Linn Victoria Scott, this popular medium entered the public record under her birth name and under those of four succesive husbands: Hatch, Daniels, Tappan, and Richmond. Her contemporaries always referred to her by the name of her current husband. In order not to confuse the reader, I generally refer to her as Cora Hatch because it was under that name that she initially created a public sensation.

she "is now twenty but looks sixteen." Similarly, Mrs. Nellie Wiltsie, a twenty-three-year-old trance speaker, was described as a "small, girl-like woman." [13] A youthful appearance, in addition to actual youth, added to a medium's credibility and to the impression she made on her audience. Observers testified over and over to the visual impact of a woman, especially a young and beautiful woman, at the podium. Cora Hatch's golden curls became among the best-documented facts of modern Spiritualism.*

Youth was also considered to reduce the motivation for fraud. "Skeptics have more faith in that which is given through children than older mediums, . . . [because] they consider there is less ability, as well as less desire, to practice trickery and deception in the child than in the adult," wrote a *Banner of Light* correspondent about Laura Ellis, who became a medium at eleven. Youth associated the medium with the innocence of childhood, just as domestic ideology contrasted women and children with the worldliness of men. The eighteen-year-old Fanny Burbank was described as "the personification of purity." "She is very childlike in her manners," observed a member of the audience, "which simplicity and innocence makes her very attractive." [14] Not all trance speakers were so young. Mediums began careers at all ages, and those who began as children often continued for decades. Many trance speakers were young matrons in their twenties, but even the thirty-year-old Achsa Sprague attracted considerable attention for her attractive appearance at the podium.

In general, Spiritualists considered the trance to be an elevated state, providing access to spirits and therefore to knowledge of the world beyond inaccessible to conscious human beings. But some questioned the accuracy of revelations received in trance. Because the ability to give a trance lecture depended on one's susceptibility to outside influences, the moral accountability of trance speakers was sometimes questioned. If trance speakers were merely passive vehicles, could they be held responsible for their behavior while in trance or for the content of their messages? The unaccountability of mediums was sometimes urged as an excuse for questionable behavior or even for fraud. When a young medium was discovered faking manifesta-

---

* An engraving, depicting Cora Hatch with flowing ringlets, bare shoulders, and a large cross hanging from a chain around her neck (see plate 9) was widely reproduced, including in the biography by Harrison D. Barrett, *Life Work of Mrs. Cora L. V. Richmond* (Chicago: Hack & Anderson, 1895), and in Emma Hardinge, *Modern American Spiritualism* (1869; reprint, New York: University Books, 1970).

tions while she was supposed to be inside a bag nailed to the floor, a leading Spiritualist explained that "it is possible for a medium, when in a trance state, to become an unconscious and irresponsible instrument in the hands of a controlling spirit." Presumably, a fraudulent spirit from the lower spheres controlled this medium.[15]

Because of the unaccountability of mediums controlled by unseen intelligences, an editorial in the *Spiritual Age* asserted that the trance was not the optimum condition for spirit communication. It viewed the trance as higher than the normal state but lower than "conscious state inspiration." The editor accepted that, "In the unconscious trance, a person may be susceptible to spirit influence, or controlled by a spirit power, and thus be used to furnish evidence of spirit existence and presence, and to give utterance to spiritual truths," but concluded that, "in a more advanced and spiritualized condition, one can do all this and more, and yet be fully awake and conscious."[16]

By questioning the trance state, critics questioned the values and assumptions that fostered female leadership. The assertion that the passivity that gave women access to spirits made them morally unaccountable undercut women's claim to spiritual authority. Two correspondents dissented from the editor's disparaging opinion of trance speaking. Their views more accurately reflect the role of the trance speaker in the spread and practice of Spiritualism. One reminded the editor that "Your patrons in this state have, as a general thing, been converts of trance speaking, and you, I think, pay those laborers a poor compliment." Trance speakers were the missionaries of Spiritualism, and their far-reaching itinerancy aided the rapid spread of the movement. Their lectures, often free to the public, might attract hundreds of people, while the séances of test mediums could accommodate only as many people as could fit around a table. "Trance speaking in an unconscious state is one of the most exalted, the most reliable, the most convincing as to its origins of any manifestation connected with the human organism," wrote the second correspondent.[17] Finally, the Spiritualist public had faith in their mediums and was unconcerned by critics' doubts about the trance state. Although more serious challenges to their leadership would emerge following the Civil War, trance speakers enjoyed the support of the mass of believers during the 1850s.

While descriptions suggest that some mediums were able to enter a trance spontaneously, trance speakers never developed consistent modes of trance behavior. According to observers, it was Cora Hatch's practice to enter the hall already in trance. During the preliminaries to her lecture, she "sat gazing upwards, with her eyes intently fixed." At the close of her lecture, "she looked and stared about her like one just awakened."[18] But other mediums who claimed to be in trance provided little evidence of an abnormal state. Because audiences were accustomed to viewing the trance as proof of spirit inspiration, a reporter describing the appearance of a lecturer in Boston felt compelled to explain that, although "Mrs. Warner is a conscious trance speaker," she "is entirely subject to the control of spirit influence while delivering her discourses." Flora Temple was described as being in trance, although she appeared to be in a normal state. Martha Hulett was described as "a conscious trance speaker" because she was able to hear what she said while she was speaking. Because the trance was viewed as enabling women to speak who were otherwise unqualified to do so, the claim of entrancement became a convention used to support women's right and ability to ascend the public platform.[19]

Trance speakers emphasized what they said rather than what they did. While test mediums might curse and swagger when controlled by the spirits of drunkards or sailors, trance speakers viewed the content of their speeches as well as the act of speaking, as inspired. High-toned trance speakers like Lizzie Doten and Achsa Sprague did not give private sittings and did not receive messages from individually identifiable spirits. Nor did they produce the common "physical manifestations" of raps or table tipping. According to Lizzie Doten, "the external phenomena of Modern Spiritualism . . . compared to the great principles underlying them, are but mere froth and foam on the Ocean of Truth." Unlike the test medium, the trance speaker might hold herself above "the external phenomena" of Spiritualism and dwell on "the great principles underlying them." Doten's description of the trance itself portrays the medium as someone who has access to the wisdom of departed spirits rather than as someone who passively communicates their views:

> The avenues of external sense, if not closed, were at least disused, in order that the spiritual perception might be quickened to the required degree, and also that the world of causes, of which the earth and its experiences are but the passing effects, might be disclosed to my vision. Certain it is that a physical change took place, effecting both my breathing and my circulation.

Some trance lectures did not even mention spiritual phenomena but were composed of religious sentiments that could have been voiced by any popularizer of a vague transcendentalism. Antebellum Americans flocked to hear trance speakers discourse on spiritual subjects just as they flocked to be enlightened by the popular lectures of Ralph Waldo Emerson.[20]

The Entrancement of the Audience

Congregationalist Antoinette Brown Blackwell made a sensation as a speaker in 1853 when she became the first woman to be ordained as a minister. She wrote to Lucy Stone that she "could get any price for lectures" after Horace Greeley reported in the *New York Tribune* that she had officiated at the first marriage to be performed by a woman. Just six years later, when she attempted to return to the lecture field following the birth of her first child, she wrote to Stone that "I have been coolly told over and over again that the time was when I stood first as a preacher but now a host of women mostly spiritualists have 'gone ahead' of me."[21] The "host of women" who superseded her on the lecture circuit between 1853 and 1859 were predominantly trance speakers. Trance speakers made their appearance in the early 1850s and served as the primary public representatives of Spiritualism during that decade.

The right of women to speak in public was hotly contested during the antebellum period. Following the historic antislavery lectures of the Grimké sisters in 1837, a few fearless reform women ventured before the public during the 1840s, most notably Ernestine Rose, Abby Kelly Foster, Lucretia Mott, and, at the end of the decade, Lucy Stone. Novelist Elizabeth Oakes Smith became a popular literary lyceum lecturer. In addition, a few women, such as the holiness preacher Phoebe Palmer and the black Methodist Jarena Lee, appeared in public as Christian evangelists.* However, the right of women to address "promiscuous assemblies," composed of both men and women, was still generally denied. Clerical opponents cited Paul's

---

* Many of the pioneer women platform speakers relied on spiritual guidance similar to that depended on by mediums. This group included Quakers who were prompted by the "inner light" and visionaries who obeyed an "inner voice." Jarena Lee, e.g., heard a voice say, "Preach the Gospel; I will put words in your mouth." Black evangelist Zilpah Elaw made her first public address in 1817 following a trance. Jarena Lee, *Religious Experiences and Journals of Mrs. Jarena Lee, Giving Account of Her Call to Preach the Gospel* (Philadelphia: Jarena Lee, 1849), 14. William Andrews, ed., *Sisters of the Spirit: Three Black Women's Autobiographies of the Nineteenth Century* (Bloomington: University of Indiana Press, 1987), 7.

injunction to the Corinthians that women should keep silent in church to argue both against women preaching and against women speaking in public in general. Because speaking in public contradicted biblical mandate, it was viewed as a subversion of God's intended ordering of the relations of men and women on earth. The General Association of Congregational Ministers of Massachusetts responded to the 1837 public appearance of the Grimké sisters with a pastoral letter describing the "dangers which at present seem to threaten the female character with widespread and permanent injury." The letter predicted that women speaking in public would lead to "degeneracy and ruin" and censured "any of that sex who so far forget themselves as to itinerate in the character of public lecturers."[22] Both advocates and opponents of women speaking in public viewed it as a fundamental issue in the debate over women's role. Conservative male religious leaders continued to debate the propriety of women speaking in mixed assemblies throughout the century.[23]

Even reform circles opposed women's public speaking. The refusal of antislavery and temperance conventions to allow women to speak provided an important catalyst to the founding of the woman's rights movement. Although radical Garrisonians supported women as speakers, the abolition movement split over the issue of women's participation, and some of the most heated feeling focused on women's right to speak in public. Oberlin College, where reform principles required that Lucy Stone be admitted as a student, refused to let her speak at commencement in 1847. Although unanimously elected by her fellow students to give a graduation address, she refused to write one rather than have it read for her by a male professor, as school policy dictated. The practice of having a man read was followed by the more proper Catherine Beecher, whose brother read her lectures, and by Emma Willard and Dorothea Dix.[24] Antoinette Brown's appearance on the platform of the World's Temperance Convention in 1853 brought the meeting to a halt. Delegates who objected to women speaking in public kept the hall in chaos for an hour and a half. In spite of derision, abuse, and severe clerical opposition, women established a presence on the American platform during the 1850s.[25]

Trance mediums were an important element in the emergence of women as public speakers during the 1850s. Although a few abolitionist women preceded them, trance speakers outnumbered reform women lecturers by the end of the 1850s. When scholar Lillian O'Connor scoured the country's archives for texts of early speeches given by women, she found speeches by only twenty-one women, all of them reformers. O'Connor included only speakers for whom she could find extant texts of speeches in contemporary publications or in the handwriting of the speaker. This may have excluded some speakers; however, her list includes some reform women who rarely spoke, such as Martha Coffin Wright and Elizabeth Cady Stanton, who did not appear in public frequently until the 1860s.[26] In a more recent study, Blanche Hersh identified fifty-one women as antebellum abolitionist feminists, only half of whom spoke in public with any regularity before the Civil War, and most of these were included in O'Connor's list of twenty-one. When the *Banner of Light* started printing lists of lecturers in 1860, it began with twenty-three women in January and listed fifty-two women lecturers by the end of the year. *The Spiritual Register for 1859* listed the names of over one hundred women trance speakers in eleven states. This did not include all the dozens of women whose careers could be followed in the Spiritualist press.[27]

Women began to deliver lectures in trance shortly after the advent of spirit communication. Mrs. G. B. Bushnell spoke in the "abnormal state" in Ohio, New York, and Pennsylvania in 1850 and was still on the lecture circuit in 1852. In Chicago, a medium named Mrs. Herrick became "an excellent but exceedingly radical lecturer" in the early 1850s. Mrs. Amanda Britt (Spence) gave trance lectures every Sunday in St. Louis, beginning in 1852. By the mid-1850s, trance lectures could be heard weekly at the regular meetings of Spiritualist societies in a number of cities. In addition, several spiritualist women, such as Cora Scott (later Hatch) in Buffalo, Achsa Sprague in South Reading, Vermont, and Charlotte M. Beebe (later Wilbour) in Milwaukee, had permanent positions as regular lecturers. Antoinette Brown Blackwell tried to secure such an arrangement where she could preach weekly reform sermons for free in New York City in 1859, but no backer would underwrite the cost of the hall. In contrast, a relatively obscure medium, Ella E. Gibson, filled a concert hall in Augusta, Maine, for six consecutive evenings. Manchester, New Hampshire, boasted seven trance speakers in 1858, five of them women. A correspondent complained to the *Banner of Light* that two of Manchester's best speakers, Emeline Houston and Susan Johnson, had gone to Massachusetts to lecture.[28]

Trance speakers received considerable attention in the press. Newspapers that found the lectures of reform women too improper to notice nonetheless covered appearances by trance speakers. Horace Greeley's *New York Tribune* alone among New York papers noticed woman's rights and abolition lectures. But, by 1858, Greeley found this practice too controversial to continue. Not even the more conservative of the antislavery papers, the *National Era,* would print an abolitionist lecture if it was delivered by a woman. Yet trance speakers received extensive press notice, both positive and negative. "She spake as woman never spake before," said the *Daily Sun* (Columbus, Ga.) of Emma Hardinge's trance lecture in that city.[29]

Spiritualists embraced the platform as an alternative to the pulpit. Trance speaker and feminist Charlotte Beebe Wilbour called the platform "the people's arena, the democratic pulpit," observing that, "A Stand-point so high and inaccessible as the Pulpit, may seem fit for the solitary despot whose empire it has sometimes served. . . . Here [on the platform] Virtue is the only strength—Reason the only test— and Spiritual Power the only exaltation."[30] Not only was the pulpit "dictatorial and authoritative," but it was also, of course, closed to women. The platform, in contrast, provided an outlet for anyone who could attract an audience, with or without church sanction. As trance speakers, women who could not speak in church took advantage of a secular format to deliver a religious message. Lizzie Doten thought the platform superior to the pulpit not only because it admitted women but also because it was a better vehicle for spiritual enlightenment. In a trance lecture on the biblical text "It is a shame for women to speak in the church," Doten exclaimed, "It is indeed a shame for woman to speak in the *Church;* and woman ought to be ashamed . . . of the church. Let woman come out from the church; and, when she comes out, the minister and all the congregation will go out with her."[31]

The sight of a lone woman confidently expounding spiritual truths enchanted American listeners. "No report can give any fair idea of the 'spirit presence' . . . of the self-possessed dignity, clearness, promptness," wrote one observer, who nevertheless remained skeptical about spirit communication.[32] Speaking mediums entranced audiences in major cities and small towns throughout the North. For listeners, the trance lecture might be both the first exposure to Spiritualism and the first exposure to a woman speaking in public; the new religion was therefore joined in the mind of the audience with the creation of a public role for women. The visibility of trance speakers as pioneer women orators was sufficient to convince the Methodist missionary W. M. Leftwich that "The first female lecturers and public speakers were spiritualists." Leftwich made this remark with disapproval in his account of his itinerancy in Missouri in the mid-1850s, confirming the chronology of the advent of trance speakers suggested by Antoinette Brown Blackwell.[33]

The impact of trance speakers reached far beyond the community of believers. They reached a broad audience, composed of the curious and the skeptical as well as the faithful. The popular writer Nathaniel Parker Willis attended a lecture by the noted medium Cora Hatch one evening when the opera he had planned to attend was canceled. He described her with admiration in the *Home Journal* as "a delicate-featured blond, of seventeen or eighteen, flaxen ringlets falling over her shoulders, movements deliberate and self-possessed, voice calm and deep, and eyes and fingers no way nervous." Willis was impressed by her beauty and her platform presence, but he was also impressed by the departure from the female role she made by speaking in public. "And very curious it was," he wrote, "to see a long haired young woman standing alone in the pulpit, her face turned upwards, her delicate bare arms raised in a clergyman's attitude of devotion, and a church full of people listening attentively while she prayed!" Willis then recalled the biblical injunction against women preaching. He knew his audience well and knew the significance that they would find in Hatch's appearance. He, however, felt that the extraordinary qualities of the speaker justified Hatch's abrogation of the biblical injunction. He explained his conclusion with an appeal to the spiritual superiority of nineteenth-century women:

> But my instinctive feeling, I must own, made no objection to the propriety of the performance. The tone and manner were of absolute sincerity of devoutness which compelled respect; and before she closed, I was prepared to believe her an exception—either that a male spirit was speaking through her lips, or that the relative position of the sexes is not the same as in the days of St. Paul. How was it with the Corinthians? Women are certainly better than we in these latter days, and as standing far nearer God, may properly speak for us, even in holy places—or so it seemed to me while listening to Mrs. Hatch.

Willis did not report the content of Hatch's lecture, explaining that it was available in the daily papers. He did dwell on her mode of presentation and most especially on her use of language. Her precise use of words and her "confident fluency" convinced Willis that "whether she speaks her own thoughts or those of other spirits—it is as nearly supernatural eloquence as the most hesitating faith could reasonably require." Willis wrote not as a Spiritualist but rather as an outsider who regarded the movement with suspicion. He reminded his readers that his past experience with spiritualism had been unsatisfactory and that "The 'Fox Sisters' and others have tried their spells on me in vain." He may not have been convinced of the reality of spirit communication by Cora Hatch's trance lecture, but he was convinced of the ability of a womanly woman to speak in public and particularly of the appropriateness of her speaking on spiritual subjects.[34]

Willis was not the only New Yorker enchanted by Cora Hatch. Although the *New York Times* thought her spirits "talked arrant transcendentalism of the diluted kind," the paper consistently reported her lectures, indicating that they did interest the public, if not the editor. She succeeded in impressing even the notorious Tammany ruffian Captain Rynders, who was on the committee from the audience that selected the topic for one of Hatch's first lectures in New York. The committee, as usual, was asked afterward whether they were satisfied with Hatch's answers to the questions they had proposed. Rynders replied that he had come believing Hatch to be a "humbug" but now had "the highest possible regard for the lady's talent." He declared that "her prayer . . . was beautiful, her theory profound, and her language eloquent." Like Willis, Rynders was not completely convinced by what Hatch said, but he was very impressed with the way she said it. Also like Willis, he changed his attitude about the appropriateness of women speaking on spiritual subjects. He declared that he had "never heard so beautiful and touching an exhortation from any pulpit."[35]

W. M. Leftwich, the Methodist missionary, agreed with Willis in associating Spiritualism's introduction of women onto the public platform with the creation of a new religous role for women. After observing that the first female lecturers in Missouri were Spiritualists, he went on to note in the same sentence that, "in the spiritualists' church, so-called, women are the high-priests; and the scriptural teachings in regard to the relation of men and women and their duties in the church are reversed." He and Lizzie Doten agreed that women should not speak in church, but for very different reasons.[36]

Reform women also responded enthusiastically to trance speakers. The suffragist Abigail Scott Duniway wrote in her newspaper, the *New Northwest,* that the trance speaker Belle Chamberlain excelled both Henry Ward Beecher and Elizabeth Cady Stanton in eloquence and logic. Duniway was sympathetic to Spiritualists because they always invited her to speak on woman suffrage at their conventions, but she was not an adherent of the movement and ridiculed mediums whose spirits directed them on questionable paths. Nevertheless, she was thoroughly impressed by trance speakers who toured the Pacific Northwest. Of medium Addie Ballou she wrote, "While we do not endorse all, or half her doctrines, we've never yet heard two men who could equal her in arguments or eloquence."[37] A hostile writer for the *New York Tribune* ridiculed the other speakers at an 1858 Spiritualist convention but found medium Amanda Britt (Spence) "an orator of rare power and accomplishment," whose speech "was far more eloquent and impressive than any other feminine address to which I ever listened." He reported that "several ladies came with streaming eyes to thank the orator and yield assent to sentiments and opinions advanced."[38]

When Paulina Wright Davis recalled the first twenty years of the campaign for woman's rights at the 1871 national convention, the only person she included in her account who had not been publicly identified with the woman's rights movement was the trance speaker Cora Hatch, then using the name of her current husband, Tappan. Davis included Hatch because she had "spoken more frequently and to larger audiences . . . than almost any other lecturer." As did most observers, Davis commented on Hatch's feminity: "Never identified with any party, she has, nevertheless, done a great work in a most womanly way." By including Hatch in her account of the woman's rights movement, Davis acknowledged the impact that trance mediums had merely because they were women who spoke in public and spoke well. Not everyone accepted the trance speakers' messages, but they were widely accepted as skilled and effective speakers.[39]

For a woman to defy convention and mount the public platform required tremendous self-confidence. Spirit mediumship emboldened women to overcome internal fears about their capabilities as well as external social strictures. The calm confidence born of spirit guidance contrasted with the insecurity that kept most women off the public platform and continued to plague some who took the giant step to the podium. Sallie Holley, for example, spoke regularly on antislavery from 1851 until the Civil War but never lost her fear of lecturing. Matilda Joslyn Gage was "trembling in every limb" when she delivered her first public lecture and spoke so softly that few could follow her carefully prepared text.[40] After this experience she confined herself principally to written statements. Susan B. Anthony became a skilled orator by the end of the 1850s but never overcame her self-doubt on the platform. Anthony questioned her ability to hold an audience, but at least she possessed sufficient volume to make herself heard. This was true of so few of her early colleagues that the impatient Anthony introduced a motion at the 1852 woman's rights convention requiring that those who could not make themselves heard give their speeches to others to read because "It is an imposition on an audience to have to sit quietly through a long speech of which they cannot hear one word." The idea that women should speak audibly in public was controversial even at the woman's rights convention. Paulina Wright Davis opposed Anthony's motion because "ladies did not come there to screech; they came to behave like ladies and to speak like ladies."[41]

Trance speakers presented a very different image of the female lecturer. Observers were surprised if a medium faltered on the platform. When the seventeen-year-old Martha Brown Sawyer spoke at the Melodeon Hall in Boston, a reporter commented that her voice had not yet matured and that she had therefore "not yet attained that pleasant volume which characterize many of our female speakers."[42] Because of their speaking skills, trance mediums were often asked to preside at funerals and weddings.

The flowing speech of trance mediums depended on a self-assurance unavailable to mid-century women who lacked spiritual inspiration. Their ability to address unknown topics chosen by the audience without preparation set them apart from other lecturers. Even the silver-tongued Lucy Stone, among the most self-assured of women reform speakers, repeated the same three lectures in rotation on her early tours. Susan B. Anthony, plagued with inconfidence as a speaker, read from a prepared text when she appeared in public in these years. In 1855, on a canvass of New York State, she read the same speech in every town, half in the evening and half in the afternoon. Anthony envied the easy eloquence of the trance speaker. "Oh, dear, dear! If the spirits would only just make me a trance medium and put the right thing into my mouth," she wrote to her coworker and confidante, Elizabeth Cady Stanton. "You can't think how earnestly I have prayed to be made a speaking medium for a whole week. If they would only come to me thus, I'd give them a hearty welcome." Fearful that she would not know what to say before an audience, she entreated Stanton to prepare a text for her to read at an upcoming convention. Anthony was undecided on the question of Spiritualism at this time, but she was full of admiration for the abilities of trance mediums.[43]

In 1857, when Cora Hatch made a sensation in New York City, the reform platform had lost many of its foremost women orators. Lucy Stone, Antoinette Brown Blackwell, and Elizabeth Cady Stanton were home with infant children. There was no woman's rights convention that year for lack of speakers. Although the *Banner of Light* also occasionally mourned the loss of a gifted speaker to marriage or motherhood, new recruits quickly filled her place. This problem was a pet peeve of Warren Chase, who complained of medium Emma Jay in 1861 that she is "not dead, but married, and mortals, not angels, are using her now." However, Emma Jay Bullene was back on the lecture circuit by 1863. New names appeared regularly in the *Banner*'s list of lecturers, replacing lost laborers in the cause.[44]

Later generations of Spiritualists would become preoccupied with sensational phenomena produced in private circles. But, before the Civil War, trance lecturers such as Cora Hatch, Lizzie Doten, and Emma Hardinge were the undisputed favorites of the Spiritualist public. Likewise, the general public, enchanted by trance speakers in the 1850s, could go elsewhere to hear a woman speak in public after the Civil War. Yet the enthusiastic response accorded to trance speakers helped open the way for women to speak in other roles. The meteoric career of the seventeen-year-old reform sensation Anna Dickinson in the 1860s, for example, mirrored the rise of popular trance speakers of the previous decade more than it resembled the careers of other reformers. Women who began as trance speakers sometimes learned to speak out of trance, and several became reform lecturers. But the progression never went in the other direction. Many reform women became Spiritualists, but none became trance speakers. Women who possessed the self-assurance to speak without spirit assistance did not seek it out later in life. Trance speaking was a transitional phase that enabled both individual women and women as a group to break through limitations on their role. It embodied a combination of feminine qualities with a departure from the feminine role that had a strong appeal to both men and women in the 1850s.

Achsa W. Sprague: A Case Study in Empowerment

In 1853, Achsa W. Sprague had been an invalid for five years. Crippled by a "scrofulous" joint disease, she lay confined to a darkened room in the village of Plymouth Notch, high in the Green Mountains of Vermont.* "Bowed down by disease, shut up from the world . . . like a prisoner chained down in his dungeon," the twenty-five-year-old former schoolteacher held little hope for her future. "But all this is now passing away," Sprague wrote in her diary on 9 February. "The chains of disease are falling off my limbs." [45] Within a few months, Sprague rose from her bed and attributed her recovery to spirits. The spirit guides that gave her the strength to rise from her sickbed also instructed her to undertake a mission that would take her far from her Green Mountain home. Sprague appeared in public as a speaking medium within a year after she began to regain the use of her limbs. Her first public lecture was in the nearby town of South Reading, on 16 July 1854.[46] She spent the rest of her life touring the country as a trance lecturer. "Having been raised from a bed of sickness . . . by Spirit agency," she wrote in her diary, "I felt it my duty to do that which has been pointed out to me by my Spirit Guides, . . . to take the position which I now occupy, that of a Public Speaking Medium." [47]

The diary and letters of Achsa Sprague provide an unusually intimate view of the inner thoughts of a trance medium both before and after her contact with Spiritualism. During the 1850s, for a woman to speak in public seemed as miraculous to many as Sprague's wonderful cure from disease. Sprague's personal papers, as well as accounts of her experiences and trance lectures in the Spiritualist press, trace the course of the concurrent miracles: her transition from a helpless invalid confined to a darkened room in rural Vermont to a popular lecturer traveling throughout the northern United States. She provides an ideal case study of the role played by mediumship in empowering a woman to assume a public career. The hundreds of impas-

---

* The village of Plymouth Notch has been preserved much as it was in Achsa Sprague's day because it became the birthplace, in 1872, of President Calvin Coolidge. Coolidge was visiting Plymouth when he learned of the death of President Warren G. Harding in 1923 and took the oath of office in the front room of his family's home. The Sprague farm, which stood across the street from the Coolidge homestead, did not survive to become part of the Plymouth Notch Historic District opened to the public by the Vermont Division of Historic Preservation.

sioned letters she evoked from friends and admirers illustrate the impact of a trance speaker on her audience.[48]

When Sprague began her journal in June 1849, she had recently become an invalid. A joint disease, probably some form of arthritis, rendered her unable to walk and sometimes prevented her from holding a pen to write. She was twenty years old and had taught school for eight years. Surrounded by invalids, Sprague chronicled both her own illness and those of relatives and friends whose health she watched anxiously as she and they underwent a variety of medical treatments. She departs from her acount of illness and treatment only to comment on the books she read (*Jane Eyre* was "very interesting"; a biography of Milton made her mind wander) and to record the names of poems she wrote (like "'Tis a Hard Life to Live" and "Invalid's Dream"). Her account is punctuated by the frequent deaths that occured in Plymouth, including that of her twenty-six-year-old brother Ephraim, who returned from Boston to languish for a year before dying of consumption in 1850.[49]

In the opening entry of her diary, Sprague vents the despondency that dominates her life before Spiritualism. "Once more I am unable to walk or do anything else; have not been a step without crutches since Sunday and see no prospect of being any better; see nothing before me but a life of miserable helplessness." Sprague's only hope for a return to an active life was a cure of her physical ailments. In her constant pursuit of medical treatment, she sought both an end to pain and debility and a return to her former independence. But her experience with doctors and medical treatment only increased her despondency. She grew to mistrust doctors and approached new treatments with skepticism. "Dr. Spencer of Clarendon . . . also examined my case, and thinks he can cure me" she wrote in her diary. "I shall take his medicine but scarce expect to receive any benefit. I have hoped until there is no chance of hope." Two months later, when the same doctor told her that her condition was improving, Sprague responded bitterly, "I shall believe it when I begin to walk."[50]

Before becoming a Spiritualist, Sprague became an expert on nonreligious approaches to healing in antebellum America. She sought cures from a variety of practitioners, often traveling great distances to see a doctor reputed to have success with difficult cases. In addition to taking the medicine various doctors prescribed for her, she wore "galvanic bands" for six weeks and was "magnetized" repeatedly by a "psychologist." Her account suggests that the consumers of health care in northern New England in the 1850s did not distinguish between "regular" or allopathic physicians and their "irregular" or sectarian counterparts. Sprague's experience showed all forms of medical care to be costly, time consuming, and ineffective. Disillusioned by the failure of medical treatment, Sprague became embittered by confinement. "I am tired to death of taking medicine and never having it do any good and think sometimes I will never try to do anything for myself again," she confided to her diary. Illness was a common, although not normative, precondition of mediumship. Sprague's experience suggests that Spiritualism may have been made more attractive by the failure of other sources of healing.[51]

Sprague did not accept her illness complacently; she rebelled against the role of invalid. Unable to walk, she rode horseback. Sprague relished this one form of independent action that allowed a temporary respite from her usual state of immobility and dependence. "Riding horseback yet," she wrote on 10 July 1849, not taking for granted that she would be able to continue, "enjoy it better than anything else." The following October, she was thrown from her horse while out riding alone. Unable to remount unaided, she lay in the field until a man from a nearby farm helped her back onto the horse. This incident is one of the few recorded humorously in her journal. Unconcerned about her potential danger as an immobilized woman lying in a field away from home, her only worry was to conceal the event. She found this display of helplessness embarrassing and probably feared that, if it were discovered, she would lose her one remaining source of independence.[51]

Having taught school from the age of twelve, Sprague was accustomed to being the sole authority in the classroom as well as contributing financially to her improverished family. In this role, Sprague enjoyed the maximum degree of autonomy available to a young woman in a mountain village in Vermont. Sprague's illness changed her from one of the most independent women in Plymouth to one of the most dependent. Instead of keeping a school where she was the mistress, she was now confined to a room in her mother's house. Her diary suggests that she found her dependence a greater trial than the physical suffering caused by her disease. She never complained of being in pain, even to her private diary. Her only references to the state of her health refer to the outcome of medical treatment or to her ability or inability to perform some action, to walk, to write, or to sew.

Sprague repeatedly lamented that her confinement was especially difficult to bear because it dashed the "bright hopes" she had held for her future. "Why can't I crush this insatiate urge for a life of action, this thirsting for knowledge?" she asked her diary.[52] Her thirst for action and knowledge suggests that she aspired to some role beyond the domestic sphere even before she became a trance speaker. But she never revealed what that bright hope might be. Instead she asked,

> Am I unreasonable that I cannot be happy? Is it the result of a com- plaining spirit that can never be satisfied? Are not poverty and sick- ness and the almost daily expectation of death in our circle, enough to crush the heart's first freshness of hope and life? . . . Is not this feeling of helplessness, this consciousness of being a burden to everyone, enough to crush the proudest spirit?[53]

By 1850, Sprague had exhausted the alternatives offered by ante- bellum medical practitioners and had given up hope of regaining her health. On 4 July she reflected bitterly on Independence Day, "How many who celebrate it realize their entire dependence upon each other and their creator?" Finally, a few days later, she asked, "What hope is there for me but in death. If I could know for sure that death would bring the higher sphere I would long for it."[54]

One of the last diary entries before her conversion to Spiritualism recounts "a discussion among us, as to whether spirits could commu- nicate with mortals." She found the conversation inspiring and as a result wrote a poem for a friend whose mother had recently died. The discussion took place at the time that news of the "Rochester Rappings" was spreading throughout the country. Sprague was quite receptive to the concept of Spiritualism. "'Tis a beautiful idea, that our departed friends are around us and with us, that they can come back to guard us from temptation, to soothe us in affliction and win us from sin," Sprague wrote in her journal. "But, if true, could the world be so sunk in wickedness? Yet . . . is it not their influence when better thoughts to the heart come back which had almost yielded to sin?"[55]

During the last years of her illness, Sprague made no entries in her journal. The disease that crippled her joints may have rendered her unable to hold a pen, or she may have lost interest out of despair. Finally, she lifted her pen again. "After . . . three years silence I un- fold these pages once more to trace upon their surface the thoughts of a long-tried heart," Sprague wrote. "How lonely, dark, desolate have passed these years of confinement, pain, suffering." But now, she told her diary, she was beginning to recover the use of her body. She began to have hope for the future, which had appeared so dark.[56]

Although Sprague dated her cure to the winter of 1853, months passed before she was strong enough to leave her room. As soon as her health started to improve, she began to receive communications from the spirits to whom she attributed her recovery. They moved her hand to write beatific visions prophesying an end to her suffering. "Come forth from thy darkness, oh thou child of sorrow," the spirits called to Sprague through her own hand. "Come forth even though thy eyes are dimmed with weeping, for thy grief shall be changed into gladness. Even as the clouds of night have fled before the first rays of the morning sun, so shall the dark clouds of sorrow soon vanish before thy returning joy." The spirits called Sprague to witness the revelation of divinity in nature. "How beautiful is the earth spread out beneath thy gate. How soft and yielding is the bright carpet beneath thy feet. . . . Look how the whole earth seems filled with glory, lit up with the radiant sunlight." As winter passed and spring came to the Green Mountains, the spirit messages were fulfilled, and Sprague left the room to which she had been confined. "Again I walked in the fields, in the woods, in the valleys and upon the mountains, gathered the flowers, listened to the music of nature, and found, like Mrs. H. M. F. Brown, that 'we are not *lone worshipers* in Nature's Temple, the beautiful and the good who have gone up into the Great Uncreated Temples are our companions.'"[57] Sprague's reflections on her state were no longer confined to the diary penned for herself alone. The previous statement appeared in *The New Era, or Heaven Opened to Man,* a newspaper devoted to the spirit phenomena to which Sprague attributed her cure.

The same spirits who freed Sprague from the "chains of disease" now inspired her voice. Within a year, she made her first appearance as a trance speaker. By the summer of 1854, she lectured regularly. For most of the next six years she toured the country as a trance lecturer, until her premature death from disease in 1862 at the age of thirty-four.

Achsa Sprague's cure and adoption of Spiritualism include several elements of a classic conversion experience. She had exhausted human remedies and viewed her situation as utterly hopeless until divine intervention caused a radical change in her state of being. Her account differs from that of a Christian conversion in that it describes not a "dark night of the soul" but rather one of the body. She is not convicted of sin—she never accepts her suffering as something that she deserves. Rather, she views her cure as a delivery from undeserved suffering and therefore a return to the natural order that had been disrupted by her illness. Although a spirit message instructed her to praise God for her years of suffering because she would one day appreciate them as "the blessing of a life," Sprague professed herself unable to comprehend this message, the meaning of which would have been clear to most Christians.[58]

The nonspiritual aspect of Sprague's recovery is difficult to interpret in retrospect because of the limited description of her physical symptoms. The determination she evinced to remain as active as possible and to seek a cure makes it unlikely that her illness was psychosomatic. Historian Leonard Twynham's diagnosis of tuberculosis of the bone is also improbable because that disease causes irreparable damage, making a cure after five years impossible. A more likely diagnosis is rheumatoid arthritis, a disease that is not uncommon in otherwise healthy women in their twenties and that can disappear after an extended period of time. Arthritis, especially among young women, has been associated by doctors with repressed anger turned inward. In arthritis, the immune system, designed to ward off threats from without, turns inward and attacks the lining of the joints. For Sprague, the return to health represents a turn outward: a shift from writing in her diary to speaking in public, a shift from the world of the home—deemed appropriate to women—to the outside world deemed appropriate to men.[59]

Sprague believed that continued improvement in her health depended on her carrying out the spirits' instructions to spread the news of spirit communication through trance lectures.[60] In a long poem, "The Angel's Visit," Sprague recounted her illness, cure, and entrance into the lecture field. The first pages of the poem describe a familiar image from her diary, "A young girl in a darkened room, / Chained by disease,—a living tomb!" The poem goes on to trace the connections in Sprague's mind that bound together her cure, the message of Spiritualism, and her mediumship:

> And stronger grew her form each day,—
> All pain and languor swept away,—
> Until, like some neglected lute,
> With broken strings all sadly mute,

That some kind hand has tuned again,
And waked to old, familiar strain,
Her heart vibrated; and each string
Seemed swept by angels' starry wings,
And gave forth songs whose every tone
Was waked by angel hands alone.
She spoke such words of heavenly truth
And life, as fitted not her youth;
And taught of angels, God and Heaven,
And said that not one tie was riven
When loved ones, called away from earth,
Awake in heaven to purer birth.
But that they come in love,
To point the weary heart above, . . .
To light with hope each weary eye,
And teach the soul it cannot die.[61]

Sprague's life as a lecturer could not have contrasted more starkly with her former confinement. Within a few months of her first lecture, she was filling halls in Boston, where local Spiritualists implored her to extend her visit. Within a year, she had addressed "overflowing" halls as far away as Michigan, and speaking engagements eventually took her to Baltimore, Philadelphia, and throughout the Midwest. From complete dependence, she attained a remarkable degree of independence for a woman of her day, supporting herself with lecture fees and traveling alone from state to state. From despondence and hopelessness, she became an enthusiastic proponent of a cheerful message, with hundreds of admirers whose letters confirm that she did in fact "light with hope each weary eye." As a trance speaker, Sprague embodied in her life the optimistic doctrines of her adopted faith.[62]

Sprague was in great demand as a speaker. "Miss Sprague is our criterion as to all that is good, great, eloquent and beautiful," wrote the man responsible for procuring Spiritualist lecturers in Terre Haute, Indiana. "Our people in Utica have fallen more deeply in love with you than before," wrote another lecture committee, entreating her to return to their city for another month. Many communities felt that the success of the movement in their area depended on Sprague's appearance. "The more I talk with the members of *Our Church* the stronger is my conviction that you are the only one that can give full satisfaction in our pulpit," wrote Benjamin Starbuck from Troy, New York. "Miss Sprague is the one we must have," echoed the Spriritualists of Burlington, Vermont.[63] While some communities tried unsuccessfully to woo her with economic incentives, she insisted that she must go where her spirits directed rather than where she would receive the largest sum. She refused several requests that she speak at the prestigious Dodsworth Hall in New York City. A friend noted Sprague's expanding career in 1858 but commented, "I know you do not do it except from *principle,* for your fame would become the more wide-spread did you seek the more conspicuous places, the cities."[64]

Much of Sprague's surviving correspondence consists of letters from Spiritualists inviting her—sometimes begging her—to lecture in their towns for periods ranging from one week to two months. Towns with Spiritualist groups normally asked her to come for a month. She was expected to speak in the principle town that invited her each Sunday and in smaller settlements in the vicinity during the week. The more Sprague traveled, the more word spread of her talents, and the demand for her services grew apace. She received fifty-seven requests to speak in 1858, seventy-one in 1859, and eighty-eight in 1860. These figures include only invitations for individual speaking engagements, not requests to speak at funerals or at the many Spiritualist conventions at which she was a featured speaker. Guest appearances had to be coordinated with her regular appointment speaking every other Sunday in South Reading. In her effort to reach as many people as possible, Sprague rarely consented to remain for a month in any location. Still, she could satisfy only a fraction of the requests. In April 1860, she wrote to the *Banner of Light* that all her Sundays were engaged until the following January. Despite her popularity, Achsa Sprague never enjoyed the renown of Emma Hardinge, Lizzie Doten, or Cora Hatch. We may assume that the fifteen or twenty Spiritualist women who ranked with her in popularity were equally in demand as speakers.[65]

Sprague's popularity as a speaker reflected the powerful impression she made on her audience. Her correspondence is full of letters such as one from Charles Townsend, husband of the trance speaker Melvina Townsend, who called her his "spiritual benefactress" because, "The first words that lifted the veil from my eyes and enabled me to desern [sic] spiritual things fell from your lips." A man who had heard Sprague speak once when she passed through his town wrote to her, "Often in the quiet hours of night . . . do you visit me in my imagination as you stood inspired before the audience in our little hall." On recalling her appearance as a speaker, he felt "deep undefined yearnings of the soul to speak in words of praise, of esteem, of affection even." Another listener who could not sleep after Sprague's lecture had a vision of her "standing before the people"[66] Other mediums evoked similar feelings. A Spiritualist admirer of Cora Hatch recalled that her "entrancing eloquence" made his "heart throb with sacred emotion." Emma Hardinge drew unwelcome attention from a man who claimed that his spirit followed her everywhere after he heard her speak.[67] The independent woman in the guise of the trance speaker enthralled her male audience.

The trance speaker's anomalous independence freed men from conventions governing their interaction with women just as it freed women to address mixed audiences.[68] Traveling alone, Sprague usually enjoyed the hospitality of the leading Spiritualist family in the town or city where she spoke. Many of these families became devoted friends who constantly urged her to return. It was not unusual for the head of the family to be smitten with the itinerant female lecturer. "Not any altar . . . nor quiet rocks and mountains stern were ought to me without the living visible spirit of the enchantress whose presence is everywhere and whose wand has quickened everything with new life and beauty and made everything vocal with music and instruction," wrote an admirer in Wisconsin.[69] Some male correspondents expressed concern over the propriety of stating the depth of their feelings for Sprague, but they risked criticism and did it anyway.[70] One married Spiritualist described his reaction to her lecture:

> I never felt so much like worshipping a mortal as I did you for the
> intelligence that spoke through you not for yourself although I might
> agree with a young man if he said you was a very comely and rather
> good looking young lady but as a Spiritualist I felt that I saw an expe-
> rience of that same power that worked so wonderfully upon the Minds
> of the early Christians which they called miraculous.[71]

As these statements testify, the visual image of a medium as she stood on the platform made an enduring impression on the audience. N. P. Willis's description of Cora Hatch "standing alone in the pulpit . . . her delicate bare arms raised in a clergyman's attitude of devotion" suggests the double impact of the medium's appearance. In addition to spiritual inspiration, trance speakers provided mid-century men with a rare opportunity to look unrestrained at an unknown woman. According to the mores of the time, male audiences probably understood the willingness of a medium to appear in public—a measure shunned by any woman with a modicum of modesty—as implying consent to be stared at. Unlike reform women, trance speakers did not dress in a manner designed to dispel this impression. Reformers favored sober Quaker-style garb. They rejected well-known author Elizabeth Oakes Smith as president of the 1852 National Woman's Rights Convention because she appeared in a fashionable dress that "left both neck and arms exposed." Susan B. Anthony, outraged by Smith's appearance, argued that "Nobody who dressed as she did could represent the earnest, solid, hard-working women of the country for whom they were making the demand for equal rights."[72]

A popular photograph (see plate 9) shows Cora Hatch in just such a dress as the one that evoked Anthony's ire. It depicts her as Willis remembered her, face upturned to heaven, flaxen ringlets flowing over bare shoulders. In addition, Hatch always wore a white rose in her belt. "Were I a medium lecturer, female, I would dress so as *not* to attract attention with outlandishness in hat, frock, wristbands, and country girl flamishness," advised one of Achsa Sprague's most avid admirers. He criticized her for wearing "innumerable flashy ribbons on [her] wrists" and a hat with "Northern light streaks." Sprague's daguerrotype portrait (see plate 10) does not reveal the color of her dress, but it shows contrasting stripes of at least three hues, suggesting a combination of bright colors that contemporaries might have associated with "country girl flamishness." Presumably, Sprague would not have elicted such fatherly advice had her appearance met her friend's standards of modesty.[73]

The public display of a colorfully dressed unconscious woman provided potent material for the imaginations of the male audience. Again unlike reform women, the public appearance of mediums did not conflict with the passivity believed to characterize female sexuality because they were understood to be unconscious. Abolitionist women were dismissed by many as traitors to their sex because they dared to stand up in public to espouse radical political views. Derisive observers commented on Susan B. Anthony's broad shoulders and suggested that the practice of women speaking in public would give rise to a third sex. But neither men nor women questioned the feminity of the beautiful Cora Hatch, ringlets bobbing about her youthful face as she expounded visions of angels.

In addition to the many friends and admirers Achsa Sprague met during her lecture tours, other men sought her acquaintance through the mail. To a Mr. Stone who asked to correspond with her, she replied that she was happy to correspond with anyone about Spiritualism. Apparently, he also asked for information that she deemed overly personal. She wrote sarcastically, "I have nothing to say about myself except that I am as *ugly looking* as nature could make me and as for my *real self*, the Internal, I shall let you draw your own conclusions from my style of writing, as I of course shall take the same *liberty* with regard to you." She was indignant when Mr. Stone sent stamps to encourage her correspondence. "I have almost a mind to send those stamps back. I wish to pay the postage on my own letters. *Perhaps you don't know I am an Advocate of Woman's Rights.* Now don't faint away." Mr. Stone may indeed have fainted, for although Sprague assured him that she never dropped a correspondent lightly, this shocking revelation concluded their brief exchange.[74]

Sprague corresponded at greater length with men who shared her enthusiasm for woman's rights. The radical Elmer Louden wrote from Indiana, "The female is taught by our *theological* teachers the ridiculous idea that the woman must *keep silent in publick* and if she will learn anything let her ask her *drunken husband* at home." Louden, who was a frequent correspondent in 1858, had never met Sprague but wanted to after reading her articles in Spiritualist papers. Only after commencing correspondence did he learn from the papers that she was a trance speaker. He so admired her views that he read one of her articles aloud to a crowd of thirty people. "I am glad to learn that you are still keeping the world of thought agitated by your *fearless* independence," he wrote to her in May. "O that there were a thousand more of the female sex to take the stand you have taken." In October, he proposed marriage to Sprague in a letter, although there is no record that they had ever met. He had not been enchanted by her appearance on the platform since he had never seen her, but the mere knowledge that she was a lecturer and did not "keep silent in publick" added to her appeal. Himself a trance speaker, he felt that "it would be adding to our present and future happiness to unite our interests as one." Whereas marrying another woman would probably have entailed giving up the freedom of his mobile style of life, marriage to the itinerant Sprague would not have interfered with his own career. He was clearly attracted by the fact that she shared the radical views about woman's role and about the relations of men and women in marriage that earned him a reputation as an advocate of free love. Louden and Sprague concurred with other free love advocates that a true marriage could occur only between two autonomous individuals and that a subservient woman could not make a good wife. Sprague's career as a trance speaker embodied Louden's ideal of an independent woman.[75]

Sprague's correspondence contains five proposals of marriage, three of which arrived in a single two-week period. This count includes only suitors who could not propose in person.[76] Apparently, an independent woman on the public platform attracted many men. Sprague's admirers were enamored, but they were not frivolous. Not one writer responded to Sprague's colorful appearance without being moved by her spiritual message. The same J. F. Parker whose poetic missives described his emotional response to visions of Sprague at night wrote in response to her article "Reply to Funeral Rites":

> I rejoice that you have the independence to plant yourself upon your interior promptings of truth and duty regardless of the prejudices of the world. . . . The clergy and those who have received their teachings . . . must yet *"go to a woman's school"* and learn that it is not the mission of any single child of the Great Father to convert himself or herself into a hearse to cart about dead forms and ceremonies.[76]

Parker was engaged by Sprague's ideas as well as by her appearance. She appealed to her audience on more than one level.

Why did Achsa Sprague refuse the many suitors who hoped to win her hand? Although some of the proposals came from men with whom she had no acquaintance, others came from men she knew well, such as the one who wrote, "I have no evil design in caressing you in the way I do, it comes from the bottom of my heart. I have told you I loved you . . . better than I do all womankind."[77] Sprague rejected matches that her friends and family viewed as desirable. "Now don't you wish you had been good?" inquired friend and sister medium Melvina Townsend when a prominent Vermont Spiritualist who had courted Sprague married a non-Spiritualist. "Well, you'll reap your rewards according to your deeds," Townsend concluded, "so I'll not trouble myself."[78] Sprague's brother-in-law thought the reform conventions she attended presented ideal opportunities for "husband-hunting." "You can't always be young and beautiful. So 'hitch on' to someone soon," he advised. When Achsa proved insusceptible to such suggestions, his friendly tone changed to recrimination. "*Your womanly greatness* . . . has changed to monstrous imperfection," he wrote. "You never can love nor be loved like a whole woman in this life."[79] While Sprague's male correspondents hoped she would some-day find a man "that will solve the mysteries of your dear self," her female friends were relieved that she avoided "the matrimonial noose," believing that she could "take care of *her self*" without a hus-band.[80]

One thing becomes abundantly clear from the extensive discussion of Achsa Sprague's marital status in her correspondence: she re-mained single by choice, a choice she was required to reassert repeat-edly. Sprague was not impervious to the satisfactions a family might offer, but she viewed her mission as a medium as answering a higher call than that voiced by her earthly suitors. "This sometimes seems like a wandering life, & the office of Medium a thankless one," she told her diary early in her career. "Yet . . . I think I can bear much of suffering, much of sorrow for the sake of truth." She viewed the hus-bandless life of an itinerant lecturer as the opposite of the life of the female invalid. "I do wish to act, to do, to live an active life and have that life one of usefulness. If I can but see the way that is right for me . . . I feel I could throw my whole soul into that work. Anything but a life of worthlessness, uselessness."[81] Melvina Townsend, at-tempting to console one of Sprague's spurned suitors, articulated her friend's reason for avoiding marriage. She explained that Achsa "loved the cause in which [she was] engaged better than anything else or *anybody*."[82]

Sprague's effect on her audience was not limited to those who hoped to marry her. Women also found themselves drawn to her in unusual ways. "Thankful and happy was I in making your acquaint-ance, for I feel that another bright star has been added to the galaxy," wrote Mirenda Randall, who found her spirit attracted to Sprague by "the power invisible."[83] The visual impact of trance speakers was greater on men. Women, after all, had many opportunities to look at each other and to hear women speak in sex-segregated prayer meet-ings, temperance societies, and church groups. Women also had ample opportunity to observe men in public roles. No objections were raised to women's presence in promiscuous assemblies addressed by male speakers. But, when a woman saw a female speaker address a mixed audience, she saw a model for the abrogation of the conven-tions that hedged her life in with limitations.

Sprague's female correspondents looked to her as an example and as a source of support in their own pursuit of independence. A lonely young woman who wore the "American costume" and supported herself by working in a milliner's shop wrote to Sprague for advice about her development as a medium. "I am impressed by my spirit guides to address you as a sister, an elder sister, hoping to get some advice from one who knows what it is to suffer for truth's sake." The young woman's description of her own persecution in her pursuit of mediumship indicates that her reference to suffering is a reference not to Sprague's extended illness but rather to Sprague's experiences as a woman who has defied conventions regarding both religion and gender roles. Sprague reassured one trance speaker who doubted her performance in public and arranged speaking engagements for another who was soon to arrive in New England from the West. Ermina Pollard, a frequent correspondent, admired Sprague's newspaper articles and hoped to publish some of her own. "How I *tremble* when I think of the *wide sea* I have launched out onto . . . the *feeble* attempt to *do good*, by writing for the *public gaze*, seems at times very like a mountain." Sprague, who wrote easily and treated the publication of her pieces lightly, provided encouragement to a few women who hoped to write for the Spiritualist press. One asked Sprague for technical assistance in punctuating a poem. Sprague's confidence in the public realm made her a model for women in a variety of roles.[84]

Women's letters, unlike those from men, recount the correspondents' desires to have Sprague's attention focused on them rather than to focus their attention on Sprague. "I need someone to whom I can open my whole soul," wrote a woman from Springfield, Illinois. "I feel that *you* will understand me." Another woman wrote Sprague, "I felt very lonely after you left, and am still pining for your loved light and lively company."[85] Sprague's successful public career brought out women's doubts about their own lives within the confines of the woman's sphere. After visiting Sprague in Vermont, Laura Washburn described her life in terms similar to those used by Sprague before she became a Spiritualist. "What I am I know not," she wrote to Sprague. "To me it seems that I am doing nothing; and to feel thus hanging upon the world without ministering to its growth or in anyway helping toward a better day is terrible. God grant that it may not long be thus." Women welcomed Sprague's religious message, which addressed their particular reservations about orthodox Protestantism. "While I shall ever cherish you as a friend," wrote a woman who had recently heard her speak, "the teachings which have fallen from your lips will never be forgotten, as they have taken deep root in my soul."[86]

Sprague viewed her mediumship as a religious vocation, not a career. When a correspondent suggested that she join him in a business partnership to exploit her talents as a medium, Sprague was appalled. "If money was my object, I might get four times what I do," she told the would-be entrepreneur. "*But money is not my object.* I would be instrumental in imparting truth and doing good. If I cannot do this, I have no wish to do anything." Sprague asserted that her "mission" as a medium was "wholly under the control of Spirits" and that "it would be useless for myself or anyone else to make any arrangements with regard to it. Unless sanctioned by the Spirits, it would be of no avail."[87]

Sprague had a reputation for sincerity. Philadelphia Spiritualist Cora Wilburn asked Sprague to address a small group, formed for the development and improvement of mediums, that could not invite speakers because it lacked resources. "I venture upon you this request," wrote Wilburn, "as I have read devotion to the cause, and earnest womanly effort in your soul. . . . I know many mediums are worshipers of mammon, but I know too, that you are not of that number." Sprague complied with this request. Other correspondents confirmed that Sprague did not choose her itinerary on the basis of pecuniary considerations. However, she made enough money lecturing to contribute to the support of her parents in 1855 and to accumulate 300 dollars in savings by 1859, which her brother-in-law invested for her at a favorable return.[88]

Although much admired by Spiritualists, Sprague had to endure the derision that met any woman who flouted convention. In "The Angel Visit," she has the audience ask,

> Why leaves she woman's lowly sphere,
> To speak where crowds these words can hear,
> When all the men of God but say,
> She doth blaspheme,—away, away?
> And thoughtless worldlings scorn to hear
> A message from the brighter sphere.[89]

Sprague departed from "woman's lowly sphere" because spirit guides explicitly encouraged her public role. Two communications from spirits survive in her handwriting.[90] Their messages directly contradict conventions that viewed women as unqualified for public leadership. The spirits, who signed themselves "Thy Guardians," left no doubts about Sprague's abilities. "Through thee come luminous revelations of divine Truth to hitherto unawakened eyes," they assured her. The spirits were especially explicit about the legitimacy of trance speaking and about Sprague's effective use of it. "Keys silver and golden are given to thee that thou mayest unlock the treasure chambers of heart and brain and lead forth embodied and garmented in rich and varied speech the loves and truths and joys of the inner life to the glad embrace of earth's children." Using the terms that conferred the authority of office on male religious leaders, the spirits called Sprague "a teacher and a priestess divinely ordained." They urged her to prepare herself for an active life, applauding her accomplishments but informing her that she had more to do. "Much have the sacred powers that guard and guide this lower sphere accomplished through thy organism though as yet thy Angel directed feet have scarcely touched the threshold of the shining portals through which thy Mission to Humanity shall inevitably lead," said the spirits.

The longer of the two messages, which continues for four pages, responds to Sprague's internal doubts about her mission, her abilities as a trance speaker, and the source of her power. The spirits assured her that they would never desert her, that they would support and empower her no matter what challenges appeared in her path. "Dost thou sometimes forget that the Power which now upholds thee is as Divine as the Divinity is Divinity"? they asked. Perhaps most important, Sprague's spirit guardians asserted that their assistance both provided the power that had allowed Sprague to overcome her debilitating illness and enabled her to pursue a path-breaking public career: "When . . . thou dost not feel the hands that ever help thee on why dost look back upon the darkened hours and say they shall return [and] say the power is almost fled. *From thee it shall not flee.*" The doubts to which the spirit message responds suggest that Sprague felt the same insecurities that might be experienced by any antebellum woman who embarked on a course so precarious as lecturing in public. The difference between Sprague and other women was that inspired messages answered her doubts. "Begin as though thou lovest that work," they advised. "We wait to help thee on. To help we said for *thou* must act." The spirits counseled action, independence, and self-reliance.

1. "The Sisters Fox, the Original Spirit Rappers."

2. Amy Kirby Post (1802–89) and Isaac Post (1798–1872) of Rochester, New York, Quaker abolitionists, early supporters of the Fox sisters, and advocates of Spiritualism.

3. Margaret Fox (1833?–93), Catherine Fox (1839?–92), and Leah Fox Fish (1818?–90).

4. The séance table.

THE BOSTON
PLANCHETTE

From the Original Pattern, first made in Boston in 1860.

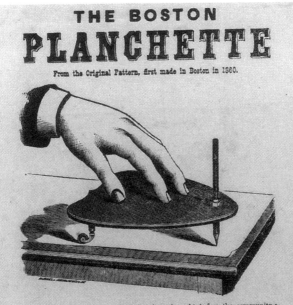

Within a few months past there has been brought before the community a little board variously noted in the papers; the BOSTON TRANSCRIPT, of May 21st, describes it as follows:

AN ASTOUNDING NOVELTY IS "PLANCHETTE,"

Which is only a little board in shape like a heart, placed on wheels or castors, with a pencil in front. When the fingers are gently placed on Planchette, in a few moments it becomes animated, moves along of its own accord, answers mental or written questions, talks with you and does many wonderful things. In November 30th number of Every Saturday, the wonder workings of Planchette are described by an English writer.

As Planchette has been extensively noticed in most of the leading papers of the day, it is unnecessary to say further of it than the following from the Boston Traveller.

Is PLANCHETTE A HUMBUG?—On this point there is a great difference of opinion. That Planchette is full of vagaries there is no question of doubt; with some it is as stubborn as Mr. Mallowney's pig, with others it is docile and quick to answer questions, interpret the thoughts of lookers on, and not only tell of past occurrences unknown to the operator, but will also give the note of warning for the future. All in all, Planchette is a wonderful institution, full of fun, puzzle and mystery and a pleasant companion in the house.

Have Planchette in the family, by all means, if you desire a novel amusement.

After various experiments to produce a wheel as a substitute for the Pentagraph, which of necessity caused Planchette to be sold at so high a price, a very neat, tasteful and durable wheel has recently been applied, which reduces the cost of Planchette one-half the former price, and for which the subscriber has exclusive control under the Patentee and manufacturers, and is now ready to fill all orders with promptness.

Planchette, black walnut board, neatly finished, - - - $1.00
Rosewood, handsome fretted work, - - - - - - - 2.00
Hollywood, beautifully painted, - - - - - - - - 3.00

FOR SALE BY

G. W. COTTRELL,
36 CORNHILL, BOSTON.

5. The Boston Planchette.

6. Fannie Davis, guided by spirit, plays organ and sings to comfort dying boy, though she has never played before.

7. Andrew Jackson Davis (1826–1910), prophet of the Harmonial Philosophy, and Mary Fenn (Love) Davis (1824–86), advocate of Spiritualism and woman's rights.

8. Emma Hardinge, medium and musician who became the historian of Spiritualism.

9. Cora L. V. Hatch, the seventeen-year-old trance speaker who enchanted American audiences in the 1850s.

10. Achsa White Sprague (1827–62),
trance lecturer, whose mediumship
ended five years of invalidism.

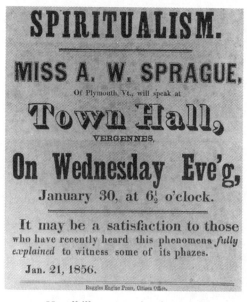

11. Handbill announcing lecture by
Achsa Sprague, 1856.

12. Spirit of "Lightheart," dissolving at the Eddy
homestead.

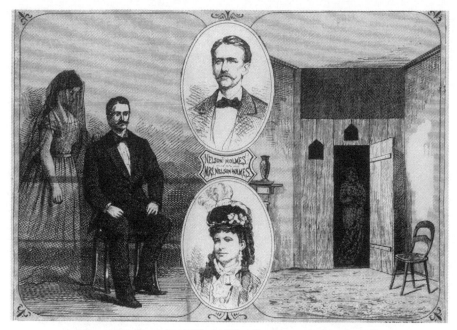

13. Materialized spirit of "Katie King," with portraits of mediums
Mr. and Mrs. Holmes, who deceived Robert Dale Owen.

14. Laura de Force Gordon (1838–
1907), trance medium who became
a well-known woman suffrage
speaker.

These documents depict the inner struggle of a woman at odds with the social strictures of her age. For Sprague wrote these messages herself, while in trance. Both the doubts and the reassurance emerged from somewhere within herself. Sprague's spirit messages provide eloquent testimony that internalized conventions presented obstacles to the expansion of women's public role as difficult to overcome as external prejudices or restrictions. "What doubting still?" Sprague asked herself in the spirit message. "It were as well to doubt at times as on to walk and think no lurking foe [*sic*]. There shall be snarls, there shall be foes. But when thou doubtest most we shall be near." Even the spirit voice had to admit that dangers faced the woman who flew in the face of convention. But that voice, the inspired voice with which Sprague spoke from the platform, believed that these dangers could be overcome.

The spirits kept their promises for seven years. From her cure in 1854 until 1861, Achsa Sprague traveled as a trance lecturer, frequently speaking in a different town every other day in her attempt to spread the Spiritualist faith. During the summer of 1861, while in Oswego, New York, to speak at a convention, Sprague was again struck by disease.* In 1862, the beloved medium died at the age of thirty-four, death bringing her career as a trance lecturer to an abrupt conclusion. But the admiration and devotion evoked by her mediumship were not easily obliterated. On the first anniversary of Sprague's death, Andrew Jackson Davis made a pilgrimage to her grave in Plymouth and described it for the *Banner of Light*. The *Banner* brought out a volume of her poems later that year. Demand for the book was so great that a second edition was issued immediately. In 1865, prominent Vermont Spiritualists gathered for a special service commemorating the eleventh anniversary of Sprague's first public trance lecture and planned to do so again the next time the date fell on the Sabbath. Ten years later, the Vermont State Spiritualist Convention, meeting at Plymouth, included a memorial service at Sprague's grave. Lecturers continued to recall her "indefatigable" labors as a trance speaker many years after her death to audiences who probably had never heard her speak.[91] As late as 1881, Sprague's

---

*While some of Sprague's correspondents referred to her fatal illness as a return of her original disease, others described it as a throat problem. If the retrospective diagnosis of arthritis is correct, then her final illness must have been distinct from the disease that caused her five years of invalidism since rheumatoid arthritis is not fatal.

spirit was cited as the author of a book received through a medium.[92] Sprague was well-enough remembered into the twentieth century to be one of the few women included in the *Dictionary of American Biography*.[93]

Within a year of her death, Sprague's spirit began to inspire other mediums. The dead Sprague addressed her friend and coworker, trance speaker Melvina Townsend, through the mediumship of Lizzie Doten: "Sister! One simple word—/ I *love* you still! / My strength shall be conferred / Your need to fill. I come to you at night / In some still hour; / And lend my spirit's might / To give you power."[94] After death, Achsa Sprague's spirit empowered other women just as her own "guardians" empowered her during her life.

5

"The Body and Soul Destroying Marriage Institution"

W hen Mary Fenn Love left the farm town of Randolph in western New York, she emancipated herself from two mammoth obstacles to her spiritual advancement: the Calvinist theology of her orthodox upbringing and an unhappy marriage. "Beware of inharmonious alliances," she warned an 1853 woman's rights convention. While most of the speakers addressed women's need for legal and economic rights, Love attributed "the chief evils of society" to "domestic uncongeniality." The following year, she traveled from her home in New York to Indiana, where more liberal laws allowed her to procure a divorce from a loveless match with Samuel Love, her husband of nine years and the father of her children. The courage and strength of conviction required for a woman to pursue such a course in the 1850s attracted the attention of Andrew Jackson Davis, whose first wife had recently died. In 1855, Mary Fenn Love married Davis, in spite of the opposition of her Baptist family. She spent the next decade trying to regain custody of her children, whose loss was the price of her freedom.[1]

Spiritualists applauded Mary Davis's identification of marriage as the root of women's oppression. The *New Era* reported that at an 1854 Spiritualist convention she did not limit herself to "the mere political and civil rights of woman; but . . . enters the very citadel of Marriage itself, and . . . looks the monster—sensuality—full in the face."[2] When Spiritualists focused their reform impulses on their own experience, they found the most serious barrier to the individual sovereignty of women in the institution of marriage as practiced in

nineteenth-century America. The women who criticized marriage
from the Spiritualist platform knew whereof they spoke. As had Mary
Fenn Davis, many had survived unhappy marriages that ended in
divorce or desertion, and all had been directly affected by the complex of social norms that surrounded the marriage institution.

Although Spiritualists agreed that marriage as they knew it was oppressive to women, few went as far as Achsa Sprague in rejecting
marriage altogether. Most Spiritualists applauded loving unions between women and men but condemned the conditions imposed on
such unions by a society that made women subservient to men. "The
present marriage law is a failure . . . fettering two beings in external-
ity, but sundering them wide as the poles in the marriage of Natures,"
pronounced Emma Hardinge in trance at Boston's Melodeon Hall.
She found marriage onerous enough to avoid it for the first fifteen
years of her mediumship but did eventually marry in 1870 at the age
of forty-seven.[3] Spiritualists recognized that a new order in which
women enjoyed complete equality must include a revision of men's
roles in relation to women and especially a reformation of the relationship between women and men in marriage. They hoped to reform marriage by applying their individualist principles to the most
intimate areas of human life. They used the same concepts that
guided their campaigns for social change to criticize the relations between husbands and wives, the choice of marriage partners, the relations of parents and children, and the nature and amount of sexual
intercourse both inside and outside marriage. The same individualism that encouraged mediumship called into question all social relations that placed one person in a position of authority over another.
The example of self-supporting mediums also drew into question the
assumption that women needed men for material support. During a
period that placed marriage on a pedestal and banned the discussion
of sexuality in public and often in private as well, Spiritualists insisted
on a frank and open analysis of the personal, political, and economic
implications of all personal and sexual relations. The critique of marriage formed the central plank of the Spiritualist woman's rights platform.

Advocates of individual sovereignty attacked the institution of marriage because it conflicted with women's self-ownership and put the
weight of the state behind slavery to oppressive customs. Spiritualists
complained that the marriage laws "robbed the wife of her child, her
property, of her name, and of her individuality." But, worst of all,

married women shared a specific disability with those legally enslaved because, once married, they lacked the legal right to control their own bodies. Both the state and the church granted husbands unlimited sexual access to their wives. Women had no legal right to refuse their husbands' sexual advances or to prevent the resulting pregnancies. In strikingly modern language, Spiritualists complained, "Rape is punished *out* of wedlock but *in it* paid no attention to." Mediums decried the "body and soul destroying marriage institution." [4]

Spiritualists believed that marriage commonly resulted from parental or social pressure, women's lack of economic alternatives, and men's lust. They wished to elevate marriage to a higher moral plane so that it would become "a soul union, not a curse." In place of conventional marriages in which women relinquished their autonomy in exchange for economic support, Spiritualists proposed an egalitarian bond based on mutual spiritual attraction. "There is no real marriage, but the marriage of affection," they insisted. Individualists as always, they replaced parental wisdom, social sanction, and economic expediency with the internal promptings of the individual heart as the basis for forming a marriage. The *Plain Guide to Spiritualism* pronounced "all marriages and all sexual cohabitings as false and infernal, unless they are based on spiritual affections and are under the purer influences of celestial harmony." [5]

Hearkening back to the Fourierist theory of "passional attraction," some Spiritualists advanced a doctrine of "spiritual affinities," arguing that the natural order contained one true mate for every individual and that the union of true affinities endured forever. Individuals who did not find their one spiritual partner on earth would find him or her in heaven. Advocates of the doctrine of affinities expounded a spiritualized view of human sexuality. Charles S. Woodruff, M.D., author of *Legalized Prostitution: or, Marriage As It Is, and Marriage As It Should Be*, considered the "Procreative power" to be "man's most Godlike attribute." He described the attraction of affinities to each other as resulting from the operation of the "two great powers in nature," magnetism and electricity. This process evinced "the God principles at work" in each human being." [6] Henry Wright concurred on the religious significance of sexuality. He found that "no man can be what he was designed to be, till by marriage, the spirit of a woman has entered into him, to refine, beautify and strengthen his peculiar nature, and assimilate it to the divine." Likewise, he viewed the influence of husbands on their wives as equally necessary to women's spiritual development. Wright understood marriage as part of a sexualized divine reality. In an article entitled "God as a Woman," he explained that, just as the man Jesus served as savior for women, so woman provided the savior for men.[7]

Spiritualists distinguished carefully between true affection and sensual attraction. "To be carnally minded is death," warned trance speaker Laura Cuppy. They argued that true marriages could result only from spiritual attraction. At a national convention, Henry Wright introduced a resolution committing Spiritualists "to avoid all customs, habits and practices that tend to develop and strengthen the animal appetites and passions at the expense of the higher and more spiritual elements of our nature." Yet Spiritualists viewed conjugal love as an exalted ideal and appropriate sexual feelings as part of the natural order that drew affinities together. "All the passions . . . are, in their ideal conception, good and noble," explained medium Charlotte Beebe Wilbour, "and only become vices when they become warped and contorted by the inadequacy of the corporeal medium through which they attempt to realize themselves in acts."[8]

Spiritualists attributed dire consequences to false marriages and hoped for great things from true ones. "The True basis of reform by which the organization [humanity] is to be perfected may be traced ultimately to the union of the sexes," wrote an Ohioan in the *Spirit Messenger*. The writer argued that drunkenness, obscenity, licentiousness, and prostitution could not be cured by methods that attacked their symptoms but left intact the false marriages that caused them. "The church or the state can make wedlock, but never marriage," the writer claimed. But he expected the "true marriage of persons of good physical organization" to result in "high moral and intellectual development, and an exalted spirituality" that would ultimately produce "a race which shall have no . . . propensity for wrong doing."[9]

Marrying for Money

Medium Lizzie Doten asserted that fewer women would marry if they had wages equal to men's and therefore had the option of supporting themselves. She advocated legislation requiring employers to pay women equal wages for equal work. Doten, dependent on her own hard-earned resources from an early age, knew how few economic alternatives women had to marriage. She had supported herself by teaching and sewing before becoming a trance speaker and writer. "The remuneration denied woman for her labor is niggardly, for by it woman is . . . driven to crime, degradation, and prostitution," Mary Fenn Davis told the huge crowd at the Rutland Convention. Spiritualists viewed women's economic independence as a prerequisite to true marriage. "Above all it is important . . . to open up the sources of industrial enterprise to woman, that she may support herself. . . . Until she can do this she cannot get the love and respect she craves." Financial necessity could not result in true marriage.[10]

Spiritualist fiction, like Lizzie Doten's short story "Marrying for Money," frequently focused on the pressure on women to enter loveless matches out of economic necessity. Epes Sargent's feminist-Spiritualist-abolitionist novel *Peculiar* described the common plight of slaves and defenseless wives forced into legal subjugation to unscrupulous men through economic exchange. It paralleled the story of a virtuous slave, sold down the river by a fickle owner, with that of an innocent white woman, "First sold by a needy parent to an old man, and then betrayed by her own uncalculating affections to a young one." The young husband feigned adoration, until his bride's expected inheritance failed to materialize. Spiritualists portrayed marriage as a perilous venture for women. "The law has no lash, no prison" for "the scoundrel who tricks a confiding woman out of her freedom," Sargent complained. "Success consecrates the crime; and the victim, when her eyes are at length opened to the extent of the deception and the misery, must continue to submit, unless she is willing to brave the ban of society and the persecutions of the law."[11]

Spiritualists saw a direct connection between economic and sexual subjugation. They compared marriage to prostitution because both gave men sexual access to women in exchange for economic support. "The law grants the husband a right to the person of his wife," said Mary Davis, "and from this has grown up the system of legal prostitution, to the gratification of lust."[12] Their critique of marriage engendered sympathy for prostitutes who worked for money. They argued that the double standard forced women into prostitution by leaving no other means of support for women shunned by society because they were the victims of seduction. Lois Waisbrooker criticized the hypocrisy of those who condoned marriage but condemned prostitution. "Women prostitute their bodies daily to the abuse of legal brutes, called husbands," she wrote, "and, *calling them virtuous,* shrink from the very touch of the garments of the more womanly woman who is prostitute illegally—forced thereto by the damnable edict of respectability, because she loved in purity of soul and *trusted illegally.*"[13]

Mediums were especially concerned by the plight of prostitutes. Emma Hardinge, the most conservative of the popular trance speakers, tried to secure the support of Spiritualists across the nation for her "Plan for a Self-Sustaining Institution for Homeless and Outcast Women." During the early 1860s, she lectured and tried to raise money for this project. Mediums Melvina Townsend and Anna Middlebrook supported the project and helped keep it before the public.[14] The project attracted a good deal of attention, including a mass meeting at Cooper Union, a petition campaign, and Hardinge's personal appeal to the New York State legislature for an appropriation. But Spiritualists refused to provide material support. A collection at the huge Abington Grove Meeting netted only twenty dollars, and Hardinge felt compelled to abandon the project until "such time as the public mind should be free to sympathize with such a movement."[15]

Hardinge's project undoubtedly suffered from Spiritualists' distaste for organizations and suspicion of permanent institutions, which doomed all such proposals. But Hardinge also received articulate opposition from her more radical coreligionists. They criticized her proposal because it treated a symptom of women's oppression while ignoring its underlying cause. Whereas landlords refused to rent to Hardinge because the inmates of her house would not be "respectable," radical women objected that this and similar proposals perpetuated the double standard by placing men and women on different "moral planes." The women's opposition shocked male proponents. "The only true method for the reform of 'outcast females' (so called)," according to medium Mary Thomas, "is not to exclude them from the world in houses of refuge or reform, but to place them on an equality with their seducers . . . extending to each equal opportunities, . . . equal sympathy as well as equal condemnation." Mrs. H. M. F. Brown and Juliet Stillman agreed that, if women had rights, could vote, and could support themselves, they would not need protection or charity. In their view, the prostitute's plight only dramatized the common situation of women in general, all of whom had to choose between sexual exploitation and destitution.[16]

Lizzie Doten also criticized Hardinge's proposal to reform prostitutes because she thought that moral reform was meaningless without economic opportunity. She urged society to provide alternatives so that women would not have to enter prostitution. Most damning of all to conventional morality, Doten suggested that many women appreciated the advantages of life in prostitution. "Kind hearted women" who attempted to aid their fallen sisters in returning to a "path of virtue" actually "envy the lot of the prostitute, as better than their own," she claimed.[17]

Perhaps mediums identified with prostitutes because they perceived parallels in the nature and conditions of their work. At a convention in Maine, a medium was controlled by a spirit who gave an account of "her unfortunate condition in the form as a prostitute at Five Points."[18] The belief that spirits took over the medium's organism and used it as a vehicle for their own ends suggests that mediumship, like prostitution, could involve relinquishing the use of one's body for pay. An unconscious woman in a séance room faced the same vulnerability encountered by prostitutes, although to a lesser extent. Medium Mattie Hull, infamous for her "free marriage" with her lecture partner Moses Hull, remarked late in life that "fully two thirds of those who go to mediums . . . go with the direct intention of being alone with a lady, and offering an insult. Others by their very first question show that they are in Spiritualism for the 'loaves and fishes'—in other words, to prostitute it to mercenary purposes."[19]

Mediums viewed their susceptibility to spirits as they did their sexuality; it was something that could be either exalted or debased, depending on the conditions under which it was practiced. In a "Defense of Mediumship," Mrs. M. J. Wilcoxen told the story of a promising young medium taken advantage of by an unscrupulous man, "one of the sharks of carnal ambition," who hoped to enrich himself at the medium's expense. Under his management, "all kinds of promiscuous magnetisms were admitted to the mediumistic circle, to say nothing of the positive, oppressive, and even tyrannizing influence of his . . . impetuous and exacting disposition." Under these conditions, the manifestations gradually "assumed the character of sheer imposture," and the medium was publicly denounced. Her mediumship discredited, she became even more dependent on her exploiter. "Too poor and lonely to make her own terms; with no means of procuring subsistence, she consented, as the sewing woman consents to the terms of her employer, with an arrow in her soul, and only a choice between the two, mediumship and proscription—shall I say prostitution?"[20]

Wilcoxen's description of the choice between mediumship and prostitution may have been realistic. Mediums, like prostitutes, were shunned by "respectable" society and excluded from other employment or from advantageous marriages because of their profession. Mediums' public roles and heterodox beliefs placed them outside accepted standards of respectability. Thus, they shared to some extent the risks prostitutes experienced because they were assumed to be "loose" women. Most important, mediums and prostitutes shared an acute awareness of the limited economic alternatives to marriage and the thin line that separated all women from destitution.

The women who agitated the reform of marriage had firsthand experience of the wrongs they attacked. Mary Fenn Davis's marital history has already been recounted. One of the most outspoken critics of marriage, Mary Gove Nichols, fled an abusive marriage, returning with her child to her father's home. In an autobiographical novel, she portrayed her first husband, Hiram Gove, as brutal and greedy. He left her in peace because he owed her father money but repossessed their daughter on her father's death. Mary was forced to kidnap her daughter and flee across the state line since the father automatically retained legal custody of the child.[21] Although little is known of the biography of Mrs. Hannah F. M. Brown, she was apparently divorced before she began her career as a newspaper editor. Warren Chase recorded that he met her in 1856 "still struggling in bondage, and waiting for freedom impatiently, which she soon after found."[22]

Cora Wilburn and Lizzie Doten, who never married, criticized the marriage-centered social order from the outside. Their difficulties as single women made them appreciate the extent to which women were coerced into marriage. Before becoming Spiritualists, both earned a meager living by sewing. According to Doten, this was not unusual for mediums."Many of us were educated in the kitchen or the workshop or on the farm. The first time I spoke in Boston, my hands were blistered with work, by which I was earning my living."[23] While Doten achieved independence as a premier trance speaker, Wilburn, an immensely popular Spiritualist author, escaped poverty only briefly. Well educated and raised in luxury in a Southern family of German Jews, Wilburn had been orphaned and left insolvent. "Now many throng around me. . . . My penned thoughts and impressions are lauded," she wrote in 1860. But this was not always the case:

Seven years ago, none praised me. . . . *I was a toiler at my needle, then,* and *aristocratic Spiritualism* knew me not. And yet, I could lay claim to

most of the attributes of *ladyhood*. I had been a dweller in sunny southern climes, unaccustomed to labor of any kind; an only child, *and a
spoiled one*. Worldly reverses made of me, (for my soul's good) one of
the sisterhood of toil. . . . Who aided me in my investigation of my
own soul's destiny? Humanity did not, but God and His ministering
spirits did.[24]

Wilburn's material success lasted only a few years; she was never able
to support herself independently after the Civil War. Although she
continued to be a much-beloved journalist, she became dependent on
the generosity of others, traveling between the homes of friends, unable to sustain a home of her own. Her experience demonstrated that
all women hovered on the brink of poverty in a society that expected
women to depend on the support of husbands.[25] Similarly, medium
Julia Schlesinger attributed to "bitter personal experience" her view
that only through individual freedom and financial independence
"can woman be lifted above the power of men of low moral character
to crush and enslave." Perhaps more than the leaders of the woman
suffrage movement, Spiritualist woman's rights advocates had personal knowledge of the oppressive results of the marriage system.[26]

Enforced Motherhood

"The most sacred and important right of woman," Spiritualists asserted, "is her right to decide for herself how often and under what
circumstances she shall assume the responsibilities and be subjected
to the cares . . . of maternity." "Man can commit no greater crime,"
they concurred, "than to impose on her a maternity . . . she is not
willing to accept."[27] If marriage was to be distinguished from prostitution, not only its economic but also its sexual basis must be transformed. When the Eighth National Woman's Rights Convention met
in 1858, Henry C. Wright congratulated its participants for having
caught up with the Spiritualists because they had finally discussed a
resolution supporting a woman's right to decide for herself whether
to bear a child. "The millions of spiritualists . . . are prepared, better
than any other class of people, to respect and vindicate woman's
rights in regard to maternity, and the relation in which it originates,"
he observed.[28] In an age without effective contraception, women inevitably linked the decision of when and how often to engage in sexual activity with the decision of when to have children. "Woman's
rights in regard to maternity" meant that most Victorian of all wom-

an's rights, the right of wives to withhold sexual access from their husbands, a right the law denied.

Spiritualists understood men's unrestrained sexual desire as a threat to women's autonomy:

> Wives are brutalized by their husband's passions, until threatened with death from physical drain of repeated pregnancy. Unwanted maternity turns mothers into murderers and abortionists. [The husband] pleads his legal rights, and the priest, the law, and the marriage institution sustain him. . . . Nothing short of giving woman the right to control her own person, and to say when and under what circumstances she is willing to take upon herself the maternal relation, will remedy this great evil.[29]

Spiritualists blamed men for enforced motherhood, with its concomitant liabilities. "There is no joy on earth compared to that of a *willing* mother, and no sorrow to that of an unwilling one. And what but *man's* animal passions ever make unwilling ones?" asked Mrs. S. H. Walls in the *Banner of Light.* To a male correspondent who blamed unwanted pregnancies on women's ignorance, she responded emphatically, "This is not so." Marriage reformers insisted that, if women controlled sexuality, there would be fewer, better children. "There is not one child in a hundred, that is begotten with the consent of the mother," argued Dr. Juliet Stillman Severance, a mother of three. She viewed enforced maternity as one more impediment to women's entering the professions or other gainful occupations. "There is no more reason why all women should be housekeepers and mothers than that all men should be farmers and fathers," she said.[30]

The declining birthrates of the period suggest that Spiritualist rhetoric reflected popular sentiment. Women bore progressively fewer children throughout the nineteenth century, and the decade 1840–50, which produced the doctrine of affinities and the spiritualized marriage, showed the greatest decline in the birthrate of any decade. Apparently, married women increasingly limited intercourse with their husbands. Spiritualist diatribes against the sexual exploitation of women by their husbands persisted even after domestic feminism and Victorian mores reduced the average number of births per woman from 7.04 at the beginning of the century to 3.56 by the end.[31]

The decline in marital fertility coincided with an ideological elevation of motherhood throughout American culture. It was precisely because Spiritualists concurred that motherhood was a sacred calling that they insisted that it must not be taken on lightly. Cora Wilburn extolled the "Holy function of reproduction." "That which should be the expression of the highest, purest love, the spiritualized actualization of the fond parental heart in the formation of angelic souls," Wilburn wrote, "is desecrated to mere animal gratification; and the child of lust and perversity is the unlooked for accident of such unholy procedure." In a poem called "The Divine Maternity," Mary Fenn Davis gave a Spiritualist version of the nineteenth-century understanding of the religious significance of motherhood. "Very near to the heart of God—. . . / Is the sacred heart of Woman—/ The nature through which alone / The Divine can become embodied, / and the spirit reach its home." Medium Ella Gibson discoursed on the spiritual significance of the three trimesters of pregnancy in a pamphlet on "soul-marriage."[32]

As Linda Gordon has observed, a broad spectrum of nineteenth-century women's groups advocated voluntary motherhood. The right of women to limit fertility was a rare point of agreement uniting radicals, mainstream suffragists, and conservative temperance and social purity advocates. Although Spiritualists shared little with conservative women's groups, they sound remarkably similar on this issue. Spiritualism contributed leaders to two other movements concerned with voluntary motherhood: Lucinda Chandler to social purity and Alice Stockham to sex education. Spiritualists differed from other groups in opposing enforced maternity earlier in the century and in insisting on a frank discussion of the issue. Unconcerned by the delicacy of the topic, they occasionally risked jail to assert the need for a graphic discussion of sex and procreation.[33]

Free Love

While Spiritualists disagreed about whether marriage was morally salvageable, their agreement on the immorality of marriage as practiced in mid-century America led to the charge that they advocated free love. *Free love* is a problematic term for the historian because it was more frequently an accusation leveled at others than a positive self-identification. Generally understood to mean opposition to marriage as an institution, many who applied the label to themselves fell far short of this extreme position. Proponents used it to refer to their opposition to marriage laws that discriminated against women, while detractors used it as a synonym for promiscuity or infidelity. Similar to the term *communist* in twentieth-century America, free love often denoted a basic undermining of accepted values. Support for marriage as an institution became a litmus test by which conservatives (the *New York Times*, e.g.) judged the morality of reformers. Those wary of radicals classed Spiritualists, socialists, and woman's rights advocates together as sympathizers with the bogeyman of radicalism, free love.[34]

The accusation of free love was a common weapon in the arsenal of Spiritualism's enemies. John Ellis, who dedicated his five-hundred-page exposé of free love to "the advocates of Christian marriage," concluded that approximately four million Spiritualists in the United States were "all more or less committed to the doctrine of Free Love." He charged that, "even though he does not practice it, the Spiritualist is bound to uphold the doctrine, since it is part of his peculiar creed." The suspicious public who feared free love believed that it threatened the family and the structure of society.[35]

While the term *free love* was infamous in mid-century America, the actual doctrines advocated by its adherents were usually quite tame. Free love in the nineteenth century did not imply the principle of sexual permissiveness that the phrase suggests to the twentieth-century reader. Rather, it referred to the belief that the morality of sexual intercourse depended on freely experienced compelling mutual desire—that is, love—*not* on whether the parties were married. It applied strict tests of morality to all sexual relations, whether within or without lawful marriage. Far from advocating casual or frequent sexual contacts, "free lovers" concurred with other health reformers that Americans had far too much sex, most of it within marriage. Vivian Grey wrote to the *Social Revolutionist* that sexual slavery in marriage destroyed the health of American women because submitting to sex without love was physically debilitating. Following the advice of Spiritualist free love theorist Thomas Low Nichols would result in a married couple having intercourse only as often as they had children. Because the conjugal rights described by marriage laws were generally understood to guarantee a man's sexual access to his wife rather than a woman's sexual access to her husband, free love meant the freedom of women to refuse their husbands' sexual advances, a potentially powerful source of autonomy in an age without contraception and with little notion of sexual satisfaction for women.[36]

Spiritualist free love advocates advanced the controversial doctrine as one aspect of woman's emancipation, as a remedy for abusive marriages. "Where woman is degraded by a drunkard or a sensualist's rule, let her make herself free," advised a popular Spiritualist writer. In keeping with their anarchist tendencies, Spiritualists believed that state sanction could not impute morality to a sexual relation. Only lovers brought together by God-given natural impulses acted morally. If husband and wife ceased to feel true love for each other, they should cease sexual contact and live as brother and sister. Free love proponents called for liberalized divorce laws because they believed that if spouses did not love each other sexual contact became immoral, even within a lawful marriage.[37]

Most Spiritualists did not support free love, but most free love advocates were Spiritualists, so the movements were widely linked in the popular mind. Notably, figures such as Mary Gove Nichols and Victoria Woodhull espoused Spiritualism during their brief phases as free love activists, although they later recanted their unorthodox stands on both sex and religion. This radical minority benefited from Spiritualists' commitment to free speech and expressed its position as a consistent application of the familiar concept of individual sovereignty. When a speaker at a New York State convention claimed that Spiritualism had nothing to do with "Free-Love, Abolition or Women's Rights," *Agitator* editor Mrs. H. M. F. Brown asked, "What has it to do with anything if it ignores the discussion of the three great questions of the day?"[38]

Radical Spiritualists agreed that Spiritualism had everything to do with these three movements and all for the same reason: free love, abolition, and woman's rights all sought to liberate the individual from physical and spiritual domination by others and from the oppressive power of the state. Each movement spelled out one set of results of the consistent application of the principle of individual sovereignty. Spiritualist socialist Alfred Cridge argued, "The philosophy of Spirit existence . . . clearly demonstrates the necessity of freedom in all relations, to Spiritual progress." Because he believed that "the sexual, conjugal, and parental relations" were "the most important that human beings can sustain to each other," he viewed complete freedom as especially important in these areas. Cridge argued that "discordant social relations operate to attract low spirits" because the spouse who attained a high level of spiritual development would be exposed to the spirits attracted by the spouse at a lower level. Mediums in particular could suffer from the influence of "low spirits" attracted by a spouse. Spiritual progress, Cridge concluded, depended

on two conditions that could be created only by the practice of free
love:

> first; power to dissolve all uncongenial and false relations;—to indi-
> vidualize, and disintegrate ourselves from the incongruous mass to
> which we are held, not by inward attraction, but by the outward forces
> of law and physical necessity. . . . This constitutes the elements of indi-
> vidual Sovereignty or FREEDOM. The second step is to co-operate; to
> follow our attractions; to form true business and domestic relations;—
> or, in other words, to LOVE. Thus we obtain the elements of Freedom
> and Love, forming, in combination, FREE-LOVE. This then, being the
> essence of Spiritual progress, FREE LOVE is the doctrine of Spiritual-
> ism.[39]

Cridge has been identified by a historian of free love as an opponent
of the movement because he believed that marriage was the symptom,
not the cause, of social oppression. Yet he clearly advocates free love
in this passage.

During the 1850s, a surprising array of Spiritualists accepted the
label "free lover" without rejecting marriage as an institution. Only a
handful of extremists wanted to abolish marriage altogether, while
many Spiritualists accepted a definition of free love that respected
marriage and proposed to elevate it to a higher level. In fact, far from
avoiding marriage, advocates of free love engaged in it more frequently than those who waited "until parted by death" to marry
again. They believed that marriages should be easier to terminate,
not more difficult to contract. They advocated free love because they
wanted to free marriage from the debasing interference of the state
and of pecuniary interests; they did not want to abolish it. Spiritualists Thomas and Mary Gove Nichols, Alfred and Annie Denton
Cridge, and Lois Waisbrooker advocated free love because they
viewed marriage as a sacred institution and believed that false marriages were immoral and should be more easily dissolved.[40]

An exchange regarding "Marriage and Individual Sovereignty" in
the *Vanguard* directly addressed the question of whether marriage
was the cause or the symptom of women's oppression. John Patterson,
editor of the *Vanguard's* predecessor, the *Social Revolutionist*, criticized
editors Alfred and Anne Denton Cridge for being unfaithful to individualist principles by being married. According to Patterson, marriage, including the Cridge marriage, was "incompatible with the individual sovereignty of woman." Alfred Cridge replied that the
problem lay with the oppression of women, not with the institution

of marriage. Cridge appealed to both individual and social reform as solutions to women's disabilities rather than to the abolition of marriage. He attributed the oppression of women in marriage to the low level of development of the particular spouses, not to the institution of marriage. He cited himself and his wife as evidence for the compatibility of matrimony with self-sovereignty in the case of enlightened individuals and, "hence, we infer, for others who are developed above the sphere of despotism, and congenially mated." Cridge asserted that those who had not attained his own level of individual development "will be despotic in any relation." To alleviate the disabilities suffered by married women, Cridge prescribed woman's rights. "When woman has her rights, her slavery is annihilated—not her marriage. Woman is deprived of her rights because she is a woman, not because she is married."[41]

Patterson retorted that women could never be free within marriage. He compared granting rights to women within marriage to alleviating the conditions of slaves without abolishing slavery. "Any rights a woman gains within marriage are at the whim of her husband." Patterson's position was the more accurate portrayal of the law. Single women lost many rights with their "legal death" on marriage. They lost the rights to own property, to enter into contracts, and to conduct business without the consent of their husbands, not because they were women, but because they were married.[42]

Anne Denton Cridge also disagreed with Patterson's condemnation of her marriage, but on different grounds from her husband. She agreed that marriage had restricted her freedom because it had resulted in the birth of a child. However, she argued that marriage had also freed her because she wanted a child, and marriage gave her the opportunity to have one. This intimate journalistic meeting of the personal and the political ended abruptly with the unexpected death of the Cridge baby. Discussion of the morality of the Cridge marriage gave way to expositions of parental grief in the pages of the *Vanguard*.[43]

Anne Denton Cridge wanted self-sovereignty, but she also wanted a family and knew by experience that the latter goal might require some compromise of the first. Spiritualists who advocated free love in addition to marriage, rather than as an alternative, recognized the potential victimization of women in the context of sexual freedom. Transient alliances might deprive women of the opportunity to have children or leave them unable to support their offspring. By attacking

women's disabilities within marriage while simultaneously elevating
the ideal of marriage as a spiritual union, Spiritualists hoped to free
women from threats to their autonomy both in marriage and outside it.[44]

Newspaper editor Mrs. H. M. F. Brown illustrates free love proponents' support for marriage. A longtime advocate of free love, she
sought a license to perform weddings from the state of Illinois as a
representative of the Religio-Philosophical Society. She received the
license and officiated at Spiritualist weddings. When a young couple
came forward and asked to be married at the annual "Festival" of the
Religio-Philosophical Society in 1865, Mrs. Brown obliged. She "dealt
some severe blows against the marriage laws," detailing the numerous
legal disabilities to which marriage exposed women. "She pled for the
equality of wife and husband before the law as they are before God."
Brown censured parents who "suffered their children to rush
blindly to the marriage altar," condemning "Mothers and fathers
[who] sell their beautiful innocent daughters for homes, a main-
tenance, and positions." In a final rhetorical flourish, Mrs. Brown concluded that false marriages were the root cause of all the "heart-
aches, the suicides, the jealousies, elopements, insanity, drunkenness, and in fact all the ills and curses that call for prisons, asylums, doctors and preachers."[45]

Brown followed this bitter indictment of the marriage laws with a
glowing description of the "peace, good-will and holy aspirations"
produced by *"true* soul unions." She reminded the bride and groom
that "wedded hearts had no need of legislation to keep them together,
they were bound by natural, by eternal laws, and could not, would
not, *dis*-unite." After further remarks, Mrs. Brown performed the
marriage, in a ceremony similar to the Quaker rite. She directed the
couple to link right hands in recognition that "your hearts are already
united, and that you only ask public recognition of the marriage already registered in heaven." She then pronounced them husband and
wife. Each week, the *Religio-Philosophical Journal* reported the names
of couples committed to free love principles by participating in this
unusual rite. Spiritualists turned the meaning of the marriage ceremony on its head by making it an occasion for the declaration of
woman's freedom rather than her subjugation.[46]

The rejection of marriage was more characteristic of communitarian movements led by charismatic male mediums than of free love as
expressed by independent Spiritualists. Free love was most closely

identified with John Murray Spear's Kiantone community in upstate New York, with the non-Spiritualist Oneida community inspired and governed by John Humphrey Noyse, with the activities of Stephen Pearl Andrews and Thomas and Mary Gove Nichols at Josiah Warren's Modern Times on Long Island, and with the socialist Berlin Heights Community in Ohio.[47] These experiments made temporary alliances viable because the community replaced the couple as the source of permanent care for children. Mary Gove Nichols saw the cooperative economic and social arrangements of Modern Times as offering "a new future for women." In order for women to realize health and freedom, purity and happiness, she argued, they must be self supporting; "so long as man feeds, he must control." Modern Times proposed cooperative nursery, laundry, and cooking facilities to ensure women's freedom *and* to provide for the inhabitants' material needs.[48] Yet, with all the material objections to transient relationships answered, Nichols still considered marriage "a sacrament," which could not be made by law. "If any should wish to separate and form new unions, I doubt not they will do so, and not live in falsehood and discord." Still, she observed that most at Modern Times were "loyal husbands and wives, because they preferred to be." In the long run, utopian free love communities proved too short lived to fulfill their promise to provide women with an alternative to marriage for the raising of children. When communities practiced free love as understood by the general public, few Spiritualists condoned the situation. Even the radical Elmer Louden, who found so much about free love attractive, was repelled by a visit to the Berlin Heights community and professed himself "perfectly content to let them wallow in their licentiousness."[49]

At the Rutland Free Convention, infamous for its free love debates, the medium Mrs. Julia Branch presented the antimarriage position. "It is woman's privilege to accept or refuse any love that comes to her," proclaimed Mrs. Branch, "and when her love has died out, she is no longer a fit partner for the man who has taken her to his heart." She proposed to substitute a resolution stating "that the slavery and degradation of woman proceeds from the institution of marriage" for the more moderate resolution on egalitarian marriage adopted by the predominantly Spiritualist convention. But Branch backed down when pressed as to whether she wished to be interpreted as advocating the exercise of male lust unrestrained, a result that most Spiritualists viewed as inevitable if marriage was abolished altogether.[50]

Whereas a few were willing to advocate sexual relations outside marriage, very few were willing to put their views into practice, or at least to do so openly. Even "varietist" free lovers, who believed that true love could occur with more than one person in a lifetime, never advocated promiscuity. Spiritualist author and lecturer Moses Hull announced his free love views in 1873 in *Woodhull and Claflin's Weekly.* He believed that people needed changes of sex partners just as they needed changes of scenery. His wife concurred, and they dissolved their marriage by mutual proclamation. Hull soon announced his "free marriage" to his lecture partner, Mattie Sawyer. They considered their union to be a marriage, although contracted without benefit of judge or clergy. Likewise, Spiritualists Leo Miller and Mattie Strickland entered into a notorious free union in 1876 because they believed that they were spiritual affinities, not because they sought a temporary sexual relation.[51]

Because the term *free love* had no clear definition, reformers often said that they accepted free love if it meant one thing but not if it meant another. The meaning of the term differed depending on whether it was being used as an accusation or a description. "There are two meanings of Free Love, one high and holy . . . , another low, debased . . . meaning . . . free lust," said trance speaker Lizzie Doten. She attributed the latter meaning to misguided male Spiritualists. "The man with a badly regulated love principle will go to a woman, and . . . let her know that a sentiment of affinity draws him toward her. . . . And they charge this self delusion to Spiritualism. Distrust the Spiritualism that says it is so." While Doten did not deny the doctrine of affinities, she asserted that a "properly regulated love principle will not entertain the idea of possession of another man's wife." She was prepared to support free love so long as it did not compromise marriage.[52] Trance speaker Achsa Sprague, on the other hand, decried marriage but refused the label "free love." *"You decidedly misunderstand me,"* she wrote to a newspaper to correct the impression that she taught free love. "I only spoke against the injustice of *all* Laws, the Laws of marriage among them," Sprague declared, in an explanation that would have confirmed to many that she did in fact advocate free love.[53]

"Free-love, as I accept it, is to love in my Father's world all that is lovable, admirable and good," wrote Cora Wilburn. Wilburn, a social conservative known for her sentimental fiction and poetry, viewed free love as a stand against all oppression:

I protest . . . against all forms of slavery, against the sale of my black brother and sister . . . against the education and sale of maidens for the marriage altar . . . against the tyranny of labor, as it is enjoined in our northern cities, in our factories, in our households . . . ; the hardheartedness of landlords, the tasking of the wretched seamstress, the burdening of orphans and widows with the double weight of humiliation and toil, . . . the starvation wages that force young women into the paths of degradation.

Wilburn hoped that free love would eradicate "the saddest captivity of all" by bringing "release from the dominion of the senses, . . . liberty from the bondage of the passions, . . . the resurrection of the soul life of love and freedom from the environments of gross, debasing sensualism."[54] While Wilburn understood the absence of sensual desire as freedom, others might interpret it as repression, the antithesis of Spiritualist individualism. Wilburn's interpretation of free love clarifies how the espousal of the infamous doctrine could be part of the assertion of a conservative domestic ideology. "Woman's mission in this age is with the spiritual faculties," Wilburn claimed; "she has been long even as the beast of burden; she had been the unholy idol, the fashionable goddess; she must become the true woman, the pure angel, now!"[55]

Spiritualist free love proponents clearly did not intend to increase men's sexual access to women or to condone sex outside marriage. They condemned the betrayer of innocence who seduces a young girl on a promise of marriage and then disappears, leaving her a victim of the double standard.[56] Spiritualists showed their sympathy to victims of male lust in their response to the much-publicized divorce suit of the young medium Cora Hatch. The seventeen-year-old trance speaker convinced a New York court to grant her a divorce because her husband and manager, Benjamin Hatch, took advantage of her youth to abuse her both financially and sexually. Benjamin Hatch responded with a pamphlet titled *Spiritualist Iniquities Unmasked,* which attributed the breakup of his marriage to his wife's mediumship. He accepted the reality of spirit communication but claimed that mediumship always led to marital discord because only the lowest "class" of spirits remained close enough to earth to influence mediums. He accused mediums generally of infidelity, named specific instances, and assigned the cause to the practice of Spiritualism.[57]

Spiritualists jumped to defend the honor of their mediums and the practice of their faith. The public discussion of the unseemly details of Cora Hatch's conjugal relations drew tremendous sympathy from the Spiritualist public. While the secular press applied the double standard of morality to Cora, as they would to any woman who sought a divorce, the Spiritualist press defended her action. "This result of the marriage of a girl but sixteen years of age, of pure benevolent disposition, with a man nearly three-fold her years, of an avaricious, mercenary cast of character, has been long anticipated."[58] Other mediums responded with trance lectures in Cora's support. Lizzie Doten spoke in trance on the text "Let he that is without sin among you cast the first stone." Without mentioning names, she blamed marital difficulties on the "badly regulated love principle" of errant husbands and urged that a woman of "delicate nature . . . craving sympathy" who goes astray receive sympathy, not condemnation. Emma Hardinge responded with a trance lecture entitled "Marriage," critical of the marriage laws, which the *Banner of Light* declared the most able yet given about a subject "on which so much happiness and misery depends."[59] Twelve years (and two additional marriages) later, Cora Hatch won praise for her divorce suit from woman's rights advocate Paulina Wright Davis, who recalled that Cora "practically protested false and unholy marriage, because purity and harmony were necessities of her life."[60]

Spiritualists' critique of marriage and Free Love itself were part of the nineteenth-century elevation of the roles of wife and mother and increased respect for the domestic sphere. Discussing the relation between free love and marriage, Alfred Cridge claimed, "We are free not because we have risen above [marriage], but because we have risen up to it."[61] Once again, Spiritualists pushed Victorian mores to their logical extreme. If marriage were indeed so sacred as nineteenth-century moralists claimed, then it needed no legal sanction to regulate it. If motherhood were a sacred calling, it could not be entered into involuntarily. Spiritualists drew radical implications from domestic ideals.

Late Nineteenth-Century Sex Radicalism

Probably the nineteenth-century figure most closely associated with free love is Victoria Woodhull. Her extreme antimarriage position, however, was not typical of free love advocates. As Hal Sears has observed, her short-lived but widely publicized free love agitation in the early 1870s marked a watershed in the widespread discussion of sexual alternatives in nineteenth-century America, after which the topic's respectability greatly diminished.[62] Within a few years, Woodhull fled to a respectable marriage in England (her third) and denied her earlier views. Yet the Spiritualist sex radicals who had been discussing alternatives to traditional marriage for twenty years before Woodhull continued to do so for twenty years after her notoriety made the term *free love* almost unmentionable. Juliet Stillman Severance and fellow Spiritualist J. H. Cook still wrote "scientific" articles on "the number and duration of sex-loves" in the 1880s, when few reformers not dedicated exclusively to sex radicalism would touch the subject. The serious attention paid by Spiritualists as a group to the critique of marriage suggests that both men and women among them were dissatisfied with sexual relations in the nineteenth century.[63]

One figure stands out among Spiritualist lecturers who continued to agitate for the reform of marriage and sexuality long after entrenched Victorian values made their activities scandalous and sometimes illegal. Lois Waisbrooker was described by a contemporary as "a she Abraham Lincoln" whose compelling oratory evoked the image of Sojourner Truth, Margaret Fuller, and the actress Charlotte Cushman rolled into one. She described herself as an "untrammeled Spiritualist speaker," devoted to the intertwined reforms of woman's rights, free love, and Spiritualism. Waisbrooker's personal history remains mysterious, but she had clearly experienced the economic and social liabilities of unmarried women.[64] With no husband in evidence, she attempted to support her children by working as a domestic servant, but poverty and illness forced her to give them up to be raised by others. At the age of twenty-six, she resolved to pursue her education and became a teacher in black schools before the Civil War, a task then as disreputable as was her future career as an advocate of Spiritualism and free love. A brief second marriage when she was thirty convinced her of the immorality of the marriage laws. The content of Waisbrooker's prolific writings may provide clues to her biography. The seduction and betrayal of young women and the victimization of unwed mothers by the double standard constantly recur as themes in both her fiction and her nonfiction. Waisbrooker drew critical attention to the relation between the sexual and the economic exploitation of women in *The Sexual Question and the Money Power* and in her account of a feminist utopia, *A Sex Revolution*.[65]

"If I am what I am told by those on the other side . . . then for this cause came I into the world . . . to declare the truth as I see it," Waisbrooker wrote in the introduction to one of her books.[66] The "truth" as Waisbrooker saw it was that women were victimized by every aspect of contemporary morality. They suffered from the double standard that held them to stricter standards of behavior than men; they suffered from economic discrimination that forced them into loveless marriages; and they suffered from the belief that women were naturally passionless and that the presence of sexual desire reflected a lack of virtue. Waisbrooker believed that women's emancipation required both the restraint of male passion and the release of female sexual impulses.

Waisbrooker's attitude toward sexuality reflected her firm belief that the natural world, including natural human impulses, revealed the divine order of creation. Because desire was a natural property of human beings, she viewed it as good. Further, she insisted that each of us must accept our own sexuality in order to attain full self-respect, which she saw as "an absolute requirement as a basis for a noble character." Because she believed all humans experienced sexual desire, she saw society's negative attitudes toward sex as degrading to the self-images of all people. Women suffered most from this view because sexual desire was less acceptable in women than in men. "I came to womanhood with the idea that purity was without desire, and when my own nature awoke I despised myself because I could not subdue it," Waisbrooker quoted from "one of the most conscientious women" she knew.[67] Waisbrooker's insistence that human sexuality must be accepted in order to allow for self-respect shows the distance Spiritualism had traveled from the religious worldviews that preceded and surrounded it. Protestant orthodoxy asserted that salvation required a consciousness of oneself as inherently sinful by virtue of one's descent from Adam through the tainted process of sexual reproduction. In contrast, Waisbrooker believed that a consciousness of oneself as good, including a consciousness of one's sexuality, was a prerequisite to moral character and behavior. Far from abandoning the contemporary elevation of femininity, Waisbrooker insisted that the true woman had sexual feelings and that her purity was compromised by society's insistence that she deny them.

Waisbrooker tied her free love views directly to her religious beliefs. She attributed her ability to cut through the dishonesty and deception of conventional morality to Spiritualism's direct access to truth. As a Spiritualist, she believed that she was "no longer sitting in the shadow of reflected light, but clothed with the sun, with direct power." In her book *The Occult Power of Sex,* she argued that the magnetic forces that made spirit communication possible also powered the sex drive that drew individual men and women together. This same force was the source of religious enthusiasm. The "yearnings of youth," Waisbrooker contended, could be satisfied either by sex or by religion, and it was because they knew this that the clergy attempted to control sexuality. Waisbrooker viewed her struggle to emancipate human beings from uncongenial marriages and sexual relations and her struggle to emancipate souls from the dogma of conventional religion as one and the same.[68]

Waisbrooker was first arrested under the Comstock Antiobscenity Act in 1892. She was accused of printing obscene matter in her Kansas newspaper, *Foundation Principles,* which expounded "Humanitarian Spiritualism." The offending material consisted of an exchange between the editor and a male correspondent. The man described himself as an uncongenially wed middle-aged lawyer. He sought Waisbrooker's advice about his sexual relationship with a thirty-year-old unmarried woman because the woman wanted to discontinue their affair. "I love her dearly and do not want to do that which will cause her pain or regret, and yet we were made for each other, and for no other, and we need that exchange of sexual vitality that can only be had by free and unrestricted intercourse." The correspondent proposed that he and his lover occasionally meet away from home for a day or two, in order to enjoy the benefits of their sexual contact. He contended that "our relations are and would be pure and right according to the true law of nature" and clearly hoped that Waisbrooker would affirm his view and support the continuation of his relationship.[69]

Waisbrooker reprinted the letter in full in order to vent her opposition to the views of its author and of those who "think we are demanding freedom that we may revel in sensual pleasure." Instead of supporting the writer's call for freedom, she condemned his hypocrisy for remaining in a loveless marriage and seeking secret sex outside it. "What is the matter, my good sir, that you cannot adjust conditions so that you can fearlessly and openly take your loved one by the hand in the face of the world?" She castigated him for wanting to "secure the pleasure without the risk" by continuing the clandestine affair. "Should exposure follow, you, a man, can stand it, but where would she be in the eyes of the community? Do you *love* her and yet would subject her, through her love for you, to such a risk? If you cannot stand by her now, you could not stand then."[70]

Waisbrooker saw the source of her correspondent's dilemma *not* in the social sanctions against extramarital sex but rather in his willingness to remain in a loveless marriage. As a solution, she prescribed the dissolution of his false marriage, which would free him to follow his heart. She attributed his problem not to his lover's unwillingness to continue their affair in secret but to his own moral weakness for being unwilling to brave social ostracism and seek a divorce. Her solution moved the onus of loyalty to reform principles off the woman's shoulders and placed it squarely on those of her married lover.

Lois Waisbrooker's views illustrate the possible differences between men's and women's understandings of free love. The correspondent subscribed to Waisbrooker's paper and read her writings but used the concepts he found there to support the traditional double standard of morality that allowed men to seek sexual alliances outside marriage without risking the social respectability of the married state. Waisbrooker's response criticized both the inconsistency of the lawyer's position with free love principles and his sexism in wanting to subject his female partner to risks he himself was not willing to assume. For many male proponents, the attraction of free love lay in its promise of freer sexual contact; for women, the doctrine might more accurately be defined as freedom *not* to love, except in very limited circumstances in which they exercised complete control of their own actions.

Spiritualists' willingness to enter "the citadel of marriage" and criticize society's most dearly held beliefs exacted stiff penalties from the advocates of free love. For Lois Waisbrooker, the price was repeated arrests, culminating in her prosecution at the age of seventy-six for publishing an article condemning "The Awful Fate of Fallen Women," which a Washington State court judged obscene in 1902.[71] Free love could exact a more personal toll from a woman whose husband's interpretation of the doctrine differed from her own. Mary Fenn Davis ultimately fell victim to the same principles that liberated her from a loveless marriage years before. In 1885, her husband and coworker, Andrew Jackson Davis, informed her that he had misinterpreted the spirit messages of thirty years ago and that she was not in fact his spiritual affinity. His true affinity had appeared in a young woman who was his fellow student at the United States Medical College in New York. The announcement cost the founder of the Harmonial Philosophy much of his reputation in reform circles, where his wife was as highly esteemed as he. But the sixty-year-old Mary

Fenn Davis, true to her principles, received the news with apparent equanimity and did not fight the ensuing divorce. However, she went into a physical decline from which she never recovered. She assumed her mother's maiden name, Fenn, and died a year and a half later.[72]

6

Mediums versus Medical Men

When Spiritualists attempted to discover the meaning of equal rights by stringent application of the principle of individual sovereignty, they did not limit themselves to social or political concerns. They found additional roadblocks to women's autonomy in the physical conditions of their lives. They proposed to free women from cumbersome clothing that restrained their limbs and organs, from medical theories that encouraged them to view themselves as weak, and from barriers to their participation in the healing professions. Spiritualists joined reformers who focused on health in extending self-sovereignty to include what one ate, what one wore, and what sort of treatment one received when ill. All these, they contended, must follow the laws of nature rather than the dictates of society.

The female body became one locus of the cultural debate about the role and capabilities of women. Most observers agreed that the health of American women was poor and getting worse. Catherine Beecher's 1855 survey of her acquaintances revealed a "terrible decay of female health all over the land."[1] Opponents of woman's rights argued that women's generative organs inclined them toward disease and debility, making it impossible for women to enter society on an equal footing with men. Emancipation, in their view, was impossible because restrictions on woman's role resulted directly from her physiology, especially from her reproductive system. In contrast, Spiritualists joined health reformers in arguing that women were naturally healthy but that ill health resulted from the artificial restrictions imposed by civilization on women's natural physical abilities. They found the source of women's debility in social conventions that dictated loveless marriages and repeated unwanted pregnancies as well as restrictive clothing, an unhealthful diet, and a lack of exercise. The emancipation of women, for Spiritualists, was a health issue, providing the only remedy for physical suffering.

These two opposing views of women's bodies reflected two different approaches to health in general. Medical practice in nineteenth-century America included an array of techniques whose practitioners fell into two broad categories: "regular" or "orthodox" physicians, who based their treatments on the study of anatomy and on physical examinations, and "irregular" or "sectarian" physicians, who based their practice on a particular system of medicine ranging from homeopathy to botanical cures and patent medicines. The ineffectiveness of regular therapeutics coupled with a general distrust of experts with elite education convinced state legislatures to repeal most laws favoring orthodox practitioners during the Jacksonian period. As a result, all practitioners enjoyed the same lack of state regulation during the period before the Civil War. But by the century's close the regulars had secured a monopoly on medical therapeutics from the state, and the practice of competing systems of healing became illegal. In campaigning for their medical monopoly, regulars aimed one attack of their battle against sectarians at the presence of women as healers throughout the sectarian movements.[2]

The two poles of opinion about women's bodies had their roots in divergent views of nature that tied sectarian healing to heterodox religion and regular medicine to Protestant orthodoxy. While sectarians looked to nature as an ally in the healing process, regulars viewed nature as presenting problems that must be cured or controlled.[3] Orthodox religion and orthodox medicine reinforced a similar worldview in which human beings in their natural state were seen as flawed from birth and in need of assistance from officially sanctioned authority figures trained in a specialized body of knowledge. While orthodox clergy portrayed the human soul as inevitably prone to sin, orthodox physicians portrayed the human body, especially the female body, as inherently prone to disease. Just as ministers traditionally found a tendency toward sin in woman's moral anatomy because of Eve's instrumental role in tempting Adam into disobedience in the Garden of Eden, so doctors associated woman's physical anatomy with a tendency toward pathology. The emerging male medical establishment alleged that a disease-prone reproductive system governed woman's physiology, resulting in inevitable physical frailty that dictated a severely restricted sphere of action.[4] Regular doctors joined the clergy in asserting the appropriateness of women remaining within their "sphere," the clergy basing their arguments on the Bible, the doctors basing theirs on the body. Doctors and ministers agreed that both physical and spiritual ill health in women resulted from disobedience. They prescribed obedience to a male authority figure as a cure for the degenerative tendencies of body and soul.

While all sectarian medical movements attacked the practices of regular doctors, Spiritualists incorporated heterodox healing into an integrated worldview that added a critique of the medical establishment to their critiques of the establishment in religion, politics, and society. Spiritualists opposed orthodox medicine with the same fervor with which they opposed orthodox theology, and with some of the same arguments. Because they viewed each individual as embodying the image of God and the laws of nature, they viewed health, like godliness, as the natural condition of human beings, which only misguided human intervention could destroy. Disease, according to Andrew Jackson Davis, reflected discord. A cure would result from the restoration of harmony of the individual with the laws of nature. Because harmony was a spiritual as well as a physical quality, it could be restored more effectively by the Harmonial Philosophy than by physical therapeutics. "Atheism is not more destitute of the divine qualities of intuitive wisdom than are the various systems of medicine of that restorative principle which alone can summon the spirit of health," Davis explained. Because he located the source of disease in spiritual disharmony, he attributed most diseases to mental origins. However, because mental disharmony resulted in real physical disease, he encouraged the use of trained, albeit irregular, physicians.[5]

Just as they insisted that individuals had direct access to religious truth without intervention by scripture, clergy, or sacrament, Spiritualists also insisted that individuals had direct access to health without the "heroic" interventions of regular physicians. Spiritualists equated laws designed to give regulars a monopoly on medical practice with laws regarding the establishment of religion. Thomas Hazard of Rhode Island compared the legislative campaign of the "old blood-letting, opium, and drugging school" with the contemporaneous campaign to amend the Constitution to declare the United States a Christian nation, the combined results of which would "consign as merchandise . . . the souls of men to one branch of the conspirators, and their bodies by mutual compact to the other." Hazard devoted the first fifty pages of his *Family Medical Instructor* to descriptions of the pain and suffering caused by bloodletting and narcotics administered by regulars in contrast to the benign techniques of "unlettered" practitioners. He cautioned Spiritualists to beware of conspiracies of doctors and ministers to "incarcerate innocent healing mediums" in insane asylums, not an unwarranted concern given that regulars defined mediumship as a disease.[6]

In addition to insisting that women were naturally healthy, Spiritualists also asserted that women were better suited than men to act as healers. They believed that spirit communication, through women's mediumship, could cure the diseases of the physical body just as it healed rents in the social fabric and cured rifts between the living and the dead. In medicine as in religion, Spiritualists took the opposite extreme from the orthodox position, turning for healing not to men with training but to women with vision.[7]

Medical Mediums

The desire for relief from physical suffering joined the desire for relief from the emotional anguish of bereavement in drawing investigators to Spiritualism. As the technological advances of the nineteenth century increased expectations about the ability of human beings to harness natural forces and control the physical world, the therapeutic capabilities of physicians made little progress. In part to fulfill their patients' desires for therapy that would produce immediate observable results, orthodox physicians relied on "heroic" bleedings and purgings as well as narcotics and alcohol. Although bloodletting was on the decline by mid-century, physicians continued to prescribe opium and alcohol and to subject even infants and children to toxic doses of mercury until well after the Civil War. The greatest challenge to regular doctors and their heroic treatments came from homeopathists, whose sweet-tasting medicines in "infinitesimal doses" provided a pleasant alternative to the regimen of poisons prescribed by regulars.[8]

For those whose diseases proved no more susceptible to the sugar pills of the homeopathist than to the dangerous prescriptions of the regulars, physically benign religious or mental healing offered a rational alternative. For victims of disease like Achsa Sprague, who had exhausted the ineffective physical therapies available in nineteenth-century America, only the hope of a cure by spirits remained. "Medical mediums" and "clairvoyant physicians," most of them women, appeared throughout the country, offering an attractive choice of treatment for consumers of medical care. Some examined patients in trance, dispensing remedies prescribed by spirit doctors. Others healed through the laying on of hands charged with spirit forces, while still others used the clairvoyant state to see inside the diseased body. Spiritualism adopted from mesmerism the notion that entranced individuals could heal disease. But while mesmerism attributed the healing agency enabled by trance to a universal mesmeric fluid, Spiritualists transformed the healing trance into a form of mediumship.[9]

Mediums offered a wide variety of medical services. The clairvoyant physician Mrs. J. C. Dutton maintained two offices in Cleveland, one on the east side and one on the west. She described her healing technique: "while in clairvoyant state examines patients, discovers the nature of their disease, prescribes proper homeopathic, Botanical and Electro-magnetic remedies." In addition to office visits, she offered to send her own medicinal formula, which promised to cure fever or ague in one week. Another Cleveland practitioner offered to treat disease through clairvoyance and through the laying on of hands. A Boston "midwife and ladies' physician" announced in the *Banner* that she had engaged a trance medium to assist in her practice. She also announced that she accepted indigent cases. In the advertising columns of Spiritualist newspapers, healing mediums offered consultations through the mail to those who enclosed one dollar and a lock of their hair.[10]

While trance speakers relied on the free listing of lecturers in Spiritualist periodicals to apprise the public of their whereabouts, healing mediums paid for advertisements and listed themselves in city directories. Americans in need of medical treatment flocked to take advantage of the therapeutic alternatives offered by Spiritualists. Dr. Main's Institute "for healing under the guidance of spirits" announced that it treated ninety-eight inpatients as well as handling seven thousand office visits during its first year of operation in 1857. Dr. Main proudly announced a net profit of two thousand dollars. The author of the *Plain Guide to Spiritualism* advised the formation of healing circles in every community because, he said, there were not enough healing mediums to go around. The midwestern activist Elmer Louden wrote to the *Banner* in the hope of convincing some healing medium to move from Boston to Illinois. Noted trance speakers Cora Hatch and Melvina Townsend began as healing mediums.[11]

Mediums did prescribe medicines, but they avoided the purgatives, stimulants, and narcotics used by regular doctors. When Isaac Post was unwell, a clairvoyant who was an old family friend wrote that she had "felt inclined to look after him and his prospects and discovered a considerable debility, the result of billious derangement." In her clairvoyant state, she "thought he needed some bitters prepared as follows, orange peel, cammomile, etc. and gin."[12] Mrs. Semantha Mettler patented and distributed nationally medicines bearing her name and made according to recipes revealed to her by spirits. Her medicines and her practice with her husband as "Psycho-Magnetic Physicians" allowed Mettler to support her family and accumulate substantial real estate. Mettler's patent medicine success preceded that of the famous Lydia Pinkham by twenty years. Lydia Pinkham did not attribute her recipe to spirits, but her faith in the superiority of her own vegetable compound to the prescriptions of the regulars derived from the progressive Quaker heritage that led her into abolition and Spiritualism.[13] Sarah Danskin called herself a physician of the "New School" because she had been the "pupil and medium" of the spirit of Benjamin Rush for ten years. She also offered for sale "the American Lung Healer, prepared and magnetized by Mrs. Danskin."[14]

Spiritualist practitioners emphasized the difference between their techniques and those of orthodox physicians. One ad in the *Banner of Light* offered the services of a husband and wife medical team who felt "no sympathy with the legalized medical institution" and offered to treat patients instead "with a store of Eclectic, Botanic, Thompsonian and Patent medicines."[15] Mary Robbins Post wrote to Amy and Isaac of a medium who "extolled the virtues of her remedy and contrasted her cure with others who had been treated by the first rate doctors who almost invariably give calomel." Post expressed satisfaction that the medium "dwelt on the pernicious effects of calomel," a purgative that caused mercury poisoning, but feared that a sick relative's "faith in doctors prescriptions will remain though he order calomel every night for a week." Another correspondent of Amy Post's described how the prescriptions of a male doctor (tincture of opium and snuff) "dried my throat out so I could not swallow." She then went to a medium whose treatment was "mainly magnetic" and felt "much better in every way."[16] Spiritualist healers proudly described the medicines they administered as mild in comparison to the strong drugs used by regulars. While regular doctors relied on prescriptions as the basis of therapy, Spiritualists placed their faith in the laws of nature as the most potent therapeutic agent. "Medicines cannot impart the principle of health any more than a book can convey the light of wisdom," explained Andrew Jackson Davis. He warned sufferers that there were no infallible remedies and urged them to place their confidence in the "*Self-Healing Energies* that impregnate every fiber . . . of the organism." [17]

Animosity between healing mediums and regular physicians pervades the biography of Mrs. J. H. Conant, medium of the *Banner of Light* free circle for seventeen years. Her biographer describes the near death of the medium from an overdose of morphine prescribed by a physician who wrote the incorrect dose because he was himself "under the influence of stimulants." The overdose was administered to the unconscious woman by her husband, who had faith in the doctor who prescribed it. When apprised of the result of his prescription, the physician acknowledged his mistake and gave his patient up for dead. But Mrs. Conant prescribed for herself in trance, and, as soon as she received the medicine "of a simple nature" that she requested, she speedily recovered. Mrs. Conant continued to sit "for medical examinations only" each afternoon after her services as a test medium were engaged exclusively by the *Banner*. [18]

Medical mediums, like mediums in general, were predominantly female. Spiritualists viewed women as specially suited to the healing profession. Just as they found a warrant for women's religious leadership in accepted stereotypes about women's natural piety, they found a justification for the medical training of women in the common view that women had inherent nurturing qualities. In an address entitled "Woman the Physician," Mary Nichols argued that woman was suited to healing because she was loving, whereas "man has had the strength to be a surgeon, poisoner, destroyer, hangman." [19] "Who shall do this work better than woman? Woman, who has suffered most at the hands of materia medica," editorialized the Spiritualist *New Era* on Marenda Randall's receipt of the M.D. in 1855. Randall viewed women as especially suited to medical practice because of their personal experience with the health consequences of a social system that forced women into marriages in which they could not control access to their own bodies. "Every medical man *knows*—if he does not every medical *woman* does—that the penalty of God's *laws*, which those human laws compel us to violate, directly *kill* ninety-nine hundredths of the female world." In Randall's view, women needed sound medical care more than men did because they suffered more harshly from the ills of society.[20]

Spiritualists viewed the training of women as medical professionals as a step in progress toward living by the laws of nature. Their hostility toward regular physicians and support for female practitioners made them supportive of any women who entered the medical field, whether orthodox or sectarian. "Notwithstanding the opposition of conservative scientists . . . [we] can see no limit to the power of woman to enter the chambers of knowledge. . . . Every institution should be opened to her," wrote the Spiritualist eclectic Dr. Alcinda Wilhelm.[21] A number of Spiritualists were associated with the beginnings of the Woman's Medical College of Philadelphia, the first woman's medical school, founded in 1850. The Longshores, a Philadelphia Quaker family, played a prominent role both in founding the college and in the rise of Spiritualism in Philadelphia. The original impetus for the founding of the college was said to have resulted from the interest in medicine shown by the first president's sister-in-law, Hannah Myers Longshore. Longshore, a member of the Woman's Medical College's first graduating class, became its first female faculty member in 1853, the same year she sat weekly in one of Philadelphia's first séance circles. She was joined at the weekly séances by her husband, the vice-president of the college's Board of Trustees, by her sister-in-law, Anna Longshore, another early graduate who would go on to become a world-renowned women's health lecturer, and by one of her medical students, Rebecca B. Thomas.[22]

As the Woman's Medical College of Philadelphia struggled to increase its acceptance by the medical establishment, it expelled its unorthodox members, including its founders, the Longshores. The Longshores went on to start another medical school, this time explicitly irregular: the Penn Medical University identified its approach as "eclectic," indicating that it taught its students to utilize a variety of therapeutic approaches. The interests of the new school's students and faculty are indicated by the subjects of theses accepted for graduation. In addition to more conventional medical subjects, several theses address woman's role as a physician, several focus on electricity as a therapeutic agent, and one discusses "Mind and Matter." Spiritualists transferred their loyalty to the new school. At least seven active Spiritualists graduated from the Penn Medical University during its early years: Marenda Randall, Alcinda Wilhelm, Rebecca B.

Thomas, Caroline Hinckley Spear, Annie Stambach, Samuel B. Britton, and Horace Dresser. All but Rebecca Thomas became well-known speakers on the Spiritualist platform.[23]

Just as trance speakers swelled the ranks of America's first group of women on the public platform, so medical mediums were well represented among the first women to receive formal medical training. Marenda Randall, Achsa Sprague's sister-in-law, had practiced "botanic obstetrics" in Woodstock, Vermont, for fifteen years. Following the advent of her mediumship, she decided to travel to Philadelphia to attend the Penn Medical University. After receiving the M.D., she set up a practice in Philadelphia in which she offered patients eclectic medical treatment in addition to healing "by magnetic or spiritual influence by touch."[24] Caroline Hinckley Spear also traveled to Philadelphia for medical education. In 1858, she had accompanied the medium John Murray Spear to his community at Spirit Springs in upstate New York as his amanuensis and had borne his illegitimate child. In 1863, Spear divorced his wife and married Caroline Hinckley. A few years later, she graduated from the Penn Medical University and was appointed to its faculty. By 1870, she and her husband had moved to California, where she joined in organizing the first woman suffrage organization.[25]

Spiritualists joined the general health reform movement in arguing that disease could be prevented by living according to the laws of nature. Spiritualists like Henry C. Wright, Mary Gove Nichols, Mary Tillotson, and Paulina Wright Davis played a role in health reform beyond Spiritualist circles.[26] Spiritualists acknowledged the kinship between their health reform goals and those of others who challenged the medical establishment. During the Civil War, Louisa Patterson, secretary of the Progressive Spiritualists of Cadiz, Indiana, offered a resolution to provide Union soldiers with an alternative to allopathic medical care. The convention drafted a statement asking President Lincoln to allow soldiers to return home to be nursed by wives and mothers rather than remaining in dangerous army hospitals under the care of regular physicians.[27] Even the first women regulars found themselves allied with heterodox practitioners against the male medical establishment, which tried to maintain a monopoly to the exclusion of both groups. Dr. Marie Zakrzewska, pioneer regular physician, was refused office space because the landlord assumed that a female practitioner must be a medium. Female regulars sympathized with reformers' opposition to the repressive orthodox view of women's physiology, and Spiritualists returned the compliment. "We like to see these female doctors," said a speaker at the annual festival of the Religio-Philosophical Society. "They prove the powers of woman to be equal to man."[28]

Health Reform

Although Spiritualism's critique of orthodox medicine offered hope to patients of both sexes, Spiritualists focused their attention on overcoming barriers to women's health. They espoused a variety of reforms aimed at freeing women from socially constructed restrictions on their physical motion and development, including dress reform, gymnastics, temperance, vegetarianism, and water cure. Health reform appealed to woman's rights advocates because it contradicted the association of femininity with physical frailty and ill health. "In order that the spirit may grow and develop properly," argued Dr. Juliet Stillman, "it is necessary that the body should be kept in a healthy condition." She maintained that dress and health reform were necessary both to the advancement of women and to the advancement of Spiritualism.[29]

While mediums freed individuals from pain and disease, Spiritualist reformers proposed specific reformations of personal life that they believed would free the population generally from illness and suffering. Spiritualists appealed to the "Laws of Life," as written in the "book of nature," as guides to maintaining health as well as curing disease. Americans read Spiritualist medical advice in Mrs. Lucina Tuttle's *The Clairvoyant's Family Physician* and in the *Harbinger of Health* by Andrew Jackson Davis. Here they received advice on preventive medicine consistent with modern recommendations for the avoidance of America's worst health hazards: cancer, heart disease, and alcoholism. Spiritualist health reformers, following an earlier generation of dietary reformers led by Sylvester Graham, advised vegetarianism as well as abstinence from tea, coffee, tobacco, and alcohol. They decried the use of narcotics and advised regular exercise and fresh air.[30]

Andrew Jackson Davis's *Progressive Annual* listed not only Spiritualist lecturers but also practicing women physicians, women instructors in light gymnastics, "practical dress reformers" who wore the "American costume" (composed, like the bloomer, of a short skirt over loose trousers), and speakers on the freedom and equality of the sexes.

Demonstrating Spiritualists' faith in women's physical strength, Mary Davis's daughter provided instruction in "light gymnastics," following Dio Lewis, at the Spiritualist Belvidere Seminary run by the popular poet Belle Bush. Davis defended women's participation in gymnastics as an aid to health and fitness. The *Banner of Light* printed a lively series of articles in which dress reformers advocated "Riding Astride" as a healthful and appropriate activity for women and discussed what women should wear when they did it.[31]

"Dress reform will eradicate the worst slavery of American women," claimed Andrew Jackson Davis's *Herald of Progress*. Dress reform applied only to women, no attempt being made to alter the standard male costume. Spiritualist lecturer Louise T. Whittier refused invitations to speak on Spiritualism in order to give priority to dress reform. She apologized to the readers of the *Banner of Light* for refusing their many requests but insisted that "physical reform" must accompany spiritual emancipation. As a plank of the Spiritualist woman's rights platform, dress reform represented larger concerns than mere physical freedom. Dress reformers viewed women's fashions as morally debasing because they distorted the female form in order to appeal to male sensuality. Spiritualists hoped that dress reform, like marriage reform, would alleviate the devastating health effects of male lust. Trance speaker Miss A. S. Knox condemned the "false education of girls" because it led to "woman's present condition of slavery to fashion."[32]

Confining clothes kept women in their "place" and restricted women's movement so as to render them incapable of venturing outside their "sphere." Replacing traditional attire with reform dress indicated independence of spirit as well as a desire for physical freedom. The editors of the *Vanguard* thought that an applicant's decision to wear bloomers showed "evidence of sufficient intellectual capacity" to exceed the usual feminine role and succeed as a typesetter on their paper. Displaying one's radicalism so visibly required courage. Spiritualist William Denton recalled that, when he met his future wife, Elizabeth Foote, in the mid-1850s, he "had considerable trouble . . . shielding her from insult" because she wore the bloomer. Foote, who worked as a compositor on the *Type of the Times* (a paper advocating phonetic spelling, one of the less urgent items on the Spiritualist reform agenda), expressed her progressive life-style in her dress.[33]

Only a minority of mediums and lecturers actually donned the American costume. Most trance speakers preferred traditional femi-

nine garb, more appealing to the public. Spiritualists and other reformers agreed in principle that women should be freed from the
bonds of fashion, but the practitioners of dress reform found a more
receptive audience among Spiritualists. The rejection of the reform
dress was the first concession to expediency on the part of the non-
Spiritualist reformers who would go on to lead the woman suffrage
movement. Stanton and Anthony wore the bloomer briefly but soon
gave up the new costume because it attracted ridicule, not because
they no longer believed in the principles that caused them to adopt
it. As always, the small cadre of Spiritualist dress reformers put principles before pragmatism. They continued to wear and to advocate
the reform dress long after most reformers abandoned it. At one
Spiritualist convention, the husband of a popular medium "heard it
remarked that if diet and dress reform were discussed here, it would
hurt the cause." "But," he concluded, "if the cause were hurt so easily,
let it die." [34] The *Banner of Light* and Spiritualist conventions provided
forums for discussion of dress reform between the demise of the National Dress Reform Association in 1863 and the founding of the
American Free Dress League by Spiritualist Mary Tillotson in 1875. [35]

Spiritualists universally condemned "the baleful influence of tobacco and alcohol." Although they objected to the intolerance and
sectarianism of the evangelical temperance movement, they unanimously supported its goal. Trance speaker Warren Chase participated
in the temperance movement in the early 1850s but abandoned it
because of its "religiously bigoted spirit." He regretted the adoption
of the movement by the Protestant churches because "whatever reform the clergy took hold of was poisoned to death, for their kid
gloves soon crowded off the hardened hands of labor, without which
there could be no success." The quarterly conference of the North-
western Association of Spiritualists resolved that "as our spiritual
growth depends to a great extent upon the physical, that we should
strive by living in accordance with natural laws to promote healthy
conditions, and that the use of all stimulating drinks and tobacco
should be discontinued by all lovers of purity and progress." Like
other temperance advocates, they decried the victimization of wives
and daughters legally subject to drunken husbands and fathers. Even
vegetarianism could be seen as a women's issue by health reformers
who depicted meat eating as a form of male violence. "All kinds of
brutes are eaten by man," Juliet Stillman told a Spiritualist convention. "Even little singing birds do not escape his rapacity." [36]

In water cure, Spiritualists found a medical system in sympathy with their reform orientation. Also called hydropathy, water cure was a therapeutic approach imported from Europe in 1843 that relied on the internal consumption and external application of cold water for the prevention and cure of all diseases. Spiritualists, as well as other antebellum reformers, embraced water cure because of its appeal to the laws of nature embodied in each human being as the source of healing and because of the reform principles of its leaders. Hydropathy relied on the natural curative tendencies of the individual rather than on intervention by an authoritative medical expert. The editor of the Spiritualist *Vanguard* commended the Cottage Grove water cure, where proprietors Dr. Routh and wife were "radical reformers and spiritualists." Water cure establishments provided a fertile environment for the development of many of the ideas advocated by Spiritualist health reformers.[37]

At water cures, reform dress, diet, and ideas were the norm rather than the exception. Hydropathic retreats held special sympathy for unorthodox approaches to childbirth. Regular physicians and reformers agreed that the sedentary habits of middle-class women led to ill health and made pregnancy and childbirth more difficult. Orthodox doctors treated the resulting symptoms with heroic bleedings, purgings, and dosings, while hydropathists treated the cause with healthful living in order to make intervention unnecessary. The hydropathic regimen of fresh air, exercise, loose clothing, and cold water safeguarded the health of mother and child from intervention by "obstetrically ignorant" orthodox doctors who bled hemorrhaging women from the arm and dosed parturient mothers with toxic preparations. Andrew Jackson Davis claimed that the majority of married women suffered from the results of malpractice during confinement. He blamed their misfortune on the practice of employing male doctors. "Beautiful souls," wrote Davis, "always shrink from the wretched practice of 'doctoring' a child into existence." While regular doctors waged war against the employment of female midwives, Davis agreed with many sectarians that female birth attendants were necessary to preserve the health of mother and child. He viewed the employment of regular physicians as harmful both because of their gender and because their Calvinist perspective portrayed pain in childbirth as inevitable. "Our 'Orthodox Brethren' teach that woman's physiological sufferings are unavoidable . . . that woman's menstruational and childbearing pains are the result of an 'original sin,'" Davis explained.

"We," he told his renders, "read the Book of Nature with a different light." Regulars insisted on weeks or months of bedrest following childbirth, leaving previously healthy women severely depleted. The refusal to give up their bodies to the heroic treatments and months of confinement prescribed by regular doctors was one more way in which Spiritualist women insisted on individual sovereignty.[38]

Water cures contradicted convention by encouraging women to focus on their own needs rather than the needs of others. Often located in picturesque pastoral settings, water cure establishments freed women from domestic cares and from the watchful eye of "tyrant custom." Such conditions proved ideal for the discovery of talents incompatible with domestic duties, such as mediumship. A quarterly convention of speakers and mediums met at the Avon Spring Water Cure in New York State in 1869, where the proprietor made arrangements for participants to board at the cost of one dollar per day. The assembled mediums recommended the Avon cure as providing "favorable surroundings and conditions" for "the unfoldment of all phases of mediumship." Miss Marrieta Munson was sent to a water cure to be treated for "lung fever" in 1854. There she met a medium who said she would recover and become a medium herself. They remained at the cure together for six months. Spirits informed Munson that she had been cured on condition that she become a public medium. When she returned home and forgot the terms under which she had been cured, she was reminded by an attack of typhoid fever. She then joined in practice with a healing medium. The medium Mrs. Bushnell made a living by exercising her clairvoyant powers at a water cure.[39]

One of Spiritualism's most avid advocates of both health reform and woman's rights was the hydropathic doctor Juliet Stillman Severance. In 1857, she enrolled in the Hygeo-Therapeutic College in New York City, run by R. T. Trall, who introduced hydropathy in America. A Baptist in good standing when she began medical school, Stillman soon attended her first séance and received convincing evidence of spirit communication. The spirits quickly empowered her to espouse controversial positions. In the college debate society, she and one other argued a position opposed by the whole society. "When I rose to speak I was positively controlled," Stillman recalled. "And, to show the power that was used through me, I will state that, not withstanding the professors and students were all opposed to my argument, I received the vote of the house." On her graduation, Juliet Stillman embarked on a career of constant controversy as a "Hydropathic and Magnetic Physician and Accoucheur," Spiritualist lecturer, and woman's rights and health reform radical. She adopted the reform dress in 1852 and wore it throughout the 1850s and 1860s while practicing medicine in Wisconsin and Iowa and lecturing throughout the Midwest. When she first practiced in De Witt, Iowa, the local regular doctors launched a campaign against her. In 1865, she created a stir at a Minneapolis medical convention, where, as chair of the committee on resolutions, she introduced a clause "favoring magnetism as a therapeutical agent."[40]

Stillman bore three children by her first husband. There is no record of whether this first marriage and family occurred before or after her graduation from medical school at the age of twenty-five and the beginning of her lengthy public career as doctor and lecturer. In 1869, she married her Spiritualist coworker A. B. Severance, without interrupting her tireless service as organizer and speaker at Spiritualist conventions. The *Religio-Philosophical Journal* noted that her marriage was accompanied by a shift "from bloomers and boots, to short dresses and shoes," implying that she still shunned conventional clothing. Even among her coreligionists, her consistent reform views generated contention. Called "a radical of the radicals" by a contemporary source, Juliet Stillman Severance championed Victoria Woodhull in 1872 as an agent of "social freedom" and continued to advocate radical sexual ideals long after Woodhull had abandoned them.[41]

An occasional investigator objected to the amount of time devoted to woman's rights and health reform at Spiritualist conventions. After one of Juliet Stillman Severance's more graphic health reform lectures, a Mr. Kellogg protested that they ought to be discussing Spirits, not social issues. "I suppose the majority . . . came here . . . to hear about Spiritualism, not about bloomerism, sweetbreads, and potatoes," he complained. Apparently Mr. Kellogg was incorrect, for he was then treated to a trance lecture by Miss Knox, who "spoke at length of the laws of life, birth and death, and the necessity of woman being elevated to a position equal with man." Next, the convention heard a letter from Mrs. Daniel, editor of the *Rising Tide,* in which she expressed her hope that the conference would discuss woman's rights and marriage "and every social wrong . . . probing to the very center, at whatever cost it may be to the sensitive feelings of those present."[42]

Spiritualists' advocacy of health reform may seem inconsistent with Andrew Jackson Davis's claim that all disease originated in the mind. If disease was mental in origin and could be cured by adopting a harmonious mental outlook, why should one be concerned with the physical conditions of life? The Spiritualist vision of a harmonious natural order depicted the union of mind and body. Because Spiritualists believed that spirits had bodies and that those bodies were perfected versions of the bodies we have while living, they gave the body greater ultimate importance than religious outlooks that viewed physical life as fleeting and unimportant. But placing such importance on the body presented other problems for a religion that maintained that spirits could pass through walls and mysteriously transport themselves from one sphere of the universe to another. As the century wore on, these hazier regions of Spiritualist cosmology would draw criticism from other metaphysical movements. Spiritualist involvement in health reform may be difficult to explain from the point of view of their beliefs about the nature of the body, but it is easy to explain in terms of their commitment to woman's rights, their antiauthoritarianism, and their anti-Calvinism. Spiritualists hoped that health reform, like spirit communication, would allow people to live as reflections of a benign and harmonious natural world, in which sin, evil, and disease had no place.

Spiritualism and Allied Causes of Nervous Derangement

Spiritualism's attack on orthodox medicine and the worldview of which it was a part did not go unanswered. Regularly trained physicians fighting to bar a host of sectarian medical systems from practice took Spiritualism seriously both as a source of competition and as a manifestation of disease. Male doctors attacked women in general during this period as unfit to practice medicine, or any other profession, because of an anatomical proclivity to hysteria. The medical attack on mediums was a special case, and an especially vehement one, of the medical attack on women in general. Doctors who viewed the female organization as inherently pathological saw mediums, who exemplified so many feminine qualities, as prime examples of pathology. Not coincidentally, mediums also constituted a highly visible and vocal case of the assertion of the rights and the wisdom of women practicing healing and using heterodox methods in their practice.

Mrs. A. T. Harris wrote to the *Banner of Light* that, when she returned
to Northfield, Vermont, in 1859 after a two-year absence, healing mediums had replaced regular physicians. Previously, attempts were
made to "banish them from town. . . . Now, among 6 allopathics, are
one reformer and 5 healing mediums." Whether Spiritualists actually
threatened the dominance of regular doctors is unclear, but they
voiced competitive ambitions.[43]

The well-known neurologist William Alexander Hammond, a professor at New York's City University and at Belleview Hospital, addressed the pathology of mediumship in the *North American Review* in
1870. He revised this article into a monograph, *The Physics and Physiology of Spiritualism,* in which he denied the reality of Spiritualist phenomena, attributing its appearance to suggestion and sleight of hand.
He explained the behavior of mediums as symptoms of "hypnosis . . .
hysteria, catalepsy, and ecstasy." Hammond gave examples from ancient history in which men manifested these conditions. But all the
cases he presented from his own practice described female patients
and strongly associated mediumship with hysteria—believed by doctors of the period to be a disease of the female reproductive organs
("womb-disease"). Thus, he believed in the abstract that men could
"suffer" from mediumship, but in his own practice he could identify
the disease only in females.[44]

In 1876, Hammond took "the opportunity presented by the demand for a new edition" of *The Physics and Physiology of Spiritualism* to
enlarge it into *Spiritualism and Allied Causes of Nervous Derangement,* a
work of 366 pages, including chapters devoted to each phase of mediumship (speaking, healing, physical, etc.) and a chapter on fasting
girls, who attributed their ability to survive without food to spirit
agency. The book upheld the same arguments advanced in the earlier
volume but showed Hammond's continued interest in the subject.
The new edition showed familiarity with a wide range of mediumistic
behavior, apparently gathered from personal observation. But investigation did not alter Hammond's views. "At most of the spiritualistic
meetings which I have attended," he wrote, "there have been hysterical phenomena manifested."[45]

William B. Carpenter, registrar of the University of London, devoted a chapter to Spiritualism and mesmerism in his popular *Principles of Mental Physiology* in 1874. In 1876, Alfred Russel Wallace's
defense of Spiritualism from the chair of the Anthropological Section
of the British Association made it an issue in the transatlantic scien-

tific community. In the wake of the well-publicized fraud trial of medium Henry Slade in London and increased concern about Spiritualism among scientists, Carpenter treated the subject further in *Mesmerism, Spiritualism &c. Historically and Scientifically Considered*. Carpenter attended séances with Alfred Russel Wallace but did not share Wallace's enthusiasm for what he saw. Like Hammond, he attributed public demonstrations to fraud. In place of hysteria, Carpenter found the motivation for fraud in "the fostering influence of pecuniary temptations" in paid mediums and in malice in unpaid mediums. "For it is well known to those who have had adequate opportunities of observation," he wrote, "that there is a class of persons (especially, I am sorry to have to say, of the female sex) who have an extraordinary proclivity to deceit . . . and who enjoy nothing better than 'taking-in' older and wiser people." Although Carpenter's claim that Spiritualism resulted from women's deceptiveness provided a less complex explanation than Hammond's for mediumistic behavior, he joined in associating it closely with femininity. "Every medical practitioner . . . has met with cases in which young ladies have imposed in this way, by feigning disease, not only upon their families, but upon their previous doctors."[46]

R. Frederic Marvin, "Professor of psychological medicine and medical jurisprudence in the New York Free Medical College for women," finally named the disease of which Spiritualism was the symptom. He identified a form of insanity that he labeled "mediomania, or the insanity of mediums." He found that "mediomania" was a "very ancient form of derangement—the name is modern, the phenomena ancient." Relying heavily on Hammond, Marvin associated mediumship with the natural pathology of female organs. Because the female reproductive system was "more complex" than the male, "those forms of insanity which are associated with derangements of that system are more frequent among women than among men." Marvin found that "mediomania, while it often attacks men . . . more frequently assails women, and is generally preceded by a genito or venerio-pathological history." "The word mediomania," he concluded, "though not actually synonymous with the word utromania, is very closely allied with it in meaning."[47]

Both Hammond and Marvin associated disease of the female reproductive system, and so mediumship, with women's willful departure from traditional roles. Hammond attributed the appearance of mediumistic hysteria in one case to his patient's "excessive mental exertion, she having contracted a taste for philosophy, in the study of which she indulged to a great extent."[48] Following the influential work of Dr. Edward H. Clarke, these doctors asserted that, if women used their brains to attempt the mental exertion required for higher education, they would overtax their systems and suffer gynecological disease.[49] Marvin, taking this reasoning a step further, claimed that departure from traditional feminine roles was not the cause but rather the symptom of reproductive disease. He viewed mediumship as a manifestation of a medical disorder causing rebellion against gender roles.

> Utromania frequently results in mediomania. . . . The angle at which the womb is suspended in the pelvis frequently settles the whole question of sanity or insanity. Tilt the organ a little forward—introvert it, and immediately the patient forsakes her home, embraces some strong ultraism—Mormonism, Mesmerism, Fourierism, Socialism, oftener Spiritualism. She becomes possessed by the idea that she has some startling mission in the world. She forsakes her home, her children, her duty, to mount the rostrum and proclaim the peculiar virtues of free-love, elective affinity, or the reincarnation of souls.[50]

In the angle of the uterus, Marvin discovered the source of sympathy between religious and political radicalism that has eluded so many historians. The *Banner of Light* responded to his novel theory by hurling back at the doctors all the charges made in the medical "War Against Spiritualism." It found the scientists "guilty of the grossest *charlatanry* and humbug in their 'toe-joint,' 'utero-maniac' and 'epileptic' theories." And, true to form, the *Banner* accused the doctors of being unscientific: "The fraudulent medium—if such exists—who ekes out a subsistence by *imitating* veritable facts in a deceptive way is less a criminal than the malicious sociologist who denies the facts that others, of unquestionable veracity and intelligence, have tested and witnessed."[51]

Much of what was at stake in the debate between mediums and medical men concerned the appropriateness of women exercising will. Marvin makes it clear that for a woman to believe that she can exercise her will in order to accomplish a "mission in the world" is a symptom of disease. Many therapeutic innovations in the treatment of diseases of women during this period, like Weir Mitchell's "Rest Cure," involved the subjugation of the will of the female patient to that of her male doctor.[52] Spiritualists envisioned a more egalitarian relationship between patient and practitioner in which the patient was encouraged to exercise the self-healing properties of her own nature. In his discussion of gynecological disease, Andrew Jackson Davis presents the will as the most important element in women's recovery of health. Interestingly, he prescribes the use of the will to cure the very disease that Marvin thought caused mediumship: prolapsis uteri. The way he states his advice suggests that he knew it contradicted conventional wisdom: "The Treatment we propose is radical and positive . . . the paragon of all remedies, the faultless curative power within the pharmacy of immortal mind, is *the Will*. Let every Sister, whether daughter or mother . . . diseased or healthy . . . exercise this immaculate energy."[53]

Spiritualists and physicians both associated the physical characteristics leading to mediumship with the female body. Spiritualists, however, viewed these characteristics as fostering revelation, while doctors viewed them as pathology. One Spiritualist described nineteenth-century women as "physically inactive, sedentary, and non-manifestational" yet found that the resulting weakness made them good vehicles for spirit communication. Two competing schools of healing voiced competing interpretations of the physical nature of mediumship. The view of mediumship espoused by regular doctors was an extension of their view of female physiology as inherently pathological. In contrast, a columnist in the *American Spiritualist* explained, "We are not to consider the negative condition a manifestation of disease. . . . Without susceptibility and impressibleness, control by spirit power would be impossible."[54]

How could Spiritualists reconcile this celebration of female weakness and passivity with their assertions that women were naturally strong and healthy? As Spiritualists struggled with the cultural vocabulary of Victorian ideas about gender and stretched them to their limits, they bumped up against the contradictions inherent within them. After all, nineteenth-century norms portrayed women both as paragons of virtue who had the moral power to influence men to resist evil and simultaneously as weak, will-less hysterics in need of protection both from the world and from the pathological tendencies of their own physiology. Spiritualists made virtues out of both feminine stereotypes, salvaging a moral role for women out of either activity or passivity.

7

"No Organization Can Hold Me"

T he paradoxes and tensions within Spiritualism began to undermine its significance for woman's rights and reform during the 1870s and 1880s.[1] The movement that had played such a dramatic role in encouraging women's leadership saw the suppression of women within its own ranks. Spiritualists felt the same pulls that drew other postwar reformers away from their radical past toward a more moderate application of individualist principles. Instead of calling for a restructuring of society based on the sovereignty of each individual, many reformers now campaigned for government control of personal behavior to eliminate specific vices. As the century advanced, the distinctiveness of Spiritualism's social program faded, owing in part to its success, however limited, in several areas. The spread of liberal theology and the loosening of some restrictions on appropriate activities for women reduced the distance between Spiritualism and other visions of society. The increase in reform women speaking in public after the Civil War diminished the social significance of trance speaking. Although still controversial, a woman's appearance on the public platform no longer attracted interest in and of itself.

Meanwhile, within Spiritualism, a variety of attacks on mediumship evinced a devaluing of the feminine qualities so prized in the movement's early years. Sensational mediums replaced trance speakers as Spiritualism's biggest attraction, and mediumship itself therefore ceased to challenge accepted gender roles. The new sensationalism attracted figures anxious to gain personal benefit from its newsworthiness, including Victoria Woodhull and Helena Blavatsky. Sensationalism and self-agrandizement generated a reaction against mediumship that contributed to the founding of the new religion of Christian Science. The Spiritualism of the last quarter of the century lacked the radical thrust of the early movement.

The Debate over Organization

Striking changes in Spiritualist attitudes appeared in the debate over organization. In its first decades, Spiritualism's insistence on individual freedom in all things prevented its adherents from establishing formal structure, organization, or leadership of any kind. Faith alone bound believers together. Spiritualists feared that organization would routinize their faith just as it had that of so many groups before. They recalled the active presence of spirit in the early years of Methodism and Quakerism and lamented how institutionalization stilled the spirit and restricted freedom of conscience in these bodies. "Other religions have succeeded in forming popular organizations," they complained, "and the results have been priestcraft and slavish adherence to the tyrant St. Custom." Spiritualists avoided such pitfalls by shunning organization altogether.[2]

Advancing a nationwide movement without formal association generated obvious difficulties. A loosely affiliated group of believers could not construct buildings, conduct schools, or support speakers. The cry rose frequently, most often from men with leadership ambitions, that the cause required an organization capable of unified action. As early as 1851, the editor of the *Spirit Messenger* advocated organization in his newspaper. The spiritual freedom that appealed to so many Americans conflicted with the ambitions of zealous leaders who advocated any measure that would promote the cause.[3]

Spiritualism's inherent antinomianism predisposed believers against all structures of authority. Mediums' objections to organization were part of the anarchist heritage they shared with other antebellum radicals. Opposition to organization produced its own "ism" within abolition in the 1840s ("No-organizationism"). In 1852, the National Woman's Rights Convention, still dominated by radicals, debated and defeated a proposal for a national organization. "What organization in the world's history has not encumbered the unfettered actions of those who created it?" Angelina Grimké Weld inquired of the convention. She opposed formal association in the same language that advocates of free love used to oppose marriage. "We are bound together by the natural ties of spiritual affinity. . . . We need no external bonds to bind us together, no cumbrous machinery to keep our minds and hearts in unity of purpose and effort." Ernestine Rose compared organizations to Chinese foot binding, and Lucy Stone said she "had had enough of thumb-screws and soul screws never to wish to be placed under them again." They all used religious associations as examples of the oppression resulting from organization.[4]

Most reform activists accepted the expediency of organizations after the Civil War, but the legacy of free conventions made it difficult for many Spiritualists to participate in pro-organization postwar reform movements. In 1869, Lucy Stone abandoned her antiorganization position and shocked the die-hard nonresistant Amy Post by asking her to serve as a delegate to the first convention of the American Woman Suffrage Association. Post replied that she could not in good conscience participate in a convention composed of invited or elected delegates, one that therefore lacked a free platform. "I think dear friend that the spirit of *freedom* and *equality* has taken root and grown too tall with the mass of the people, for them to accept any outside position," she wrote to Stone. "They surely will soon grow weary of being seated out oneside, admitted as mere listeners—no *rights*—no *vote*—no *voice*." Post clearly protested as a matter of principle, not of personal desire, as she herself would unquestionably have been elected as a delegate representing her own Rochester Equal Suffrage Association. Post's commitment to the values of pre-Civil War radical reform alienated her from younger, more goal-oriented suffragists. "Oh! I do not want to be an outsider in this glorious cause, I want to be folded and sheltered in your beneficent arms and hearts, but how can I go back into the bondage of exclusiveness?" Post asked Stone.[5] The conflict between ardent individualism and longing for fellowship plagued Post in the woman's rights movement just as it had within Quaker meetings.

Proposals for organization generated heated debates at Spiritualist conventions and often resulted in adoption of equivocal resolutions. The 1859 Vermont State Spiritual Convention tried to reconcile contradictory positions by resolving to "carefully avoid combinations for any improper purpose such as limiting individual freedom, controlling each other's opinions, or avoiding personal responsibility." However, the convention found that organization, carefully controlled, had its place. Its resolution affirmed "the propriety and desirableness of association for . . . mutual aid and encouragement in true life, promoting friendly and fraternal intercourse and interest in each other's welfare, and co-operating in the support of public meetings." Spiritualists' commitment to individualist principles clashed with their earnest desire to advance their cause.[6]

In spite of ideological reservations, Spiritualists mustered enough sentiment in favor of united action to gather in their first national convention in Chicago in 1864. The convention endorsed the usual spectrum of reform causes, but debate over the formation of a national organization dominated the five-day meeting. The topic evoked so much controversy that little other business could be conducted. Initially, men contributed most to the discussion. Only one woman participated in the early debates, opposing organization in trance. Medium Lizzie Doten, vice-president of the convention, was not sure how she felt. But on the final day of the convention, which was completely devoted to the topic, Amanda Britt Spence made an argument that united mediums against organization. She identified organization with "positive," that is, masculine, characteristics, applying the view that "positive" qualities were inconducive to spirit communication to groups as well as to individuals. She warned mediums that "she had ever found that spirits were averse to organization of any kind; even a positive mind will often prevent spiritual manifestations." Finally, the convention appointed a committee to consider the formation of an organization and report to another national convention in one year's time.[7]

When the Second National Convention assembled at Philadelphia in 1865, the pro-organization forces immediately moved to form a permanent association, a clear challenge to the leadership of mediums. In contrast to the free conventions and open platforms characteristic of Spiritualism's first fifteen years, the Second National Convention was limited to delegates, officially designated by local groups to represent their views. Eighteen officers, seventeen men and nonmedium lecturer Mary Fenn Davis, presided over the convention. The assembly excluded mediums from committees because of their "want of practicality." In response, mediums reasserted the antiauthoritarian values that justified their leadership and united against organization. The *Banner of Light* reported that Cora Hatch "trusted the attempt at organization would be a failure, and her purpose in attending the Convention was to make it a failure." "I am *bitterly* opposed to religious organizations of any kind—to anything that fetters or binds the human mind," she told the convention. Medium Melvina

Townsend concurred. "Just so sure as we have an organization of faith we shall have despotism, and not be allowed to speak what is objectionable to others," she warned.[8] Mediums understood that formal association threatened their role because it recognized masculine leadership qualifications rather than the passive characteristics that linked mediumship and femininity. "This plan is *man's* work, the production of *men's* brains. . . . I see nothing of woman about this plan," complained Lizzie Doten. "Your organization will be a dead thing next year. It is said, we shall have creeds if we adopt this plan; but we had better have creeds than this. We are acting from policy, not principle."[9]

Finally, the trance speakers lost the debate, and the American Association of Spiritualists was voted into existence. In spite of mediums' impassioned opposition, the motion to form a permanent organization carried, although many abstained from voting. Not surprisingly, the pro-organization forces were better organized and had the votes to pass the motion. The debate took place in the men's arena, and their position triumphed. Although Lizzie Doten recounted antiorganization visions and a medium from Baltimore was influenced by her control to "assail very severely the order of the convention," men dominated as delegates, and they voted for organization. Lizzie Doten withdrew from the convention.[10]

In spite of her refusal to participate in a permanent organization, Lizzie Doten returned to the national convention the following year to argue for the rights of mediums. She felt that the newly formed American Association of Spiritualists was incompatible with the full freedom of conscience necessary to permit individuals to act on information received from spirits. "No organization can hold me," she told the 1866 convention.[11] Although she refused to be a delegate to the convention because delegates represented other people, not themselves, the trance speaker was so popular that she was invited to address the convention anyway. The decision on the part of the convention organizers to invite her to speak even though she opposed the convention itself and would surely say so from the platform suggests that her views were shared by a sizable antiorganization constituency that a national organization could not afford to alienate.

Lizzie Doten's arguments against organization explicitly linked it with the suppression of female leadership. She portrayed the movement toward organization as a shift away from the Spiritualist understanding of what attributes qualified religious leaders. She reminded her audience of the Philadelphia convention at which women and mediums were excluded from the business committee because they were not practical. Doten complained that "the tendency throughout the whole of that convention was to exclude women from the Committees." She viewed this as a step backward that contradicted the progressive goals of Spiritualism. "Oh, women of the nineteenth century, think of that from a Spiritualist Platform!" the shocked Doten cried out. Her criticism of the convention met with universal applause. She was especially incensed by the "Committee on the Address," charged to produce an address on Spiritualism for general distribution. Editor Mrs. M. M. Daniel wrote the address, but it was published over the names of the entire committee. Laughter and applause greeted Doten's accusation that "that address, which has gone out to the whole world, arose from a woman's inspiration, though the world does not know it, for a man's name stands first among the signatures to that Address." [12]

The breakdown for and against organization divided normal speakers from trance speakers more fully than it divided men from women. Women who had the same leadership qualities as men joined men in advocating a system of organization that rewarded assertiveness over passivity. Like male leaders, female normal speakers such as physicians Juliet Stillman, Alcinda Wilhelm, and Annie Longshore Potts claimed professional or educational qualifications. Lois Waisbrooker, a normal speaker who favored organization, applauded the delegate system because "individuals, having 'especial missions,' axes of their own to grind, will not be permitted to mar the action of the convention." Accustomed to public derision, normal speakers knew they could make it in a man's world. Trance speakers were less certain. They were not sure whether they would find adequate freedom for their spirits inside an organization. They depended on the trance state to liberate their voices and justly feared that they would be silenced in an organization that elevated traditional leadership skills. [13]

The third national convention in 1866, the first of the American Association of Spiritualists, included no trance speakers on its program. Three men gave lectures in the normal state, and Miss Susie Johnson spoke in favor of "practical work," urging Spiritualists to come out from Unitarian churches and build their own halls. Veteran J. M. Peebles criticized the absence of trance speakers from the program. "We would like to see at future conventions . . . certain times set apart for the immortals to entrance their mediums. It would be just to the invisible world."[14] Instead of giving mediums space on the program, the convention questioned their integrity in a long discussion of the legitimacy of "dark circles." The convention debated a motion to require the *Banner of Light* and the *Religio-Philosophical Journal* to report both sides when such a manifestation caused controversy.

After the convention, Melvina Townsend gave the medium's perspective in the *Banner of Light*. She felt that the problems that created a need for scrutiny of dark circles resulted not from women's dishonesty but rather from men's greed. She said that if she were a medium for physical manifestations (rather than a trance speaker and healing medium) she would want them to be investigated. However, she reminded Spiritualists that mediums could be more easily "psychologized" than other people; that is, they possessed unusual sensitivity to the influence of thoughts of other people, living or dead. She blamed the existence of fraudulent manifestations on men's attempts to exploit mediums for their own profit. On behalf of her sister mediums, she described the psychological vulnerability of the women on whom the Spiritualist faith depended:

> We go before the public; we stand before a great cloud of psychological influences that rolls in upon us. We go with our earnest natures strong for the right, determined to do everything that is for the best, and that will add to our reputation and the reputation of Spiritualism; but coming into contact with those strong psychological influences that you, my brothers, are in the habit of dealing out to us, we lose our position before the world for a time. . . . I call upon men everywhere to make a nobler use of their psychological powers than they have done. Do not drag us down to destruction any more.

Townsend explained that either an investigator's desire to witness a particular manifestation or a manager's desire for the financial benefits of satisfying investigators could be strong enough to influence a medium psychologically. "But," Townsend insisted, "there is no real consciousness to do wrong." Townsend viewed the debate over mediumship at the national meeting as an explicit attack on women.[15]

Advocates of organization made some attempts to assure the equality of women within the new association. At the 1864 convention, the organizing committee recommended that the nominating committee be composed of one man and one woman from each state. But, as modern affirmative action efforts have shown, the decision to appoint equal numbers of men and women cannot work unless the prejudices embedded within the required qualifications are reassessed. Recognition of mediumship equalized the presence of men and women in Spiritualist leadership; decreasing respect for mediums threw the balance off again. Twenty men and eleven women sat on the nominating committee in 1864, and female participation in leadership of the organization continued to decline as it became more structured.[16]

While Spiritualism continued to prosper as a popular movement, attendance at national conventions dwindled, rarely exceeding two hundred. The Fourth National Convention in Cleveland was uneventful, featuring typical lectures by H. C. Wright on nonresistance and by Juliet Stillman on health reform. The year 1868 produced a similarly predictable convention, notable only for its location—Rochester's Corinthian Hall—the site of the Fox sisters' first public demonstration.[17] Arguments over internal organization once again dominated the Sixth National Convention at Buffalo, at which normal speaker Mrs. H. F. M. Brown was the only female officer for the second year in succession. The convention focused on the apportionment of delegates and debated the founding of a college, the pet project of a few leaders. This new proposal was yet another attack on women's leadership, as it valued education over inspiration. A Mrs. Parkhurst observed, "The best speeches were made by those who were taught from the spirit-world—persons who never had a college education." Sarah Horton gave the convention's single trance lecture, in which she objected to portrayals of Spiritualism as a "religion of the head" and characterized it instead as a "religion of the heart." Both Horton and Parkhust objected to the organization's attempt to adopt values that would exclude women from leadership: education, organization, and hierarchy.[18]

Mediums lost the battle over the formation of a national organization, but they and their followers won the war. After six national conventions, it was clear that the fledgling American Association of Spiritualists would never become a representative body of American Spiritualists. It simply lacked the allegiance of the majority of believers. The *Banner of Light* expressed faith in the good-will of the association's officers but skepticism about their ability to generate enthusiasm for a national organization. The editors complained that, while the association's conventions should attract thousands of investigators, they drew only a few speakers and mediums instead, whom the paper dubbed "impractical but useful persons." In 1870, the Seventh Annual Convention occurred without the *Banner's* support and mer-ited only a brief report in its pages. One delegate proclaimed it a success in the efforts of those who went but a failure because of poor attendance.[19]

Under these demoralized conditions, Spiritualists first saw the fresh face of Victoria Woodhull. The 1871 Eighth National Convention of the American Association of Spiritualists did not get the attendance hoped for, but it did hear a paper by a previously unknown speaker that generated much interest. The notorious Woodhull was an unconventional reformer and sometime revolutionary, best known for her flamboyant life-style, her physical beauty, and her Wall Street brokerage house. Woodhull's decision to run for president of the United States in 1871 brought to her attention a number of existing movements for which she felt sympathy and that had the potential to advance her candidacy. These included woman suffrage, socialism, and Spiritualism. Following her surprise appearance and victory at the Woman Suffrage Convention in Washington, Woodhull received an invitation to the Spiritualist convention because a recent biographical sketch emphasized her youthful mediumistic experiences. The convention forthwith elected her president, much to the surprise of all present.[20]

Woodhull's unexpected election to the presidency of the only representative body of American Spiritualists drew the ire of veteran leaders. For the most part, they condemned her not for the radicalism that had gained her national notoriety but for opportunism. Hudson Tuttle charged that Woodhull took advantage of the convention, that she was not a delegate, had never attended a convention before, and came for the sole purpose of being elected president. He claimed that her election was illegal because she received a bare plurality but was declared president with forty-three votes. It is difficult to dispute Tuttle's account of Woodhull's election. Her appearance followed close on the heels of the National Woman Suffrage Association Convention in Washington, D.C., at which she upstaged the regular program, and her participation in the formation of Section 12 of the socialist International Workingman's Association (commonly known as the First International), both of which offered great potential for Woodhull's self-promotion.[21] Tuttle charged that "the Troy convention was used as the means whereby to prostitute spiritualism to the support of unparalleled selfishness" and that Woodhull had tried to identify all Spiritualists as her personal supporters at the woman suffrage convention.[22]

A few months later, Woodhull issued a call for a "People's Convention" to start a new political party and formally nominate her for president. She scheduled her convention to coincide with the upcoming annual meeting of the National Woman Suffrage Association. The call took two forms, one attributed to the National Woman Suffrage Association, signed by Elizabeth Cady Stanton, Susan B. Anthony, Isabella Beecher Hooker, and Matilda Joslyn Gage, the other from Victoria Woodhull, and sixty individuals. The signers of the second call included popular mediums and leading Spiritualists, apparently most of the forty-three who voted for Woodhull at the Troy convention, as well as her cohorts in Section 12 of the First International.[23] Susan B. Anthony immediately repudiated Woodhull's call and Woodhull's unauthorized use of her name. Stanton and Hooker still supported Woodhull, but the single-minded suffragist Anthony stymied Woodhull's intention of usurping the suffrage platform by having the gas lights turned off when Woodhull took the podium. Woodhull rented a nearby hall, where the "People's Convention" promptly nominated her for president of the United States. She claimed support for her nomination from all three groups she had courted during the previous year: suffragists, socialists, and Spiritualists. Both suffragists and socialists severed connections with her after this, but the American Association of Spiritualists, tiny and troubled, continued to reelect her.[24]

Woodhull's election to the presidency of the decrepit American Association of Spiritualists by forty-three votes did not make her a leader in the movement. Among Spiritualists in New York for the competing conventions, Mary Fenn Davis, Andrew Jackson Davis, and Laura de Force Gordon remained loyal to Susan B. Anthony and the National Woman Suffrage Association.[25] However, Woodhull's office in the Spiritualist association, combined with her extreme social radicalism, did make her a heroine to some Spiritualists. Spiritualist suffragists Laura Cuppy Smith, Addie Ballou, and Moses Hull gave full allegiance to Woodhull and her candidacy for president of the United States.

In 1872, the American Association of Spiritualists reelected Woodhull with thirty-one votes. She declined, but her declination was not accepted. She then gave a powerful speech, her third in the three-day conference. To illustrate the hypocrisy of a society that preached conventional morality but practiced free love, she described the extramarital affair between the extraordinarily popular minister Henry

Ward Beecher and his parishioner Mrs. Elizabeth Tilton.[26] This revelation ultimately gained Woodhull greater infamy than her social
radicalism, but her initial mention of it drew little attention beyond
the convention. Following her address, she proposed a resolution designed to identify the organization with her views. "That the American Association of Spiritualists hereby declare that religious, political
and social freedoms are the fundamental principles of all improvement of human life." This mild resolution would never before have
generated controversy, but, when tied to Victoria Woodhull, it fright-
ened usually bold Spiritualists.[27] Moderate medium Emma Hardinge
objected that "Mrs. Woodhull's election as president of the American
Association of Spiritualists therefore involves a supposed recognition
of her principle and procedures by every American Spiritualist."
Hudson Tuttle agreed with Hardinge because Woodhull had been
elected by a delegate convention based on the principle that elected
leaders represented the views of those who elected them; therefore,
by electing Woodhull, they had bound themselves to be represented
by her views. Woodhull supporter Anna Middlebrook argued both
that the election did not commit all other Spiritualists to Woodhull's
views and that those views should be accepted. "I do not understand
that kind of Spiritualism that ignores woman suffrage, social reform,
labor reform, and kindred topics; and I should be ashamed to be
identified with a cause that did not mean to work for suffering humanity through these channels." Middlebrook suggested that others
join the Catholics, "who, while they believe in the communion of the
saints, keep the masses in ignorance." Woodhull's election also drew
charges of ballot fraud.[28]

Dissatisfied by the lack of attention to her charges against Beecher,
Woodhull published them in her own newspaper, *Woodhull and Claflin's Weekly*. This began a six-year spectacle of church councils, criminal trials, and excommunications, which ultimately showed that the
public would rather live with hypocrisy than live without Henry Ward
Beecher. By the end of it all, Victoria Woodhull relinquished both her
free love views and her thirst for publicity. A few Spiritualists remained loyal to her throughout. Laura Cuppy Smith testified as a
character witness when Woodhull was tried under the Comstock Antiobscenity Act for printing the Beecher-Tilton exposé.[29] But the infamy that accrued to Woodhull for her role in the Beecher-Tilton
scandal further reduced her small base of support among Spiritualists. When the American Association of Spiritualists reelected her in
1873, one leader proposed to split the organization between the "free

love allies of Woodhull and Hull and the True or religious or practical Spiritualists." Spiritualist groups across the country voted to condemn both Woodhull and the association and wrote to the *Banner of Light* to disassociate themselves publicly.[30]

Victoria Woodhull's election marked the demise of the American Association of Spiritualists. By the time she resigned the presidency in 1875, no one thought of trying to keep the association alive.[31] State and local organizations persisted, but as a nationwide movement Spiritualism reverted to the loose networks more consistent with its religious beliefs.[32] Woodhull's initial election resulted from the lack of interest in the organization, and her subsequent reelections doomed the association to failure because her notoriety exceeded her popularity. The antiauthoritarian pull of Spiritualist manifestations proved stronger than the ideological anarchism articulated by Victoria Woodhull. The apparent success of Spiritualist advocates of organization notwithstanding, the women who opposed it were eventually vindicated. Lizzie Doten was right that organization would lead to the exclusion of women from leadership in the movement. Lists of convention officers, delegates, and committee members show a marked decline in female leadership with the advent of organization. Ohio, for example, sent one woman in its twenty-one member delegation to the 1869 meeting of the American Association of Spiritualists.[33] Women trance speakers were also right that organization was inconsistent with the spirit of the movement and that Spiritualists espoused too many varied ideas and beliefs to be adequately represented by delegates in a national convention. Spiritualism proved insusceptible to institutionalization.

Camp Meetings and Sensational Mediumship

Although efforts to organize Spiritualists floundered, believers voted with their feet, flocking to picnics and camp meetings while they boycotted the American Association of Spiritualists. A few weeks before the poorly attended Sixth National Convention in 1869, twelve thousand people reportedly turned out for a two-day grove meeting in Abington, Massachusetts. The annual five-day camp meeting at Melrose, Massachusetts, claimed eight thousand in attendance.[34] But the crowds who thronged camp meetings at Walden Pond, Lake Pleasant, and Cape Cod were not introduced to a comprehensive program of universal spiritual and social reform. Rather, they enjoyed a festive entertainment that might include communication with departed loved ones but that had few implications for the conduct of the living.

Located on scenic lakes or beaches, camp meetings featured more entertainment and less serious discussion than the conventions of the 1850s and 1860s. Normally lasting two weeks, Spiritualist camp meetings multiplied until one was in progress somewhere in New England all summer long by the end of the 1870s. Frequently attracting five to ten thousand people on a summer Sunday, several of the camps gave rise to permanent facilities with cottages, hotels, and assembly halls.[35] Henry F. Gardner, who lost the presidency of the American Association of Spiritualists to Victoria Woodhull, enjoyed a lucrative career as a camp meeting organizer much more profitable than any benefits Woodhull reaped from her presidency.[36] Gracefully mingling sensationalism and sentimentalism, camp meetings attracted large crowds. A typical excursion might include a private sitting with a medium, a picnic at the lake front or sea shore, a concert by one or more "musical mediums," and a reform lecture by a "veteran" speaker. The free platform that formed the central attraction of Spiritualist conventions in the 1850s and 1860s became a minor feature of the camp meeting. One was more likely to go home carrying a "spirit portrait" of a departed loved one painted by a medium who had never seen a likeness of the subject than a subscription to a reform periodical.[37]

By 1874, Massachusetts hosted a three-week camp meeting at Silver Lake back to back with the two-week Lake Pleasant Camp Meeting, preceded by a two-day picnic near Salem, featuring trance speaker Laura Cuppy Smith, a merry-go-round, and a full band. In addition to their own camp meeting sites, Spiritualists met at Walden Pond and at Silver Lake, where a railroad company had erected a tent accommodating three thousand people. According to the *Boston Globe*, twenty-five hundred traveled to Silver Lake on Friday and ten thousand on Sunday, both believers and young people simply looking for a pleasant excursion. The restaurants could not accommodate the throngs. Many of the popular lecturers from the convention circuit welcomed the large audiences gathered by camp meetings. Trance speaker Lizzie Doten and William Denton, former editor of the *Social Revolutionist*, spoke frequently. But the Spiritualist public recognized them as part of a past era. The *Banner of Light* reported that the appearance of trance speaker Melvina Townsend, briefly using the married name Wood, "illustrates with old-time eloquence the power of present inspiration." Some prewar reformers objected to the festival atmosphere. Samuel B. Brittan expressed disappointment that an appeal to endow the Spiritualist Belvidere Seminary as a college netted only forty dollars at the Lake Pleasant Camp Meeting. He complained "It appears to me a very easy matter to gather . . . five to ten thousand persons in some pleasant place, to enjoy something like a holiday entertainment, but no one is prepared for any serious work, or any self-sacrifice."[38]

The triumph of the camp meetings over organization marked a triumph for mediumship. At the core of the carnival atmosphere lay the appeal of spirit manifestations, without which the event could not have occurred. But the mediums won a hollow victory, for the type of phenomena that drew huge crowds to camp meetings in the 1870s differed in important ways from the inspired trance speeches of the 1850s and 1860s. The new manifestations emphasized women's dumb passivity rather than their former role as articulate vehicles for divine truth. Although many of the trance speakers who rose to prominence in the 1850s and 1860s remained popular for several decades, the women who embarked on careers as mediums in the 1870s and 1880s did not speak in public. Instead of stepping out onto the public platform, they produced manifestations by withdrawing into cabinets, from which emerged spirit voices, spirit music, spirit hands, and eventually whole embodied spirits. Spirits no longer emboldened mediums to exceed the traditional female role. The mediums who emerged in the 1870s did not lecture, nor did they become active reformers. Some of them became involved in public controversy, but it was usually over the personal defense of their mediumship, not the defense of their sex or their principles.

Typical of the new mediums was French-American Lucie Marie Curtis Blair, whose career began in 1872. Her mediumship consisted of the ability to paint flowers while blindfolded. She toured the country giving demonstrations during the mid-1870s. She was a popular medium, meriting a spot on the program at the enormous Lake Pleasant Camp Meeting. She attracted sympathetic note in both the Spiritualist and the secular press. The sight of a blindfolded woman at an easel can hardly have had the same impact on an audience as the inspired utterances of the antebellum trance speakers.[39] Blair's appearance did not suggest to either women or men that women could do things they previously believed impossible. Another example of the 1870s-style medium was Mrs. Suydam, who gave public displays of her ability to handle fire, ostensibly made possible by the coating of her hands with an imperceptible substance by a spirit chemist. She also appeared at Lake Pleasant in 1876. Other mediums produced flowers and live doves, whose appearance they attributed to spirits. The new types of mediumship failed to challenge accepted gender roles either for the medium or for her audience. Mediumship ceased to be a source of power for women.[40]

The culmination of the sensational trend in spirit manifestations came with the popularity of "materializations." Spiritualists used the term *materialization* to refer to the appearance of fully embodied spirits. Materializations generally occurred at "cabinet séances," in which the medium withdrew into a small sealed room or closet before manifestations appeared. Although there had been earlier reports of materializations, notably at Koon's spirit room in Ohio, this type of manifestation gained wider acceptance in the 1870s. Medium Mary Andrews attained renown for materialization séances in Moravia, New York, as did Mary Hardy Pickering in Rochester, New Hampshire.[41] The most impressive materializations occurred at the Eddy homestead in Chittenden, Vermont, where five siblings acted as mediums.[42]

Devout investigators journeyed to witness this latest phase of spirit communication. Chittenden visitor J. H. Randall, in good Spiritualist tradition, urged, "Readers, you who can not believe my statements, go and see these things for your self."[43] So many investigators traveled to the Eddy homestead that Mary L. Jewett, who practiced medicine opposite the depot in nearby Rutland, opened her office to coreligionists in need of assistance en route to the village of Chittenden.[44] Mrs. A. N. Tupper spent a week at the Eddy homestead attending daily séances and reported her experience to the *Banner of Light*. At the first séance, held in the light, she saw her father, her mother, and her sister's two children, but none of them spoke to her. Then the medium was tied to his chair for the "Dark Circle," and manifestations became more raucous. Musical instruments floated about the room and played simultaneously, presumably strummed and bowed by spirits. The guitar rested on Tupper's head while playing "a beautiful piece." Finally, her little daughter Hattie, dead one year, appeared, patted Tupper on the head, kissed her, and said, "Don't cry Mamma." The next day Hattie appeared at the light circle, "dressed in pure white, with a wreath of roses about her head, and gave a beautiful piece of poetry." Hattie made similar appearances each day and told her mother that she was learning to write in verse.[45]

Materializations may have required an extraordinary readiness to believe, but they also offered an extraordinary degree of consolation. Spiritualists, especially bereaved parents, confirmed the old adage that "seeing is believing" by flocking to materialization mediums and finding their manifestations more compelling than any previously received. When an audience chose "Materialization" for the topic of an 1875 trance lecture by Cora Hatch (now Tappan), her spirit control, Adin Augustus Ballou, explained that these marvelous new manifestations distinguished "Golden Ages" from other periods of history.[46]

When materialization replaced trance speaking as the most noteworthy public manifestation of Spiritualism, the meaning of mediumship changed. Like other forms of sensational mediumship, the new manifestations emphasized the medium's passivity in new and humiliating ways and downplayed her empowerment. Test conditions frequently called for materialization mediums to be blindfolded, gagged, and bound. Laura Ellis and Mary Andrews began their séances by being tied inside a sack, which was then nailed to the floor, so that the audience could be assured that the spirit hands and figures they saw were not those of the medium. While trance speakers often traveled independently, most of the new mediums required male confederates or managers to orchestrate séances, during which the mediums neither spoke nor moved. In most cases, manifestations appeared only after the medium was securely bound and hidden in a cabinet, her effectiveness depending on invisibility and powerlessness. Mediums for materialization could not hope to inspire the same admiration that trance speakers elicited from their audiences. Letters of appreciation and admiration did not follow the appearance of a woman in a sack nailed to the floor.[47]

While materialization diluted the meaning of mediumship, it also opened Spiritualism to new and more spectacular forms of fraud and self-aggrandizement. Accounts of the Eddy family séances in the *Banner of Light* caught the attention of a bored New York attorney, Colonel Henry Steel Olcott. Olcott made a trip to Chittenden and reported his experience in the *New York Sun*. Sensing the commercial appeal of his account, another New York paper, the *Daily Graphic*, sent Olcott back to Vermont with an artist and printed his illustrated reports of the Eddy séances twice a week during the summer and fall of 1874 (see plate 12). The paper claimed these articles trebled its circulation. Olcott's accounts in turn attracted the interest of Helena Petrovna Blavatsky, a destitute Russian noblewoman, recently arrived in New York in flight from an ill-starred European past.[48] Like Victoria Woodhull, Madame Blavatsky had a history of psychic experience but associated herself with the Spiritualist movement only in hope of personal aggrandizement. One biographer has suggested that it was the popularity of Spiritualism in the United States that led her to New York in 1873.[49]

Blavatsky traveled to Chittenden in hope of attracting Olcott's attention and gaining publicity for herself as a Spiritualist. Her efforts were well rewarded. Olcott enlisted in the cause of promoting Blavatsky and her views. She helped him edit his *Graphic* articles about the Eddys into a book, and he joined her in founding the Theosophical Society in 1875.[50] At first it was unclear whether Helena Blavatsky was a friend or a foe of Spiritualism. The popular medium Emma Hardinge Britten initially allied herself with Blavatsky's new movement but by 1875 accused those who connected her with Theosophy of slander.[51] Blavatsky won praise within Spiritualism for defending the faith against the attacks of physician George Beard, etiologist of American "Nervousness," and for her role in attracting extraordinary manifestations at Chittenden. The *Spiritual Scientist,* an ailing Boston newspaper edited by E. Gerry Brown, became the organ for her views when she and Olcott helped boost circulation to keep it alive. Here she advocated ideas that gradually distinguished Theosophy from Spiritualism. While Spiritualists sought communication with the dead in general, Blavatsky and Olcott sought the secret wisdom of specific ancient magical adepts. They accepted the existence of séance manifestations but attributed them to astral projection and magical forces, not to the spirits of the dead.[52]

Perhaps Theosophy's most salient departure from Spiritualism lay in its espousal of occultism, the belief that secret or hidden knowledge can give access to magical powers. Luther Colby, current editor of the *Banner of Light,* responded to Blavatsky's innovations by denying the existence of magic. Cora Hatch Tappan pinpointed the difference between Spiritualism and Theosophy when an audience selected "The History of Occultism" as her topic for a trance lecture. She said that the word *occultism* was only a few months old, that it had been introduced by Colonel Olcott, and that it was now being confused with Spiritualism. She may have used a faulty etymology, but she was correct in asserting that American Spiritualism had never associated itself with the occult. On the contrary, Spiritualists believed that there was nothing mysterious about spirit communication, that it required no special knowledge, and that it was equally accessible to everybody. These tenets were central to the egalitarian thrust of the movement and conflicted with the emphasis on elite secret wisdom in Theosophy.[53]

While Madame Blavatsky benefited from the sensationalism of materialization, Robert Dale Owen became an unwilling victim of its newsworthiness. The well-known reformer and freethinker abandoned atheism to investigate Spiritualism during the late 1850s. He gave a valuable boost to the movement with the publication of *Footfalls on the Boundary of Another World* in 1860. Scrupulously researched and cautiously written, *Footfalls* discussed only spontaneously occurring phenomena rather than manifestations produced in the presence of mediums. The first book of its kind presented by a nationally known, non-Spiritualist publisher, it proved a huge success. Owen immediately began work on a sequel on mediumistic phenomena, but government service during the Civil War and reconstruction delayed its completion for twelve years. Finally, in 1872, Owen published *The Debatable Land between this World and the Next,* just as materializations made Spiritualism front-page news. Preceded by a long introduction addressed to the Protestant clergy urging Spiritualism as a safeguard against both secularism and Catholicism, *The Debatable Land* provided a welcome respite for those wearied by the excesses of Victoria Woodhull.[54]

Still searching for irrefutable evidence of immortality, Owen obliged when Katie King, a materialized spirit, asked for him at a Philadelphia séance. Katie called him "Father Owen," kissed him, and gave him a lock of her hair. Enchanted, Owen found this materialization credible because the mediums, Mr. and Mrs. Nelson Holmes, remained outside the cabinet in full view during Katie's appearances and therefore could not be impersonating her (see plate 13). Satisfied with his inspection of the cabinet, Owen publicly endorsed the Holmeses' materializations. He prepared an account of Katie King entitled "Touching Spiritual Visitants from a Higher Life" for the *Atlantic Monthly,* to appear as an installment of his serial autobiography. Before the article appeared in print, Owen learned that Katie King was a fraud. He met the young woman who conspired with the Holmeses to impersonate the spirit, and she returned to him some of the gifts he had presented to the charming spirit. Owen immediately withdrew his endorsement from the Holmeses' manifestations, but it was too late to remove "Touching Spiritual Visitants" from the forthcoming *Atlantic*. Editor William Dean Howells only had time to insert a disclaimer, which made both author and editor look foolish. Owen temporarily lost his sanity, and his children had him confined to an asylum.[55]

The episode shook many investigators and detracted from the credibility of materializations. But it did not disillusion committed Spiritualists. Owen himself, his sanity restored, remained faithful until death. The response of believers to the discovery of fraud is preserved in the correspondence between Mrs. Louisa Andrews of Springfield, Massachusetts, and Professor Hiram Corson, a Cornell University Shakespeare scholar. Both had witnessed the Katie King materializations and both publicly defended the accused mediums against Robert Dale Owen's disclaimer. Andrews insisted that the "bogus Katie" used to dupe Owen was "quite different from the one we saw." Her faith rested on the convincing manifestations she had witnessed, not on any particular medium. "I did not believe in the reality of what we saw because I trusted the honesty of the medium," she wrote to Hiram Corson, "and I do not doubt it now because they have been caught cheating." To the more skeptical Mrs. Corson, Andrews wrote, "I do not think anyone who has been really convinced of the reality of spirit manifestations can have that assurance shaken by the fact that spurious forms have sometimes been shown and accepted as real." Andrews, a frequent invalid, became a Spiritualist after the death of her only child. She wrote to Hiram Corson, "Since my faith in the nearness of loving and helpful spirits has been so strong I *never* feel that gloom or discontent which used often to foreshadow one in the past." In defense of materializations, she argued that "those who object to all physical manifestations cannot be affected by them as I am . . . I always felt as if lifted up into a sphere of peace and joy [illegible] while the spirits were manifesting their presence even in the simplest ways." The physical presence of her dead son helped Louisa Andrews function in the world of the living.[56]

While the Woodhull, Blavatsky, and Owen episodes displayed Spiritualist discord to the general public, Spiritualism struggled with internal conflicts. As spirit manifestations became more sensational and therefore harder to believe, mediums were subjected to vicious personal attacks from within their own ranks. A faithful Spiritualist public was understandably angered when they believed that mediums intentionally deceived them. Once mediums began to traffic in materialization, fraud was much easier to prove and certainly required the medium's conscious collusion. Incorrect messages could be attributed to the effect of a variety of psychological forces on an unconscious medium. But nothing could remove the guilt from a medium who donned a wig in a spirit closet to impersonate a beloved deceased parent or child. Public wrath poured out on mediums from within Spiritualism during the 1870s.

Spiritualists spent the decade preoccupied with accusations of fraud and attempts to vindicate specific mediums. Almost every issue of the *Banner* discussed these. Mediums attacked each other. Mrs. J. M. Carpenter exposed Annie Eva Fay by demonstrating Fay's feats without the assistance of spirits. Carpenter said that she exposed Fay to "keep separate the true from the false in Spiritualism." Carpenter claimed that she was always glad to have her own mediumship tested because "I do not desire to be self-deceived nor to deceive others." Washington Danskin observed that "discord, jealousies and selfish animosity are being spread abroad every week in our journals." Instead of raising their voices to promote universal freedom and progress, Spiritualists who accepted materializations spent the 1870s raising defense funds for the trials of prominent mediums accused of fraud.[57]

While sensational manifestations might or might not shake the faith of investigators, they presented definite problems to longtime leaders identified with a movement now gaining publicity for questionable phenomena. Andrew Jackson Davis was the first important Spiritualist to attack the new manifestations. Throughout the 1870s, he waged an unsuccessful campaign to assert the primacy of his philosophical system over the spirit manifestations that had spread its fame. He inaugurated the effort with the publication of *The Fountain with Jets of New Meaning* in 1870, which questioned the notion that departed spirits waited in readiness at any moment to be summoned by mediums or circles. Finally, in 1878, appalled by increasing sensationalism and by the "magical Spiritualism" of Madame Blavatsky, Davis attempted to sever Harmonial Philosophy from Spiritualism. "While harmonizing in essentials, Modern Spiritualism and Harmonial Philosophy directly antagonize in the sphere of public uses," Davis wrote, hoping to dissociate himself from the mass marketing of sensational phenomena. A small group followed him out of Spiritualism

into the First Harmonial Association of New York, but his philosophy
without spirit manifestations proved no more viable in 1878 than in
1848.[58]

No other major figures left Spiritualism over materializations, but
many expressed cautious skepticism over the direction of their movement. John C. Bundy, editor of the *Religio-Philosophical Journal,* joined
Davis's attempt to return to Spiritualism to its basic philosophy but
refused to go along in condemning séances altogether.[59] A struggle
emerged between Spiritualism's two major organs, the *Banner of Light*
always endorsing the most popular manifestations while the *Religio-
Philosophical Journal* argued for strict test conditions. Veteran trance
speakers expressed doubts about the new manifestations. Addie Ballou criticized Laura Ellis for her sensationalism.[60] Lizzie Doten attended eighteen séances at the Eddy homestead and found the materializations unsatisfactory. "While I have no positive evidence that
fraud has been practiced, yet there were many things that appeared
exceedingly doubtful," she wrote to the *Banner of Light.* She recommended that the Eddys either admit an occasional observer to their
cabinet or give up materialization séances. "In my 17 years experience in Spiritualism, I have learned that all communications from
spirits through human agency must necessarily partake largely of the
frailties, weaknesses, and errors of poor human nature," she wrote,
gently questioning the veracity of the Eddys' manifestations. When
Elizabeth Foote Denton criticized materializations, she wrote as a
loyal Spiritualist asking that strict standards of proof be used to secure the legitimacy of all phenomena. The *Banner* gave her critique
space on its front page but attacked her inside in an editorial titled
"Mrs. Denton Against Spiritualism." Materializations divided believers and left mediumship suspect even within Spiritualism.[61]

Christian Science versus Spiritualism

Perhaps the most serious challenge to mediumship came from the
new religious movement Christian Science. Christian Science accepted much of Spiritualism's basic outlook but rejected mediumship
altogether. Founded in 1875 by Mary Baker Eddy, one difference between Christian Science and Spiritualism was immediately evident in
the presence of a single founder figure who produced an authorita-

tive text that formed the basis of the faith. In the first edition of *Science and Health*, the Christian Science "text-book," Mary Baker Eddy treated the more substantive differences between Christian Science and Spiritualism in a lengthy chapter entitled "Imposition and Demonstration."* In it, Eddy took the claims of mediumship seriously and showed extensive familiarity with Spiritualist practice. "We have investigated the phenomena called mediumship both to convince ourself of its nature and cause and to be able to explain it," she wrote, "and have succeeded in the first instance but may have failed in the latter."[62] In addition to the claims of mediumship, Eddy took very seriously the concerns that prompted Americans to investigate Spiritualism. She tried to provide a comprehensive meaning system that would address those same concerns without recourse to spirit communication.

Christian Science emerged from a social context in which Spiritualism enjoyed wide acceptance. Many assumed Eddy to be a medium because she was a woman who healed without medicines or surgery.[63] But, in fact, like her first teacher, the mental healer Phineas Pankhurst Quimby, Eddy viewed her own approach to healing as thoroughly distinct from Spiritualism. Even before she defined her new faith, Eddy addressed "P. P. Quimby's spiritual science healing disease as opposed to deism or Rochester-Rapping Spiritualism" in one of her first public lectures.[64] Two years later, in 1866, Eddy's effort to heal herself after a fall on the ice led to her discovery of the principles of Christian Science. In spite of her own firm rejection of Spiritualism, she found the first sympathetic audience for her new faith among those whose interest in unorthodox metaphysics drew them to investigate Spiritualism. While committing her new views to paper in *Science and Health*, Mary Baker Eddy lived in two different Spiritualist boarding houses, where politeness compelled her to take a seat at the séance table. At the third Spiritualist home in which she resided while writing *Science and Health*, she converted her hostess to Christian Science. In 1868, Eddy advertised for students in the *Banner of Light*, offering to teach "healing on a *principle of science*," using "no medicine, electricity, physiology or hygiene." Nothing in the ad sug-

---

* "Imposition and Demonstration" was retitled first "Christian Science and Spiritualism" and eventually "Christian Science Versus Spiritualism," under which name it constitutes chapter 4 of the current authorized edition of *Science and Health*.

gested that she was a Spiritualist, but its presence in the *Banner* would have led potential students to assume that Eddy's system would at least be in sympathy with Spiritualist practices.[65]

Christian Science addressed the same basic needs that drew investigators to Spiritualism: it provided consolation for the bereaved by denying the reality of death, hope for the sick by denying the reality of disease, and support for the irrelevance of Calvinism by denying the reality of evil. Christian Science, like Spiritualism, claimed to be scientific, making recourse to empirical evidence. Also like Spiritualism, Christian Science consciously opposed itself to the doctrines of orthodoxy in both religion and medicine. It kept women out of the examining rooms of regular physicians, probably a health advantage during this period. Like Spiritualism, Christian Science further conflicted with regular medicine by encouraging women to become healers and by proposing an egalitarian relationship between healer and patient, in which anyone healed by Christian Science could go on to become a practitioner.

The most significant point on which Christian Scientists concurred with Spiritualists and differed from other Christians was in the belief that there is no change at death. However, Christian Science rejected the Spiritualist view that the continuity of life after death is proved by physical evidence of spirit presence. To answer the Spiritualist assertion that spirit manifestations show that we continue to have bodies after we die, Christian Scientists asserted that we never really had bodies to begin with, that the only part of the individual that ever really existed was the spirit, before or after death. Eddy called Spiritualists "gross materialists" because they based their belief in the immortality of the soul on manifestations that showed the continuity of individual characteristics, including physical characteristics, after death. "They make personality spirit . . . and, rejecting a personal God, make a God of persons . . . persons called spirits," Eddy explained. In contrast, she declared, "There is but one Spirit."[66]

Eddy's call to monotheism may sound like a reassertion of orthodoxy, but it accompanied an unorthodox transcendental understanding of God that formed the distinctive doctrine of her faith. Christian Science proclaimed that God is good and God is all. According to Eddy, God is the only substantial reality, and whatever is not God is insubstantial and nonexistent. Thus, evil does not exist but only reflects our false belief in its existence. Christian Science practice rested on the belief that correct thoughts, which rejected the erroneous belief in the reality of evil, could change material conditions. Illness, pain, and misfortune resulted from incorrect thoughts and could be cured by thoughts in harmony with the divine mind. This teaching further advanced the Spiritualist view that the world ultimately reflected a benign divine reality and that the welfare of human beings depended on being in harmony with the divine order. Christian Science concurred in the view that people are inherently good, each embodying God within, in contrast to the orthodox Christian doctrine of a fallen humanity in need of salvation.[67]

The historian Sydney Ahlstrom coined the term *harmonialism* to describe a cosmological outlook that can be traced from Swedenborgianism through Spiritualism to Christian Science and New Thought. The Christian Scientist historian Stephen Gottschalk takes issue with Ahlstrom's inclusion of Christian Science in the category harmonialism, arguing that Christian Science should be seen as a more orthodox Christian expression that acknowledges the need for salvation through Christ, although understood in a distinctive way. This disagreement is important for a discussion of Spiritualism because it bears on the extent to which Christian Science should be seen as growing out of Spiritualism and the extent to which it should be seen as a departure from the cosmological context in which it developed.[68]

In my view, both interpretations provide valuable insights for understanding the relation between Christian Science and Spiritualism. I concur with Ahlstrom in locating the origins of Christian Science in the same line of historical development that stretched from Swedenborgianism through Spiritualism to New Thought. Eddy used terms that had been developed in the writings of Andrew Jackson Davis. Concepts such as the "Father Mother God," "Christ Principle," and the definition of God as principal rather than person, which became quite important in Christian Science, would have been familiar to Eddy's Spiritualist readers, who might have taken their use as a sign of continuity with Davis's thought. Eddy probably referred to a number of sources during the composition of *Science and Health*, but the non-Spiritualist sources were obscure or unpublished, while the works of Andrew Jackson Davis were well known and widely read. Eddy assumed that the readers of *Science and Health* would be familiar with Spiritualism and that they would see in it apparent attractions about which she must disillusion them. These aspects of Eddy's teaching suggest that it should be seen as a development that followed directly from Spiritualism.[69]

More support for Ahlstrom's interpretation comes from the difficulty Eddy had in convincing her followers that Spiritualism and Christian Science were utterly incompatible. The two movements blended sympathetically in *The Soul: A Monthly Journal Devoted to the Theories and Phenomena of Soul, Mind and Intelligence,* published in Boston during the 1880s. One medium attended Eddy's course with her husband, A. J. Swarts. Mr. Swarts then attempted to teach Christian Science at Spiritualist camp meetings and at the "Spiritual Science University" he founded in Chicago. The errant student stated that he followed Eddy's teachings "to a fair extent, yet I cannot ignore Mediumship, Clairvoyance or Magnetism, in their proper office."[70] Eddy saw no need to explain the difference between Christian Science and any other contemporary religious movement, but convincing students to reject Spiritualism required constant reiteration. "Is spiritualism or mesmerism included in Christian Science?" Eddy asked rhetorically in a publication designed to provide answers to frequently asked questions. "They are wholly apart from it," was her clear reply.[71] The amount of attention Eddy devoted to distinguishing her movement from Spiritualism suggests that she viewed Spiritualism as the religion with which her own faith could be most easily confused.

On the other hand, Gottschalk's interpretation of Christian Science as stemming from Protestant orthodoxy is helpful in emphasizing the focus on evil present in Christian Science but absent from other harmonial groups. Mary Baker Eddy had no doubt that the mortal, human aspects of each person reflected the total depravity of Adam's legacy. Although Eddy believed that evil did not exist, she was preoccupied with fighting the dangerous temporal effect of the belief in evil. This concern gave her cosmology a very different tone from Spiritualism, which had virtually nothing to say about evil. From her conviction that mind could control matter, Eddy concluded that, if thoughts could heal, they could also harm. She feared the "mental malpractice" of those who wished her ill and attributed her husband's death to arsenic placed in his body by the malicious thoughts of her enemies. Eddy taught that spiritual phenomena resulted from the power of the medium's mind to read the thoughts of investigators and, in some cases, to actualize them in material form. She viewed mediumship as potentially destructive and in need of scrutiny because it demonstrated the power of the human mind to control matter in ways that could be used against others.[72]

This view of mediumship formed the core of Eddy's critique of Spiritualism, one of the most salient penned by a nineteenth-century author. The text of *Science and Health* shows the reader a well-informed and respectful author familiar with a wide variety of mediumistic phenomena as well as with the writing of Andrew Jackson Davis. Eddy describes having witnessed manifestations, trance speaking, and attempts at healing through clairvoyance and even quotes from the *Banner of Light*. While most critics attributed manifestations either to fraud or to the credulity of investigators, Eddy explained the phenomena without questioning the integrity of either the investigator or the medium. "The reader must make due distinction between mediumship and the individual," Eddy explained; "there are undoubtedly noble purposes in the hearts of noble women and men who believe themselves mediums."[73]

Most critics of Spiritualism ridiculed investigators as well as mediums. Laced with compassion for the anguish that prompted investigation, Eddy's critique acknowledged the reality and the value of every heartfelt experience that led believers to Spiritualism. "Mediums have a strong hold on the sympathies of those who mourn the loss of friends," Eddy wrote. "In the sorrow of bereavement . . . they turn the gushing emotions into the belief they are not separated, and this comfort comes to the mourner like heaven's benediction, gaining a strong foothold in the minds of millions." Hers is a critique that could be read with interest by a sincere Spiritualist.[74]

Perhaps most important in appealing to an audience sympathetic to Spiritualism, Eddy did not dismiss the possibility of spirit communication out of hand. Rather, she argued that real spirit communication would not address the senses, as Spiritualists claimed, but would appear without matter. If it were in fact possible to see spirits, Eddy told her readers, we would see them all the time and have no need of mediums to facilitate communication. Eddy left open the possibility that true spiritual manifestations, obtained without mediumship, could occur. "What are termed spiritual manifestations, as progress compels the change, will be found not mediumship, but openly defined, and when confined within the limits of harmony . . . it will be time to consider them demonstrations of science, but not until then. These manifestations at present are the results of tricks or belief."[75]

Eddy's analysis of trance speaking also acknowledged the effectiveness of Spiritualism. She recognized that speaking mediums in trance could give lectures of which they would be incapable in a normal state. She attributed the extraordinary abilities of trance speakers to the power of their belief that external intelligences spoke through them.

> When eloquence proceeds from the belief a departed "spirit" is speaking, and can say what the so-called medium is incapable of uttering, or even knowing alone, the fetters of mind are unclasped, and forgetting her ignorance, by believing others are speaking for her, becomes eloquent beyond her usual self, and because she believes the one spirit is helping her. Now destroy this belief of aid, and the old limits personal sense assigns are resumed, and she says I am incapable of "words that glow" because I am uneducated.[76]

Eddy's keen appreciation of the tangible impact of Spiritualism on believers' lives made her arguments accessible to some whose sympathies would not allow them to entertain critiques based on ridicule of mediums or investigators. For the sick or bereaved who found what they were looking for in the séance room but had difficulty accepting Spiritualist claims about the source of what they saw, Christian Science provided an explanation that did not question the integrity of their experience. This approach had a special potential to influence a group more important within Spiritualism than in most religious groups: the as-yet-unconvinced investigator.

Eddy's attack on mediumship allowed her to build a movement that could assign her a unique leadership position. Under Eddy's leadership, Christian Science became a tightly organized movement, with a firm structure ensuring the continuity of her own teachings as the sole basis of the church. Mary Baker Eddy's role as founder and author of the authoritative "text-book" *Science and Health* meant that the new movement could not countenance the extreme individualism so central to Spiritualism. In Christian Science worship, selections from *Science and Health* and from the New Testament replaced sermons, and those who presided were called "readers" rather than "ministers" because their function was to read the words of Mary Baker Eddy, not to interpret scripture on their own. Where Spiritualists emphasized personal spiritual knowledge, Christian Scientists emphasized doctrinal uniformity.

While mediumship implied that women as a group had natural qualities of spiritual leadership, Christian Science asserted that one woman had unique spiritual attributes. Although the new movement produced in its founder one of the most important female religious leaders in American history, it discouraged other women from following her example. Christian Science did empower women within certain well-defined limits; it asked them to lead worship services, to become healers, and to assume a variety of public roles within their church. However, Eddy censured any who emulated her by aspiring to religious authority in any way comparable to hers. She prohibited the use of writings on Christian Science other than her own and limited the terms of readers to three years so that no local leader could ever attract a personal following. The authoritative role of Eddy's teachings left no outlet for the creativity of other leaders and forced Eddy to expel several powerful women who were among her most effective advocates. Christian Science promoted the exclusive authority of one woman rather than promoting women's leadership as a principle. Lacking Spiritualism's individualist base, Christian Scientists had no religious motivation to become reform activists. The boundless energy that Spiritualists poured into their many cherished social reforms Christian Scientists devoted to building their own movement.[77]

Mary Baker Eddy's critique of Spiritualism as materialistic drew added salience from the timing of its publication. The appearance of *Science and Health* in 1875 coincided with the duping of Robert Dale Owen by the materialized spirit of Katie King and with Olcott and Blavatsky's publicization of the materializations at the Eddy homestead, followed by the founding of the Theosophical Society. Both the Spiritualist public and the public at large were disillusioned by the sensationalism of materializations. While Theosophy drew off a small group of intellectuals interested in esoteric knowledge and the ancient wisdom of the East, Christian Science, at the opposite extreme, provided a religious alternative cleansed of any possible association with sensational manifestations or with the occult. Eddy's critique of spirit manifestations as materialistic echoed new concerns voiced by many who would previously have defended the phenomena. Among these was Mary Fenn Davis, who published *Danger Signals: An Address on the Uses and Abuses of Modern Spiritualism*, also in 1875. In it she decried popular misconceptions about the true nature of Spiritualism and asserted its opposition to the materialism implied by materialization séances.[78]

In sensational mediumship, the dangers of basing women's leadership on stereotyped feminine qualities came to the fore. What, after all, was the difference between a lovely young woman charming a man into showering her with gifts and favors duirng a séance, as Ka-

tie King did to Robert Dale Owen, and doing the same during an
afternoon tea, as did conventional Victorian young ladies? Mary Fenn
Davis warned against the exaggerated passivity of the new mediumship. "It is an abuse of Spiritualism to *yield up selfhood* in the absorbing
investigation of the phenomena," she told her audience. She cautioned mediums to accept spirit guides as friends and teachers only.
"If we allow this inward joy to sweep away our strength, if we become
entirely passive to the will of spiritual beings, and instead of cultivat-
ing within ourselves positive goodness, content ourselves with negative goodness only, we open the avenues through which low and discordant influences can easily reach our natures." Finally, she called
Spiritualists back to the principle of individual sovereignty that made
mediumship a source of power for women in the 1850s and 1860s.
"It is dangerous and destructive to lay aside our own judgment in
obedience to any authority outside ourselves."[79] Without the ideological backing that tied Spiritualism to radical reform in the earlier period, mediumship ceased to empower women as individuals or to be a
model of women's power and independence to those who witnessed it.

Like the move toward organization in the 1860s, the attacks on mediumship during the 1870s marked a questioning of the value of the
feminine qualities that had been so admired in the mediums and
trance speakers of Spiritualism's first decades. The less innocent postwar public appreciated the conflict between the feminine ideals of
purity and passivity that apparently went unnoticed before the Civil
War. Even the mediums' defenders admitted that feminine qualities
could lead to immorality. In 1878, leader A. E. Newton observed that
"a keenly susceptible medium, having no dishonest or unworthy mo-
tive, is *liable* to be prompted, perhaps I should say *impelled*, by the
mental action of surrounding persons, in or out of the body, to acts
of deception or other immoralities."[80] The doubts about mediumship
that concerned only the few leaders participating in the American
Association of Spiritualists in the late 1860s became the preoccupation of all Spiritualists in the 1870s.

As mediumship sustained attacks from every direction, fewer
women felt the promptings of heavenly communications. Indeed,
with damning criticism emanating from both inside and outside spiritualist ranks, mediumship, especially public mediumship, lost many
of the benefits women previously derived from it. Where it once
helped women to overcome self-doubt, it could easily become a
source of humiliation and embarrassment to those who attempted the
sensational manifestations expected in the 1870s. By 1875, the name

of the annual "Mediums and Speakers Convention" had to be changed because so few in attendance were mediums. A correspondent complained of the lack of mediums to the *Banner of Light,* observing that many mediums no longer practiced their gifts and that those who left public life were not being replaced by new laborers. Spiritualism distinguished itself less and less among religious groups by fostering female leadership.[81]

In addition to the founding of Christian Science by Mary Baker Eddy, the public notoriety accorded to Blavatsky and Woodhull may seem to indicate an increase in women's leadership during the 1870s, but in fact the scandal that surrounded both figures undermined Spiritualism's claim that woman's nature suited her to be a teacher of religion. Blavatsky and Woodhull confirmed the public's worst fears about the dangers of exposing female sexuality to the amoral public sphere. In the popular mind, the passivity believed to be inherent in woman's nature made Woodhull and Blavatsky pawns for the spread of licentiousness, not vehicles for revelation. Although Woodhull achieved widespread fame and Blavatsky became the founder of a religious movement that still exists today, both figures, as did Mary Baker Eddy, emphasized their own leadership rather than the empowerment of women in general.

Under these conditions, Spiritualism ceased to be a locus of either spiritual or political power for women. The new manifestations lacked the potential to be vehicles for the social criticism delivered by trance speakers. Medium Melvina Townsend nostalgically recalled the "days gone by when angel Achsa Sprague stood as a queen of power."[82] As women lost visibility on the Spiritualist platform, their concerns played a smaller role in the movement's priorities. The 1878 meeting of the Vermont State Spiritualist Association exemplified changes in the movement. A discussion of "What should we Spiritualists do for the benefit of humanity?" recommended "home influence" as the first step toward social uplift, a far cry from the sweeping reforms advocated twenty years before. Lamenting the changes in Spiritualism, Thomas Middleton "spoke forcibly on the apparent reluctance of the female portion of the audience to speak in conference." Mrs. S. A. Wiley closed with "a radical yet sympathetic address," a qualification formerly unnecessary among Vermont Spiritualists. Spiritualism continued to thrive, but its new position in the American religious landscape presented fewer challenges to the status of women.[83]

"The Same Hand that Guided Me Here Will Hold Me There"

T he attractions of communication with the dead proved too strong to be wiped away by the scandals and defections of the 1870s.[1] Spiritualism enjoyed a resurgence during the 1880s, but it never resumed its earlier role as a central agent of feminism. While no other group competed for that role at mid-century, by the 1880s a broad and increasingly evangelical suffrage campaign overshadowed what remained of Spiritualist agitation. As a movement, Spiritualism lost much of its radical thrust, but, as a faith, it continued to support individual radical activists. The generation of women empowered by Spiritualism did not lose their inspiration when the movement ceased to provide it. Instead they continued to speak out for controversial causes, using skills gained within Spiritualism on a variety of campaigns for women's emancipation. For example, while the Woodhull scandal rocked local Spiritualist organizations, Mary Fenn Davis and trance speaker Charlotte Beebe Wilbour were occupied by their roles as vice-president and president of the new organization of literary women, Sorosis.[2] Attacks on mediumship in the 1870s failed to diminish the strength of conviction of a generation of Spiritualists committed to woman's rights.

Spiritualism and Woman Suffrage

Woman suffrage benefited more than any other movement from the self-confidence women gained in Spiritualism. During the last quarter of the nineteenth century, Spiritualism and suffrage engaged in a two-way exchange. The heterodox religion attracted many women who had already come to prominence as leaders in the suffrage movement. Even as the woman's rights movement drifted from its individualist origins and the political thrust of Spiritualism diminished, many suffrage leaders found meaning in a religion that reinforced the self-ownership of women. Although the mere advocacy of woman's rights no longer required divine sanction by the end of the century, devoting one's life to the cause was still a risky undertaking. As suffrage narrowed, Spiritualism continued to validate a creative nonconformity for its leaders. The other side of the exchange occurred when the dynamic speaking mediums of the Civil War period transferred their talents to the suffrage cause. Most continued to speak in trance but spoke for suffrage in a conscious state as well. The ranks of the trance lecturers provided a corps of experienced female speakers for the suffrage campaign.

California suffragists relied almost exclusively on trance speakers during 1870, the first season of general agitation in that state. Of the nine women listed in the *History of Woman Suffrage* as holding suffrage meetings during the 1870 campaign, six also appear in the *Banner of Light*'s "List of Lecturers." Of the remaining three, only one cannot be positively identified as a Spiritualist. The single man on the list, John A. Collins, served as president of the Society of Progressive Spiritualists in San Francisco. He was the only man to serve as an officer of California's first suffrage organization. One of the speakers, Mrs. H. M. F. Brown, was on salary as missionary of the American Association of Spiritualists, and another, Mrs. F. A. Logan, had just finished a year as missionary for the Minnesota State Spiritualist Association.[3] Coreligionists thought a third California speaker, Addie Ballou, exceptionally talented. A sister speaker recalled, "Where cold intellect has failed to reach the heart she takes captive many a soul with her woman-love." These were experienced speakers nurtured within Spiritualism. They had joined the suffrage movement in 1870 while it still shared much of the broad Spiritualist woman's rights program. But once involved, they remained active even when the suffrage movement veered from its earlier basis.[4]

. The women of California did not hesitate to choose trance mediums when they selected their most effective speakers. They sent mediums Laura de Force Gordon, Laura Cuppy Smith, and Caroline Spear to present the first woman suffrage petition to the California legislature. When the state senate considered a woman suffrage bill, advocates sent Laura Gordon and Addie Ballou together with the state superintendent of the Woman's Christian Temperance Union, Sarah M. Severance, to advance their cause. The California State Suffrage Association elected Laura de Force Gordon president from 1884 to 1894, during which time she attended a number of national conventions. Medium Elizabeth Kingsbury founded the Southern California Woman Suffrage Association in 1885 and presided over it until she returned East five years later. During the 1888 political campaign, both parties employed trance speakers to take their case to the all-male electorate. The Democrats hired Laura de Force Gordon, and the Republicans hired Addie Ballou.[5]

The biography of Laura de Force Gordon (see plate 14) typified the course that many women followed from trance medium to suffragist. As a teenager, Laura de Force led the itinerant life of a traveling trance speaker, touring throughout New York and New England as well as her native Pennsylvania. She was a popular speaker, sharing top billing with Lizzie Doten at the Abington Grove meeting in 1860.[6] "The people of Decorah are unusually exercised under the spiritual exercises of Miss Force," a local newspaper reported after she gave a spontaneous lecture on "Astronomy," the subject selected by her audience.[7] Her marriage in 1862 at the age of twenty-three did not interrupt her speaking career but did exacerbate the feelings of homesickness she had always felt while in the lecture field.[8] "To the poor, earnest hearted itinerant, dollars and cents, sufficient to supply present or even future wants, is poor remuneration for the sacrifice of conjugal, fraternal, or social enjoyments of home," she wrote in 1863. "Naught but the hope of benefiting society by their labors, could retain them in the lecturing field."[9]

When Laura de Force Gordon and her husband moved to California in 1868, she took the opportunity of their westward journey to "benefit society by her labors" along the route. As a trance medium, she could speak on whatever the occasion demanded. In one town in Nevada, she lectured on Spiritualism at the court house and on temperance at the Methodist church and gave a third lecture on woman suffrage at which she took subscriptions to Stanton and Anthony's newspaper, the *Revolution*.[10] Her first lecture in San Francisco provided the initial impulse toward the founding of the California Woman Suffrage Society in 1870. For the next two years, she traveled throughout the Northwest as a woman suffrage lecturer and was nominated for the state senate while still publicly identified as a Spiritualist.[11] During the next decade, she divorced her husband for adultery, became one of the first two women admitted to the California bar, and built a successful legal practice. At some point after the mid-1870s, she lost faith in the spirit guides who empowered her first decades of public speaking. Firmly established in a respectable career, Laura de Force Gordon no longer needed assistance from external intelligences. In 1905, two years before her death, she identified herself as an agnostic, "with leanings toward Theosophy."[12] While many mediums followed Laura Gordon into the suffrage campaign, it is difficult to tell how many followed her out of Spiritualism once they arrived there. The record does show, however, that communication with the dead became a less urgent priority for trance speakers who found prominent roles in the suffrage movement.

The California suffrage campaign may have had unusual opportunities to utilize trance speakers because mediums and radicals responded disproportionately to the call of the West during the last quarter of the nineteenth century. Radical Spiritualists used geographic mobility as one more way to abrogate convention: they moved to the West, where society enjoyed relative freedom from traditional values and institutions.[13] Spiritualist Abbigail Bush, the first woman to chair a woman's rights convention, moved to California by 1869 and was followed by Fanny Green McDougall, Elizabeth Lowe Watson, Laura de Force Gordon, Hannah Brown, and a host of other radicals.[14] The stories of many of the characters in this book end on the West Coast. Lois Waisbrooker ended her days at the anarchist colony of Home, Washington.[15] Annie Denton Cridge (whose baby's death began her mediumship and this narrative) left her family in Washington, D.C., to grow oranges in Riverside, California, in 1870, both to raise money for publication of her four-volume manuscript and "to demonstrate that the self-salvation of women lies in the culture of the soil." According to her husband, who remained East to collect his salary, she died there in 1874 from overwork, separation from the reform field, and "the misery of the isolated household." He reported to the *Banner of Light* that both his son and his daughter practiced Spiritualism and talked with their dead mother.[16]

Although the dominance of Spiritualists in the California suffrage movement may be a special case, suffrage also shared leaders with Spiritualism in older states with strong Protestant establishments where greater risks accrued to association with religious heterodoxy than in California. In Connecticut, New Jersey, Indiana, New York, and Michigan, mediums and their supporters played important roles in state campaigns. Throughout the country, the suffrage movement benefited from Spiritualism's best speakers.[17]

While mediums moved onto the suffrage platform, suffragists received a warm welcome at Spiritualist gatherings. Most picnics and camp meetings found a slot for suffrage between entertainments. The *Banner of Light* briefly introduced a "Woman's Rights Department" and published a copy of a suffrage petition in 1873 for readers to cut out and send to their legislators.[18] During the 1890s, Susan B. Anthony balked public opinion every summer to participate in Woman Suffrage Day at Lily Dale, a regular feature of the program at the Spiritualist resort founded by Anthony's old cohorts in the North Collins Yearly Meeting of Progressive Friends. Other Woman's Day speakers at Lily Dale included Anna Howard Shaw, Harriet Stanton Blatch, Charlotte Perkins Gillman, Ida Husted Harper, and Margaret Sanger.[19] Suffragist editor Abigail Scott Duniway told readers of the *New Northwest* that she liked to notice Spiritualism in her columns because "unlike all other religious bodies . . . they invite us to their platforms." She spoke on suffrage every summer at Oregon's Spiritualist grove meetings.[20]

Spiritualism was only one small factor contributing to the rise and progress of the suffrage movement, but it is helpful to understanding the inner struggles of some of its leaders. Spiritualism never enjoyed numerical dominance among suffragists. Mainstream Protestants, many of them associated with Christian reform efforts, provided greater numbers to the movement. However, important suffragists strongly identified with evangelicalism adopted Spiritualism toward the end of their lives. Even the loyal Methodist Frances Willard became an interested investigator, and Paulina Wright Davis, Isabella Beecher Hooker, Mary Livermore, and May Wright Sewall, for example, all died secure in the knowledge that they had communicated with those who had gone before them.[21] The Spiritualist faith continued to attract leaders working for social change even after the religious movement lost much of its political focus. Sewall adopted Spiritualism in 1897 following a visit to Lily Dale at which she communicated with her recently deceased second husband. For the next twenty-three years, she concealed her almost daily communication with spirits, fearing it might compromise her credibility as a reformer. Finally, two weeks before her death in 1920, she revealed her faith and authorized publication of a book she had secretly written about her Spiritualist experiences.[22]

As the twentieth century dawned, it found the aging Susan B. Anthony still laboring for woman suffrage, the cause to which she had devoted half a century. Having envied the inspired eloquence of her Spiritualist coworkers when she began her work, she now appreciated the certainty their faith gave them as her generation approached death. Now in her eighties, Anthony wrote to her friend, the medium and suffragist Elizabeth Lowe Watson, that their journeys "must soon come to an end" and wondered what awaited them beyond this life. "You think you know—but I do not, only that I have the *faith* that the same hand that has guided me here—will continue to hold me there." Although still voicing an investigator's uncertainty, Anthony expected the same power that led her to dedicate her life to woman's emancipation to govern her fate after death.[23]

The Legacy of Radical Individualism

In addition to providing support and trained speakers for the suffrage movement, Spiritualism fostered another group of female leaders who worked for woman's rights. These were radical reformers whose views distanced them from the increasingly conservative suffrage movement. Most had been young activists before the war and remained loyal to the broad woman's rights program of the 1850s. During the 1870s and 1880s, suffrage leaders chose to tone down their radical views and Garrisonian roots in order to gain popular support for suffrage, especially among churchgoing women. Spiritualists complained that the woman's rights movement had "surrendered to the control of Orthodoxy" to avoid "the scandal of free love which attaches to all who want to make marriage better for women." In Illinois, Spiritualists assisted an attempt to keep the cause of suffrage in radical hands but were defeated, in part because of their perennial disorganization. "However," a Spiritualist newspaper maintained, "a few independent workers, not at all identified with the organic movement, are still doing (not saying) more for the cause than those to whom the work is committed in trust as its guardians."[24]

These "independent workers" were the indefatigable Spiritualist woman's rights advocates discussed in chapter 3, who still maintained their commitment to individual sovereignty and to the broad reform agenda that it dictated. Although they spoke and wrote in favor of woman suffrage, many became identified with movements espousing a broader reorganization of society. The hydropathic physician Juliet Stillman Severance became involved in the labor movement. In addition to serving as president of state Spiritualist associations in Illinois, Wisconsin, and Minnesota, she served in three presidential nominating conventions of the Labor Party, introduced the woman suffrage plank at the 1888 convention that formed the Union Labor party, and served for three years as master workman of the Knights of Labor. As well as asserting the need to include woman's rights in the program of various radical movements, Severance fought the growing conservatism among feminists. She opposed, for example, the proposal of the Woman's Social Science Association to make castration "the penalty for misused sexuality" to prevent the reproduction of every "drunkard, . . . person guilty of incest, every felon, idiot, and wife-beater." Severance argued from the antebellum romantic view that benign natural laws embodied in the individual should be allowed to proceed unhindered. "I cannot see that the destruction of any organ that executes the perverted will of badly regulated minds can be other than an interference with the chances for development of the individual, which should be the grand consideration and aim, not their destruction," she wrote in the anarchist periodical *Liberty* in 1883.[25]

Never forsaking woman's rights or Spiritualism, trance speaker Addie Ballou became a leader of Bellamy nationalism and socialism in California.[26] Lois Waisbrooker combined both movements with activism in anarchism and free speech. Editor Julia Schlesinger believed that "in order to be free women must be financially independent," so she combined her mediumship with a campaign for economic justice for women. She used her Spiritualist journal, the *Carrier Dove,* to promote suffrage and expose poverty in San Francisco and to attack the excesses of wealthy families.[27] These women, like most Spiritualist reformers, were first and foremost activists. They combined diverse affiliations, all of which they saw as necessary to the progress of society. Although each showed firm commitment to the campaigns in which she participated, it would be incorrect to lift out any one "ism" as dominating their concerns. Committed to a thorough overhaul of society, they advocated a host of causes with equal ardor. Even Cora Hatch (now Richmond), still a well-known medium as she neared fifty, petitioned the governor of Illinois for clemency for the Haymarket anarchists in 1887.[28] Spiritualism provided a continuing rallying point for radical women whose personal and political programs were incompatible with the increasingly conservative suffrage movement.

Historians have judged nineteenth-century reformers harshly for bowing to expediency in order to gain implementation of the measures they proposed. The woman suffrage movement, especially, has been criticized for making the ideological concessions necessary to create the broad coalition that led to its eventual victory.[29] In contrast, Spiritualists' staunch refusal to compromise their convictions for any reason won them the title "fanatic" both from their contemporaries and from twentieth-century authors. To dismiss Spiritualists as a "lunatic fringe" is to ignore the significant ways in which their faith reflected the values of Victorian America. Every practice or idea developed within Spiritualism was an extreme form of an idea already afloat in American culture. Ever uncompromising, Spiritualists asked other Americans to make consistent application of their beliefs about the continuity of the personality after death, the natural piety of women, the reunion of families in heaven, the sacrality of the marriage bond, and the autonomy of individual conscience. By the end of the century, the success of moderate versions of the Spiritualist program would be evident in the abolition of slavery, the triumph of liberal theology, drastically transformed attitudes toward death and mourning, the "feminization of American religion," and the emergence of a popular movement for woman's rights. By aggressively asserting radical positions on the spectrum of contemporary cultural trends, Spiritualism dislodged the center of public opinion from traditional views and contributed to the success of religious and social liberalism.[30]

Though Spiritualism contributed to the disestablishment of America's Calvinist heritage, its own doctrines remained permanently outside the pale of acceptable public opinion. While a broad spectrum of the population found the promise of communication with the dead attractive and welcomed some of the trends that Spiritualism encouraged, only a fraction of these accepted the full implication drawn by Spiritualists that spirit communication superseded Christian revelation. The number of Americans who wanted to talk to the dead and who investigated the possibility of doing so always exceeded the number who were willing to forgo the hope of achieving salvation through Christ. America's identity as a Christian nation became more firmly entrenched than ever as the twentieth century opened. As broad as

Spiritualism's appeal was, its critique of Christianity as inherently oppressive was as controversial in 1900 as it had been in 1848.

Because of these factors, Spiritualism provides a test case of the probable fate of the suffrage movement if it had not made the compromises it did. The leaders of the suffrage movement have been criticized by twentieth-century historians for straying from the comprehensive radicalism that characterized the early years of woman's rights agitation. Historians have been most critical of suffragists' compromises of principle regarding issues of class and race. However, religion was probably the issue that could most easily have destroyed the nineteenth-century suffrage coalition. Suffragists' refusal to extend their critique of inequality to include institutional Christianity won them their largest organizational ally, the Woman's Christian Temperance Union, but it nearly cost them the participation of Elizabeth Cady Stanton and ultimately did alienate leader Matilda Joslyn Gage. Religious radicalism was part of the antebellum reform program that suffragists sacrificed in order to make their cause more acceptable. Spiritualist woman's rights advocates, in contrast, persisted in pressing the full array of antebellum demands, including the condemnation of Christianity as inherently hierarchical and therefore oppressive to women. They never swerved from their early socialist or free love views and maintained racial attitudes more egalitarian than those held by mainstream suffragists. As a result, they were spurned by turn-of-the-century reform movements and excluded from the public discussion of social issues. Had the suffragists followed a similar course, their movement might have met with a similar fate at the hands of historians: instead of being criticized, Spiritualists have been either ridiculed or ignored.[31]

Ironically, Spiritualism's role in expanding American ideological alternatives dwindled as a result of the success of the campaigns it had done so much to advance. The concurrent success and failure of Spiritualism is evident in the contrasting choices made by two young women from Rockford, Illinois, separated in time by a crucial decade and a half. In 1857, Martha Hulett, a seventeen-year-old farmer's daughter, made a sensation by speaking in trance in Rockford and the neighboring towns. Fifteen years later, Alta C. Hulett, age eighteen, probably Martha's relative, lectured in the same Illinois towns on her right to practice the profession for which she had prepared but from which she was excluded because of her sex: law. Alta Hulett authored the legislation that permitted women to practice law in Illinois and became the first woman admitted to the Illinois bar. If these two women were related, or even if they were not, they present a revealing comparison. In 1857, an independent young woman needed the support of invisible intelligences to justify her public appearance. In 1873, a woman similarly situated spoke to defend her right to participate in a highly respected profession for which she had trained in the traditional manner. In 1857, the speaker and her audience attributed her eloquence to spirits; in 1873, she spoke on her own authority. The trance speaker's role in opening the public platform to women helped make possible the use of the platform to demand further expansion of women's opportunities two decades later. Because spirit guidance enabled one generation of women to become public speakers, the next generation of women activists did not require the same assistance. The advances made by trance speakers made their existence unnecessary.[32]

Spiritualism helped a crucial generation of American women find their voice. It produced both the first large group of female religious leaders and the first sizable group of American women to speak in public. Whether one views the medium's voice as inspired by an external intelligence or by some remote region of her own mind, the trance state liberated it. Trance removed the power of social sanctions both inside and outside the medium's psyche. Some authors, most notably Ann Douglas, have argued that the "feminization of American culture" reflected in Spiritualism perpetuated women's restricted role and produced a morally impotent sentimental culture.[33] The history of Spiritualism suggests, on the contrary, that the identification of piety with femininity could aid in the expansion of women's options and contribute to the potency of a comprehensive moral idealism. More women stepped beyond conventional female roles because of Spiritualism than they would have without it. In mediumship and in its inherent individualism, Spiritualism held up a model of women's unlimited capacity for autonomous action to the men and women of nineteenth-century America.

Finally, Spiritualism's enduring appeal to reformers, and to others, lay in its unique ability to satisfy the one dear hope that no other movement could: the abolition of death. As part of the cultural vocabulary of the reformers who had their roots in abolition, Spiritualism remained sufficiently familiar to be available as a possible interpretation of experience but did not have such weight that it enforced itself on them. When faced with personal losses, reformers continued

to turn to Spiritualism for consolation. Second generation suffragist
Alice Stone Blackwell recalled that, when her mother, Lucy Stone,
was approaching death in 1893, "something was said about her possibly coming back to communicate with those she had left." Stone,
who had already expressed her confidence that when woman suffrage was granted she would "know it on the other side," replied, "I
expect to be too busy to come back." Stone's disclaimer not withstanding, her bereft husband, Henry Blackwell, "sat night after night alone
in her room in the dark, to see if her spirit might come to him." "But,"
daughter Alice Stone Blackwell recorded, "there was no voice or to-
ken, and neither he nor I could put any faith in the mediums who
professed to bring us messages from her."[34] Henry Blackwell did not
believe in mediums, but he did want to talk to his wife. For Blackwell,
as for many Americans, the bonds of love uniting him to a human
companion proved stronger than the dictates of reason that told him
that her voice was stilled. Long after the cultural milieu that produced a religion of radical individualism vanished from the scene,
Spiritualism continued, and continues today, to attract those unable
to accept that death marks a final separation from cherished friends.

ABBREVIATIONS

AIPFP   Amy and Isaac Post Family Papers, University of Rochester Department of Rare Books and Special Collections.

AWS   Achsa W. Sprague Papers, Vermont Historical Society, Montpelier.

BL   *Banner of Light* (Boston, Mass.).

HWS   *History of Woman Suffrage,* ed. Elizabeth Cady Stanton, Susan B. Anthony, Matilda Joslyn Gage, 4 vols. (New York: Fowler & Wells, 1881–1902).

LMC   *The Collected Correspondence of Lydia Maria Child, 1817–1880,* ed. Patricia Holland and Milton Meltzer, microfiche ed. (Millwood, N.Y.: Krause Microform, 1980).

MJPP   Mary and Joseph Post Papers, private collection.

NAW   *Notable American Women,* ed. Edward T. James, Janet Wilson James, and Paul Boyer, 3 vols. (Cambridge, Mass.: Harvard University Press, 1975).

"Sprague's Diary"   Leonard Twynham, ed., "Selections from Achsa Sprague's Diary and Journal," *Proceedings of the Vermont Historical Society* 9 (1941): 131–84.

NOTES

Introduction

1. Anne Denton Cridge, "Obituary of Denton Cridge," *Vanguard* 1 (1857): 222.
2. Anne Denton Cridge, "Experiences of a Skeptical Medium," *Vanguard* 1 (1857): 260.
3. Cridge, "Obituary of Denton Cridge," 222.
4. *Social Revolutionist* 1 (1856): 24, 41, 57. *Vanguard*, 18 December 1858, 1.
5. The best modern account of Spiritualism is R. Laurence Moore, *In Search of White Crows* (New York: Oxford University Press, 1977). Although Spiritualism dated its origins to 1848, it did not settle on its name until 1852. Ernest Joseph Isaacs, "A History of Nineteenth-Century American Spiritualism as a Religious and Social Movement" (Ph.D. diss., University of Wisconsin, 1975), 102–3. From the United States, the movement spread to England, Western Europe, and throughout the British colonies. In many parts of the world, it merged with spiritualistic practices of African origin. For examples of these, see Irving Zaretsky and Cynthia Shambaugh, *Spirit Possession and Spirit Mediumship in Africa and Afro-America: An Annotated Bibliography* (New York: Garland Publishing, 1978).
6. Elizabeth Cady Stanton, Susan B. Anthony, and Matilda Joslyn Gage, eds., *History of Woman Suffrage* (herafter cited as *HWS*), 4 vols. (Rochester, N.Y.: Fowler & Wells, 1881–1902), 3:530. The statement about female leadership appears in the chapter on Michigan compiled by Spiritualist Catharine A. F. Stebbins (3:514).
7. Fred Folio (pseud.), *Lucy Boston: or, Women's Rights and Spiritualism, Illustrating the Follies and Delusions of the Nineteenth Century* (Auburn, N.Y.: Alden & Beardsley, 1855).
8. Mary Farrell Bednarowski, "Nineteenth-Century American Spiritualism: An Attempt at a Scientific Religion" (Ph.D. diss., University of Minnesota, 1973), passim.
9. Charles E. Rosenberg, *No Other Gods: Science and American Social Thought* (Baltimore: Johns Hopkins University Press, 1976), 2.

10. Robert Luther Thompson, *Wiring a Continent: The History of the Telegraph Industry in the United States, 1832–1866* (Princeton, N.J.: Princeton University Press, 1947), 16–19.

11. For an interesting discussion of electricity and Spiritualism by a nineteenth-century intellectual who found electricity "mysterious," see Lydia Maria Child to Harriet Winslow Sewall, 11 July 1880, and Lydia Maria Child to Lucy Searle, 3 January 1862, *The Collected Correspondence of Lydia Maria Child, 1817–1888* (hereafter referred to as *LMC*), ed. Patricia Holland and Milton Meltzer, microfiche ed. (Millwood, N.Y.: Kraus Microfilm, 1980).

12. Emma Hardinge, *Modern American Spiritualism* (1869; reprint, New York: University Books, 1970), 45. Charles S. Woodruff, M.D., *Legalized Prostitution: or, Marriage As It Is, and Marriage As It Should Be, Philosophically Considered* (Boston: Bela Marsh, 1862), 158. Ann King to Amy Post, 11 April 1853, Amy and Isaac Post Family Papers (hereafter referred to as AIPFP), University of Rochester Library, Department of Rare Books and Special Collections. Isaac Post, *Voices from the Spirit World* (Rochester, N.Y.: C. H. McDonell, 1852), xiii.

13. Robert Darnton, *Mesmerism and the End of the Enlightenment in France* (Cambridge, Mass.: Harvard University Press, 1968), 10–15.

14. Rosemary R. Ruether and Eleanor McLaughlin, introduction to *Women of Spirit: Female Leadership in the Jewish and Christian Traditions*, ed. Rosemary R. Ruether and Eleanor McLaughlin (New York: Simon & Schuster, 1979), 16–28.

15. Shirley MacLaine, *Out on a Limb* (New York: Bantam Books, 1984), 163.

16. See, e.g., Ken Wilber, "There Is No New Age," *One Earth, the Findhorn Foundation Magazine* 8 (Summer 1988): 12–15; and Dennis Stillings, "Channels: Strip-miners of the Psyche," *Utne Reader* 21 (May–June 1987): 104–7.

Chapter One

1. The title of this chapter is taken from Waterloo Friends, *Proceedings of the Yearly Meeting of Congregational Friends* (Auburn, N.Y.: Henry Oliphant, 1850), 9, 20.

2. Isaac Post to Joseph and Mary Robbins Post, 23 November [1848?], Mary and Joseph Post Papers (hereafter referred to as MJPP), private collection. Ann Leah Fox Fish Brown Underhill went by the name of Leah. Whitney Cross, *The Burned Over District* (Ithaca, N.Y.: Cornell University Press, 1950), 16.

3. Amy Post to Joseph Post [1850s?], MJPP. Frederick Douglas to Amy Post, 11 April [1848?], AIPFP. Both Douglas and Amy Post deeply regretted the rift in their friendship that resulted from their disparate responses to the rappings. See Frederick Douglas to Amy Post, March 1850, and 15 January 1875, AIPFP. See Charles Powell Ray, "Register of the Family Papers of Isaac and Amy Kirby Post, 1817–1918," August 1978, manuscript in the University of Rochester Department of Rare Books and Special Collections. See also Nancy A. Hewitt, "Amy Kirby Post: 'Of whom it

was said, "being dead, yet speaketh,"'" *University of Rochester Library Bulletin* 37 (1984): 5–21.

4. Isaac Post to Joseph and Mary Robbins Post, 23 November [1848?], MJPP. For early accounts of the Hydesville rappings, see Eliab Wilkinson Capron, *Singular Revelations: Explanation and History of the Mysterous Communion with Spirits* (Auburn, N.Y.: Finn & Rockwell, 1850); Adelbert Cronise, *The Beginnings of Modern Spiritualism in and Near Rochester* (Rochester: Rochester Historical Society, 1925); J. B. Campbell, M.D., *Pittsburgh and Allegheny Spirit Rappings* (Allegheny, Pa.: Purviance & Co., 1851), 28–31, 80. On the Fox sisters, see Ernest Isaacs, "Fox, Ann Leah, Margaret, and Catherine," in *Notable American Women* (hereafter cited as *NAW*), ed. Edward T. James, Janet Wilson James, and Paul Boyer, 3 vols. (Cambridge, Mass.: Harvard University Press, 1975), 1:655–57; and William George Langworthy Taylor, *Katie Fox, Epoch Making Medium and the Making of the Fox-Taylor Record* (New York: G. P. Putnam's Sons, 1933).

5. Isaac Post to Amy Post, 22 May 1848, AIPFP.

6. Isaac Post to Joseph and Mary Robbins Post, 23 November [1848?], AIPFP.

7. Robert Doherty, *The Hicksite Separation* (New Brunswick, N.J.: Rutgers University Press, 1967), chap. 2. *Proceedings of the Annual Meeting of the Friends of Human Progress Held at Waterloo, N.Y.* (Oswego, N.Y.: Pryne & Stickney, 1854), 3, as quoted in Nancy A. Hewitt, *Women's Activism and Social Change* (Ithaca, N.Y.: Cornell University Press, 1984), 184.

8. Waterloo Friends, *Proceedings* (1850), 9, 20.

9. [Isaac Post to Joseph and Mary Robbins Post,] 19 November 1849, MJPP. Sarah D. [Bills] Fish to Amy Post, 19 September 1848, AIPFP. Cronise, *The Beginnings of Modern Spiritualism*, 9. Hardinge, *Modern American Spiritualism*, 45. Campbell, *Pittsburgh and Allegheny Spirit Rappings*, 28–31, 80.

10. Isaac Post to [Joseph and Mary Robbins Post], 23 November [1848?], AIPFP. Post, *Voices from the Spirit World*, 256.

11. Isaac Post to Amy Post, 15 May 1849, AIPFP. Hewitt, "Amy Kirby Post," 11. Amy Kirby to Isaac and Hannah Post, 28 July 1825, AIPFP.

12. [Isaac Post to Joseph and Mary Robbins Post,] 19 November 1848, MJPP. Hardinge, *Modern American Spiritualism*, 43–45. A. Leah Underhill, *The Missing Link in Modern Spiritualism* (New York: Thomas R. Knox, 1885), 71.

13. Eliab Wilkinson Capron to Margaret Rutan Fox, 10 February 1850, AIPFP. *New York Tribune*, 8 June 1850. Nathaniel Parker Willis, *The Rag Bag* (New York: Charles Scribner, 1855), 184–94.

14. Hardinge, *Modern American Spiritiualism*, 71.

15. Catherine Fox to John Fox, 26 October 1850, and Catherine Fox to Amy Post, 19 June 1850, AIPFP. On Kate's homesickness, see also Catherine Fox to Amy Post, November [185–?], and Catherine Fox to Amy Post, 30 October [185–?], AIPFP.

16. *Liberator*, 3 March 1854. Garrison's *Liberator* account of the séance was reprinted as a pamphlet: William Lloyd Garrison, *Modern Phenomena* (Boston: Liberal Tract Society, 1854). He continued to sit with Leah periodically after she left public life. The spirit of Isaac Hopper, the first to appear at Garrison's 1854 sitting, also guided the hand of Isaac Post and communicated at Leah's séance table in 1863 when Garrison and Amy

and Isaac Post were present. William Lloyd Garrison to Lucy Garrison, 14 May 1863, William Lloyd Garrison Papers, Boston Public Library. On Garrison's Spiritualism, see John L. Thomas, *The Liberator: William Lloyd Garrison* (Boston: Little, Brown, & Co., 1963), 373. *Liberator*, 12 September 1851, 148; 23 January 1852, 16; 16 July 1852, 110; and 3 March 1853. Garrison's regular attendance at séances throughout the 1850s, 1860s, and 1870s may be followed in the William Lloyd Garrison Papers. See, e.g., William Lloyd Garrison to Lydia Maria Child, 6 February 1857, William Lloyd Garrison to Lucy Garrison, 17 February 1857, William Lloyd Garrison to Wendell Garrison, 14 January 1867, and William Lloyd Garrison to J. S. Adams, 31 January 1871. See also William Cooper Nell to Amy Post, 16 December 1849, 5 August 1850, and 19 February 1854, AIPFP. Samuel May accused Garrison of "a ready credulity on all subjects pertaining to Spiritualism" (Samuel May to Mr. Estlin, 1 March 1848, William Lloyd Garrison Papers, Boston Public Library).

17. *Practical Christian*, 13 August 1851, 40.
18. Post, *Voices from the Spirit World*.
19. Isaacs, "Nineteenth-Century American Spiritualism," 305–10, and "Fox, Ann Leah, Margaret, and Catherine"; Burton Gates Brown, "Spiritualism in Nineteenth-Century America" (Ph.D. diss., Boston University, 1972), 52–60, 94–98. On Kate Fox's alcoholism, see Taylor, *Katie Fox*, 154–58.
20. George Willets to Amy and Isaac Post, 13 September 1854, AIPFP. Emma Hardinge to Amy Post, 26 March [186–?], AIPFP. The book that resulted was Hardinge's *Modern American Spiritualism*.
21. Isaacs, "Ninetenth-Century American Spiritualism," 57.
22. J. H. Crawford to Achsa W. Sprague, 24 February 1859, Achsa W. Sprague Papers (hereafter cited as AWS), Vermont Historical Society, Montpelier. John S. Clacker to Isaac Post, 7 July 1849, and William Cooper Nell to Amy Post, 11 August 1848, AIPFP. Eliab Wilkinson Capron, *Modern Spiritualism* (Boston: Bela Marsh, 1855), 113. Isaacs, "Nineteenth-Century American Spiritualism," 113–14. Nathaniel Randall to Amy Post, 26 January 1852, AIPFP.
23. L. Matterson to Alva Sherman, 24 March 1852, and 28 March 1852, Sherman Safford Papers, Vermont Historical Society.
24. *Spiritual Instructions Recieved at the Meetings of One of the Circles Formed in Philadelphia* (Philadelphia: Harmonial Benevolent Association, 1852), 4. Adin Ballou, *An Exposition of Views Regarding the Principal Facts, Causes and Peculiarities Involved in Spirit Manifestations* (Boston: Bela Marsh, 1852), 167. Andrew Jackson Davis, *The Philosophy of Spiritual Intercourse* (New York: Fowler & Wells, 1851), 96.
25. E. C. Henck, *Spirit Voices: Odes, Dictated by Spirits of the Second Sphere, for the Use of Harmonial Circles* (Philadelphia: G. D. Henck, 1853), iii, 46. Another hymnal appeared the same year: J. B. Packard and J. S. Loveland, *Spirit Minstrel* (Boston: Bella Marsh, 1853).
26. Séance notebook of Charlotte Fowler Wells, 13–16, 21, Charlotte Fowler Wells Papers, Cornell University Special Collections. Greeley quote is from *New York Tribune* clipping in séance notebook. *SpiritWorld*, 15 June 1851, 200.
27. *Banner of Light* (herafter referred to as *BL*), 15 December 1866, 3. Hardinge, *Modern American Spiritualism*, 273–77.
28. *Liberator*, 21 January 1853, 12.

29. *Liberator*, 16 July 1852, 110. *BL*, 4 September 1858, 8.

30. Cora Wilburn, "Inspiration," *BL*, 18 April 1857, 3.

31. *Spiritual Age*, 13 March 1858, 2. See also Davis, *Philosophy of Spiritual Intercourse*, 96–97; and Uriah Clark, *Plain Guide to Spiritualism* (Boston: William White & Co., 1863), 172.

32. *Herald of Progress* 1 (1860): 3. Charles Beecher, *Spiritual Manifestations* (Boston: Lee & Shepard, 1879), 13. Clark, *Plain Guide*, 182.

33. Kate Field, *Planchette's Diary* (New York: J. S. Refield, 1868). Epes Sargent, *Planchette, or the Despair of Science* (Boston: Roberts Bros., 1869). *Spiritual Age*, 2 July 1859, 2. *BL*, 18 July 1868, 5, and 8 August 1868, 4. *Religio-Philosophical Journal*, 25 July 1868, 2.

34. This scenario transpired in the Quincy family of Boston. A teen-aged granddaughter of Harvard University president Josiah Quincy proved to be a gifted medium, whose manifestations commanded serious attention from family and friends. Lydia Maria Child to Sarah Shaw, 8 December 1856, and Lydia Maria Child to J. Peter Lesley and Susan Lyman Lesley, 12 December 1856, *LMC*.

35. Isaacs, "Fox, Ann Leah, Margaret, and Catherine," 656. *BL*, 11 April 1857, 6; 14 August 1875, 4; and 30 April 1864, 5.

36. H. K. Carroll, *The Religious Forces of the United States* (New York: Christian Literature Co., 1893), 350–52. The National Association of Spiritualists was founded in 1893 and continues today. Brown, "Spiritualism in Nineteenth-Century America," 203–5.

37. Brown, "Spiritualism in Nineteenth-Century America," 110–11. Frank Podmore, *Modern Spiritualism*, 2 vols. (London and New York: Charles Scribner's Sons, 1902), 1:303. Historians have also contributed estimates, but I see little basis for those proposed either in Richard William Leopold, *Robert Dale Owen: A Biography* (Cambridge, Mass.: Harvard University Press, 1940), 380; or in George Lawton, *The Drama of Life after Death: A Study of the Spiritualist Religion* (New York: Henry Holt, 1932), 156.

38. Jonathan Baxter Harrison, *Certain Dangerous Tendencies in American Life and Other Papers* (Boston: Houghton, Osgood & Co., 1880), 17. Hardinge, *Modern American Spiritualism*, 55.

39. I am currently compiling a checklist of nineteenth-century American Spiritualist periodicals.

40. "Progressive and Spiritual Books," *American Booksellers Guide* 3 (1871): 61–62.

41. For a thorough discussion of Spiritualism in American fiction, see Howard Kerr, *Mediums, Spirit-Rappers, and Roaring Radicals: Spiritualism in American Literature, 1850–1900* (Urbana: University of Illinois Press, 1972). Louisa May Alcott, *Little Women* (New York: Grosset & Dunlap, 1947), 302. Harriet Beecher Stowe to James R. Osgood, [1869,] quoted in Mary Kelly, *Private Woman Public Stage* (New York: Oxford University Press, 1984), 171.

42. Elinor Rice Hays, *Those Extraordinary Blackwells* (New York: Harcourt, Brace & World, 1967), 56–57, 87–88. Milton Allan Rugoff, *The Beechers* (New York: Harper & Row, 1981), 343–45, 520–21, 580–83; Marie Caskey, *Chariot of Fire: Religion and the Beecher Family* (New Haven, Conn.: Yale University Press, 1978), chap. 10. Abby Ann Judson, *Why She Became a Spiritualist: Twelve Lectures Delivered Before the Minneapolis Association of*

Spiritualists (Boston: Colby & Rich, 1882). Joan Jacobs Brumberg, *Mission for Life* (New York: Free Press, 1980), 161–63.

43. On Garrison, see n. 16, chap. 1, above. Gerda Lerner, *The Grimké Sisters from South Carolina* (Boston: Houghton Mifflin, 1967), 257; Sarah M. Grimké to Charlotte Fowler Wells, 29 December [18–?], Charlotte Fowler Wells Papers. On Judge Edmonds, see John W. Edmonds and George T. Dexter, *Spiritualism*, 2 vols. (New York: Partridge & Brittan, 1853–55); and Hardinge, *Modern American Spiritualism*, 94–100. *New York Tribune*, 27 May 1853, reprinted in *Practical Christian*, 18 June 1853. James Brewer Stewart, *Joshua R. Giddings and the Tactics of Radical Politics* (Cleveland: Press of Case Western Reserve University, 1970), 208–9. Carl Sandburg, *Abraham Lincoln: The War Years* (New York: Harcourt Brace, 1939), 2: 253, 261; 3: 343–46; Nettie Colburn Maynard, *Was Abraham Lincoln a Spiritualist?* (Philadelphia: Rufus C. Hartranft, 1891).

44. Lewis O. Saum, *The Popular Mood of Pre–Civil War America* (Westport, Conn.: Greenwood Press, 1980), 48–53. A recent study sees Spiritualism in northern England as dominated by "skilled working- and lower-middle-class people." Logie Barrow, *Independent Spirits: Spiritualism and English Plebians, 1850–1910* (London: Routledge & Kegan Paul, 1986), 97. Lydia Maria Child to Lucy Osgood, 18 May 1862, *LMC*. Harrison, *Certain Dangerous Tendencies*, 16–17. Jon Butler, "The Dark Ages of American Occultism, 1760–1848," in *The Occult in America: New Historical Perspectives*, edited by Howard Kerr and Charles L. Crow (Urbana: University of Illinois Press, 1983), 58–78. George Houghton to Achsa W. Sprague, 15 March 1858, AWS. See also J. R. Durfee to Achsa W. Sprague, n.d., AWS. For a discussion of Lydia Maria Child's interest in Spiritualism, see Ann D. Braude, "Spiritualism, Reform, and Woman's Rights in Nineteenth-Century America" (Ph.D. diss., Yale University, 1987), 184–201.

45. On Wilburn's Jewish upbringing, see *Agitator*, 1 April 1860, 97; and *BL*, 13 November 1869, 3. On Schlesinger, see Julia Schlesinger, *Workers in the Vineyard* (San Francisco: n.p., 1896), 32. The records, in French, of the White Star church, 1876–1901, founded by Jean Baptiste Evarerts in Door County, Wisconsin, and a copy of their hymnal are in the Special Collections of the University of Wisconsin—Green Bay. *BL*, 27 August 1859, 7. John Konrad Meidenhauer's letters in German describing the mediumship of a twelve-year-old girl in Waukesha County, Wisconsin, are held by the Wisconsin State Historical Society. Karl J. Arndt and Mary E. Olson, *German-American Newspapers and Periodicals, 1732–1955*, 2d ed. (New York: Johnson Reprint, 1965), 16.

46. The syncretistic relation between Spiritualism and twentieth-century Afro-American spiritual churches is well treated in Hans A. Baer, *The Black Spiritual Movement: A Religious Response to Racism* (Knoxville: University of Tennessee Press, 1984), 110–20. Eugene D. Genovese, *Roll Jordan Roll: The World the Slaves Made* (New York: Random House, 1975), 217, as quoted in Baer, *Black Spiritual Movement*, 114. The growing black membership in the National Spiritualist Association of America withdrew to form the National Colored Spiritualist Association in 1922. Baer, *Black Spiritual Movement*, 114. For examples of black mediums, see "Medium-

ship Among the Contrabands," *BL,* 20 August 1864, 3; "The Spiritual Contraband," *American Spiritualist,* 26 June 1869; Hardinge, *Modern American Spiritualism,* 205; and William Cooper Nell to Amy Post, 15 Januay 1851, and 25 October 1857, AIPFP.

47. Cora L. V. Daniels to Amy Post, 2 January 1866, AIPFP.

48. Hardinge, *Modern American Spiritualism,* 498. Jean McMahon Humez, ed., *Gifts of Power: The Writings of Rebecca Jackson, Black Visionary, Shaker Eldress* (Boston: University of Massachusetts Press, 1981), 33. *BL,* 25 August 1866, 3. William Cooper Nell's involvement with Spiritualism may be followed through his correspondence with Amy Post. See, e.g., 2 December 1849, 16 December 1849, and 12 April 1856, AIPFP. See also William Cooper Nell to William Lloyd Garrison, 15 September 1851, William Lloyd Garrison Papers. Warren Chase claimed Sojourner Truth had become a Spiritualist in *BL,* 2 May 1863, 4. She spoke at the National Spiritualist Convention in 1868 (*Rochester Daily Union and Advertiser,* 26 August 1868, 2) and enjoyed the friendship of popular medium Cora L. V. Scott (Hatch) Daniels. Cora L. V. Daniels to Amy Post, 2 January 1866, and Sojourner Truth to Amy Post, 18 January 1868, and 8 February 1868, AIPFP.

49. *BL,* 13 March 1858, 4; 3 April 1858, 5; 2 June 1860, 6; and 24 November 1860, 6. Louisiana Spiritualists held a statewide convention in 1868. *BL,* 12 September 1868, 4. *Christian Spiritualist,* 13 May 1854, 3. Thomas Gales Forster and J. Rollin M. Squire of New Orleans joined the *BL* editorial staff in 1857. *BL,* 14 November 1857, 4. Both traveled widely as lecturers. *BL,* 16 January 1864, 5, and 3 December 1864, 1. Forster was born in South Carolina and had been a newspaper editor in St. Louis. Carrie Grimes Forster, introduction to *Unanswerable Logic: A Series of Spiritual Discourses,* by Thomas Gale Forster (Boston: Colby & Rich, 1887). For a description of a medium in New Orleans, see also Mrs. B. G. Bushnell Marks to Amy Post, 16 January 1854, AIPFP. *BL,* 7 May 1859, 7.

50. Hardinge, *Modern American Spiritualism,* 407–16, 430–34. *BL,* 17 September 1857, 4; 16 January 1858, 5; 20 February 1858, 4; and 28 April 1866, 8. In Tennessee, the *Spiritual Magazine* was succeeded first by the *American Spiritual Magazine* and then by the *Voice of Truth,* edited by Mary Dana Shindler and Annie C. Torrey Hawks.

51. Rev. Samuel Watson, *The Clock Struck One* (Louisville, Ky.: John P. Morton, 1873). Nell Irvin Painter, introduction to *The Journal of Ella Gertrude Clanton Thomas: An Educated White Woman in War and Reconstruction,* ed. Virginia Burr (Chapel Hill: University of North Carolina Press, in press). Mary Dana Shindler, *A Southerner Among the Spirits* (Memphis, Tenn.: Southern Baptist Publication Society, 1877).

52. Hardinge, *Modern American Spiritualism,* 403–37. On Southern intellectuals, see Drew Gilpin Faust, *A Sacred Circle: The Dilemma of the Intellectual in the Old South, 1840–1860* (Baltimore: Johns Hopkins University Press, 1977), 66–67. Mary Boykin Chesnut, *A Diary from Dixie* (Cambridge, Mass.: Harvard University Press, 1980), 214. On Thomas Moore Fort, see Homer T. Fort, Jr., and Drucilla Stoval Jones, *A Family Called Fort: The Descendants of Elias Fort of Virginia* (Midland: West Texas Printing Co., 1970), 143. His copy of Thomas Lake Harris, *Epic of the Starry Heaven*

(New York: Partridge & Brittan, 1854), is now in the possession of his great-great-granddaughter Dana Lee Robert.
53. Letmid M. Kedzie to Amy Post, 1 October 1852, AIPFP.

Chapter Two

1. The title of this chapter is taken from Cora Wilburn, "My Religion," *Agitator*, 15 December 1859, 41.
2. Mary Robbins Post to Isaac Post, [1848?], Mary Robbins Post to Amy and Isaac Post, 2 February 1850, Mary Robbins Post to William Hallowell, 10 September 1850, and Mary Post to Isaac Post, 1 October 1850, AIPFP.
3. Mary Post to Isaac Post, 1 October 1850, AIPFP. Andrew Jackson Davis, *The Great Harmonia*, 4 vols. (1850), 4th ed. (Boston: Benjamin Mussey & Co.; New York: Fowler & Wells, 1853).
4. Mary Robbins Post to Amy and Isaac Post, 5 May [185–?], AIPFP.
5. Andrew Jackson Davis, *The Principles of Nature, Her Divine Revelations, and a Voice to Mankind*, (1847), 8th ed. (New York: S. S. Lyon & Wm. Fishbough, 1851). *Univercœlum and Spiritual Philosopher*, 1847–49. Robert W. Delp, "Andrew Jackson Davis: Prophet of American Spiritualism," *Journal of American History* 54 (1967): 43–56.
6. Eliab Wilkinson Capron to Margaret Rutan Fox, 10 February 1850, AIPFP. Davis, *Philosophy of Spiritual Intercourse*. For an example of the use of Davis's instructions, see *Spiritual Instructions Received at the Meetings of One of the Circles Formed in Philadelphia*, 3 and passim.
7. On Protestant theology in America at the beginning of the nineteenth century, see Sydney E. Ahlstrom, *A Religious History of the American People* (New Haven, Conn.: Yale University Press, 1972), chap. 25; and Joseph Haroutunian, *Piety versus Moralism: The Passing of the New England Theology* (New York: Henry Holt, 1932). For a fictional portrayal of the lay view of turn-of-the-century Calvinism, see Harriet Beecher Stowe, *The Minister's Wooing* (New York: Derby & Jackson, 1859).
8. Davis, *Great Harmonia*, 1: 159. Séance notes by Charlotte Fowler Wells, 36, Charlotte Fowler Wells Papers.
9. Brumberg, *Mission for Life*, 161–63.
10. Frances H[arriet Whipple] Green McDougall, *Biography of Mrs. Semantha Mettler, the Clairvoyant* (New York: Harmonial Association, 1853), 15, 18–19, 34, 58.
11. *Herald of Progress*, 17 March 1860, 5.
12. Ahlstrom, *Religious History of the American People*, 326–27, 404.
13. E. Keigwan to Lyman Draper, 20 May 1869, Draper Collection, Wisconsin State Historical Society, Madison.
14. Mrs. R. Shephard Lillie, *Two Chapters from the Book of My Life, With Poems* (Boston: John Wilson & Son, 1889), 12–13.
15. Barbara Welter, "The Cult of True Womanhood," in *Dimnity Convictions* (Athens: Ohio University Press, 1976), 21. Nancy F. Cott, "Passionlessness: An Interpetation of Victorian Sexual Ideology, 1790–1850," *Signs* 4 (1978): 219–36, and *The Bonds of Womanhood* (New Haven, Conn.: Yale

University Press, 1977), chap. 4. Rosemary Radford Ruether, "The Cult of True Womanhood," *Commonweal* 94 (1973): 127–32, 130.

16. Stowe, *The Minister's Wooing*, 25; Elizabeth Stuart Phelps, *The Gates Ajar* (Boston: Fields, Osgood & Co., 1869). Spiritualists read and endorsed the work of these authors. "To our mind the argument against endless misery was never more powerfully presented than in the following extract from *The Minister's Wooing*," editorialized the *Spiritual Age* (3 September 1859, 1). Elizabeth Cazden, *Antoinette Brown Blackwell: A Biography* (Old Westbury, N.Y.: Feminist Press, 1983), 88–90.

17. Davis, *The Principles of Nature*, 664–74. For other references to spheres, see Rev. C. Hammond, *The Pilgrimage of Thomas Paine, and Others, to the Seventh Circle in the Spirit World* (Rochester, N.Y.: D. M. Dewey, 1852); for other references to messages, see Robert Hare, M.D., *Experimental Investigation of the Spirit Manifestations* (New York: Partridge & Brittan, 1855).

18. S. C. Hewitt, *Messages from the Superior State; Communicated from John Murray, Through John M. Spear* (Boston: Bella Marsh, 1853), 119.

19. Davis, *The Principles of Nature*, 647; Hare, *Experimental Investigation of the Spirit Manifestations*, 100.

20. *New Era*, 14 September 1853, 183.

21. Ibid.

22. Cora Wilburn, "My Religion," *Agitator*, 1 April 1860, 97.

23. Beecher, *Spiritual Manifestations*. *New England Spiritualist*, 28 April 1855, 1, and 7 April 1855, 2.

24. *BL*, 30 April 1859, 5 and 14 May 1859, 7. For other accounts of excommunications, including one from Charles Grandison Finney's church in Oberlin, Ohio, see *BL*, 14 November 1863, 3; 23 July 1859, 7; and 3 March 1860, 1. Oliver Wendell Holmes, "The Professor at the Breakfast Table," *Atlantic Monthly* 3 (January 1859): 90. For a discussion of the reaction of the orthodox clergy to Spiritualism, see Moore, *In Search of White Crows*, chap. 2.

25. Lewis Bevens Schenck, *The Presbyterian Doctrine of Children in the Covenant: An Historical Study of the Significance of Infant Baptism in the Presbyterian Church in America* (New Haven, Conn.: Yale University Press, 1940), 118–19. Peter Gregg Slater, *Children in the New England Mind in Death and in Life* (Hamden, Conn.: Archon Books, 1977), 55. James Freeman Clarke, *Manual of Unitarian Belief* (1884), 13th ed. (Boston: Unitarian Sunday-School Society, 1889), 57–62, quoted in James J. Farrell, *Inventing the American Way of Death* (Philadelphia: Temple University Press, 1980), 28. Saum *Pre–Civil War America*, 44, 47–50.

26. Ralph Waldo Emerson, "Compensation," *Spirit Messenger*, 11 January 1851, 177. *BL*, 1 April 1871, 2 and 12 August 1876, 8. Lizzie Doten, *A Review of a Lecture by James Freeman Clarke on the Religious Philosophy of Ralph Waldo Emerson* (Boston: William White & Co., 1865).

27. John B. Wilson, "Emerson and the 'Rochester Rappings,'" *New England Quarterly* 41 (June 1968): 248–58, 249, quoting *The Correspondence of Henry David Thoreau*, ed. Walter Harding and Carl Bode (New York: New York University Press, 1958), 284.

28. Anne C. Rose, *Transcendentalism as a Social Movement, 1830–1850* (New Haven, Conn.: Yale University Press, 1981), 225.

29. Wilburn, "My Religion" (1 April 1860), 97.

30. Ahlstrom, *Religious History of the American People*, 483.
31. Clarence L. F. Gohdes, *The Periodicals of American Transcendentalism* (1931; reprint, New York: AMS Press, 1970), 133–34.
32. Elizabeth Peabody to William Logan Fisher, 4 July 1858, and 13 January 1862, Logan-Fisher-Fox Collection, Historical Society of Pennsylvania, Philadelphia. Georgianna Bruce to Charlotte Fowler Wells, [1850,] Charlotte Fowler Wells Papers.
33. Frank Podmore, *Modern Spiritualism*, 1:217. Winthrop Hudson, *Religion in America* (New York: Charles Scribner's Sons, 1965), 197. See also the responses to a questionnaire sent to Universalist clergy by the *Religio-Philosophical Journal*, 9 November 1878. Edwin Scott Gaustad, *Historical Atlas of Religion in America* (New York: Harper & Row, 1962), 127–29.
34. William J. Broadway, "Universalist Participation in the Spiritualist Movement of the Nineteenth Century," *Proceedings of the Unitarian Universalist Historical Society* 19, pt. 1 (1980–81): 1–15. Hewitt, *Messages from the Superior State*. Olympia Brown to Isabella Beecher Hooker, 26 June [1875–76], Isabella Beecher Hooker Correspondence, Stowe-Day Foundation, Hartford, Conn. *American Spiritualist*, 26 June 1869.
35. *BL*, 27 May 1858, 5, and 27 February 1858, 4.
36. *BL*, 13 February 1858, 6. Andrews published the *Christian Spiritualist* (Macon, Ga.). On his Universalist career, see Russell E. Miller, *The Larger Hope: The First Century of the Universalist Church in America, 1770–1870* (Boston: Unitarian Universalist Association, 1979), 312–15. J. O. Barrett, *The Spiritual Pilgrim: A Biography of James Peebles* (Boston: William White & Co., 1872); Miller, *The Larger Hope*, 823. *BL*, 1 August 1863, 8. The Fourth Annual Festival of the Religio-Philosophical Society, e.g., was held at the Universalist Meeting House in St. Charles, Illinois. *American Spiritualist*, 6 February 1869.
37. Miller, *The Larger Hope*, 226. *BL*, 26 December 1863, 2. Lydia Maria Child to Sarah Blake Sturgis Shaw, 25 October 1857, and Lydia Maria Child to Convers Francis, 25 October 1857, *LMC*.
38. *BL*, 29 October 1859, 5. Leonard Twynham, ed., "Selections from Achsa Sprague's Diary and Journal" (hereafter referred to as "Sprague's Diary"), *Proceedings of the Vermont Historical Society* 9 (1941): 162. Miller, *The Larger Hope*, 231.
39. Herman Snow, *Interesting Experiences while travelling as a colporteur with the writings of Dr. Channing in the year 1848* ([Cambridge, Mass.:] n.p., [1899]), and *Spirit-Intercourse* (Boston: Crosby & Nichols & Co., 1848); Schlesinger, *Workers in the Vineyard*, 71. William Cooper Nell to Amy Post, 16 July 1855, AIPFP.
40. John S. Clacker to Isaac Post, 7 July 1849, AIPFP.
41. Georgianna Bruce [Kirby] to Charlotte Fowler Wells [1850?], Charlotte Fowler Wells Papers.
42. Andrew Jackson Davis, *Beyond the Valley* (Boston: Colby & Rich, 1885), 129.
43. William Harlan Hale, *Horace Greeley: Voice of the People* (New York: Harper & Bros., 1950), 123–24. Glyndon G. Van Deusen, *Horace Greeley: Nineteenth-Century Crusader* (Philadelphia: University of Pennsylvania Press, 1953), 152–53.
44. Caskey, *Chariot of Fire*, 290.

45. Farrell, *American Way of Death*, 42, 39.
46. Karen Halttunen, *Confidence Men and Painted Women: A Study of Middle-Class Culture in America, 1830–1870* (New Haven, Conn.: Yale University Press, 1982), 146.
47. Davis, *Great Harmonia*, 1:157.
48. *Spirit Messenger*, 10 August 1850, 7.
49. "The Dream," *BL*, 18 April 1857, 2.
50. *Spirit Messenger*, 15 February 1851, 221.
51. Farrell, *American Way of Death*, 80.
52. Phelps, *The Gates Ajar*.
53. Ann Douglas, "Heaven Our Home," and Stanley French, "The Cemetery as a Cultural Institution," both in *Death in America*, ed. David Stannard (Philadelphia: University of Pennsylvania Press, 1975), 49–68, 69–91.
54. Map of Oak Dale Cemetery, Urbana, Ohio, surveyed by John Shoebridge Williams, 1856, John Shoebridge Williams Papers, Wisconsin State Historical Society. Williams was converted by the Fox sisters in 1851 and became a Spiritualist and reform lecturer. See his *Nature and the Bible have One Author* (Cincinnati: John Shoebridge Williams, 1861).
55. Harvey Green, *The Light of Home* (New York: Pantheon Books, 1983), chap. 7. Barbara Dod Hillerman, "Chrysallis of Gloom: Nineteenth Century American Mourning Costume," in *A Time to Mourn: Expressions of Grief in Nineteenth Century America*, ed. Martha V. Pike and Janice Gray Armstrong (Stony Brook, N.Y.: The Museums at Stony Brook, 1980), 101.
56. Davis, *Great Harmonia*, 1:171.
57. *BL*, 3 July 1858, 5. Hardinge, *Modern American Spiritualism*, 278.
58. At Hopedale Cemetery in Milford, Massachusetts, see the stones of Adin Augustus Ballou, 1852; Hannah B. Chapman, 1865; Hannah Amelia Chapman, 1867; Willie E. Heywood, 1866; Sarah Beal, 1867; Stella W. Heywood, 1871; Anna Thwing Draper, 1870; James A. Whipple, 1864; Mrs. Sarah M. Whipple, 1874; Justus Soule, 1859; Eliza Walker, 1869; Dr. Emily Gay, 1883; James M. and Sarah Emma Morey, 1913, 1902, respectively; Charlie Morey, 1857; and Wm. R. Lewers, 1865. For other examples, see the stones of Achsa W. Sprague, Plymouth, Vermont, 1862; Ebenezer, Adeline, and Nancy Eaton, Indian Mound Cemetery, Moravia, New York; and George B. Davis and Maria Houtz, Etna, New York. See also *BL*, 28 August 1858, 8. For a discussion of Spiritualist funerals and gravestones, see Braude, "Spiritualism, Reform, and Woman's Rights," 63–71.
59. *New Northwest*, 24 November 1871.
60. *BL*, 27 May 1858, 7.
61. Davis, *Great Harmonia*, 1:171

Chapter Three

1. The title of this chapter is taken from the *Agitator* (15 November 1858, 29). Letters to the editor of this feminist Spiritualist periodical were frequently signed with this closing.

2. *Vanguard* 1 (1857):220.
3. *Herald of Progress* 1 (1860): 5.
4. Lois Waisbrooker, *The Sexual Question and the Money Power* (Battle Creek, Mich., 1873), 21.
5. *HWS*, 1:67.
6. Nancy Hewitt, "Feminist Friends: Agrarian Quakers and the Emergence of Woman's Rights in America," *Feminist Studies* 12 (1986): 27–48.
7. On the fiftieth anniversary of Seneca Falls in 1898, the McClintock's parlor table was displayed on the stage of the Woman Suffrage Convention (*HWS*, 4:288). The raps were reported in George Willets to Isaac Post, 23 October 1848, AIPFP.
8. *New Era*, 2 August 1854, 158. Hardinge, *Modern American Spiritualism*, 148. *BL*, 20 April 1872, 2. On Mary Fenn (Love) Davis, see *HWS*, 1:578, 587, 593, 595; Ernest Joseph Isaacs, "Davis, Mary Fenn," in *NAW*, 1:441–42.
9. *Spirit Messenger and Harmonial Guide*, 18 October 1851, 127. *BL*, 17 September 1859, 5.
10. *HWS*, 1:75–76.
11. Nancy Hewitt, *Women's Activism*, 198–201. *HWS*, 1:69–80.
12. The catalogers of the Amy and Isaac Post Family Papers opine that Sarah D. (Bills) Fish, mother of Mary Ann Fish McClintock, was probably a relative by marriage of Ann Leah Fox Fish Underhill's first husband. She was an early convert to Spiritualism. Sarah D. (Bills) Fish to Amy Post, 19 September 1848, AIPFP. Amy and Isaac Post attributed spirit messages to Sarah Fish after her death. [Spirit of] Sarah D. (Bills) Fish to Amy and Isaac Post, 13 November 1868, AIPFP.
13. *HWS*, 3:120. Isaac Post to Joseph and Mary Robbins Post, 23 November [1848?], Abigail Bush to Amy Post, 3 May 1860, and Benjamin Fish to Amy Post, 11 February 1869, AIPFP.
14. Ellen Carol Dubois, ed., *Elizabeth Cady Stanton / Susan B. Anthony: Correspondence, Writing, Speeches* (New York: Schocken Books, 1981), 76. On Sarah Grimké, see Lerner, *The Grimké Sisters*, 257; and Sarah M. Grimké to Charlotte Fowler Wells, 29 December [18–?], Charlotte Fowler Wells Papers. On the Motts' investigations of Spiritualism, see Joseph Post to Isaac Post, 21 March 1868, AIPFP; Magaret Hope Bacon, *Valiant Friend* (New York: Walker & Co., 1980), 234; and *Spiritual Instructions Received at the Meetings of One of the Circles Formed in Philadelphia*, 127.
15. Ray Allen Billington, ed., *The Journal of Charlotte Forten: A Free Negro in the Slave Era* (New York: W. W. Norton & Co., 1981), 57, 93. William Cooper Nell to Amy Post, 22 August 1852, and 12 April 1856, AIPFP.
16. To identify and interpret radical abolitionists, I have relied on Lewis Perry, *Radical Abolition: Anarchy and the Government of God in Antislavery Thought* (Ithaca, N.Y.: Cornell University Press, 1973). Lawrence J. Friedman has identified an overlapping group as the "insurgent Boston clique." Of the twenty members of this "intimacy circle," eight adopted Spiritualism, four may have, one died before 1848, and seven rejected it. Lawrence J. Friedman, *Gregarious Saints: Self and Community in American Abolitionism, 1830–1870* (Cambridge, Mass.: Cambridge University Press, 1982), 45–47. On the split in abolition over women's participation, see Blanche

Glassman Hersh, *The Slavery of Sex* (Urbana: University of Illinois Press, 1978), 23–29.

17. *Agitator,* 1 September 1858, 2.
18. John L. Thomas, "Romantic Reform in America, 1815–1865," *American Quarterly* 17 (1965): 656–81. David Brion Davis, "The Emergence of Immediatism in British and American Anti-slavery Thought," *Mississippi Valley Historical Review* 49 (1962): 209–30.
19. Coleman, originally a Universalist, was a Spiritualist for a number of years but eventually lost her faith, partly because she believed Spiritualism detracted from the antislavery cause. Lucy N. Coleman, *Reminiscences* (Buffalo, N.Y.: H. L. Green, 1891), 13.
20. Perry, *Radical Abolition,* chap. 3.
21. On the decline of the Non-Resistance Society, see Peter Brock, *Pacifism in the United States from the Colonial Era to the First World War* (Princeton, N.J.: Princeton University Press, 1968), 582–84. Brock views the desire of radical abolitionists to resist the Fugitive Slave Law of 1850 as a major reason for the decline of nonresistance.
22. Lewis Perry, *Childhood, Mariage, and Reform: Henry Clarke Wright, 1797–1870* (Chicago: University of Chicago Press, 1980), 32, 156–64, and *Radical Abolition,* 21, 46, 108. *Practical Christian,* 8 January 1848, 3, as quoted in Perry, *Radical Abolition,* 143. Wright's career as a Spiritualist lecturer and author may be followed throughout the Spiritualist press, beginning with the *Spiritual Philosopher,* 28 December 1850, and ending with "God as a Woman," *BL,* 4 June 1870, 2, followed by an account of his funeral three months later, *BL,* 3 September 1870, 5. *American Booksellers Guide* 3 (1871): 61–62. For Wright's séance with Leah Fish, see *Practical Christian,* 13 August 1851, 40.
23. Harrison D. Barrett, *Life Work of Mrs. Cora L. V. Richmond* (Chicago: Hack & Anderson, 1895), 68. On the woman's rights activities of Abby H. Price, see *HWS,* 1:218, 242, 532; *Practical Christian,* 27 March 1852, 93, and 20 November 1852, 59; Paulina Wright Davis, *A History of the National Women's Rights Movement, for Twenty Years* (New York: Journeyman's Co-Operative Association, 1871), 26.
24. The *Practical Christian* first noticed the Fox sisters on 3 February 1849, 3. See also 25 May 1849, 3; 2 February 1850, 3; 1 February 1851, 2; and 8 November 1851, 54. Ballou, *An Exposition,* 215–39. On Ballou's and Hopedale's response to the death of Adin Augustus, see Adin Ballou, *Autobiography of Adin Ballou, 1803–1890* (Lowell, Mass.: Vox Populi Press, 1896), 376–79; *Practical Christian,* 14 February 1852, and 28 February 1852.
25. Ballou presided at the Convention of Media and Manifestationists, Boston, August 1852 (*Practical Christian,* 14 August 1852, 30), and at the Spiritualist Convention at Worcester, Massachusetts, 29 and 30 September 1852, at which John Murray Spear and E. D. Draper served as vice-presidents (*Practical Christian,* 9 October 1852, 46). Spear left Hopedale to exercise his mediumship more fully. He published several volumes of communications and led an unsuccessful attempt to found a Spiritualist community in western New York. On Spear, see Perry, *Radical Abolition,* 218–22; John Murray Spear, *The Educator: Being Sugestions, Theoretical and*

Practical, Designed to Promote Man-Culture and Integral Reform, with a View to the Ultimate Establishment of a Divine Social State on Earth, ed. Alonzo E. Newton (Boston: Office of Practical Spiritualists, 1857); and Lawton, *Life after Death,* 618–23.

26. *Radical Spiritualist,* 1 January 1860, 69, and 1 October 1859, 45. *Radical Spiritualist,* 1 March 1860, 83; Brock, *Pacifism,* 443; Perry, *Radical Abolition,* 275–78.

27. *Practical Christian,* 16 June 1853, 16. Madeleine B. Stern, *The Pantarch: A Biography of Stephen Pearl Andrews* (Austin: University of Texas Press, 1986), 78. *Social Revolutionist* 1 (1856): 104; Warren Chase, *The Life-Line of the Lone One* (Boston: Bella Marsh, 1857), 195.

28. *Vanguard* 1 (1857): 237.

29. Albert J. Wahl, "The Progressive Friends of Longwood," *Bulletin of the Friends Historical Society* 42 (1953): 14–15.

30. Sarah Thayer to Amy Post, 29 April 1857, AIPFP. On Thayer's background, see Isaac Hicks to Amy Post, 15 July 1866, and Sarah E. Thayer to Amy Post, 15 September 1869, AIPFP. Benjamin Starbuck to Isaac Post, 8 December 1856, AIPFP.

31. Chase, *Life-Line,* 275.

32. Pennsylvania Meeting of Progressive Friends, *Proceedings* (New York: Oliver Johnson, 1858), 12, 104, 105. *Vanguard* 1 (1857): 222. Pennsylvania Meeting of Progressive Friends, *Proceedings* (New York: Oliver Johnson, 1859), 8, 31. Only the Pennsylvania meeting, although it endorsed investigation, failed to accept the manifestations unequivocally.

33. "Sprague's Diary," 151. Benjamin Starbuck to Isaac Post, 14 November 1865, and 8 December 1856, AIPFP. *BL,* 23 July 1857, 5; 17 September 1857, 5; 28 November 1857, 6; and 3 April 1858, 5. Pennsylvania Meeting of Progressive Friends, *Proceedings* (1858), 105. Charlotte Beebe (Wilbour) married and moved to New York in 1860, where she became a founder of Sorosis along with Mary Davis. *Herald of Progress,* 4 February 1860, 5.

34. *HWS,* 1:312; *BL,* 29 August 1863, 8; 28 November 1863, 3; and 10 June 1865, 3; *Religio-Philosophical Journal,* 10 July 1969. Pennsylvania Meeting of Progressive Friends, *Proceedings* (New York: Oliver Johnson, 1860), 51. *BL,* 23 May 1863, 5.

35. *BL,* 4 June 1859, 4; 3 September 1859; 27 August 1857, 5; 9 August 1862, 5, and 30 August 1862, 3.

36. Allen C. Thomas, "Congregational or Progressive Friends: A Forgotten Episode in Quaker History," *Bulletin of Friends' Historical Society of Pennsylvania* 10 (1920): 29–30.

37. H. D. Barrett, *Cassadaga; its history and teachings* (Meadville, Pa.: Gazette Printing Co., 1891), 11–13. *American Spiritualist,* 7 August 1869, 114. *BL,* 11 January 1868, 3.

38. *BL,* 29 November 1862, 3; 28 November 1863, 3; 15 October 1864, 8; 10 June 1865, 3; and 25 August 1866, 3.

39. Wilbur H. Siebert, *Vermont's Anti-slavery and Underground Railroad Record* (1937; reprint, New York: Negro Universities Press, 1969), 74. Thomas Powers, another important "conductor" on the underground railroad in Vermont, may have been a Spiritualist. His son, John D. Powers, began keeping scrapbooks of clippings from Spiritualist newspapers around

1868, eight years before his father's death. John D. Powers Scrapbooks, Vermont Historical Society. Siebert, *Vermont's Anti-slavery Record*, 91, 96, 97. Lillie Buffum Chace Wyman and Arthur Crawford Wyman, *Elizabeth Buffum Chace, 1806–1899: Her Life and Its Environs* (Boston: W. B. Clarke Co., 1914), 107. Elizabeth Buffum Chace was a member of the New England Non-Resistance Society. Brock, *Pacifism*, 565.

40. Ann King to Amy Post, 12 August 1860, AIPFP.
41. *Agitator*, 15 August 1858, 4.
42. Pennsylvania Meeting of Progressive Friends, *Proceedings* (New York: John F. Trow, 1856), 65.
43. Pennsylvania Meeting of Progressive Friends, *Proceedings* (1858), 104–5. A. Day Bradley, "Progressive Friends in Michigan and New York," *Quaker History* 52 (1963): 101.
44. *Agitator*, 15 August 1858, 4. Pennsylvania Meeting of Progressive Friends, *Proceedings* (1859), 7.
45. Clark, *Plain Guide*, 88–89. *BL*, 18 August 1860, 8.
46. "The Convention at Rutland," *Liberator*, 2 July 1858, 106. *Spiritual Age*, 22 May 1858, 3; *Liberator*, 4 June 1858, 91; *BL*, 15 May 1858, 5, and 3 July 1858, 8. *Spiritual Age*, 3 July 1858, 2.
47. Rutland Free Convention, *Proceedings of the Free Convention held at Rutland, Vt., June 25th, 26th, 27th, 1858* (Boston: J. B. Yerrington & Son, 1858), 9–10.
48. Ibid.
49. *BL*, 3 July 1858, 8. Rutland Free Convention, *Proceedings*, 147, 178–84, 31–32.
50. Rutland Free Convention, *Proceedings*, 138.
51. *Liberator*, 2 July 1858, 106.
52. Garrison, Coleman, Higginson, Nell, and the Grimkés are discussed elsewhere in the text. Wyman and Wyman, *Elizabeth Buffum Chace*, 107. Betsey Mix Cowles to Amy Post, 1 December 1850, AIPFP. On Jackson, see Lydia Maria Child to Harriet Sargent, 19 November 1861, *LMC*. On Loring, see Lydia Maria Child to J. Peter Lesley and Susan Lyman Lesley, 12 December 1856, and Lydia Maria Child to Francis George Shaw, 25 August 1876, *LMC*. On Johnson, see *Spiritual Instructions Received at the Meetings of One of the Circles Formed in Philadelphia*, 172.
53. *BL*, 25 June 1857, 4. Tho⁀ ⁀s Wentworth Higginson, *The Rationale of Spiritualism* (New York: T. J.   ⁀wood, 1859), and *The Results of Spiritualism* (New York: S. T. Munson, 1859).
54. *Spiritual Age*, 25 September 1858, 2. *Liberator*, 29 March 1861, 3, as quoted in Perry, *Childhood, Marriage, and Reform*, 158. *BL*, 23 August 1873, 8, and 25 September 1858, 8.
55. *Liberator*, 4 November 1853, and 20 January 1855.
56. William Cooper Nell to Amy Post, 21 November 1854, AIPFP. *HWS*, 1:820, 824. Perry, *Radical Abolition*, 222.
57. Coleman, *Reminiscences*, 24–25. *HWS*, 1:825, 619. William Cooper Nell to Amy Post, 2 January 1855, AIPFP. *BL*, 17 September 1859, 5.
58. *Radical Spiritualist* 1 (1859): 44, 53, 60. *Herald of Progress*, 28 April 1860, 2.
59. *BL*, 10 July 1858, 4.
60. E. R. Place, "Spiritualism and Anti-Slavery," *Liberator*, 23 July 1858, 119.

61. *Herald of Progress,* 4 February 1860, 4, and 31 March 1860, 4.
62. *Liberator,* 10 July 1863, 112; 24 July 1863, 118, 120; and 7 August 1863, 128.
63. *Agitator,* 1 August 1858, 6.
64. For example, at the 1851 Woman's Rights Convention in Akron, Ohio, Spiritualists included President Frances Dana Gage, Vice-President Lucius A. Hine, Secretary Marius Robinson, and Business Committee members Betsey Mix Cowles and Mrs. E. R. Coe. *Proceedings of the Woman's Rights Convention Held at Akron, Ohio, May 28 and May 29, 1851* (Cincinnati: Ben Franklin Book and Job Office, 1851), 3.
65. Ellen Dubois views the woman's rights movement as ancillary to the abolition movement until 1869, when the founding of an independent woman's movement was marked by the creation of the National Woman Suffrage Association. Ellen Carol Dubois, *Feminism and Suffrage* (Ithaca, N.Y.: Cornell University Press, 1978), chap. 6.
66. *BL,* 25 August 1866, 3.
67. *Social Revolutionist* 1 (1856): 103. Chase, *Life-Line,* 133. *Agitator,* 15 August 1858, 4.
68. *American Spiritualist,* 30 January 1869, 3. *BL,* 28 July 1866, 4.
69. Emma Hardinge, *Six Lectures On Theology and Nature* ([Chicago?]: n.p., 1860), 154. *HWS,* 3:561; Steven M. Buechler, *The Transformation of the Woman Suffrage Movement: The Case of Illinois, 1850–1920* (New Brunswick, N.J.: Rutgers University Press, 1986), 57–60. *BL,* 26 July 1862, 8. *Religio-Philosophical Journal* 1 (1865): 1.
70. *Religio-Philosophical Journal* 1 (1865): 1.
71. On Lois Waisbrooker, see Hal D. Sears, *The Sex Radicals* (Lawrence: Regents Press of Kansas, 1977), 231–34.
72. The exception was Mary Fenn (Love) Davis, whose woman's rights activities may be followed in *HWS,* under both her first and second married names.
73. *Revolution* 1 (1869): 221, 357. Pam McAllister, "Women in the Lead: Waisbrooker's Way to Peace," introduction to *A Sex Revolution,* by Lois Waisbrooker (1893; reprint, Philadelphia: New Society Publications, 1985), 38–46.
74. *HWS.* The fourth volume was edited by Susan B. Anthony and Ida Husted Harper.

Chapter Four

1. Barbara Welter, "The Cult of True Womanhood," 21.
2. *BL,* 10 November 1866, 2.
3. R. Laurence Moore has observed the compatibility between mediumship and the cult of true womanhood and investigated the relation between the accepted qualities of femininity and the role of medium in *In Search of White Crows,* chap. 4, "The Medium and Her Message: A Case of Female Professionalism."
4. A. E. Sluper to Achsa W. Sprague, 1 September 1857, AWS.

5. *BL*, 21 September 1861, 8.

6. Hardinge, *Six Lectures*, 10.

7. *BL*, 18 September 1875, 1. Schindler, *A Southerner Among the Spirits*. For other examples of spirit direction of mediums' careers, see "History of Mediums," *BL*, 29 May 1858, 7.

8. For descriptions of large meetings where women spoke in trance and men spoke in the "normal" state, see e.g., "South Royalton Convention," *Christian Spiritualist*, 27 September 1856; "Picnic at Abington," *BL*, 25 September 1858, 8; and "Convention of Spiritualists at Plymouth," *BL*, 13 August 1859, 4.

9. On the qualifications of men for the public platform during this period, see Donald M. Scott, "The Popular Lecture and the Creation of a Public in Mid-Nineteenth-Century America," *Journal of American History* 66 (March 1980): 791–809.

10. *BL*, 3 April 1858, 5. *Christian Spiritualist*, 13 January 1855.

11. *BL*, 11 February 1860, 4–5.

12. Hatch's sugar-coated biography glosses over her marital history but is helpful on other particulars. See Barrett, *Mrs. Cora L. V. Richmond*, 8, 122, 127, 146–65. The chronology of the biography is confirmed by contemporary accounts. See *Practical Christian*, 25 February 1853; *New York Times*, 11 April 1857, and 28 May 1857.

13. *BL*, 3 July 1858, 8; 21 November 1857, 5; 25 July 1857, 5; 22 October 1859, 6; 5 May 1860, 5; and 14 November 1863.

14. *BL*, 27 May 1865, 2–3. Ermina H. Pollard to Achsa W. Sprague, 21 March 1858, AWS.

15. *BL*, 12 May 1866, 3.

16. *Spiritual Age*, 15 January 1859, 2.

17. Ibid.

18. *New York Times*, 8 January 1859.

19. *BL*, 22 October 1864, 4; 3 July 1858, 8; and 5 May 1860, 6.

20. Achsa W. Sprague to Mr. Stone, 1 May 1854, AWS. Lizzie Doten, *Poems from the Inner Life* (Boston: William White & Co., 1864), vi, xvii–xviii, as quoted in Mary Farrell Bednarowski, "Lizzie Doten: Literary Spiritualist" (Master's thesis, Duquesne University, 1969), 24.

21. Cazden, *Antoinette Brown Blackwell*, 85; Antoinette Brown Blackwell to Lucy Stone, 14 April 1859, as quoted in ibid., 122–23.

22. "The General Association of Massachusetts (Orthodox) to the Churches Under Their Care" (1837), reprinted in Alice S. Rossi, ed., *The Feminist Papers: From Adams to de Beauvoir* (New York: Columbia University Press, 1973), 305–6. See also Barbara Brown Zikmund, "The Struggle for the Right to Preach," in *Women and Religion in America*, vol. 1, *The Nineteenth Century*, ed. Rosemary Radford Ruether and Rosemary Keller (New York: Harper & Row, 1981), 193–241.

23. For the dates when the various Protestant churches opened leadership positions to women, see Virginia Lieson Brereton and Christa Ressmeyer Klein, "American Woman in Ministry: A History of Protestant Beginning Points," in *Women of Spirit*, ed. Ruether and McLaughlin, 301–32.

24. *Liberator*, 29 May 1840; Lillian O'Connor, *Pioneer Women Orators: Rhetoric in the Ante-bellum Reform Movement* (New York: Columbia University Press, 1954), 37, 25–28.

25. Doris G. Yoakam, "Woman's Introduction to the American Platform," in *A History and Criticism of American Public Address,* ed. William Brigance (New York: McGraw-Hill Book Co., 1943), 1:153–89. Alice Stone Blackwell, *Lucy Stone: Pioneer of Woman's Rights* (Boston: Little, Brown & Co., 1930), 60–123. *HWS,* 1:152–60.

26. O'Connor, *Pioneer Women Orators,* 41–42.

27. Blanche Glassman Hersh, *The Slavery of Sex: Feminist Abolitionists in America* (Urbana: University of Illinois Press, 1978). Uriah Clark, ed., *The Spiritual Register for 1859—Facts, Philosophy, Statistics of Spiritualism* (Auburn, N.Y.: U. Clark, 1859).

28. Hardinge, *Modern American Spiritualism,* 347–49; Isaacs, "Nineteenth-Century American Spiritualism," 113, 118; Nathaniel Potter, Jr., to Amy Post, 12 February 1850, and B. G. Bushnell Marks to John Robinson, 13 December 1852, AIPFP. Ira Button Eddy, manuscript reminiscences, Chicago Historical Society. Hardinge, *Modern American Spiritualism,* 356. *New England Spiritualist,* 23 June 1855, 3. *BL,* 3 September 1857; 12 June 1858, 7; and 26 June 1858, 7.

29. O'Connor, *Pioneer Women Orators,* 127–29. *BL,* 11 February 1860, 4. For a collection of press notices on a trance lecturer, see Leonard Twynham, "Achsa W. Sprague," *Proceedings of the Vermont Historical Society* 9 (1941): 347–59.

30. *Brittan's Journal of Spiritual Science, Literature, Art and Inspiration* 2 (1874): 244–51.

31. *BL,* 11 February 1860, 5.

32. Nathaniel Parker Willis, *The Convalescent* (New York: Charles Scribner, 1859), 305.

33. Rev. W. M. Leftwich, *Martyrdom in Missouri* (St. Louis: Southwestern Book and Publishing Co., 1870), 38–39.

34. Willis, *The Convalescent,* 303–6.

35. *New York Times,* 8 January 1859, p. 4, col. 5; 11 April 1857, p. 1, cols. 1–2; 28 May 1857; 23 January 1858; 8 January 1859, p. 5, col. 2.

36. Leftwich, *Martyrdom in Missouri,* 38–39.

37. *New Northwest,* 12 September 1873, 2 and 3 July 1874, 4.

38. *New York Daily Tribune,* 27 September 1858. On the career of Mrs. Amanda Britt (later Spence), see Hardinge, *Modern American Spiritualism,* 356.

39. Davis, *The National Women's Rights Movement,* 29.

40. William H. Pease and Jane H. Pease, "Holley, Sallie," in *NAW,* 2:205–6; O'Connor, *Pioneer Women Orators,* 88.

41. Ida Husted Harper, *The Life and Work of Susan B. Anthony* (Indianapolis: Hollenbeck Press, 1898), 1:75, 3:1126.

42. *BL,* 13 March 1858, 5.

43. Blackwell, *Lucy Stone,* 93. Harper, *Susan B. Anthony,* 123. Dubois, ed., *Stanton/Anthony Correspondence,* 62, 76–77.

44. *BL,* 2 March 1861, 3, and 3 October 1863, 2.

45. "Sprague's Diary," 147.

46. Walter J. Coates, "The Transcendental Poetess of Plymouth," *Driftwind* 2 (1927): 6.

47. "Sprague's Diary," 147.

48. The Achsa W. Sprague Papers held by the Vermont Historical Society are, as far I can ascertain, the only extant personal papers of a nineteenth-century Spiritualist medium. In 1941, the Vermont historian Leonard Twynham published "Sprague's Diary." At that time, Twynham stated that he had the diary in his possession as well as numerous other Sprague writings, including a four-volume manuscript poem, and that he planned to publish a volume of Sprague's writings. The volume never materialized, and my search has not yielded the location of the original diary or of any of the manuscripts Twynham mentioned. I have therefore relied on the printed diary. Sprague wrote frequently for the Spiritualist press during her lifetime, and a collection of poetry, *The Poet and Other Poems* (Boston: William White & Co., 1864), appeared shortly after her death.

49. "Sprague's Diary," 132, 134, 136, 143.

50. Ibid., 132–33.

51. Ibid., 136, 139–41, 146, 134.

52. Ibid., 133, 136.

53. Ibid., 141.

54. Ibid., 136.

55. Ibid., 146.

56. Ibid., 147.

57. *New Era*, 19 July 1854, 152.

58. Ibid., 153.

59. Sanford Meyerowitz, "The Continuing Investigation of Psychosocial Variables in Rheumatoid Arthritis," in *Modern Trends in Rheumatology*, vol. 2, ed. Allan G. S. Hill (London: Butterworths, 1971), 95–96.

60. "Sprague's Diary," 151.

61. Sprague, *The Poet*, 299–300.

62. *New England Spiritualist*, 7 April 1855, 2; 14 April 1855, 1–2; 19 May 1855, 3; and 9 June 1855, 2.

63. J. W. Hitchcock to Achsa W. Sprague, 20 April 1860, Lyman L. Curtis to Achsa Sprague, 28 September 1858, Benjamin Starbuck to Achsa W. Sprague, 29 January 1857, and Mrs. Elizabeth Brown to Achsa W. Sprague, 12 July 1858, AWS.

64. Benjamin Starbuck to Achsa W. Sprague, 1 June 1857, and Ermina H. Pollard to Achsa W. Sprague, 21 March 1858, AWS.

65. *New England Spiritualist*, 23 June 1855, 3; draft of letter to BL on reverse of Myron E. Cole to Achsa W. Sprague, 9 April 1860, AWS.

66. Charles G. Townsend to Achsa W. Sprague, 6 January 1858, J. F. Parker to Achsa W. Sprague, 16 March 1858, and Benjamin Gleason to Achsa W. Sprague, 12 September 1859, AWS.

67. Barrett, *Mrs. Cora L. V. Richmond*, 183. Moore, *In Search of White Crows*, 115.

68. Most trance speakers traveled alone. Fictional accounts often portray mediums as being under the control of fathers or husbands who arranged their engagements and used hypnosis to place them in trance before each lecture. Based in part on the notorious Benjamin Hatch, first husband and probable exploiter of Cora Hatch, the older man who profits from a young woman's mediumship appears in Henry James's *The Bostonians* (1886) and in William Dean Howells's *The Undiscovered Country* (1880).

However, the sources indicate that most itinerant mediums traveled unaccompanied, even if they were married. Spiritualists showed suspicion of some men who did accompany mediums. "You ask how we like Mrs. Hatch? Very much and *Mr.* Hatch very little," Benjamin Starbuck wrote to Achsa Sprague, 1 June 1857, AWS. See also Kerr, *Mediums and Spirit-Rappers,* 143, 201.

69. Ethan Allen Hitchcock to Achsa W. Sprague, 24 January 1861, AWS.
70. Thomas Richmond to Achsa W. Sprague, 27 June 1860, and Francis Barry to Achsa W. Sprague, 24 June 1860, AWS.
71. R. D. Searle to Achsa W. Sprague, 23 May 1859, AWS.
72. Harper, *Susan B. Anthony,* 72.
73. J. H. Crawford to Achsa W. Sprague, 3 February 1860, AWS. The daguerrotype of Sprague reproduced here (see plate o) is probably the one she sat for while engaged as a speaker in Boston in April 1856 at the age of twenty-eight. See "Sprague's Diary," 170.
74. Achsa W. Sprague to Mr. Stone, 1 May 1854, and 4 June 1854, AWS.
75. E[lmer] B. Louden to Achsa W. Sprague, 4 February 1858, 25 April [1858?], 27 May 1858, and 6 October 1858, AWS.
76. Ansel Eddy to Achsa W. Sprague, 8 December 1856, J. R. King to Achsa W. Sprague, 15 September 1858, Luther Henry to Achsa W. Sprague, 20 September 1858, and 1 October 1858, E[lmer] B. Louden to Achsa W. Sprague, 6 October 1858, and D. C. Warren to Achsa W. Sprague, 25 August 1860, AWS. In addition, a letter from Sprague's brother-in-law reports that "that *Awful Detestible* Maxim, who has broken 'thousand women's hearts' (you say) says he wants to marry you." Nathan Randall to Achsa W. Sprague, 16 February 1860, AWS.
76. I have been unable to locate this article. It was published either in the *World's Paper* or in the *Green Mountain Freeman,* or possibly in both. J. F. Parker to Achsa W. Sprague, 23 May 1858, AWS.
77. D. C. Warren to Achsa W. Sprague, 25 August 1860, AWS.
78. M[elvina Townsend] to Achsa W. Sprague, 28 July 1859, AWS.
79. Brother and Sister [Nathan Randall and Sarah Sprague Randall] to Achsa W. Sprague, 9 September 1858, and Nathan Randall to Achsa W. Sprague, 3 September 1860, AWS.
80. Dorius Fox to Achsa W. Sprague, 5 August 1860, Delia Pollard to Achsa W. Sprague, 3 July 1861, and Mrs. Ada H. Merrill to Achsa W. Sprague, 4 February [18–?], AWS.
81. "Sprague's Diary," 151.
82. Luther Henry to Achsa W. Sprague, October 1858, AWS. Sprague also discouraged the marriage of her older sister, Orvilla, to the widower Jarius Josslyn and composed a long poem to advance her view. Orvilla married him anyway. Personal communication from the great-granddaughter of Jarius Josslyn, Mrs. Barbara B. Chiolino, 4 October 1988.
83. M[irenda] C. Randall to Achsa W. Sprague, 11 July 1858, AWS.
84. Almedia B. Fowler to Achsa W. Sprague, 17 March 1862, M[elvina] S. Townsend to Achsa W. Sprague, 30 November 1860, Laura McAlpin to Achsa W. Sprague, 19 January 1861, Ermina H. Pollard to Achsa W. Sprague, 16 January 1858, and Lucy A. Cooke to Achsa W. Sprague, 20 December 1855, AWS.

85. Sarah B. Worthen to Achsa W. Sprague, 23 February 1860, and Maria Richmond to Achsa W. Sprague, 5 March 1860, AWS.
86. Laura Washburn to Achsa W. Sprague, 15 October 1860, and Martha to Achsa W. Sprague, 16 February 1860, AWS.
87. Achsa W. Sprague to Mr. Maynard, 7 March 1855, AWS.
88. Cora Wilburn to Achsa Sprague, 9 March 1858, and Lewis G. Davis to Achsa W. Sprague, 24 January 1858, AWS. "Sprague's Diary," 155. John M. Steen to Achsa W. Sprague, 26 December 1859, AWS.
89. Sprague, *The Poet*, 301.
90. These undated messages are in folder no. 18, AWS.
91. *BL*, 11 July 1863, 3; 7 May 1864, 4; 14 May 1864, 5; 16 July 1864, 3; 24 December 1864, 5; 25 March 1865, 7; 5 August 1865, 3; 26 June 1875, 8; and 11 April 1868, 8; *Present Age*, 30 April 1870, 4; *BL*, 8 April 1876, 8.
92. Athaldine Smith, *Achsa W. Sprague and Mary Clark's Experiences in the First Ten Spheres of Spirit Life* (Springfield, Mass.: Star Publishing Co., 1881). Although the early poems attributed to Sprague's spirit are consistent with her views and style of writing, nobody familiar with Sprague's career could have attributed to her the messages in this book. This suggests that Sprague's name and reputation were familiar even to those who became Spiritualists after Sprague's death.
93. Leonard Twynham, "Achsa Sprague," *Dictionary of American Biography* (New York: Charles Scribner's Sons, 1935), 17:469–70.
94. *BL*, 2 May 1863, 3. Other poems by Sprague were received by mediums Doten, Townsend, and Cora Hatch. *BL*, 26 September 1863, 8; 14 November 1863, 4; and 25 July 1868, 2.

Chapter Five

1. *HWS*, 1:587. Isaacs, "Davis, Mary Fenn." Andrew Jackson Davis, *The Magic Staff; An Autobiography* (New York: J. S. Brown & Co., 1857), 494–95, 502–4, 507–12, 533–52. See also Isaacs, "Nineteenth-Century American Spiritualism," 216.
2. *New Era*, 2 August 1854, 158.
3. *Spiritual Age*, 19 February 1859, 3. E. J. Dingwall, "New Introduction" to *Modern American Spiritualism*, by Hardinge, xv.
4. *Religio-Philosophical Journal* 1 (1865): 1. *BL*, 16 January 1864, 3.
5. *Universe*, 28 August 1869, 72. *Social Revolutionist* 1 (1856): 104. Clark, *Plain Guide*, 121.
6. Woodruff, *Legalized Prostitution*, 162, 158.
7. Henry C. Wright, *Anthropology; or, The Science of Man: In Its Bearings on War and Slavery, and on Arguments from the Bible, Marriage, God, Death, Retribution, Atonement and Government, in Support of These and Other Social Wrongs* (Cincinnati, 1850), 28–29, as quoted in Perry, *Radical Abolition*, 224–25. *BL*, 4 June 1870, 2.
8. *BL*, 30 May 1863, 2, and 2 November 1867, 1. *Herald of Progress*, 4 February 1860, 2.

9. *Spirit Messenger,* 29 March 1851, 268.
10. Lizzie Doten, "A Plea For Working Women," *BL,* 10 May 1862, 4. Giles Stebbins, "Two Golden Volumes—Poems by Elizabeth Doten," *Arena* 16 (1896): 229. *BL,* 10 July 1858, 8. *Social Revolutionist* 1: (1856): 103.
11. Lizzie Doten, *My Affinity and Other Stories* (Boston: William White & Co., 1870), 179–228. Epes Sargent, *Peculiar: A Tale of the Great Transition* (New York: G. W. Carleton & Co., 1863).
12. *BL,* 10 July 1858, 8.
13. Waisbrooker, *The Sexual Question,* 14.
14. *BL,* 11 August 1860, 3; 18 August 1860, 8; and 15 September 1860, 6.
15. *BL,* 3 June 1860, 4; 13 April 1861, 4; 15 June 1861, 8; 19 September 1863, 8; and 13 April 1867, 1.
16. *BL,* 8 August 1868, 3, and 30 May 1863, 2.
17. Doten, "A Plea For Working Women." For a similar view, see Lois Waisbrooker to Amy Post, 25 April 1867, AIPFP.
18. *BL,* 21 February 1863, 8.
19. Schlesinger, *Workers in the Vineyard,* 60.
20. *Religio-Philosophical Journal,* 13 March 1869, 2.
21. Taylor Stoeher, *Free Love in America* (New York: AMS Press, 1979), 9.
22. Chase, *Life-Line,* 265.
23. *BL,* 4 November 1865, 8.
24. *Agitator,* 1 February 1860, 70.
25. Wilburn's educational level is suggested by her writing and by her translations of contemporary German authors for *BL* and other Spiritualist papers. On her popularity, see, e.g., *BL,* 5 March 1864, 3. On her financial difficulties, see *BL,* 7 March 1863, 5, and 2 January 1864, 5.
26. Schlesinger, *Workers in the Vineyard,* 30. On the supportive husbands of abolitionist woman's rights advocates who became suffragists, see Hersh, *The Slavery of Sex,* chap. 7.
27. *BL,* 10 July 1858, 3.
28. *Spiritual Age,* 5 June 1858, 2. Wright frequently addressed "the reform of parentage" at Spiritualist conventions. His books *Marriage and Parentage: or, the Reproductive Element in Man, as a Means to his Elevation and Happiness,* 2d ed. (Boston: Bela Marsh, 1855), and *The Unwelcome Child; or, The Crime of an Undesigned and Undesired Maternity* (Boston: Bela Marsh, 1858) influenced many of his coreligionists. *Agitator,* 1 July 1858.
29. *Banner of Progress,* 1 February 1868, 3.
30. *BL,* 9 March 1867. *Universe,* 28 August 1869, 72.
31. Daniel Scott Smith, "Family Limitation, Sexual Control, and Domestic Feminism in Victorian America," *Feminist Studies* 1 (Winter–Spring 1973): 40–57.
32. *BL,* 22 August 1863, 2. *Spiritual Age,* 6 November 1858, 2. Ella E. Gibson, *Humanitarianism: the Origin of Mind, and Soul Marriage* (Bangor, Maine: Samuel S. Smith, 1856), 10.
33. Linda Gordon, *Woman's Body, Woman's Right* (New York: Penguin Books, 1977), chap. 5.
34. Sidney Ditzion, *Marriage, Morals and Sex in America: A History of Ideas* (New York: Bookman Associates, 1953), 157.
35. Dr. John B. Ellis [pseud.], *Free Love and Its Votaries; or American Socialism Unmasked* (New York: United States Publishing Co., 1870), 405. See also

Reverend William H. Ferris, "Review of Modern Spiritualism," *Ladies Repository* 16 (January–June 1856): 46–52, 88–92, 139–44, 229–33, 297–304, 364–70; Capron, *Modern Spiritualism*, 380–81; Asa Mahan, *Modern Mysteries Explained and Exposed* (Boston: J. P. Jewett & Co., 1855), 282–90.

36. *Social Revolutionst* 2 (1856): 137. Stephen Nissenbaum, *Sex, Diet and Debility in Jacksonian America* (Westport, Conn.: Greenwood Press, 1980), 161, 162. Gordon, *Woman's Body, Woman's Right*, chap. 5.

37. Cora Wilburn, "My Religion," *Agitator*, 15 March 1860, 90.

38. Kerr, *Mediums and Spirit-Rappers*, 91–97. *Agitator*, 1 August 1858, 6.

39. Alfred Cridge, "Spiritualism, Socialism, and Free Love," *Social Revolutionist* 1 (1856): 124.

40. Stoehr, *Free Love. Social Revolutionist* 1 (1856): 53. Those who opposed marriage altogether included John Patterson, Francis Barry, Austin Kent, Julia Branch, and Stephen Pearl Andrews, none of them influential Spiritualists.

41. *Vanguard* 1 (1857): 164, 187, 218.

42. Ibid., 218.

43. Ibid., 222.

44. Ibid., 164. Anne Denton Cridge's autobiography was serialized in the *Social Revolutionist* and the *Vanguard. Vanguard* 1 (1857): 219, 222.

45. *Religio-Philosophical Journal* 1 (1865): 1.

46. Ibid.

47. Hardinge, *Modern American Spiritualism*, 233–34. See also John Humphrey Noyes, *History of American Socialisms* (New York: J. P. Lippincott & Co., 1870).

48. *Nichols's Journal of Health, Water-Cure, and Human Progress*, July 1853, 31.

49. *Nichols's Journal of Health, Water-Cure, and Human Progress*, October 1853, 53. E[lmer] B. Louden to Achsa W. Sprague, 25 April [1858?], AWS.

50. *BL*, 10 July 1858, 8. Julia Branch's speeches at the Rutland Convention and its sequel in Utica suggest that she was among the most radical and most eloquent reformers of her day. However, she apparently made little imprint on the historical record. Besides these two appearances, I have located no other mention of her in the Spiritualist press, which was unlikely to ignore such a firey speaker. She does appear in Benjamin Hatch's list of unfaithful mediums (B[enjamin] F. Hatch, *Spiritualist Iniquities Unmasked, and, the Hatch Divorce Case* [New York: B. F. Hatch, 1859], 15) and at a New Jersey Spiritualist convention in 1865, at which she apparently took a more conservative position (*New York Tribune*, 15 August 1865).

51. Sears, *The Sex Radicals*, 88–89.

52. *BL*, 2 April 1859, 5.

53. Achsa W. Sprague to Mr. Harvey, n.d., AWS.

54. Cora Wilburn, "My Religion," *Agitator*, 1 March 1860, 82.

55. Wilburn, "My Religion," (15 March 1860).

56. This is a central theme of Lois Waisbrooker's novels *Helen Harlow's Vow* (1870; reprint, New York: Murray Hill, 1887) and *Alice Vale: A Story for the Times* (Boston: William White & Co., 1869) and of Lizzie Doten's story "My Affinity," in *My Affinity*.

57. Hatch, *Spiritualist Iniquities Unmasked*.

58. *BL*, 2 October 1858, 5. On general press coverage, see *BL*, 25 September 1858, 5.

59. *BL,* 2 April 1859, 4, 5.
60. Davis, *The National Women's Rights Movement,* 29.
61. *Vanguard* 1 (1857): 218.
62. Sears, *The Sex Radicals,* 23. Victoria Woodhull's activities within Spiritualism will be discussed in the next chapter. Eventually, free love became discussable again, but the early debates all had to be repeated. See, e.g., the sympathetic treatment under "Family" in William D. P. Bliss, *The Encyclopedia of Social Reform* (New York: Funk & Wagnalls, 1897), 599–602.
63. *Lucifer,* 10 April 1885, 2.
64. Born Adeline Eliza Nichols, Waisbrooker's son's last name was Fuller, and she had assumed the name Lois Waisbrooker by 1869, when her first publication, *Alice Vale,* appeared. Her son's name could be his father's, whether married to Waisbrooker or not, or it could be a foster parent's. Waisbrooker was probably the name of the man to whom she was married briefly during the late 1850s. Sears, *The Sex Radicals,* 231–34. James C. Malin, *A Concern about Humanity: Notes on Reform, 1872–1912 at the National and Kansas Levels of Thought* (Lawrence, Kans.: James C. Malin, 1964), 117–31. Pam McAllister, "Women in the Lead," 34–46.
65. Waisbrooker, *The Sexual Question,* and *A Sex Revolution.*
66. Lois Waisbrooker, *My Century Plant* (Topeka, Kans.: Independent Publishing Co., 1896), 10.
67. Ibid., 170.
68. Ibid., 17, 55–56.
69. Sears, *The Sex Radicals,* 233. Waisbrooker, *My Century Plant,* 237, 240.
70. Waisbrooker, *My Century Plant,* 240.
71. Sears, *The Sex Radicals,* 233–34.
72. Isaacs, "Davis, Mary Fenn." Davis, *Beyond the Valley,* 209, 286–93.

Chapter Six

1. Catherine Beecher, *Letters to the People on Health and Happiness* (New York: Harper & Bros., 1855), 121.
2. Barbara Ehrenreich and Deirdre English, *For Her Own Good: 50 Years of Experts' Advice to Women* (Garden City, N.Y.: Doubleday/Anchor Books, 1978), 49, 54–61.
3. Catherine L. Albanese, "Physics and Metaphysics in Nineteenth-Century America: Medical Sectarians and Religious Healing," *Church History* 55 (1986): 489–502.
4. Carroll Smith-Rosenberg and Charles Rosenberg, "The Female Animal: Medical and Biological Views of Woman and Her Role in Nineteenth-Century America," *Journal of American History* 60 (September 1973): 332–56.
5. Andrew Jackson Davis, *Harbinger of Health; Containing Medical Prescriptions for the Human Body and Mind* (New York: A. J. Davis, 1861), 409.
6. Thomas R. Hazard, *Civil and Religious Persecution in the State of New York: A Family Medical Instructor* (Boston: Colby & Rich, 1876), 66.
7. For a discussion of other ways in which Spiritualism challenged orthodox medicine, see Joan Jacobs Brumberg, *Fasting Girls: The Emergence of Ano-*

rexia Nervosa as a Modern Disease (Cambridge, Mass.: Harvard University Press, 1988), 74–77.

8. Charles Rosenberg, "The Therapeutic Revolution: Medicine, Meaning, and Social Change in Nineteenth-Century America," in *The Therapeutic Revolution*, ed. Morris Vogel and Charles Rosenberg (Philadelphia: University of Pennsylvania Press, 1979), 18. Sarah Stage, *Female Complaints: Lydia Pinkham and the Business of Women's Medicine* (New York: W. W. Norton & Co., 1979), 58.

9. Frank Podmore, *Mesmerism and Christian Science: A Short History of Mental Healing* (Philadelphia: George W. Jacobs & Co., 1909), 218.

10. *American Spiritualist*, 30 January 1869, 4. *BL*, 12 June 1858, 8.

11. *BL*, 17 October 1857, 4. Clark, *Plain Guide*, 174. *BL*, 20 May 1865, 3. For other accounts of Spiritualist healers, see Hardinge, *Modern American Spiritualism*, 269, 279–80; and Julia Craft Smith, *The Reason Why; or, Spiritual Experiences of Mrs. Julia Craft Smith, Physician, assisted by her Spirit Guides* (Boston: Julia Craft Smith, 1881).

12. Mrs. J. W. [Bushnell] Marks to Amy and Isaac Post, 9 August 1855, AIPFP.

13. McDougall, *Biography of Mrs. Semantha Mettler. Greer's Hartford City Directory for 1860–61* (Hartford, Conn.: Elihu Geer, 1860), 181, 313. See also Achsa Sprague's account of the Mettler family in "Sprague's Diary," 148. Stage, *Female Complaints*, 18–26.

14. *BL*, 31 July 1880, 8.

15. *BL*, 4 June 1857, 6.

16. Mary Robbins Post to Amy and Isaac Post, 26 October 1854. [No name] to Amy and Isaac Post, 31 May 1863, AIPFP.

17. Davis, *Harbinger of Health*, 31.

18. John W. Day, *Biography of Mrs. J. H. Conant, the World's Medium of the Nineteenth Century* (Boston: William White & Co., 1873), 35–36. *BL*, 11 April 1857, 6.

19. *Nichols' Journal*, 25 March 1854, 4.

20. *New Era*, 10 February 1855, and 18 November 1854, 2.

21. *BL*, 1 October 1864, 5.

22. Gulielma Fell Alsop, M.D., *History of the Womans' Medical College, Philadelphia, Pennsylvania, 1850–1950* (Philadelphia: J. B. Lippincott & Co., 1950), 36. *Spiritual Instructions Received at the Meetings of One of the Circles Formed in Philadelphia*, 12. "Longshore, Hannah E. Myers," in *NAW*, 2:426–28. Harold J. Abrahams, *Extinct Medical Schools of Nineteenth-Century Philadelphia* (Philadelphia: University of Pennsylvania Press, 1966), 205, 214, 230. On Anna Longshore Potts, see Frances E. Willard and Mary Livermore, *A Woman of the Century: Fourteen Hundred-Seventy Biographical Sketches* (Buffalo, N.Y.: Charles Wells Moulton, 1893). *HWS*, 1:389.

23. Alsop, *History of the Woman's Medical College*, 64. Abrahams, *Extinct Medical Schools*, 210, 227, 229. On Hannah Longshore's allegiance to eclecticism, see Regina Markell Morantz-Sanchez, *Sympathy and Science: Women Physicians in American Medicine* (New York: Oxford University Press, 1985), 59.

24. *New Era*, 10 February 1855, and 17 February 1855.

25. Ernest C. Miller, "Utopian Communities in Warren County, Pennsylvania," *Western Pennsylvania Historical Magazine*, 49 (October 1966): 307. *BL*,

27 November 1858, 5. Abrahams, *Extinct Medical Schools*, 427. *HWS*, 3:754–55.

26. Morantz-Sanchez, *Sympathy and Science*, 33–34, 40–43.

27. *BL*, 29 August 1863, 8.

28. Mary Roth Walsh, *"Doctors Wanted: No Women Need Apply"* (New Haven, Conn.: Yale University Press, 1977), 80. *BL*, 26 July 1862, 8.

29. *BL*, 28 January 1865, 2.

30. Mrs. Lucina Tuttle, *The Clairvoyant's Family Physician* (New York: Fowler & Wells, 1850); Davis, *Harbinger of Health*, 176. For a review of Tuttle, see *Spirit Messenger*, 16 November 1850, 117.

31. *The Progressive Annual for 1862, Comprising an Almanac, a Spiritualist Register, and a General Calendar of Reform* (New York: A. J. Davis, 1862), 50; *Progressive Annual for 1863* (New York: A. J. Davis, 1863), 41. *BL*, 21 December 1867, 3. "Housework and Exercise," *The Ladies' Own Magazine*, May 1869, 149. *BL*, 29 August 1863, 3.

32. *Herald of Progress*, 28 April 1860, 5. Clark, *Plain Guide*, 88–89. *BL*, 16 January 1864, 3, and 9 August 1862, 3.

33. *Vanguard* 1 (1857): 331. J. H. Powell, *William Denton, the Geologist and Radical: A Biographical Sketch* (Boston: J. H. Powell, 1870), 29.

34. *Vanguard* 1 (1857): 220. *BL*, 9 August 1862, 3.

35. On dress reform, see William Leach, *True Love and Perfect Union: The Feminist Reform of Sex and Society* (New York: Basic Books, 1980), 243–51; and Jane B. Donegan, *"Hydropathic Highway to Health": Women and Water-Cure in Antebellum America* (New York: Greenwood Press, 1986), 135–61.

36. Chase, *Life-Line*, 199. *American Spiritualist*, 30 January 1869, 3. *BL*, 26 July 1862, 8. See, e.g., the strong temperance resolution passed by the Illinois State Spiritualist Association in 1868. *BL*, 15 August 1868, 3.

37. Susan E. Cayleff, *Wash and Be Healed: The Water-Cure Movement and Women's Health* (Philadelphia: Temple University Press, 1987); Donegan, *"Hydropathic Highway to Health"*; Kathryn Kish Sklar, "All Hail to Pure Cold Water!" in *Women and Health in America: Historical Readings*, ed. Judith Walzer Leavitt (Madison: University of Wisconsin Press, 1984), 246–54. *Vanguard* 1 (1857): 108.

38. Davis, *Harbinger of Health*, 411–13. Donegan, *"Hydropathic Highway to Health,"* 75, 85.

39. *American Spiritualist*, 30 January 1869, 2. *BL*, 7 March 1869, 3. *BL*, 25 September 1858, 8. George Willets to Amy Post, 13 September 1854, AIPFP.

40. *Universe*, 21 August 1869, 64. "Juliet Stillman Severance," in *Woman of the Century*, by Willard and Livermore, 642–43.

41. Willard and Livermore, *Woman of the Century*, 643. *Religio-Philosophical Journal*, 10 July 1869, 8, and 2 March 1872, 6.

42. *BL*, 26 July 1862, 8.

43. *BL*, 16 April 1859, 6.

44. William Alexander Hammond, *The Physics and Physiology of Spiritualism* (New York: Appleton & Co., 1871), 34.

45. William Alexander Hammond, *Spiritualism and Allied Causes of Nervous Derangement* (New York: G. P. Putnam's Sons, 1876), 256. On "fasting girls," see Brumberg, *Fasting Girls*. For a Spiritualist account of a medium who survived for forty-five days without nourishment, see the description of Frances Davis in *BL*, 4 September 1858, 4.

46. William B. Carpenter, *Principles of Mental Phsyiology* (New York: Appleton, 1874), and *Mesmerism, Spiritualism &c. Historically and Scientifically Considered: Being Two Lectures Delivered Before the London Institution* (New York: Appleton & Co., 1877), 103, 107, 108. See also John J. Cerullo, *The Secularization of the Soul: Psychical Research in Modern Britain* (Philadelphia: Institute for the Study of Human Issues, 1982), 28–34; Allan Gauld, *The Founders of Psychical Research* (New York: Schocken Books, 1968), 83–86; Brian Inglis, *Natural and Supernatural: A History of the Paranormal* (London: Hodder & Straughton, 1977).

47. R. Frederic Marvin, M.D., *The Philosophy of Spiritualism and the Pathology and Treatment of Mediomania. Two lectures read before the New York Liberal Club* (New York: Asa K. Butts & Co., 1874), 35, 38.

48. Hammond, *Physics and Physiology,* 28.

49. Edward H. Clarke, *Sex In Education; or, A Fair Chance for the Girls* (Boston: James R. Osgood & Co., 1873).

50. Marvin, *Mediomania,* 7.

51. *BL,* 13 May 1876, 4.

52. Ehrenreich and English, *For Her Own Good,* 91–104. Carroll Smith-Rosenberg, "The Hysterical Woman: Sex Roles and Role Conflict in Nineteenth-Century America," in *Disorderly Conduct: Visions of Gender in Victorian America* (New York: Oxford University Press, 1985), 207.

53. Davis, *Harbinger of Health,* 411.

54. *BL,* 10 November 1866, 2. *American Spiritualist,* 30 January 1869, 1.

Chapter Seven

1. The title of this chapter is taken from *BL,* 6 October 1866, 3.

2. *BL,* 14 April 1866, 1. *Religio-Philosophical Journal,* 3 September 1870, 6.

3. *Spirit Messenger,* 31 May 1851, 345.

4. Perry, *Radical Abolition,* 113–17. *HWS,* 1:540–41.

5. Amy Post to Lucy Stone, 5 November 1869, AIPFP.

6. *BL,* 17 September 1859, 5. See also *BL,* 11 August 1860, 4, and 18 August 1860, 8.

7. *BL,* 3 September 1864, 8; 17 September 1864, 8; and 24 September 1864, 8. Achsa Sprague expressed her opposition in the *New England Spiritualist,* 12 May 1855, 3.

8. *BL,* 19 August 1865, 8; 28 October 1865, 4; 4 November 1865, 8; and 4 November 1865, 8. Cora Hatch was using her maiden name, Cora Scott, following her divorce from Benjamin Hatch.

9. *BL,* 11 November 1865, 8.

10. *BL,* 11 November 1865, 8; 4 November 1865, 8; and 18 November 1865, 8.

11. *BL,* 6 October 1866, 3.

12. *BL,* 6 October 1866, 3.

13. *BL,* 19 August 1865, 8.

14. *BL,* 8 September 1866, 1, 8.

15. *BL,* 29 September 1866, 3.

16. *BL,* 20 August 1864, 4.

17. *BL*, 2 November 1867, 1; 16 November 1867, 1; 27 September 1868, 3; and 3 October 1868, 4; *Rochester Union and Advertiser*, 27, 28, 29 August 1868.

18. *BL*, 25 September 1869, 3.

19. *BL*, 8 January 1870, 8, and 22 October 1870, 3.

20. Theodore Tilton wrote his sympathetic biographical sketch in the hope of placing Woodhull in his debt so that she would not reveal his wife's adultery with Henry Ward Beecher. The strategy proved unsuccessful. Theodore Tilton, "Victoria C. Woodhull: A Biographical Sketch," *Golden Age Tract No. 3* (New York: Golden Age, 1871). Emanie Sachs, "*The Terrible Siren*": *Victoria Woodhull (1838–1927)* (New York: Harper & Bros., 1928), 103–9, 121–22. Victoria Woodhull awaits a dispassionate biography, so secondary sources must be used with care. *BL*, 30 September 1871, 4, 8.

21. At the suffrage convention, Woodhull upstaged the regular proceedings by securing an audience with the House Judiciary Committee for a woman suffrage memorial, making her the first woman to testify before a congressional committee. Her stirring speech won the adoration and devotion of Elizabeth Cady Stanton, Susan B. Anthony, and Isabella Beecher Hooker. *HWS*, 2:443–82. Samuel Bernstein, *The First International in America* (New York: Augustus M. Kelley, 1962), 63, 112–17.

22. *Religio-Philosophical Journal*, 17 February 1872, 1. Although I have found no record of a previous direct association of Woodhull with Spiritualism, *Woodhull and Claflin's Weekly* already provided a forum for radical Spiritualists, who had not had their own organ since the *Vanguard* and the *Social Revolutionist* in the 1850s. Columnists included the *Vanguard*'s editors, Alfred and Anne Denton Cridge, and veteran free love advocates C. M. Overton and Francis Berry. The Progressive Society of Spiritualists of New York advertised in the paper (*Woodhull and Claflin's Weekly*, 26 November 1870, 16).

23. Notably, Laura Cuppy Smith, Anna Middlebrook, Melvina S. Townsend Hoadley, Addie Ballou, C. Fannie Allyn, Horace Day, Horace Dresser, Newman Weeks, L. K. Coonley, J. H. W. Toohey, H. T. Child, Alfred Cridge, Moses Hull, Dorus Fox, and H. F. Gardner. *BL*, 13 April 1872, 8; *Woodhull and Claflin's Weekly*, 20 April 1872.

24. Bernstein, *First International*, 134–35. Harper, *Susan B. Anthony*, 412–15. Helen Krebs Smith, *The Presumptuous Dreamers: A Sociological History of the Life and Times of Abigail Scott Duniway (1872–1876)* (Lake Oswego, Oreg.: Smith, Smith & Smith, 1983), 2:5–11.

25. *New Northwest*, 31 May 1872, and 7 June 1872. *BL*, 21 December 1872, 3.

26. Altina L. Waller, *Reverend Beecher and Mrs. Tilton: Sex and Class in Victorian America* (Amherst: University of Massachusetts Press, 1982). Sachs, "*Terrible Siren*," 169–77.

27. *BL*, 28 September 1872, 8.

28. *BL*, 30 March 1872, 3.

29. M. M. Marberry, *Vicky: A Biography of Victoria Woodhull* (New York: Funk & Wagnalls, 1967), 119. A few Spiritualist conventions continued to send their proceedings to *Woodhull and Claflin's Weekly*. *BL*, 4 July 1873, 2, and 1 November 1873, 2.

30. *BL,* 27 September 1873, 2; 18 October 1873, 8; 25 October 1873, 3; 1 November 1873, 3; 15 November 1873, 2; 22 November 1873, 3; and 6 December 1873, 3.
31. *BL,* 28 August 1875, 8.
32. Some local groups organized in order to procure the legal benefits enjoyed by other religious groups, such as authority to solemnize marriages. Mrs. A. D. Wiggin organized Spiritualists in Los Angeles and received a license to marry. But, in Massachusetts, the state refused to authorize local societies to grant marriage licenses because there was no uniform accepted practice among Spiritualists. *BL,* 16 July 1870, 4, and 19 March 1870, 3.
33. *American Spiritualist,* 7 August 1869.
34. *BL,* 4 September 1869, 8.
35. Lily Dale, a Spiritualist summer camp on Cassadaga Lake in Chataqua County, New York, still has a thriving program from 1 July to Labor Day, housed in the same buildings pictured in Barrett, *Cassadaga,* which also describes other camp meeting sites. See also Merle W. Hersey, *Seventy-fifth Anniversary of the Lily Dale Assembly, 1879–1954* (Lily Dale, N.Y., 1954). Recent Lily Dale programs have included neurolinguistic programming, lectures on the worldview of the Seneca Indians, meditation led by Alan Watts, and tai-chi classes in addition to classes on mediumship development and clairvoyance. A smaller summer camp that still meets is the Freeville Assembly. For its history, see *Official Program* (Freeville, N.Y., 1917).
36. *BL,* 9 September 1876, 8; 23 September 1876, 2; and 28 July 1877, 8.
37. See, e.g., *American Spiritualist,* 7 August 1869, 113.
38. *BL,* 4 July 1874, 5; 16 August 1873, 5; 3 August 1878, 8; and 23 September 1876, 3.
39. Lucy C. Blair Scrapbooks, 1871–73, 42 and passim, American Antiquarian Society, Worcester, Mass.
40. *BL,* 5 August 1876, 4; 26 August 1876, 8; and 4 November 1876, 8.
41. On Mary Andrews, see *Rochester Union and Advertiser,* 2 July 1873, 2; *BL,* 16 March 1872, 1; 8 June 1872, 1; 1 February 1873, 2; 20 September 1873, 3; and 3 July 1875, 4. On Mary Hardy Pickering, see *BL,* 19 January 1878, 4; 9 March 1878, 8; 16 March 1878, 4; 4 May 1878, 8; and 13 July 1878, 1.
42. Webster, Horatio, William, Adelia, and Alice Eddy. *BL,* 18 April 1874, 1.
43. *Religio-Philosophical Journal,* 13 June 1874.
44. *BL,* 16 May 1874, 3.
45. *BL,* 18 April 1874, 1.
46. *BL,* 6 November 1875, 8.
47. Colonel Olcott's book about the Eddy family included illustrations of the medium gagged and bound to a chair. *BL,* 9 November 1867, 5. Henry S. Olcott, *People From the Other World* (Hartford, Conn.: American Publishing Co., 1875).
48. Marion Meade, *Madame Blavatsky: The Woman Behind the Myth* (New York: G. P. Putnam's Sons, 1980), 110–25. Bruce F. Campbell, *Ancient Wisdom Revealed: A History of the Theosophical Movement* (Berkeley: University of California Press, 1980), 20–22. Leopold, *Robert Dale Owen,* 395.

49. Meade, *Madame Blavatsky*, 97. Blavatsky wrote that she came to the United States because it was "the cradle of modern Spiritualism." *Spiritual Scientist*, 3 December 1874, 148–49, reprinted in Helena Petrovna Blavatsky, *Collected Writings*, vol. 1, *1874–1878* (Wheaton, Ill.: Theosophical Press, 1966), 47.

50. Olcott, *People From the Other World*. Meade, *Madame Blavatsky*, 132.

51. *BL*, 18 December 1875, 3.

52. Meade, *Madame Blavatsky*, 150. Blavatsky's articles in the *Spiritual Scientist* are reprinted in her *Collected Writings*, 1:85–162.

53. Blavatsky, *Collected Writings*, 1:126–43. *BL*, 26 August 1876, 1.

54. Robert Dale Owen, *Footfalls on the Boundary of Another World* (Philadelphia: J. B. Lippincott & Co., 1860). Leopold, *Robert Dale Owen*, 328–335, and *The Debatable Land between this World and the Next* (New York: G. W. Carleton & Co., 1872).

55. Robert Dale Owen, "Touching Spiritual Visitants from a Higher Life. A Chapter of Autobiography," *Atlantic Monthly* 35 (January 1875): 57–69. Leopold, *Robert Dale Owen*, 321–39. Kerr, *Mediums and Spirit-Rappers*, 112–18.

56. Louisa Andrews to Hiram Corson, 15 December 1874, Louisa Andrews to Caroline Rollin Corson, 22 December 1874, Louisa Andrews to Hiram Corson, 23 March 1875, and Louisa Andrews to Hiram Corson, 20 August 1875, Hiram Corson Papers, Cornell University Special Collections.

57. *BL*, 25 September 1875, 3 and 6 May 1876, 8.

58. *Religio-Philosophical Journal*, 21 December 1878. Delp, "Andrew Jackson Davis," 50–52.

59. Robert W. Delp, "American Spiritualism and Social Reform," *Northwest Ohio Quarterly* 44 (Fall 1972): 93–94.

60. *Present Age*, 4 March 1871. *BL*, 8 April 1871, 3.

61. *BL*, 11 September 1875, 8, and 13 May 1876, 1, 4.

62. Mary Baker Glover [Eddy], *Science and Health* (Boston: Christian Scientist Publishing Co., 1875), 84.

63. Robert Peel, *Mary Baker Eddy*, 3 vols. (New York: Holt, Rinehart & Winston, 1966–77), 1:317.

64. Ernest Sutherland Bates and John V. Dittemore, *Mary Baker Eddy: The Truth and the Tradition* (New York: Alfred A. Knopf, 1932), 96–97. For Quimby's views on Spiritualism, see Horatio W. Dresser, ed., *The Quimby Manuscripts* (New York: Thomas Y. Crowell, 1921), 76–79, 188, 239.

65. Peel, *Mary Baker Eddy*, 1:211, 219–22. *BL*, 20 June 1868, and 4 July 1868.

66. [Eddy], *Science and Health* (1875), 66, 71–72.

67. Mary Baker Eddy, *Science and Health With Key to the Scriptures* (Boston: Christian Science Publishing Co., 1934), 339, 468.

68. Stephen Gottschalk, "Christian Science and Harmonialism," in *The Encyclopedia of the American Religious Experience*, ed., Charles H. Lippy and Peter W. Williams (New York: Charles Scribner's Sons, 1988) 2:901. Another Christian Science historian locates the cultural context of the movement in a transcendental effervescence that stretched from Ralph Waldo Emerson to Andrew Jackson Davis but insists on the independent biblical origins of Eddy's ideas. Robert Peel, *Christian Science: Its Encounter with American Culture* (New York: Henry Holt & Co., 1958).

69. For a comparison of *Science and Health* with the work of Andrew Jackson Davis and Emanuel Swedenborg, see Hermann S. Ficke, "The Source of Science and Health," *Bibliotheca Sacra* 85 (1928): 417–23. Most discussions of the sources of *Science and Health* have focused on Eddy's reliance on the work of Phinea Pankhurst Quimby. The number of accusations of plagiarism to which Eddy has been subjected suggests that *Science and Health*, like many religious texts, represents an original synthesis drawing on a number of sources. See Dresser, ed., *The Quimby Manuscripts*. The *American Booksellers Guide* estimated that Andrew Jackson Davis's work sold ten thousand volumes annually during the 1870s. "Progressive and Spiritual Books," *American Booksellers Guide* 3 (1871): 61–62.

70. Peel, *Mary Baker Eddy*, 2:160, 206, 225–28.

71. Mary Baker G. Eddy, *Miscellaneous Writings, 1883–1896* (Boston: Joseph Armstrong, 1897), 34.

72. Ibid., 2. Peel, *Mary Baker Eddy*, 2:113–17. [Eddy,] *Science and Health* (1875), 84–85.

73. [Eddy,] *Science and Health* (1875), 74, 75, 78–80, 88.

74. Ibid., 70.

75. Ibid., 70, 66, 64.

76. Ibid., 78.

77. The most notable expulsions were those of Emma Curtis Hopkins, Ursula Gestefeld, and Augusta Stetson, all of whom became religious leaders in their own right after being severed from the Christian Science church. Interestingly, Eddy accused the popular Stetson, whom many assumed would succeed her as leader of the church, of Spiritualism. Peel, *Mary Baker Eddy*, 2:177–80, 3:231–35, 329–43. "Gestefeld, Ursula Newell," in *NAW*, 2:27–28; "Hopkins, Emma Curtis," in *NAW*, 2:219–20; "Stetson, Augusta Emma Simmons," in *NAW*, 3:364–66. Charles S. Braden, *Spirits in Rebellion: The Rise and Development of New Thought* (Dallas: Southern Methodist University Press, 1963), 138–49.

78. Mary F[enn] Davis, *Danger Signals: An Address on the Uses and Abuses of Modern Spiritualism* (New York: A. J. Davis & Co., 1875), 5, 17.

79. Ibid., 28.

80. *BL*, 15 June 1878, 3.

81. *BL*, 25 September 1875, 2.

82. *BL*, 1 June 1872, 2.

83. *BL*, 19 October 1878, 3.

Conclusion

1. The title of this chapter is taken from Susan B. Anthony to Elizabeth Lowe Watson, 1 April 1902, Mary McHenry Keith Papers, California Historical Society.

2. The twelve original founders of Sorosis included at least one other Spiritualist, the actress Kate Field, author of *Planchette's Diary*. Wilbour continued devotion to both suffrage and Spiritualism until her permanent departure for Paris in 1875. *HWS*, 3:403, 406; *BL*, 8 July 1871, 4; Charlotte

B. Wilbour, "The Platform," *Brittan's Journal of Spiritual Science, Literature, Art and Inspiration* 2 (1874): 244–51. On Sorosis, see Karen J. Blair, *The Clubwoman as Feminist: True Womanhood Redefined, 1868–1914* (New York: Holmes & Meier, 1980).

3. The six listed in the *BL* were Laura de Force Gordon, Laura Cuppy Smith, Mrs. H. M. F. Brown, Addie L. Ballou, Mrs. F. A. Logan, and Paulina Roberts. *HWS*, 3:755; *BL*, 1 January 1870, 3. The other two Spiritualists were Caroline Hinkley Spear and Elizabeth Anne Kingsbury. On John A. Collins, see Schlesinger, *Workers in the Vineyard*, 47; *HWS*, 3:754–55.

4. *BL*, 6 November 1869, 3. *BL*, 30 October 1869, 8.

5. *HWS*, 4:485, 495, 479. On the mediumship of Elizabeth Anne Kingsbury, see *BL*, 18 June 1857, 6, and 28 November 1857, 6; Elizabeth Anne Kingsbury to Amy Post, 24 June 1862, AIPFP. On her suffrage work, see Gayle Ann Gullett, "Feminism, Politics, and Voluntary Groups: Organized Womanhood in California, 1886–1896" (Ph.D. diss., University of California, Riverside, 1983), 147–50.

6. *BL*, 3 December 1859, 7, and 3 June 1860, 4. Laura de Force's manuscript diary of her travels as a trance speaker is in the possession of her living relatives and is not currently available to researchers.

7. *Rochester Union and Advertiser*, 3 December 1859, 2.

8. *BL*, 14 March 1863, 8; 11 July 1863, 3; 12 September 1863, 3; 10 June 1865, 4; and 31 March 1866, 3.

9. *BL*, 28 February 1863, 2.

10. *BL*, 24 October 1868, 3.

11. "Gordon, Laura de Force," in *NAW*, 2:68–69. *HWS*, 3:756. *New Northwest*, 25 August 1871, 1, 4.

12. See draft biography corrected by Gordon in the John M. Winterbotham Papers, Wisconsin State Historical Society.

13. Sandra Sizer Frankiel, *California's Spiritual Frontiers* (Berkeley: University of California Press, 1988), 32–34.

14. On Bush, see Benjamin Fish to Amy Post, 11 February 1869; *HWS*, 3:120, 4:298, 345. On McDougall, see *HWS*, 3:764, 977; and her obituary by S. B. Britten, *BL*, 24 August, 1878, 1. On Brown, see *BL*, 26 June 1875, 3.

15. Sears, *The Sex Radicals*, 232.

16. *BL*, 15 May 1875, 6. Philadelphia leader Selden then became a California state senator in the 1870s. *BL*, 25 August 1866, 3, and 14 August 1875, 5. Thomas Lake Harris, who founded several unsuccessful Spiritualist communities in the eastern United States between 1850 and 1870, finally settled in California in 1875, where his Fountain Cove community survived into the 1930s. Isaacs, "Nineteenth-Century American Spiritualism," 316–20.

17. Isabella Beecher Hooker, Lita Barney Sayles, and Frances Ellen Burr in Connecticut; Mary Davis and Elizabeth A. Kingsbury in New Jersey; Agnes Cook, Mary Thomas Clark, and Cora Bland in Indiana; Amy Post, Sarah Hallock, Mary Hallowell, Sarah Willis, and Charlotte Beebe Wilbour in New York; Newman Weeks in Vermont; and Catharine Ann Fish Stebbins and Giles Stebbins in Michigan.

18. *BL,* 6 April 1872, 8; 16 August 1873, 2, 8; 23 August 1873, 8; 18 January 1873, 4; and 6 December 1873, 3.

19. Harper, *Susan B. Anthony,* 2:710, 3:1259. Barrett, *Cassadaga,* 11. Hersey, *Seventy-Fifth Anniversary of the Lily Dale Assembly,* 49–51. The Freeville Assembly also held an annual Woman Suffrage Day. See *Official Program* (1917).

20. *New Northwest,* 12 September 1873, 2; 27 October 1871, 3; and 3 July 1874, 4.

21. John C. Bundy to Frances Elizabeth Willard, 28 January 1881, 2 June 1882, and 5 October 1885, John C. Bundy Papers, University of Illinois at Chicago. On Paulina Wright Davis, see Harriet Winslow Sewall to [Lydia Maria Child], 4 July [1874?], Lydia Maria Child Papers, Boston Public Library. Mary Livermore to Lillian Whiting, correspondence 1899–1901, Mary Livermore Letters, Boston Public Library.

22. May Wright Sewall, *Neither Dead Nor Sleeping* (Indianapolis: Bobbs-Merrill Co., 1920), 10 and passim. James Stephens, "May Wright Sewall: An Indiana Reformer," *Indiana Magazine of History* 78 (1982): 273–95.

23. Susan B. Anthony to Elizabeth Lowe Watson, 1 April 1902, Mary McHenry Keith Papers, California Historical Society. When Anthony died in 1906, Elizabeth Lowe Watson responded in verse, "She is not dead but more alive / Than in her fairest earthly days." Harper, *Susan B. Anthony,* 3:1604.

24. Buechler, *The Transformation of the Woman Suffrage Movement,* 67–76. *BL,* 26 November 1870, 8.

25. Willard and Livermore, *Woman of the Century,* 643. *Liberty,* 14 April 1883, 1.

26. Mari Jo Buhle, *Women and American Socialism, 1870–1920* (Urbana: University of Illinois Press, 1983), 78, 141; Reda Davis, *California Women: A Guide to Their Politics, 1885–1911* (San Francisco: California Scene, 1967), 138–39.

27. On Waisbrooker, see Sears, *The Sex Radicals,* 229–34. Schlesinger, *Workers in the Vineyard,* 30–31. Robert W. Delp, "American Spiritualism and Social Reform," 94–95.

28. On Hatch, see Barrett, *Mrs. Cora L. V. Richmond,* 478–79.

29. Aileen S. Kraditor, *The Ideas of the Woman Suffrage Movement, 1890–1920* (Garden City, N.Y.: Anchor Books, 1971), 39. Buechler, *The Transformation of the Woman Suffrage Movement,* 201.

30. Barbara Welter, "The Feminization of American Religion, 1800–1860," in *Dimnity Convictions.*

31. William O'Neil, *Everyone Was Brave: A History of Feminism in America* (New York: Quadrangle Books, 1971), ix. Kraditor, *Ideas of the Woman Suffrage Movement,* 64–75. Angela Y. Davis, "Woman Suffrage at the Turn of the Century: The Rising Influence of Racism," in *Women, Race and Class* (New York: Random House, 1981), 110–26. Matilda Joslyn Gage, *Woman, Church and State* (1893), introduction by Sally Roesch Wagner (Watertown, Mass.: Persephone Press, 1980), xxix–xxxvii. Harper, *Susan B. Anthony,* 3:1255.

32. In 1862, Martha Hulett married, moved to Michigan with her husband, and assumed his name, Perry. She apparently spoke infrequently after

this. In 1875, the Illinois bar admitted M. Frederika Perry, of Coldwater, Mich., on the motion of Alta Hulett. I cannot confirm whether M. Frederika Perry and Martha Hulett Perry were the same person or whether Martha and Alta were blood relatives, but some connection seems likely. On Martha Hulett Perry, see *BL*, 23 July 1857, 5; 5 May 1860, 6; 20 September 1862, 8; 7 November 1863, 3; and 20 July 1867, 1. On Alta Hulett and M. Frederika Perry, see *HWS*, 3:572–75. My thanks to Beverley Whitehead, registrar of the Rockford Museum Association, for help in trying to identify Martha and Alta Hulett.

33. Ann Douglas, *The Feminization of American Culture* (New York: Alfred A. Knopf, 1977).

34. Blackwell, *Lucy Stone*, 278, 287.

REFERENCES

Primary Sources

MANUSCRIPT COLLECTIONS AND SCRAPBOOKS

American Antiquarian Society, Worcester, Mass.:
  Lucy C. Blair Scrapbooks
  Abigail Kelly Foster Papers
Boston Public Library:
  Lydia Maria Child Papers
  William Lloyd Garrison Papers
  Mary Livermore Letters
Chicago Historical Society:
  Ira Button Eddy, manuscript reminiscences
Cornell University Special Collections:
  Caleb M. Carr Letters
  M. M. Cass Papers
  Hiram Corson Papers
  Charlotte Fowler Wells Papers
Historical Society of Pennsylvania, Philadelphia:
  Logan-Fisher-Fox Collection
  Claude W. Unger Collection
Private collection:
  Mary and Joseph Post Papers
Rowland E. Robinson Memorial Association:
  Letters of Rowland T. Robinson and Ann King
Smith College, Sophia Smith Collection:
  William Lloyd Garrison II Diaries
Stowe-Day Foundation, Hartford, Conn.:
  Isabella Beecher Hooker Correspondence
Syracuse University, George Arents Research Library:
  Constance Pierpont Noyes Robertson Papers
University of Illinois at Chicago, Department of Special Collections:
  John C. Bundy Papers

University of Rochester Library, Department of Rare Books and Special Collections:
  Amy and Isaac Post Family Papers
Vermont Historical Society, Montpelier:
  Achsa W. Sprague Papers
  John D. Powers Scrapbooks
  Sherman Safford Papers
  Townsend Family Papers
Wisconsin State Historical Society, Madison:
  Draper Collection
  John Shoebridge Williams Papers
Yale University, Sterling Memorial Library, Department of Manuscripts and Archives:
  Andrew Jackson Davis Papers

NEWSPAPERS AND PERIODICALS

Agitator (Cleveland). 1858–59.
American Spiritual Magazine (Memphis, Tenn.). 1875–77.
American Spiritualist [*Ohio Spiritualist*] (Cleveland). 1868–72.
Antislavery Bugle (Salem, Ohio). 1850–54.
Banner of Light (Boston). 1857–1885.
Banner of Progress (San Francisco). 1867–68.
Buchanan's Journal of Man (Cincinnati). 1849–56.
Christian Banker (Chicago). 1853.
Christian Spiritualist (New York). 1854–56.
Facts (Boston). 1882–87.
Gallery of Spirit Art (Brooklyn, N.Y.). 1883.
Heat and Light (Boston). 1851.
Herald of Progress (New York). 1860–64.
Hull's Crucible (Boston). 1871–77.
Ladies Own Magazine (Indianapolis). 1869.
Liberator (Boston). 1850–60.
Little Bouquet (Chicago). 1874.
Lucifer. The Lightbearer (Valley Falls, Kans.). 1883–96.
New Era; or Heaven Opened to Man (Boston). 1853–56.
New England Spiritualist (Boston). 1855–56.
New Northwest (Seattle). 1871–77.
Nichols' Journal (New York). 1853–54.
New York Times. 1857–59.
New York Tribune. 1850–53.
Olive Branch (Utica, N.Y.). 1883.
Optimist and Kingdom of Heaven (Anderson, Ind.). 1864–68.
Practical Christian (Hopedale, Mass.). 1846–57.
Present Age (Kalamazoo, Mich.; Chicago). 1868–72.
Progressive Annual (New York). 1862–65.
Radical Spiritualist (Hopedale, Mass.). 1858–60.
Religio-Philosophical Journal (Chicago). 1865–80.
Revolution (New York). 1868.
Rising Tide (Independence, Iowa). 1860–65.
Rochester Daily Union and Advertiser. 1868.

Sacred Circle (New York). 1854–56.
Shekinah (Bridgeport, Conn.). 1851–53.
Social Revolutionist (Greenville, Ohio). 1856–57.
Soul (Boston). 1888.
Spirit Messenger (Springfield, Mass.). 1850–53.
Spiritual Age (New York). 1858–59.
Spiritual Eclectic (Boston; Portland, Maine). 1860.
Spiritual Magazine and Harmonial Guide (Memphis, Tenn.). 1875.
Spiritual Philosopher (Boston). 1850.
Spiritual Reformer (Hopedale, Mass.). 1859–62.
Spiritual Telegraph (New York). 1853–57.
Spiritual Universe, Radical Advocate, and Journal of Reform (Cleveland). 1854–1855.
Spiritualist (Appleton, Wis.; Janesville, Ohio). 1868.
Spiritualist Register (Auburn, N.Y.). 1857–61.
Univercœlum and Spiritual Philosopher (New York). 1847–49.
Universe. A Journal of Literature, the Spiritual Philosophy, Woman's Independence, etc. (Chicago; New York). 1868–70.
Vanguard (Dayton, Ohio; Richmond, Ind.; Cleveland). 1857–59.
White Banner (Philadelphia). 1869.
World's Paper (Sandusky, Vt.). 1857.

CONVENTION AND ORGANIZATION PROCEEDINGS

American Spiritualist Association. *Address to the Public.* Chicago: Printed for the Association by the *Religio-Philosophical Journal*, n.d.
———. *Constitution and Some of the Resolutions Adopted at the Fifth Annual Convention held at Rochester, New York, August 25–28, 1868.*
Freeville Assembly. *Official Program.* Freeville, N.Y., 1917.
New England Spiritualist Association. *Constitution and By-Laws, List of Officers and Address to the Public.* Boston, 1854.
Pennsylvania Meeting of Progressive Friends. *Proceedings of the Pennsylvania Meeting of Progressive Friends, Held at Longwood, Chester County, Fifth Month, 1856.* New York: John F. Trow, 1856.
———. *Proceedings of the Pennsylvania Yearly Meeting of Progressive Friends held at Longwood, Chester County, 1859.* New York: Oliver Johnson, 1859.
———. *Proceedings of the Pennsylvania Yearly Meeting of Progressive Friends held at Longwood, Chester County, 1860.* New York: Oliver Johnson, 1860.
———. *Proceedings of the Pennsylvania Yearly Meeting of Progressive Friends, Held at Longwood, Chester County, Fifth Month, 1857.* New York: John F. Trow, 1857.
———. *Proceedings of the Pennsylvania Yearly Meeting of Progressive Friends, Held at Old Kinnett, Chester County, Fifth Month, 1853.* New York: John F. Trow, 1853.
———. *Proceedings of the Pennsylvania Yearly Meeting of Progressive Friends, Including Four Sermons by Theodore Parker.* New York: Oliver Johnson, 1858.
Proceedings of the Woman's Rights Convention Held at Akron, Ohio, May 28 and 29, 1851. Cincinnati: Ben Franklin Book and Job Office, 1851.
Queen City Park Spiritualist Camp Meeting. *Program.* South Burlington, Vt., 1896.

Rules and Regulations of a Spiritualist Association, at their Rooms, 15 Brattle Street, Boston. Boston: Geo. C. Rand & Avery, 1856.
Rutland Free Convention. *Proceedings of the Free Convention held at Rutland, Vt., June 25th, 26th, 27th, 1858.* Boston: J. B. Yerrington & Son, 1858.
Waterloo Friends. *Proceedings of the Yearly Meeting of Congregational Friends Held at Waterloo, N.Y., From the 3rd to the 5th of Sixth Month, inclusive, 1850.* Auburn, N.Y.: Henry Oliphant, 1850.
———. *Proceedings of the Yearly Meeting of the Friends of Human Progress, Held At Waterloo, Seneca Co., N.Y.* Rochester, N.Y.: C. W. Hebard & Co., 1859.

BOOKS AND ARTICLES

Arthur, Timothy Shay. *The Angel and the Demon: A Tale of Modern Spiritualism.* Philadelphia: J. W. Bradley, 1858.
Ballou, Adin. *Autobiography of Adin Ballou, 1803–1890.* Lowell, Mass.: Vox Populi Press, 1896.
———. *An Exposition of Views Regarding the Principal Facts, Causes and Peculiarities Involved in Spirit Manifestations, Together With Interesting Statements and Communications.* Boston: Bela Marsh, 1852.
———. *Memoir of Adin Augustus Ballou.* Hopedale, Mass.: Community Press, 1853.
Barett, Harrison D. *Cassadaga; its history and teachings. With histories of Spiritualist Camp Meetings and Biographies of Cassadaga Pioneers and Others.* Meadville, Pa.: Gazette Printing Co., 1891.
———. *Life Work of Mrs. Cora L. V. Richmond.* Chicago: Hack & Anderson, 1895.
Beecher, Catherine. *Letters to the People on Health and Happiness.* New York: Harper & Bros., 1855.
Beecher, Charles. *Spiritual Manifestations.* Boston: Lee & Shepard, 1879.
Blackwell, Alice Stone. *Lucy Stone: Pioneer of Woman's Rights.* Boston: Little, Brown & Co., 1930.
Blavatsky, Helena Petrovna. *Collected Writings.* Vol. 1, *1874–1878.* Wheaton, Ill.: Theosophical Press, 1966.
Brownson, Orestes. *The Spirit-Rapper: An Autobiography.* Detroit: Nourse, 1884.
Campbell, J. B., M.D. *Pittsburgh and Allegheny Spirit Rappings: Together With a General History of Spiritual Communications.* Allegheny, Pa.: Purviance & Co., 1851.
Capron, Eliab Wilkinson. *Modern Spiritualism, its facts and fanaticisms, its consistencies and contradictions.* Boston: Bela Marsh, 1855.
———. *Singular Revelations: Explanation and History of the Mysterious Communion With Spirits.* Auburn, N.Y.: Finn & Rockwell, 1850.
Carpenter, William B. *Mesmerism, Spiritualism &c. Historically and Scientifically Considered: Being Two Lectures Delivered Before the London Institution.* New York: Appleton & Co., 1874.
Chase, Warren. *The Life-Line of the Lone One: or, Autobiography of the World's Child.* Boston: Bela Marsh, 1857.
Child, Lydia Maria. *The Collected Correspondence of Lydia Maria Child, 1817–1888.* Edited by Patricia Holland and Milton Meltzer. Microfiche ed. Millwood, N.Y.: Kraus Microfilm, 1980.

Clark, Uriah. *Plain Guide to Spiritualism: A Hand-Book for Sceptics, Inquirers, Clergyman, Believers, Lecturers, Mediums, Editors....* Boston: William White & Co., 1863.

———, ed. *The Spiritual Register for 1859—Facts, Philosophy, Statistics of Spiritualism.* Auburn, N.Y.: U. Clark, 1859.

Coleman, Lucy N. *Reminiscences.* Buffalo, N.Y.: H. L. Green, 1891.

Correspondence Between the Believers in the Harmonial Philosophy in St. Louis and the Rev. Dr. N. L. Rice. Cincinnati: Printed for the Friends of Progress of Cincinnati by Longley Bros., 1854.

Cridge, Alfred. *Epitome of Spirit-Intercourse: . . . Its Relation to Christianity, Insanity, Psychometry, and Social Reform.* Boston: Bela Marsh, 1854.

Cridge, Annie Denton. *Man's Rights; or, How Would You Like It? Comprising Dreams.* Boston: William Denton, 1874.

Cronise, Adelbert. *The Beginnings of Modern Spiritualism in and Near Rochester.* Rochester, N.Y.: Rochester Historical Society, 1925.

Davis, Andrew Jackson. *Beyond the Valley; A Sequel to the Magic Staff: An Autobiography.* Boston: Colby & Rich, 1885.

———. *The Great Harmonia.* 4 vols. 1850. 4th ed. Boston: Benjamin Mussey & Co., New York: Fowler & Wells, 1853.

———. *Harbinger of Health: Containing Medical Prescriptions for the Human Body and Mind.* New York: A. J.Davis, 1861.

———. *The Magic Staff: An Autobiography.* New York: J. S. Brown & Co., 1857.

———. *The Philosophy of Spiritual Intercourse; Being an Explanation of Modern Mysteries.* New York: Fowler & Wells, 1851.

———. *The Principles of Nature, Her Divine Revelations, and a Voice to Mankind.* 1847. 8th ed. New York: S. S. Lyon & Wm. Fishbough, 1851.

Davis, Mary F[enn]. *Danger Signals: An Address on the Uses and Abuses of Modern Spiritualism.* New York: A. J. Davis & Co., 1875.

Davis, Paulina Wright. *A History of the National Women's Rights Movement, for Twenty Years.* New York: Journeyman's Co-Operative Association, 1871.

Day, John W. *Biography of Mrs. J. H. Conant, the World's Medium of the Nineteenth Century.* Boston: William White & Co., 1873.

Discussion of Modern Spiritualism, between Dr. J. G. Fish (a Spiritualist) and T. H. Dunn (a Christadelphian) held at Corinthian Hall, Rochester, June 3–9. Rochester, N.Y.: Morse & Owens, 1872.

Doten, Lizzie. *My Affinity and Other Stories.* Boston: William White & Co., 1870.

———. *Hesper the Home Spirit.* Boston: Tomkins, 1858.

———. *Poems from the Inner Life.* Boston: William White & Co., 1864.

———. *Poems of Progress.* Boston: William White & Co., 1871.

———. *A Review of a Lecture by James Freeman Clarke on the Religious Philosophy of Ralph Waldo Emerson, delivered in Lyceum Hall, Boston, March 6, 1865.* Boston: William White & Co., 1865.

Dresser, Horatio W., ed. *The Quimby Manuscripts.* New York: Thomas Y. Crowell, 1921.

Eddy, Mary Baker G. *Miscellaneous Writings, 1883–1896.* Boston: Joseph Armstrong, 1897.

———. *Science and Health.* Boston: Christian Scientist Publishing Co., 1875.

———. *Science and Health.* Vol. 2. Lynn, Mass.: Dr. A. G. Eddy, 1878.

———. *Science and Health With Key to the Scriptures.* Boston: Joseph Armstrong, 1898.

———. *Science and Health With Key to the Scriptures.* Boston: Christian Science Publishing Co., 1934.

Edmonds, John W., and George T. Dexter. *Spiritualism.* 2 vols. New York: Partridge & Brittan, 1853–55.

Ellis, Dr. John B. [pseud.]. *Free Love and Its Votaries; or American Socialism Unmasked, Being an Historical and Descriptive Account of the Rise and Progress of the Various Free Love Associations in the United States, and of the Effects of Their Vicious Teachings Upon American Society.* New York: United States Publishing Co., 1870.

Ficke, Hermann S. "The Source of Science and Health." *Bibliotheca Sacra* 85 (1928): 417–23.

Field, Kate. *Planchette's Diary.* New York: J. S. Refield, 1868.

Fisher, William Logan. *Progressive Friends: An Account of the Fourth Annual Meeting of the Progressive Friends, with some Observations on their Principles and Prospects.* N.p., 1856.

Folio, Fred [pseud.]. *Lucy Boston: or, Women's Rights and Spiritualism, Illustrating the Follies and Delusions of the Nineteenth Century.* Auburn, N.Y.: Alden & Beardsley, 1855.

Forster, Thomas Gale. *Unanswerable Logic: A Series of Spiritual Discourses.* Boston: Colby & Rich, 1887.

Forten, Charlotte. *The Journal of Charlotte Forten: A Free Negro in the Slave Era.* Edited by Ray Allen Billington. New York: W. W. Norton & Co., 1981.

Further Communications from the World of the Spirits, on Subjects Highly Important to the Human Family. By Joshua, Soloman, and Others, including the Rights of Man, by George Fox. Given Through a Lady. 2d ed. New York: John Mayer, 1862.

Gage, Matilda Joslyn. *Woman, Church and State.* 1893. With an introduction by Sally Roesch Wagner. Watertown, Mass.: Persephone Press, 1980.

Garrison, William Lloyd. *Modern Phenomena.* Boston: Liberal Tract Society, 1854. (First published in *Liberator,* 3 March 1854.)

Gibson, Ella E. *Humanitarianism: the Origin of Mind, and Soul Marriage.* Bangor, Maine: Samuel S. Smith, 1856.

Hammond, Rev. C. *The Pilgrimage of Thomas Paine, and Others, to the Seventh Circle in the Spirit World.* Rochester, N.Y.: D. M. Dewey, 1852.

Hammond, William Alexander. *The Physics and Physiology of Spiritualism.* New York: Appleton & Co., 1871.

———. *Spiritualism and Allied Causes of Nervous Derangement.* New York: G. P. Putnam's Sons, 1876.

Hannaford, Phebe A. *Daughters of America: or, Women of the Century.* Augusta, Maine: True & Co., 1883.

Hardinge, Emma. *Modern American Spiritualism: A Twenty Years' Record of the Communion Between Earth and the World of the Spirits.* 1869. Reprint. New Hyde Park: University Books, 1970.

———. *Six Lectures On Theology and Nature.* [Chicago?]: n.p., 1860.

Hare, Robert, M.D. *Experimental Investigation of the Spirit Manifestations, Demonstrating the Existence of Spirits and Their Communion With Mortals.* New York: Partridge & Brittan, 1855.

Harper, Ida Husted. *The Life and Work of Susan B. Anthony.* Indianapolis: Hollenbeck Press, 1898.

Harrison, Jonathan Baxter. *Certain Dangerous Tendencies in American Life and Other Papers.* Boston: Houghton, Osgood & Co., 1880.

Hatch, B[enjamin] F. *Spiritualist Iniquities Unmasked, and, the Hatch Divorce Case.* New York: B. F. Hatch, 1859.

Hazard, Thomas R. *Civil and Religious Persecution in the State of New York: A Family Medical Instructor.* Boston: Colby & Rich, 1876.

Henck, E. C. *Spirit Voices: Odes, Dictated by Spirits of the Second Sphere, for the Use of Harmonial Circles.* Philadelphia: G. D. Henck, 1853.

Hersey, Merle W. *Seventy-fifth Anniversary of the Lily Dale Assembly, 1879–1954.* Lily Dale, N.Y. 1954.

Hewitt, S. C. *Messages from the Superior State; Communicated from John Murray, Through John M. Spear.* Boston: Bella Marsh, 1853.

Higginson, Thomas Wentworth. *The Rationale of Spiritualism, being two extemporaneous lectures delivered at Dodsworth's Hall, Dec. 5, 1858.* New York: T. J. Ellinwood, 1859.

———. *The Results of Spiritualism, A Discourse delivered at Dodsworth's Hall, Sunday, March 6, 1859.* New York: S. T. Munson, 1859.

History of the Mysterious Noises, Heard at Rochester and Other Places, supposed to be Spirit Communications together with many Psychological Facts and new developments. Rochester, N.Y.: D. M. Dewey, 1850.

Hooker, John. *Some Reminiscences of a Long Life.* Hartford, Conn.: Belknap & Warfield, 1899.

Horn, Henry J. *Strange Visitors: A Series of Original Papers Dictated Through a Clairvoyant.* New York: G. W. Carleton & Co., 1869.

Howells, William Dean. *The Undiscovered Country.* Boston: Houghton, Mifflin & Co., 1880.

Jackson, Rebecca. *Gifts of Power: The Writings of Rebecca Jackson, Black Visionary, Shaker Eldress.* Edited by Jean McMahon Humez. Boston: University of Massachusetts Press, 1981.

James, Henry. *The Bostonians.* 1886. New York: Modern Library, 1956.

Judson, Abby Ann. *Why She Became a Spiritualist: Twelve Lectures Delivered Before the Minneapolis Association of Spiritualists.* Boston: Colby & Rich, 1882.

Leftwich, Rev. W. M. *Martyrdom in Missouri.* St. Louis: Southwestern Book and Publishing Co., 1870.

Light on the Way. With an introduction by James Freeman Clarke. Boston: Ticknor & Co., 1886.

Lillie, Mrs. R. Shephard. *The Religious Conflict of the Ages and Other Addresses.* Boston: Colby & Rich, 1889.

———. *Two Chapters from the Book of My Life, With Poems.* Boston: John Wilson & Son, 1889.

Logan, Mrs. John A. *The Part Taken by Women in American History.* Wilmington, Del.: Perry-Nalle, 1912.

McDougall, Frances H[arriet Whipple] Green. *Biography of Mrs. Semantha Mettler, the Clairvoyant: Being a History of Spiritual Development and Containing an Account of the Wonderful Cures Performed Through Her Agency.* New York: Harmonial Association, 1853.

———. *The Envoy: From Free Hearts to the Free.* Pawtucket, R.I.: Juvenile Emancipation Society, 1840.

———. *Memoirs of Eleanor Eldridge.* Providence, R.I.: P. T. Albro, 1847.

Marvin, R. Frederic, M.D. *The Philosophy of Spiritualism and the Pathology and Treatment of Mediomania. Two lectures read before the New York Liberal Club.* New York: Asa K. Butts & Co., 1874.

Maynard, Nettie Colburn. *Was Abraham Lincoln a Spiritualist? or, Curious Revelations from the Life of a Trance Medium.* Philadelphia: Rufus C. Hartranft, 1891.

Noyes, John Humphrey. *History of American Socialisms.* New York: J. P. Lippincott & Co., 1870.

Olcott, Henry S. *People From the Other World.* Hartford, Conn.: American Publishing Co., 1875.

Owen, Robert Dale. *The Debatable Land between this World and the Next.* New York: G. W. Carleton & Co., 1872.

———. *Footfalls on the Boundary of Another World.* Philadelphia: J. B. Lippincott & Co., 1860.

———. "Touching Spiritual Visitants from a Higher Life. A Chapter of Autobiography." *Atlantic Monthly* 35 (January 1875): 57–69.

Phelps, Elizabeth Stuart. *Beyond the Gates.* New York: Houghton, Mifflin & Co., 1883.

———. *The Gates Ajar.* Boston: Fields, Osgood & Co., 1869.

———. *The Gates Between.* New York: Houghton, Mifflin & Co., 1887.

Powell, J. H. *William Denton, the Geologist and Radical: A Biographical Sketch.* Boston: J. H. Powell, 1870.

Post, Isaac. *Voices from the Spirit World, being Communications from Many Spirits, by the Hand of Isaac Post, Medium.* Rochester, N.Y.: C. H. McDonell, 1852.

Report of the Mysterious Noises, heard in the House of Mr. John D. Fox, in Hydesville, Acadia, Wayne Co. Authenticated by the Certificates and Confirmed by the Statements of Citizens of that Place and Vicinity. N.p., n.d.

[Richmond,] Cora Linn [Scott Hatch] Daniels. *As It Is to Be.* Franklin, Mass.: Cora Linn Daniels, 1892.

Richmond, Thomas. *God's Dealing With Slavery.* Chicago: Religio-Philosophical Publishing House, 1870.

Sargent, Epes. *Peculiar: A Tale of the Great Transition.* New York: G. W. Carleton & Co., 1863.

———. *Planchette, or the Despair of Science.* Boston: Roberts Bros., 1869.

Schlesinger, Julia. *Workers in the Vineyard: A Review of the Progress of Spiritualism, Biographical Sketches, Essays, and Poems.* San Francisco: n.p., 1896.

Sewall, May Wright. *Neither Dead Nor Sleeping.* Indianapolis: Bobbs-Merrill Co., 1920.

Shelhamer, M[ary] T[heresa]. *Life and Labor in the Spirit World.* Boston: Colby & Rich, 1885.

Shindler, Mary Dana. *A Southerner Among the Spirits.* Memphis, Tenn.: Southern Baptist Publication Society, 1877. Reissued. Boston: Colby & Rich, n.d.

Simms, William Gilmore. *The Letters of William Gilmore Simms.* Edited by Mary Simms Oliphant. Columbia: University of South Carolina Press, 1954.

Smith, Athaldine. *Achsa W. Sprague and Mary Clark's Experiences in the First Ten Spheres of Spirit Life.* Springfield, Mass.: Star Publishing Co., 1881.

Smith, Francis H. *My Experience, or Footfalls of a Presbyterian to Spiritualism.* Baltimore: n.p., 1860.

Smith, Julia Craft. *The Reason Why; or, Spiritual Experiences of Mrs. Julia Craft Smith, Physician, assisted by her Spirit Guides.* Boston: Julia Craft Smith, 1881.

Snow, Herman. *Interesting Experiences while travelling as a colporteur with the writings of Dr. Channing in the year 1848.* [Cambridge, Mass.:] n.p., [1899].

———. *Spirit-Intercourse: containing incidents of personal experience while investigating the new phenomena of spirit thought and action; with various communications through himself as medium. . . .* Boston: Crosby & Nichols & Co., 1853.

Spear, John Murray. *The Educator: Being Suggestions, Theoretical and Practical, Designed to Promote Man-Culture and Integral Reform, with a View to the Ultimate Establishment of a Divine Social State on Earth.* Edited by Alonzo E. Newton. Boston: Office of Practical Spiritualists, 1857.

Spiritual Instructions Received at the Meetings of One of the Circles Formed in Philadelphia, for the purpose of Investigating the Philosophy of Spiritual Intercourse. Philadelphia: Harmonial Benevolent Association, 1852.

Sprague, Achsa W. *I Still Live: A Poem for the Times.* Oswego, N.Y.: Oliphant, 1862.

———. *The Poet and Other Poems.* Boston: William White & Co., 1864.

———. "Selections from Achsa Sprague's Diary and Journal." Edited by Leonard Twynham. *Proceedings of the Vermont Historical Society* 9 (1941): 131–84.

Stanton, Elizabeth Cady, and Susan B. Anthony. *Elizabeth Cady Stanton/Susan B. Anthony: Correspondence, Writing, Speeches.* Edited by Ellen Carol Dubois. New York: Shocken Books, 1981.

Stanton, Elizabeth Cady, Susan B. Anthony, and Matilda Jocelyn Gage. *History of Woman Suffrage.* 4 vols. New York: Fowler & Wells, 1881–1902.

Stebbins, Giles. "Two Golden Volumes—Poems by Elizabeth Doten." *Arena* 16 (1896): 228–37.

Stowe, Harriet Beecher. *The Minister's Wooing.* New York: Derby & Jackson, 1859.

Taylor, Sarah E. L., ed. *Fox-Taylor Automatic Writing, 1869–1892: Unabridged Record.* Minneapolis: Tribune–Great West Printing Co., 1932.

Taylor, William George Langworthy. *Katie Fox, Epoch Making Medium and the Making of the Fox-Taylor Record.* New York: G. P. Putnam's Sons, 1933.

Thomas, Ella Gertrude Clanton. *The Journal of Ella Gertrude Clanton Thomas: An Educated White Woman in War and Reconstruction.* Edited by Virginia Burr. With an introduction by Nell Irvin Painter. Chapel Hill: University of North Carolina Press, in press.

Torrey, Elizabeth R. *Reply to the Rev. Dr. W. P. Lunt's Discourse Against the Spiritual Philosophy.* Boston: Bela Marsh, 1855.

Underhill, A. Leah. *The Missing Link in Modern Spiritualism.* New York: Thomas R. Knox, 1885.

Waisbrooker, Lois. *Alice Vale: A Story for the Times.* Boston: William White & Co., 1869.

———. *Helen Harlow's Vow.* 1870. Reprint. New York: Murray Hill, 1887.

———. *My Century Plant.* Topeka, Kans.: Independent Publishing Co., 1896.

———. *A Sex Revolution.* 1893. With an Introduction by Pam McAllister. Reprint. Philadelphia: New Society Publications, 1985.

────. *The Sexual Question and the Money Power.* Battle Creek, Mich., 1873.

Walker, Mrs. Dr. *Reminiscences of the Life of Charlotte Cushman, compiled from Various Records, by Mrs. Dr. Walker, her chosen medium.* Boston: William P. Tenney, 1876.

Watson, Rev. Samuel. *The Clock Struck One, and Christian Spiritualist, being a Synopsis of Spirit Intercourse by an Episcopal Bishop, Three Ministers, Five Doctors, and Others at Memphis, Tenn., in 1855.* Louisville, Ky.: John P. Morton, 1873.

Wilbour, Charlotte Beebe. *Soul to Soul: Lectures and Addresses delivered by Charlotte Beebe Wilbour during the years 1856–58.* New York: G. W. Carleton & Co., 1872.

Willard, Frances E., and Mary Livermore. *A Woman of the Century: Fourteen Hundred-Seventy Biographical Sketches Accompanied By Portraits of Leading American Women in All Walks of Life.* Buffalo, N.Y.: Charles Wells Moulton, 1893.

Willis, Nathaniel Parker. *The Convalescent.* New York: Charles Scribner, 1859.

────. *The Rag Bag.* New York: Charles Scribner, 1855.

Woodruff, Charles S., M.D. *Legalized Prostitution: or, Marriage As It Is, and Marriage As It Should Be, Philosophically Considered.* Boston: Bela Marsh, 1862.

Wright, Henry Clarke. *Marriage and Parentage: or, the Reproductive Element in Man, as a Means to his Elevation and Happiness.* 2d ed. Boston: Bela Marsh, 1855.

Wyman, Lillie Buffum Chace, and Arthur Crawford Wyman. *Elizabeth Buffum Chace, 1806–1899: Her Life and Its Environs.* Boston: W. B. Clarke Co., 1914.

Secondary Sources

Abrahams, Harold J. *Extinct Medical Schools of Nineteenth-Century Philadelphia.* Philadelphia: University of Pennsylvania Press, 1966.

Ahlstrom, Sydney E. *A Religious History of the American People.* New Haven, Conn.: Yale University Press, 1972.

Ahlstrom, Sydney E., and Robert Bruce Mullin. *The Scientific Theist: A Life of Francis Ellingwood Abbot.* Macon, Ga: Mercer Press, 1987.

Albanese, Catherine L. "Physics and Metaphysics in Nineteenth-Century America: Medical Sectarians and Religious Healing." *Church History* 55 (1986): 489–502.

Alsop, Gulielma Fell, M.D. *History of the Woman's Medical College, Philadelphia, Pennsylvania, 1850–1950.* Philadelphia: J. B. Lippincott & Co., 1950.

Andrews, William, ed. *Sisters of the Spirit: Three Black Women's Autobiographies of the Nineteenth Century.* Bloomington: University of Indiana Press, 1987.

Bacon, Margaret Hope. *Valiant Friend: The Life of Lucretia Mott.* New York: Walker & Co., 1980.

Baer, Hans A. *The Black Spiritual Movement: A Religoius Response to Racism.* Knoxville: University of Tennessee Press, 1984.

Barrow, Logie. *Independent Spirits: Spiritualism and English Plebians, 1850–1910.* London: Routledge & Kegan Paul, 1986.

Bates, Ernest Sutherland, and John V. Dittemore. *Mary Baker Eddy: The Truth and the Tradition.* New York: Alfred A. Knopf, 1932.

Bednarowski, Mary Farrell. "Lizzie Doten: Literary Spiritualist." Master's thesis, Duquesne University, 1969.
———. "Nineteenth-Century American Spiritualism: An Attempt at a Scientific Religion." Ph.D. diss., University of Minnesota, 1973.
———. "Outside the Mainstream: Women's Religion and Women Religious Leaders in Nineteenth-Century America." *Journal of the American Academy of Religion* 48 (1980): 207–31.
———. "Spiritualism in Wisconsin in the Nineteenth Century." *Wisconsin Magazine of History* 59 (1975): 2–19.
———. "Women in Occult America." In *The Occult in America: New Historical Perspectives*, edited by Howard Kerr and Charles L. Crow, 177–95. Urbana: University of Illinois Press, 1983.
Bernstein, Samuel. *The First International in America*. New York: Augustus M. Kelley, 1962.
Blair, Karen J. *The Clubwoman as Feminist: True Womanhood Redefined, 1868–1914*. New York: Holmes & Meier, 1980.
Bourginon, Erika. "World Distribution and Patterns of Possession States." In *Trance and Possession States*, edited by Raymond Prince, 3–32. Montreal: R. M. Bucke Memorial Society, 1966.
Braden, Charles S. *Spirits in Rebellion: The Rise and Development of New Thought*. Dallas: Southern Methodist University Press, 1963.
Bradley, A. Day. "Progressive Friends in Michigan and New York." *Quaker History* 52 (1963): 95–103.
Braude, Ann D. "Spiritualism, Reform, and Woman's Rights in Nineteenth-Century America." Ph.D. diss., Yale University, 1987.
Broadway, William J. "Universalist Participation in the Spiritualist Movement of the Nineteenth Century." *Proceedings of the Unitarian Universalist Historical Society* 19, pt. 1 (1980–81): 1–15.
Brock, Peter. *Pacifism in the United States from the Colonial Era to the First World War*. Princeton, N.J.: Princeton University Press, 1968.
Brown, Burton Gates. "Spiritualism in Nineteenth-Century America." Ph.D. diss., Boston University, 1972.
Brumberg, Joan Jacobs. *Fasting Girls: The Emergence of Anorexia Nervosa as a Modern Disease*. Cambridge, Mass.: Harvard University Press, 1988.
———. *Mission for Life: The Judson Family and American Evangelical Culture*. New York: Free Press, 1980.
Buechler, Steven M. *The Transformation of the Woman Suffrage Movement: The Case of Illinois, 1850–1920*. New Brunswick, N.J.: Rutgers University Press, 1986.
Buhle, Mari Jo. *Women and American Socialism, 1870–1920*. Urbana: University of Illinois Press, 1983.
Butler, Jon. "The Dark Ages of American Occultism, 1760–1848." In *The Occult in America: New Historical Perspectives*, edited by Howard Kerr and Charles L. Crow, 58–78. Urbana: University of Illinois Press, 1983.
Campbell, Bruce F. *Ancient Wisdom Revealed: A History of the Theosophical Movement*. Berkeley: University of California Press, 1980.
Carroll, H. K. *The Religious Forces of the United States*. New York: Christian Literature Co., 1893.
Caskey, Marie. *Chariot of Fire: Religion and the Beecher Family*. New Haven, Conn.: Yale University Press, 1978.

Cayleff, Susan E. *Wash and Be Healed: The Water-Cure Movement and Women's Health.* Philadelphia: Temple University Press, 1987.

Cazden, Elizabeth. *Antoinette Brown Blackwell: A Biography.* Old Westbury, N.Y.: Feminist Press, 1983.

Cerullo, John J. *The Secularization of the Soul: Psychical Research in Modern Britain.* Philadelphia: Institute for the Study of Human Issues, 1982.

Coates, Walter J. "The Transcendental Poetess of Plymouth." *Driftwind,* vol. 2 (1927).

Cross, Whitney. *The Burned Over District: The Social and Intellectual History of Enthusiastic Religion in Western New York, 1800–1850.* Ithaca, N.Y.: Cornell University Press, 1950.

Darnton, Robert. *Mesmerism and the End of the Enlightenment in France.* Cambridge, Mass.: Harvard University Press, 1968.

Davis, Angela Y. *Woman, Race and Class.* New York: Random House, 1981.

Davis, David Brion. "The Emergence of Immediatism in British and American Anti-slavery Thought." *Mississippi Valley Historical Review* 49 (1962): 209–30.

———. "Slavery and Sin." In *The Antislavery Vanguard: New Essays on Abolitionists,* edited by Martin Duberman, 3–31. Princeton, N.J.: Princeton University Press, 1965.

Davis, Reda. *California Women: A Guide to Their Politics, 1885–1911.* San Francisco: California Scene, 1967.

DeLeon, David. *The American as Anarchist: Reflections on Indigenous Radicalism.* Baltimore: Johns Hopkins University Press, 1978.

Delp, Robert W. "American Spiritualism and Social Reform, 1847–1900." *Northwest Ohio Quarterly* 44 (Fall 1972): 85–99.

———. "Andrew Jackson Davis: Prophet of American Spiritualism." *Journal of American History* 54 (1967): 43–56.

Ditzion, Sidney. *Marriage, Morals and Sex in America: A History of Ideas.* New York: Bookman Associates, 1953.

Doherty, Robert. *The Hicksite Separation: A Sociological Analysis of Religious Schism in Early Nineteenth Century America.* New Brunswick, N.J.: Rutgers University Press, 1967.

Donegan, Jane B. *"Hydropathic Highway to Health": Women and Water-Cure in Antebellum America.* New York: Greenwood Press, 1986.

Douglas, Ann. *The Feminization of American Culture.* New York: Alfred A. Knopf, 1977.

Dubois, Ellen Carol. *Feminism and Suffrage: The Emergence of an Independent Women's Movement in America, 1848–1869.* Ithaca, N.Y.: Cornell University Press, 1978.

Ehrenreich, Barbara, and Deirdre English. *For Her Own Good: 50 Years of Experts' Advice to Women.* Garden City, N.Y.: Doubleday/Anchor Books, 1978.

Farrell, James J. *Inventing the American Way of Death.* Philadelphia: Temple University Press, 1980.

Faust, Drew Gillpen. *A Sacred Circle: The Dilemma of the Intellectual in the Old South, 1840–1860.* Baltimore: Johns Hopkins University Press, 1977.

Flexner, Eleanor. *A Century of Struggle: The Woman's Rights Movement in the United States.* Cambridge, Mass.: Harvard University Press, 1975.

Fornell, Earl W. *The Unhappy Medium.* Austin: University of Texas Press, 1964.

Frankiel, Sandra Sizer. *California's Spiritual Frontiers: Religious Alternatives in Anglo-Protestantism, 1850–1910.* Berkeley: University of California Press, 1988.
Freeman, James Dillet. *The Household of Faith: The Story of Unity.* Lee's Summit, Mo.: Unity School of Christianity, 1951.
Friedman, Lawrence J. *Gregarious Saints: Self and Community in American Abolitionism, 1830–1870.* Cambridge, Mass.: Cambridge University Press, 1982.
Fuller, Robert C. *Mesmerism and the American Cure of Souls.* Philadelphia: University of Pennsylvania Press, 1982.
Gauld, Allan. *The Founders of Psychical Research.* New York: Schocken Books, 1968.
Gaustad, Edwin Scott. *Dissent in American Religion.* Chicago: University of Chicago Press, 1973.
———. *Historical Atlas of Religion in America.* New York: Harper & Row, 1962.
Genovese, Eugene D. *Roll Jordan Roll: The World the Slaves Made.* New York: Random House, 1975.
Gohdes, Clarence L. F. *The Periodicals of American Transcendentalism.* 1931. Reprint. New York: AMS Press, 1970.
Goldfarb, Russell M., and Clare R. Goldfarb. *Spiritualism and Nineteenth-Century Letters.* Rutherford, N.J.: Fairleigh Dickinson University Press, 1978.
Gordon, Linda. *Woman's Body, Woman's Right: A Social History of Birth Control in America.* New York: Penguin Books, 1977.
Green, Harvey. *The Light of the Home.* New York: Pantheon Books, 1983.
Gullett, Gayle Ann. "Feminism, Politics, and Voluntary Groups: Organized Womanhood in California, 1886–1896." Ph.D. diss., University of California, Riverside, 1983.
Hale, William Harlan. *Horace Greeley: Voice of the People.* New York: Harper & Bros., 1950.
Halttunen, Karen. *Confidence Men and Painted Women: A Study of Middle-Class Culture in America, 1830–1870.* New Haven, Conn.: Yale University Press, 1982.
Haroutunian, Joseph. *Piety versus Moralism: The Passing of the New England Theology.* New York: Henry Holt, 1932.
Hays, Elinor Rice. *Those Extraordinary Blackwells: The Story of a Journey to a Better World.* New York: Harcourt, Brace & World, 1967.
Hersh, Blanche Glassman. *The Slavery of Sex: Feminist Abolitionists in America.* Urbana: University of Illinois Press, 1978.
Hewitt, Nancy A. "Amy Kirby Post: 'Of whom it was said, "being dead, yet speaketh."'" *University of Rochester Library Bulletin* 37 (1984): 5–21.
———. "Feminist Friends: Agrarian Quakers and the Emergence of Womans' Rights in America." *Feminist Studies* 12 (1986): 27–48.
———. *Women's Activism and Social Change: Rochester, New York, 1822–1872.* Ithaca, N.Y.: Cornell University Press, 1984.
Howe, Daniel Walker. "American Victorianism as a Culture." *American Quarterly* 27 (1975): 507–32.
Hudson, Winthrop. *Religion in America.* New York: Charles Scribner's Sons, 1965.
Inglis, Brian. *Natural and Supernatural: A History of the Paranormal.* London: Hodder & Straughton, 1977.

Isaacs, Ernest Joseph. "A History of Nineteenth-Century American Spiritualism as a Religious and Social Movement." Ph.D. diss., University of Wisconsin, 1975.

James, Edward T., Janet Wilson James, and Paul Boyer, eds. *Notable American Women*. 3 vols. Cambridge, Mass.: Harvard University Press, 1975.

Kerr, Howard. *Mediums, Spirit-Rappers, and Roaring Radicals: Spiritualism in American Literature, 1850–1900*. Urbana: University of Illinois Press, 1972.

Kerr, Howard, and Charles L. Crow, eds. *The Occult in America: New Historical Perspectives*. Urbana: University of Illinois Press, 1983.

Kraditor, Aileen S. *The Ideas of the Woman Suffrage Movement, 1890–1920*. Garden City, N.Y.: Anchor Books, 1971.

Lain, David. *Guns and Rain: Guerillas and Spirit Mediums in Zimbabwe*. Berkeley: University of California Press, 1985.

Lawton, George. *The Drama of Life after Death: A Study of the Spiritualist Religion*. New York: H. Holt & Co., 1932.

Leach, William. *True Love and Perfect Union: The Feminist Reform of Sex and Society*. New York: Basic Books, 1980.

Leavitt, Judith Walzer, ed. *Women and Health in America: Historical Readings*. Madison: University of Wisconsin Press, 1984.

Leopold, Richard William. *Robert Dale Owen: A Biography*. Cambridge, Mass.: Harvard University Press, 1940.

Lerner, Gerda. *The Grimké Sisters from South Carolina*. Boston: Houghton Mifflin, 1967.

Lewis, I. M. *Ecstatic Religion*. Hammondsworth: Penguin Books, 1971.

Malin, James C. *A Concern about Humanity: Notes on Reform, 1872–1912, at the National and Kansas Levels of Thought*. Lawrence, Kans.: James C. Malin, 1964.

Marberry, M. M. *Vicky: A Biography of Victoria Woodhull*. New York: Funk & Wagnalls, 1967.

Meade, Marion. *Madame Blavatsky: The Woman Behind the Myth*. New York: G. P. Putnam's Sons, 1980.

Meltzer, Milton. *Tongue of Flame: The Life of Lydia Maria Child*. New York: Thomas Y. Crowell, 1965.

Miller, Ernest C. "Utopian Communities in Warren County, Pennsylvania." *Western Pennsylvania Historical Magazine* 49 (October 1966): 301–17.

Miller, Russell E. *The Larger Hope: The First Century of the Universalist Church in America, 1770–1870*. Boston: Unitarian Universalist Association, 1979.

Moore, R. Laurence. *In Search of White Crows: Spiritualism, Parapsychology, and American Culture*. New York: Oxford University Press, 1977.

Morantz-Sanchez, Regina Markell. *Sympathy and Science: Women Physicians in American Medicine*. New York: Oxford University Press, 1985.

Nelson, Geoffrey K. *Spiritualism and Society*. London: Routledge & Kegan Paul, 1969.

Nissenbaum, Stephen. *Sex, Diet and Debility in Jacksonian America: Sylvester Graham and Health Reform*. Westport, Conn.: Greenwood Press, 1980.

O'Connor, Lillian. *Pioneer Women Orators: Rhetoric in the Ante-bellum Reform Movement*. New York: Columbia University Press, 1954.

O'Neil, William. *Everyone Was Brave: A History of Feminism in America*. New York: Quadrangle Books, 1971.

Peel, Robert. *Christian Science: Its Encounter with American Culture.* New York: Henry Holt & Co., 1958.
———. *Mary Baker Eddy.* 3 vols. New York: Holt, Rinehart & Winston, 1966–77.
Perry, Lewis. *Childhood, Marriage, and Reform: Henry Clarke Wright, 1797–1870.* Chicago: University of Chicago Press, 1980.
———. *Radical Abolition: Anarchy and the Government of God in Antislavery Thought.* Ithaca, N.Y.: Cornell University Press, 1973.
Pike, Martha V., and Janice Gray Armstrong. *A Time to Mourn: Expressions of Grief in Nineteenth Century America.* Stony Brook, N.Y.: The Museums at Stony Brook, 1980.
Pivar, David. *Purity Crusade: Sexual Morality and Social Control, 1868–1900.* Westport, Conn.: Greenwood Press, 1973.
Podmore, Frank. *Mesmerism and Christian Science: A Short History of Mental Healing.* Philadelphia: George W. Jacobs & Co., 1909.
———. *Modern Spiritualism: A History and a Criticism.* 2 vols. London and New York: Charles Scribner's Sons, 1902.
Ray, Charles Powell. "Register of the Family Papers of Isaac and Amy Kirby Post, 1817–1918." August 1978. Manuscript in the University of Rochester Department of Rare Books and Special Collections.
Reigel, Robert. *American Feminists.* Lawrence: University of Kansas Press, 1963.
Rose, Anne C. *Transcendentalism as a Social Movement, 1830–1850.* New Haven, Conn.: Yale University Press, 1981.
Rosenberg, Charles E. *No Other Gods: Science and American Social Thought.* Baltimore: Johns Hopkins University Press, 1976.
———. "The Therapeutic Revolution: Medicine, Meaning, and Social Change in Nineteenth-Century America." In *The Therapeutic Revolution: Essays in the Social History of American Medicine,* ed. Morris Vogel and Charles Rosenberg. Philadelphia: University of Pennsylvania Press, 1979.
Ruether, Rosemary R. "Women in Utopian Movements." In *Women and Religion in America.* Vol. 1, *The Nineteenth Century,* 46–100. New York: Harper & Row, 1981.
Ruether, Rosemary R., and Eleanor McLaughlin, eds. *Women of Spirit: Female Leadership in the Jewish and Christian Traditions.* New York: Simon & Schuster, 1979.
Rugoff, Milton Allan. *The Beechers: An American Family in the Nineteenth Century.* New York: Harper & Row, 1981.
Sachs, Emanie. *"The Terrible Siren": Victoria Woodhull (1838–1927).* New York: Harper & Bros., 1928.
Saum, Lewis O. *The Popular Mood of Pre–Civil War America.* Westport, Conn.: Greenwood Press, 1980.
Schenck, Lewis Bevens. *The Presbyterian Doctrine of Children in the Covenant: An Historical Study of the Significance of Infant Baptism in the Presbyterian Church in America.* New Haven, Conn.: Yale University Press, 1940.
Scott, Donald M. "The Popular Lecture and the Creation of a Public in Mid-Nineteenth-Century America." *Journal of American History* 66 (March 1980): 791–809.
Sears, Hal D. *The Sex Radicals: Free Love in High Victorian America.* Lawrence: Regents Press of Kansas, 1977.

Siebert, Wilbur H. *Vermont's Anti-slavery and Underground Railroad Record.* 1937. Reprint. New York: Negro Universities Press, 1969.

Sklar, Kathryn Kish. "All Hail to Pure Cold Water!" In *Women and Health in America: Historical Readings,* edited by Judith Walzer Leavitt, 246–54. Madison: University of Wisconsin Press, 1984.

Slater, Peter Gregg. *Children in the New England Mind in Death and in Life.* Hamden, Conn.: Archon Books, 1977.

Smith, Daniel Scott. "Family Limitation, Sexual Control, and Domestic Feminism in Victorian America." *Feminist Studies* 1 (Winter–Spring 1973): 40–57.

Smith, Helen Krebs. *The Presumptuous Dreamers: A Sociological History of the Life and Times of Abigail Scott Duniway (1872–1876).* 2 vols. Lake Oswego, Oreg.: Smith, Smith & Smith, 1983.

Smith-Rosenberg, Carroll. *Disorderly Conduct: Visions of Gender in Victorian America.* New York: Oxford University Press, 1985.

Smith-Rosenberg, Carroll, and Charles Rosenberg. "The Female Animal: Medical and Biological Views of Woman and Her Role in Nineteenth-Century America." *Journal of American History* 60 (1973): 332–56.

Stage, Sarah. *Female Complaints: Lydia Pinkham and the Business of Women's Medicine.* New York: W. W. Norton & Co., 1979.

Stannard, David, ed. *Death in America.* Philadelphia: University of Pennsylvania Press, 1975.

Stephens, James. "May Wright Sewall: An Indiana Reformer." *Indiana Magazine of History* 78 (1982): 273–95.

Stern, Madeleine B. *The Pantarch: A Biography of Stephen Pearl Andrews.* Austin: University of Texas Press, 1968.

———. *The Phrenological Fowlers.* Norman: University of Oklahoma Press, 1971.

Stoehr, Taylor. *Free Love in America: A Documentary History.* New York: AMS Press, 1979.

Thomas, Allen C. "Congregational or Progressive Friends: A Forgotten Episode in Quaker History." *Bulletin of Friends' Historical Society of Pennsylvania* 10 (1920): 21–31.

Thomas, John L. "Antislavery and Utopia." In *The Antislavery Vanguard: New Essays on Abolitionists,* edited by Martin Duberman, 240–69. Princeton, N.J.: Princeton University Press, 1965.

———. *The Liberator: William Lloyd Garrison.* Boston: Little, Brown & Co., 1963.

———. "Romantic Reform in America, 1815–1865." *American Quarterly* 17 (1965): 656–81.

Thompson, Robert Luther. *Wiring a Continent: The History of the Telegraph Industry in the United States, 1832–1866.* Princeton, N.J.: Princeton University Press, 1947.

Twynham, Leonard. "Achsa Sprague." In *Dictionary of American Biography,* 17:469–70. New York: Charles Scribner's Sons, 1935.

———. "Achsa W. Sprague." *Proceedings of the Vermont Historical Society* 9 (1941): 347–59.

Tyler, Alice Felt. *Freedom's Ferment: Phases of American Social History from the Colonial Period to the Outbreak of the Civil War.* New York: Harper & Row, 1944.

Van Deusen, Glyndon G. *Horace Greeley: Nineteenth-Century Crusader.* Philadelphia: University of Pennsylvania Press, 1953.

Wahl, Albert J. "The Progressive Friends of Longwood." *Bulletin of the Friends Historical Society* 42 (1953): 13–32.

Waller, Altina L. *Reverend Beecher and Mrs. Tilton: Sex and Class in Victorian America.* Amherst: University of Massachusetts Press, 1982.

Walsh, Mary Roth. *"Doctors Wanted: No Women Need Apply."* New Haven, Conn.: Yale University Press, 1977.

Walters, Ronald G. *American Reformers, 1815–1860.* New York: Hill & Wang, 1978.

Welter, Barbara. *Dimnity Convictions: The American Woman in the Nineteenth Century.* Athens: Ohio University Press, 1976.

Wilber, Ken. "There Is No New Age." *One Earth, the Findhorn Foundation Magazine* 8 (Summer 1988): 12–15.

Wilson, John B. "Emerson and the 'Rochester Rappings.'" *New England Quarterly* 41 (June 1968): 248–58.

Yoakam, Doris G. "Woman's Introduction to the American Platform." In *A History and Criticism of American Public Address,* edited by William Brigance, 1:153–89. New York: McGraw-Hill Book Co., 1943.

Zikmund, Barbara Brown. "The Struggle for the Right to Preach." In *Women and Religion in America,* vol. 1, *The Nineteenth Century,* edited by Rosemary Radford Ruether and Rosemary Keller, 193–241. New York: Harper & Row, 1981.

INDEX

Abington Grove Meeting, 122
Abolition movement, 11, 61, 93, 163; and
     "come-outers," 61–62; and Quakers,
     xvii, 12, 68–69; Spiritualism and, 29–
     30, 57, 60–61, 72, 74–81; and woman's
     rights movement, xvi, xx, 76–79
Abortion, xxiv, xxv, xxviin11, xxviin12
Affinities, doctrine of, 119, 126, 134
African Americans, xxiii, 29
African religious beliefs, 28–29
Agitator (Hannah M. F. Brown), 61, 76, 80,
     129
Agitator (Mary Livermore), 80n
Ahlstrom, Sydney, 185, 186
Albanese, Catherine L., xviii
Alcott, Louisa May, 27
Amedy, Rosa, 85
American Anti-Slavery Society, 61, 74–75
American Association of Spiritualists,
     166–73 passim, 190
"American Dress" (costume), 80, 151, 152
American Free Dress League, 153
American Spiritualist, 161
American Woman Suffrage Association,
     164
Anderson, Mr., 29
Andrews, L. F. W., 47, 75
Andrews, Louisa, 180
Andrews, Mary, 176, 177
Andrews, Stephen Pearl, 74, 133
Andrews, William, 90n
Anthony, Susan B., xxi, 59–60, 66, 108,
     153, 171, 197; *History of Woman
     Suffrage*, 2–3, 81; at Lily Dale, 196; as

an orator, 97; *Revolution*, 80, 194; and
     Women's Loyal League, 77
Antislavery movement. *See* Abolition
     movement
Arminianism, 38, 46
Atlantic Monthly, 179–80
Automatic writing, 18, 34
Avon Spring Water Cure, 155

Ballou, Addie, 96, 171, 182, 193, 194, 198
Ballou, Adin, 63–64
Bancroft, George, 16
Banner Free Circle, 25, 148
Banner of Light, 25, 27, 29, 47, 66, 98, 106,
     115, 152, 153, 168, 173, 176–77, 182,
     191, 195; advertisements in, 25, 146,
     147, 183; on American Association of
     Spiritualists, 169–70; in defense of
     mediums, 160; "list of lecturers," 92,
     193; neutrality on abolition, 75, 76, 79;
     quoted, 85, 87, 136, 158, 165, 174–75;
     stand on woman's rights, 79, 196;
     "Woman's Rights Department," 196
Baptist, xviii, xx
Barker, Joseph, 21–23
Barnum's Hotel (N.Y.C.), 16
Barrett, Harrison D., 87n
Beard, George, 178
Beebe, Charlotte M., 65, 66, 92, 93, 120,
     192
Beebe, Emily, 85
Beecher, Catherine, 91, 142
Beecher, Charles, 24, 27
Beecher, Henry Ward, 50, 52, 171–72

Beecher, Lyman, 50
Belvidere Seminary, 152, 175
Berlin Heights Community, 133
Bible, 43, 43n; injunction against women
  preaching, 90–91, 93, 94
Blacks, Spiritualism and, 28–29, 30
Blackwell, Alice Stone, 202
Blackwell, Antoinette Brown, xxi, 39,
  39n–40n, 90, 91, 92, 94, 98
Blackwell, Henry, 27, 202
Blackwell family, 27
Blair, Lucie Marie Curtis, 175
Blatch, Harriet Stanton, 196
Blavatsky, Helena, 162, 178–79, 189, 191
Blood-letting, 144, 145
Bloomers, 80, 152, 153
Books, Spiritualism in, 26–27, 80. *See also*
  Literature
Boston Globe, 174
Branch, Julia, 71, 133
Brekus, Catherine, xix
Bridge, Louisa, 55
Britt, Amanda. *See* Spence, Amanda Britt
Britten, Emma Hardinge. *See* Hardinge,
  Emma
Britton, Samuel B., 150, 175
Brook Farm, 16, 45
Brown, Antoinette. *See* Blackwell,
  Antoinette Brown
Brown, E. Gerry, 178
Brown, Mrs. Hannah M. F., 68, 78, 103,
  122, 124, 169, 193, 195; and the
  Agitator, 76, 80, 129; as critic of
  marriage, 132
Brown, Olympia, 40n, 47
Bruce, Georgianna. *See* Kirby, Georgianna
  Bruce
Bryant, William Cullen, 16
Buffum family (R.I.), 67
Bullene, Emma Jay, 85, 98
Bundy, John C., 182
Burbank, Fanny, 87
Burleigh, Charles, 68
Burns, Ken, xxi
Burtis, Sarah Anthony, xxi, 59
Bush, Abigail, 11, 59, 195
Bush, Belle, 152
Bush, Henry, 11
Bushnell, Mrs. G. B., 19, 92, 155

Butler, Jon, xviii, 28
Butler, Judith, xix
Butts, Bryan J., 64

California State Suffrage Association, 194
California Woman Suffrage Society, 194
Calvinism, 33, 35–36, 199; rejection of,
  33–40, 43–44, 184
Camp meetings, 173–82
Capron, Eliab, 15, 16, 19, 59, 60
Carpenter, Mrs. J. M., 181
Carpenter, William B., 158–59
Carrier Dove, 198
Carroll, Bret, xvii
Caskey, Marie, 50
Cassadaga, xviii
Catholicism: and infant damnation, 37–
  38; Spiritualism and, xxiii, 30. *See also*
  Christianity
Cemeteries, rural, 51, 52, 53
Chace, Elizabeth Buffum, 73
Chamberlain, Belle, 95–96
Chandler, Lucinda, 127
"Channels," 8–9
Channing, William Ellery, 48
Channing, William Henry, 45
Chase, Warren, 48, 64, 78, 98, 124, 153
Chesnut, Mary, 30
Child, Lydia Maria, 28, 48
Childbirth practices, 154–55
Christianity, 4, 36, 62; liberal denomina-
  tions, 43–49; and Spiritualism, 30, 42–
  43, 199–200. *See also* Protestantism;
  Religion
Christian Science, 7, 163; vs. Spiritualism,
  xviii, 182–89
Christian Spiritualist, 30
Church Women United, xxiii
Civil War, xx
Clairvoyant's Family Physician, The, 151
Clark, Mary Thomas. *See* Thomas, Mary
Clarke, Dr. Edward H., 160
Clarke, James Freeman, 44
Clothing reform. *See* Dress reform
Cluer, Susie, 86
Colby, Luther, 75, 178
Coleman, Lucy, 59, 62, 73, 74
Collins, John A., 192
Collinson family, 22–23

ANN BRAUDE teaches at the Harvard Divinity School. She is co-editor of *Root of Bitterness: Documents of the Social History of American Women* and author of *Women and American Religion.*